Training Activities that Work

Increase Interaction to
Engage, Learn and Inspire

Volume 1

Training Activities that Work

Increase Interaction to
Engage, Learn and Inspire

Volume 1

Catherine Mattiske

Alison Asbury

Melanie Barn

Denise Gaul

Susan Giddens

Emma Lambert

Diana McLeod

Aly Rumbelow

Elizabeth Tighe

tpc™

TPC - The Performance Company Pty Ltd
PO Box 639
Rozelle NSW 2039
Sydney, Australia
ACN 077 455 273
email: info@tpc.net.au
Website: www.tpc.net.au

National Library of Australia
Cataloguing-in-Publication data

Mattiske, C, Asbury, A, Barn, M, et al
Copyright © 2014 By Catherine Mattiske

Training Activities that Work: Increase Interaction to Engage, Learn and Inspire, Volume 1
Includes index
ISBN 978-1-921547-62-1
1. Occupational training. 2. Learning. I. Title.
370.113
Printed in USA
Distributed by TPC - The Performance Company - www.tpc.net.au
For further information contact TPC - The Performance Company, Sydney Australia on +61 9555 1953 or TPC - The Performance Company, California on +1 818-227-5052, or email info@tpc.net.au

TPC books are available at special quantity discounts to use as premiums and sales promotions or for use in corporate training programs. To contact a representative, please email us at sales@tpc.net.au

Dedication

To every trainer, I have trained

To every participant, those trainers have trained

To every change, those participants have made

To the transformation, that comes from training excellence.

Catherine Mattiske

Table of Contents

About the Author:

Catherine Mattiske

Catherine Mattiske is a leading training professional, author and publisher, with an internationally acclaimed career spanning 30 years across an array of industries including banking, insurance, pharmaceutical, biotechnology and retail.

Mattiske established 'The Performance Company', a leading edge training and consulting organization, in 1994. The Performance Company has offices in Sydney, Los Angeles and in New York and London.

Mattiske created the ID9® process which is a constructivist approach to learning design that encourages collaborative experiential learning. ID9® is used globally by trainers and instructional designers for rapid development of all types of learning interventions and training programs.

Catherine Mattiske has earned a reputation for helping clients achieve their personal and business goals across Australia, the USA, United Kingdom, Europe, Africa, New Zealand and Asia.

Mattiske's client list has a global reach, including high profile Fortune 100 and 500 companies.

Catherine Mattiske is an accomplished author and publisher. The best-selling, 'Train for Results' (Allen and Unwin), was on academic reading lists worldwide and published in its 3rd Edition. As a publisher, Catherine Mattiske released the 26 part 'Learning Short-takes®' series in 2009 and in 2014 adds the 27th title to this series.

Recognized globally for her achievements in business and for her contribution to the field of training, Catherine Mattiske is a member of the US Congressional Business Advisory Council. Mattiske has been awarded for her influence to US business and has also been nominated on several occasions for the prestigious Australian Business Woman of the Year.

For further details: www.tpc.net.au

Catherine Mattiske

CEO and Founder - The Performance Company (TPC), Australia

About the Co-authors

Alison Asbury

Chapter 7 - Bridging Tasks for Participants - Learning and Review Activities

Melanie Barn

Chapter 5 - During Course: Review Activities - End of Day / Start of Day

Denise Gaul

Chapter 2 - During Course: Learning Activities

Susan Giddens

Chapter 9 - Supporting the Learning - Activities for Managers and Trainers

Emma Lambert

Chapter 1 - Pre-Course Activities for Participants

Chapter 8 - Post-course Activities for Participants

Diana McLeod

Chapter 3 - During Course: Mini Review Activities

Aly Rumbelow

Chapter 6 - During Course: Review Activities - End of Course

Elizabeth Tighe

Chapter 4 - During Course: Review Activities - Post-Lunch

The eight co-authors of this book embarked on the **Certified ID9® Professional – Level 3 (Platinum)** course, known in the training industry as ID9® Platinum, facilitated by Catherine Mattiske. They are professional corporate trainers, facilitators, and managers and are both subject-matter experts in professional corporate training and within their chosen industry.

Before ID9® Platinum they achieved the status of Certified ID9® Professionals – firstly at level 1 (ID9® Silver) then level 2 (ID9® Gold). This book is the product of a continuing learning activity conducted during the ID9® Platinum program, a 12 week learning journey that is described in more detail in the Introduction of the book. Each of the co-authors brought their wealth of training experience into the ID9® Platinum program and advanced their knowledge throughout the 12 weeks of training. They combined their experience and knowledge to create a rich library of learning and review activities which they now freely share with you, the reader.

The eight co-authors all hold senior training positions within global organizations, have all traveled extensively and trained participants worldwide. Collectively, they hold a wealth of knowledge about the training profession and put that knowledge into use on a daily basis within each of the organizations for which they work.

The book has been written with the express intent that regardless of the reader's subject matter expertise, industry or content focus area, the learning and review activities can be implemented into the reader's training programs. While the book is primarily targeted to professional development in a corporate setting it is equally valuable for trainers, teachers, facilitators, educators and subject matter experts (SMEs) who are called upon to train in all industries and vocations.

As part of this journey each co-author agreed that they wish that they had owned this book **Training Activities that Work** as a quick and instant reference guide of ideas for designing training programs throughout their own training careers.

Further information about each co-author forms the introduction of each chapter.

Acknowledgements

To each of my co-authors I would like to thank you for the opportunity of working with you not only during ID9® Platinum but for the previous years that led us to today.

To Alison Asbury, Melanie Barn, Denise Gaul, Susan Giddens, Emma Lambert, Diana McLeod, Aly Rumbelow and Elizabeth Tighe you are not simply participants on one of my training courses but eight professional women who I'm proud to have such a close association with and always be united through this group achievement. Each of you have taught me innumerable lessons and during our time together we've laughed (often hysterically), worked through mazes of complexity, trusted each other as we dived into unchartered learning processes, and together, navigated to what has become a huge achievement for each of you individually and collectively.

Finally, and no less importantly, to all of our families and friends who have displayed endless patience and provided an infinite support for this endeavor, thank you.

Catherine Mattiske

Introduction

By Catherine Mattiske

How the book came into being

One evening I was sitting with my husband talking about work, our careers and what we'd like to do in the future in a similar conversation husbands, wives, partners, families and friends have worldwide. Our conversation steered towards what Malcolm Gladwell termed the 'tipping point' and what were the significant events that influenced my career in training.

The first 'tipping point' stood out as being the launch pad for increased credibility, global recognition and as the driver to many client's decision to bring me into their company to train their trainers, write their instructional design and engage my company, The Performance Company (TPC), broadly across their global or local organizations. This tipping point for me was when Allen & Unwin published my first book Train for Results. Allen & Unwin's association commenced in 2001 at an industry networking function during an icebreaker activity where delegates had the opportunity to meet others. The first part of the activity was the 'normal introduction', you know, "Hi I'm Catherine, I'm a trainer from Sydney Australia, blah blah. I met three people in about 2 minutes, none of whom I remember clearly. Then the facilitator changed the rules and asked us to meet one more person, in a second round of the activity, this time we were asked to use a very interesting and intriguing introduction. A man carrying an orange briefcase came straight over to me and introduced himself to me as a spy. I enquired out of curiosity on why a spy was attending a training network event to which he told me that he was a book publisher spying on the meeting looking for his next author. I then introduced myself as an author who was thinking about writing a book. Four hours later he had asked me to sign a book contract and I had a publisher. That night was the 'tipping point' that changed the trajectory of my career.

Was this a spark of fate? Why was it me who met the man with the orange briefcase? There were 250 people in the room doing the activity, and he introduced himself to me. The questions remain unanswered and always will. However, what remains is the tremendous opportunities that have resulted from a seemingly chance encounter and the ensuing publication of not only that first book, Train for Results (published in 2002), but from the other books I've written since, this book being the 28th and the first that I have co-authored.

The second 'tipping point, was the launch of the TPC Virtual Classroom™ and training ID9® the nine-step instructional design program, in a non-traditional classroom setting. I had trained ID9® Level 1 (Silver) and ID9® Level 2 (Gold) both in the new exciting virtual setting where participants joined their live classes from all points of the globe. I developed a way to increase learning retention and learning application far beyond anything I had achieved in a traditional classroom setting – something that still surprises me.

Each of the co-authors of this book had achieved their ID9® Silver and Gold certification programs and they had registered for the third step in the process: Certified ID9® Professional – Level 3 (Platinum) via TPC Virtual Classroom™. After working with each participant, some for years, I knew them as highly talented training professionals who collectively had trained thousands of participants and made significant impact to the organizations in which they currently work and throughout their training careers with previous companies. During this conversation with my husband I shared how I wanted to provide ID9® Platinum participants with something tangible during the Platinum course that would potentially change the trajectory of their careers, just like the man with the orange briefcase had done for me. The idea struck me: during the ID9® Platinum course participants would consolidate their learning and together we would author a book and publish it. This book is the tangible result of the ID9® Platinum course and forges a standard in the future that all ID9® Platinum participants will achieve their Certified ID9® Professional – Level 3 (Platinum) and also become published authors.

From idea to reality

What a great idea: publish a book representing a tangible product of the efforts that each participant had already put into their ID9® Silver and Gold certification and would expand during the ID9® Platinum program. The idea of the book would bring together not only their learning from all of the ID9® courses but also teach the perhaps unexplored discipline of writing, editing and co-authoring challenges which none of them had previously undertaken. I was beyond excitement with the vision and the possibilities that may open up for my eight participants as it did for me when my first book was published in 2002.

So then to the reality. The planning began well before any of the ID9® Platinum course sessions started. I set a very clear aim for the book: publish a book for professional trainers who are in search of meaningful, practical and 'not-just-for-fun' learning and review activities, written by trainers, for trainers.

The important foundation stone – ID9® methodology and process

Linking the ID9® methodology to the book became the foundation stone:

1. engaging participant's managers, then

2. engaging participants via **pre-course work** and **during their course** with learning and review activities, and

3. keeping participant motivation alive while maximizing learning application through participant **post-course work** and manager follow-up.

This structure has become the structure of this book.

Beginning the journey

Before the course started my eight participants, all from different parts of the world, independently decided to have a post-ID9® Gold meeting to compile all of the activities that they had created during their ID9® Gold course. They had planned this meeting completely independently with their aim that they didn't lose the great ideas that they had gathered during ID9® Gold. This meeting was well after they had achieved their ID9® Gold certification and before ID9® Platinum. Were they psychic? Did they know that I was planning this very activity as part of the ID9® Platinum program and to then compile these ideas into a book? I decided to 'crash' their meeting.

It was 2am for me on my time zone and I logged into their WebEx call with my announcement that what they were doing in this meeting was not only a great and valuable initiative but was actually part of the ID9® Platinum process and told them my plan for them to co-author a book with me. There was a mix of reactions, none of which I planned for: shock, tears, stunned silence, thankfulness and gratitude, reeling minds thinking of possibilities, enthusiasm and the chat box in WebEx went wild with comments of joy. It was one of the greatest moments of my training career. I felt like I was the man carrying the orange briefcase at that networking meeting all those years ago who had just given them a life opportunity.

From a blank slate to the book you are now reading

The ID9® Platinum course is conducted virtually, with 6 live virtual meetings held once every 2 weeks with bridging tasks in between. In my newly revised ID9® Platinum course there was only one continuing learning activity: each participant was tasked to write one chapter, of what has become this book, over the entire 12 week ID9® Platinum program. I made a conscious effort to 'drip feed' the writing and publishing process to the group so as to not overwhelm them and to maintain learning motivation. It would be 'one step at a time' for 12 weeks.

Session 1 – Choose your chapter and write 1 activity
In the first ID9® Platinum session, on 12 June 2013, I relayed the story of the man with the orange briefcase and introduced the participants to our working icon during the Platinum program that represented all things linked to the book. Each time a task or training content linked they saw the man with the orange briefcase icon creating a consistency of purpose throughout the process.

During Session 1 of ID9® Platinum each participant nominated for a chapter which represents a part of the ID9® process. We were off and running and the activities started to be written. Topics covered in Session 1 added to each of the ID9® Silver and ID9® Gold adult learning processes, Journaling and Rico Clusters, instruction writing with behavioral learning objectives using Bloom's Taxonomy as the base, the framework of each activity's structure for the book and the obliteration of the word 'time' as a part of negative language. The book was started and in the next two weeks the participants had created a total of 8 activities – one each.

Session 2 – Keep it or Gift it

By Session 2, everyone had chosen their chapter, and had written one activity using the structured format provided. I created an arrangement called "keep it or gift it" where participants either kept the activity that they had written for their chapter or sent it as a gift to another participant for theirs.

Just this simple act created a pattern of giving for the rest of the course. During the program if someone had an idea for an activity but it didn't fit within their chapter they would write it, either in part or full, and gift it to their co-author. It was a uniting experience that overcame one of my concerns of each participant potentially feeling isolated and that they were endeavoring a solo pursuit of just their chapter. Working under this new paradigm instead the entire project became collaborative, which was beyond my expectations as their trainer.

Session 2 focused on bringing together some of the more quantifiable and researched elements of Neuro Linguistic Programming (NLP) by way of training techniques and instruction writing using predicate phrases together with an in-depth session on metacognitive reflection activities that would fuel their chapters with activity possibilities. Finally Session 2 covered variations on case studies and role plays expanding the possibilities from simply in-classroom learning activities to learning and review activities that can be placed across the entire learning process (from pre- to post-course).

You will see the tangible outcome of this session as you read the many activities that are presented in the book using metacognitive reflection, NLP techniques, case studies and role plays, all of which often challenge both novice and experienced trainers to make these techniques work in a business environment.

Session 3 – 11,000 words….Unexpected Links

After 4 weeks of the program, 10 July, the book had no title, and my eight participants had written 11,000 words in 23 activities over 50 pages. We had a brainstormed list of book titles including: Training up a Storm: Make performing the norm, Train to gain, Beyond Gold and some that I can't mention as it would put this book in a different, more risqué or comedic categories of on-line booksellers! After conducting Facebook polls, this title: **'Training Activities that Work'** was finally settled.

Session 3 was a deep dive into pre- and post-course activities for participants, participants' managers and key stakeholders, theories of learning motivation, and a final session on creating first impressions, color fundamentals and working with color across different global cultures.

It was in this session that Emma Lambert, whose focus chapter is pre- and post-course was highly engaged knowing that she could fuel her split chapter with new ideas. Susan Giddens, whos chapter is the Manager Track, was using this to create new and unique ways to engage managers in the learning process to encourage and facilitate managers to support their direct reports towards learning application. However you'll see as you read the 'during course' chapters, by Liz Tighe, Diana McLeod, Denise Gaul, Melanie Barn and Aly Rumbelow, all show the influence of this session with the link to debriefing pre-work within the session through review activities and setting up the application of learning through highly motivating in-class activities that extend into post-course work. The Bridging Task chapter by Alison Asbury also shows this learning in action where she has created potential learning and review activities linking two or more training sessions. Each learning and review activity presented in the book has one singular foundation: keep learning motivation high which maximizes the transfer and application of learning.

Session 4 – 25,000 words and a brick wall for some

6 weeks into the program and the book had grown to 119 pages and 25,000 words. As their trainer I could see that each participant was starting to change. Some were thriving in the process, others had hit 'writers block'.

During Session 4 I told the story of how I was up against my first publishing deadline and when I had only written 10,000 out of 40,000 words of my first book Train for Results. The man with the orange briefcase and I met to discuss the publishing deadline and the pressure it was putting on me to deliver. I decided that if I stayed in my current environment of busi-ness (busy-ness in my business!) I'd never make it. So, located in Australia, I flew from Sydney to Melbourne and drove to a tiny cottage in the mountains and wrote for one-week solid. Day and night I wrote. There was no mobile phone service at the cottage so once a day I went into the little village for supplies and to check my phone messages. On day 4 the Sydney office had been broken into and computers stolen and windows smashed. I decided not to go back to Sydney. My staff handled everything with professionalism without me. I only had two tasks: finish my book and keep the fire going 24 hours a day as the only form of heating in a very cold winter. I did it. Book finished, I returned to Sydney. When I arrived back into the office the following day the windows had been fixed, the insurance process well underway, new computers had arrived, and computer backups restored: business as usual. It was a great lesson: the world kept turning without me having to react, be flexible enough to change plans and never abandon my goals as others could handle things for me if needed.

Some of my eight participants had become shunted into the realization that they were part of a bigger picture than just attending the ID9® Platinum program and that they were in fact co-authoring a book which had responsibilities not just for themselves but if they 'dropped the ball' it would impact others. The challenges of eight career driven women juggling very big jobs and delivering content for the book became very real.

It became even more real when Session 4 began with graphic design options for the book cover. This was the first time that my participants had ever seen their name on a book cover. It was a mix of excitement with the pins and needles of the reality of what we were collectively doing. From the moment I showed them the graphic design options for the book and we collectively chose one, I didn't think of them any more as my participants but as my co-authors!

The rest of Session 4 covered advanced instruction writing, essential in their careers as creators of training and now as co-authors, we delved further into Bloom's Taxonomy in the Cognitive Domain and the use of metaphors and analogies in training, learning activities and review activities.

Between Sessions 4 and 5 - Breakthrough
Breakthrough! In between Sessions 4 and 5 and less than 2 months after beginning the program the book totaled 352 pages and over 54,000 words. In two weeks they had doubled the word count of the book and we now had a substantial manuscript. They were over their block.

Session 5 – 54,000 words, reflection and editing
In Session 5 we were on the home stretch. There was just one session to go after this one, so I gave them a chapter checklist to cognitively evaluate the 'worth' of each activity. You'll see that at the end of each activity in the book there's an **Adult Learning Dashboard**. Each co-author went back over each of the activities in her chapter and linked it to not only the **Base Adult Learning Process** (which you'll see on every activity) but also to which adult learning style theories, practices and methodologies are used as part of the ID9® framework. The aim of this is for trainers to quickly balance an out-of-balance course (e.g. if more kinesthetic is needed use activities that are checked ☑ Kinesthetic) or to create balance in a new course so that all adult learners, regardless of their personal learning preferences, are accommodated.

Session 5 focused on feedback and debrief and linked the advanced instruction writing from Session 4 to propel my co-authors to evaluate how each learning or review activity was professionally debriefed to provide maximum learning opportunity and traction to in turn maximize learning transfer and application. Each of my co-authors then set about to evaluate their existing debrief questions and transform them into higher-order debrief questions, which was a significant task. As a trainer reading this book, you can be sure that each of the questions written for every activity are very sound and you'll never be stuck asking probably the worst question in training: "Are there any questions?"

Finally, Session 5 finished off with the art and science of storytelling in training and the use of training themes linking our previous session on metaphors and analogies which propelled the final flurry of activities for the book, not to mention a flurry of activity in my co-authors 'real jobs' as they relayed stories of immediately undertaking rewrites of training programs in their current corporate training environments.

Between Sessions 5 and 6 – The power of synergy
Something amazing happened next. I predicted that the final book would be approximately 50,000 words and we were already past this point. My first book, Train for Results, was approximately 40,000 words so this stood to reason. Or, so I thought. In the next two weeks I thought that each co-author would trim, edit, refine but not add to their chapters very much. However, to my absolute shock, the fuel of writing started to kick in and the final push to expand and complete each chapter was happening.

Throughout the process my co-authors found their own personal rhythm, some preferring to tackle the last push alone, others in small groups and a few whole group meetings where everyone was invited and ideas flowed in upbeat virtual meetings. It was at this point that each of my co-authors solidly produced in excess of what I had asked of them and pride took over as they realized that this book would not only have their name on the front cover but be a tangible representation of their training knowledge to be shared with other trainers globally.

Session 6 – 82,000 words and still more to do
The next draft of the book totaled 82,000 words and over 400 draft pages. When I announced this during Session 6 the reaction again amazed me. There was collective shock that together my co-authors had written a book of such magnitude.

But it wasn't over yet! Session 6 advanced their knowledge by linking the popular behavioral diagnostic, DiSC, into the mix to accommodate each behavioral profile into training programs and I also provided them with new tools that would set them up with an end-to-end training process that could be used within their own business environments. Like sponges they continued to soak up new information, processes and ideas to continuously improve the learning process for their own participants, participant's managers and key stakeholders within their employer organizations.

The final book was due two weeks after Session 6 but most of my co-authors had completed early. At this point I asked them to reflect on the importance of the visibility that the book will bring each of them as an author in light of their own chapter and to make sure they are 100% complete and proud of their own chapter.

It had been 12 weeks since the start date of ID9® Platinum. 12 weeks earlier we had begun with a blank slate, zero words, zero pages, and an idea of together writing a book by trainers for trainers. 12 weeks later their work to create the draft, that has now become the book that you are reading was complete.

About my Co-Authors: Collective wisdom and experience

All of my eight co-authors of this book embarked on ID9® Platinum as trainers, managers, career women, subject-matter experts in training, specialists within their chosen industries and Certified ID9® Professionals – firstly at a Silver then at a Gold level. Each brought into the program their wealth of training experience.

All of my co-authors have other roles in life including mother, sister, daughter, wife, friend, colleague, manager, leader, niece, granddaughter, team member, neighbor, volunteer … the list is endless. They juggled all of these roles to carve out 12 weeks to focus on their own training professionalism, while still managing to achieve full-time jobs, full-time families and full-time friendships during the same 12 weeks. Furthermore, some of them simultaneously provided ID9® coaching to participants beginning their ID9® certification journey at the Silver level.

Sometimes while reviewing their work in between sessions I would read an activity and be blown away by the idea. During coaching sessions in between group sessions with each of them individually I would be silenced by their wisdom as they linked and applied ideas they had learned during the ID9® Platinum sessions, not only for this book, but also how they were applying their learnings in their day-to-day corporate work.

Now, these eight talented women, Alison Asbury, Melanie Barn, Denise Gaul, Susan Giddens, Emma Lambert, Diana McLeod, Aly Rumbelow and Elizabeth Tighe are now **Certified ID9® Professionals – Level 3 (Platinum)** and have become **published authors** in the process. Some will continue their ID9® journey becoming ID9® Coaches and Trainers in the future. However, their pinnacle achievement in the ID9® process has been their ID9® Platinum certification culminating in this book which is the tangible evidence of their effort and most importantly the application of their own learning and wisdom.

In their own words....what did you learn in the process?

During Session 6 on August 22, I asked each of them for their key learnings during ID9® Platinum. Without naming names, here's a few things what they said:

"I had no idea that we would write a book. I'm really proud about what we've done."

"It's forced me to be more grown up in training and I'm now more qualified than what I think"

"On the one hand, I was excited to hear that we are going to write a book, but on the other hand I questioned how will it come together when we're still learning, but it has."

"I've learned the truism of not what happens to you it's what you make of it and taking opportunities as they appear and help will come from unexpected sources"

"Writing a book is not necessarily enjoyable but it's extremely rewarding"

"I've learned to write properly: instructions, debrief, I'm succinct and my instructional design is so much faster"

"I've learned tangible, practical ideas that I can implement tomorrow"

"Activity, activity, activity, reinforce, reinforce, reinforce"

"Prioritize the learning and focus on it"

"You have to engage managers to get the behavior change and now I know how"

"Activities – keep the Adult Learning Base Process in mind when you develop them"

"Practice, practice, practice what I've learned and never do instructional design without the toolkit open"

"Just do it"

"I've got my Christmas present list sorted – everyone is getting our book for Christmas"

Then, unexpectedly one of the participants turned the spotlight onto me to ask what was my own take home message from the ID9® Platinum program...what did I learn? With no time to prepare or construct a planned response, this was my 'blink' response. Here's what I said...(from a transcript from the program)...

"My take home message is about RISK. Before the course I thought I want to do something that adds to the lives of these participants who will come on Platinum. I wanted to provide a real contribution to their lives in a tangible way. And so I thought of the book. The book is a contribution that I can make to participants' lives, but the biggest contribution is what that book will contribute to their own lives by each of them writing it.

When I printed the draft book today I held it I actually burst into tears. I was really proud of you all. Now when I see it, it's incredible that this is a tangible book in my hands.

That was the RISK. I was so fearful and nervous that it wasn't going to work and now to see it all done it's taught me about trusting my instincts as a trainer, and probably in the bigger picture, as a human being.

It really was a risk for me to do it because it would have been much easier just to teach the course session by session and assign lots of small bridging tasks. But, before the course started, when I saw the final participant list I thought "I've got eight smart women who can actually do this and fulfill this and make it work" and, now here it is...you've done it."

What's next...Book series/volume

Early in the process, as this ID9® Platinum group were advancing with their writing and producing such quality outcomes I made the decision to share this with others. My decision was that in the future, for all ID9® Platinum courses co-authoring a book with me will be part of the program. That way, I hope that more participants in the future, who have completed their ID9® Silver and Gold programs, can reach a similar pinnacle of achievement as this group have. I hope that for each future ID9® Platinum participant I can provide the opportunity to become a published author and potentially change the trajectory of their career and life.

About ID9®

By Catherine Mattiske

What is Instructional Design?

Instructional Design is the systematic development of training materials for both trainers and participants to ensure the quality of training delivery and achievement of learning objectives. Instructional Design is the entire process of analysis of learning needs and the development of a delivery system to meet those needs. It includes development of instructional materials and learner activities. The person who undertakes this work is the Instructional Designer.

Why is Instructional Design important to the training process?

Instructional Design is, in my opinion, the key step to quality professional training delivery. High quality Instructional Design will maximize the success of the training program. It provides the trainer with confidence to deliver the program so that the training goals and learning objectives are met. Good Instructional Design meets the needs of all adult learners regardless of their preferred learning style. Most importantly, when Instructional Design meets the learning objectives of the training program, it increases the probability that the participant will apply his or her learning and therefore change their behavior. Changing behavior by applying new skills and knowledge is the aim of all training programs and Instructional Design is the driving force to get participants to the point where they have the ability for learning application.

Components of Instructional Design

Instructional Design often begins with just a glimmer of an idea of how the end training product will look. Often the Instructional Designer (who may or may not be a subject matter expert) will need to research the subject and decide on the scope of the training program.

Needs Analysis

The preliminary step of Instructional Design is to conduct needs analysis to determine the learning gap of potential participants. This analysis is generally undertaken as part of the Internal Performance Consulting role, a role which may or may not be held by the same person undertaking the Instructional Design.

Training Goals and Objectives

Once the learning gap is established, the Instructional Design process begins with writing a clear training goal and learning objectives. The objectives state the end goal of the training program. This is the key step most important in the entire Instructional Design process. Solid learning goals and objectives mean that the complete writing and training process targeted to meet the learning objectives thus filling the gap.

Once the aim and objectives are written, then the Instructional Designer writes the program opening, then each topic including learning checks and measures and the program closing.

Creation of Training Materials

The Instructional Design deliverables include creating and documenting the program to a level of detail so that an accomplished trainer, who has subject matter expertise, is able to pick up the Instructional Design materials and deliver the program.

Program Delivery

If the training is being delivered by an electronic form, such as eLearning, the Instructional Designer designs the program, including the program aim and learning objectives, creates the topics including learning and review activities and then creates the eLearning product themselves, or hands their work over to an eLearning programmer.

Measurement of Program Effectiveness

The final step is measurement of learning success, which will be discussed in detail later in this chapter.

Instructional Design: Process Summary

Regardless of the platform by which the learning will be delivered the process is similar:
1. Needs analysis to establish the learning gap
2. Instructional Design
    a. Create training aim and learning objectives that maximize the potential of filling the learning gap
    b. Write the training program (instructor-led, eLearning or any other platform)
3. Deliver the program
4. Measure the effectiveness of the program to establish if the learning gap was filled

What is ID9®?

ID9® Defined

ID9®: Mattiske's rapid Instructional Design process.

ID9® is a constructivist approach to learning design that encourages collaborative experiential learning. The ID9® framework and process was developed by Catherine Mattiske in 1997.

ID9® is a process that builds learning through the use of learning activities and confirms new knowledge through structured review activities.

ID9® Overview

ID9® provides a comprehensive and innovative Instructional Design process for writing and creating training programs. The ID9® framework and process is suited for instructor-led programs, either in a physical or virtual classroom, eLearning, distance learning, or any other platform on which learning is delivered to produce interactive and engaging highly focused learning.

ID9® is a four-phase training framework followed by a nine step Instructional Design process that reduces Instructional Design time and increases participant retention with the aim of maximizing learning application.

Mattiske has developed ID9® based on many different adult learning principles and theoretical approaches. By using the ID9® framework and process Instructional Designers and trainers can be confident that all adult learners, regardless of their personal learning style, are catered for.

ID9® Framework – 4 phases

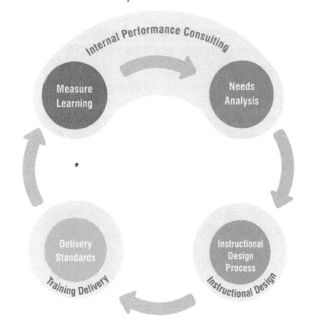

Figure 1 ID9® Framework

There are four phases to the overall ID9® framework as shown in Figure 1. The following table outlines each phase and whose role it is to deliver it:

ID9® Phase	Role
1. Needs Analysis	Internal Performance Consultant
2. Instructional Design	Instructional Designer
3. Training Delivery	Trainer
4. Measurement	Internal Performance Consultant

Three roles have been defined above; however, many trainers will wear all three hats because they have a combined role of Internal Performance Consultant, Instructional Designer and Trainer. However, in some organizations these roles are divided and different people undertake one or two of the roles. Regardless of how you work the ID9® framework is still applicable.

While the focus of **Training Activities that Work** is on providing interactive activities for the Instructional Design phase, for context, the four steps are briefly summarized below.

Step 1 – Needs Analysis

The process begins with the Internal Performance Consultant role working with their internal client group to establish the learning needs. The goal of this step is to establish 'the gap' and to define what success looks like. After this research the deliverables of this step are the training program aim, learning objectives and high level course content, identified target audience and sometimes the program duration incorporated into a training project plan and a course outline.

While **Training Activities that Work** focuses on creating learning and review activities there is an essential link to the needs analysis step. As previously stated, needs analysis is focused on determining the learning gap and designing the course aim and objectives to fill that gap. In **Training Activities that Work** each activity begins with the *learning activity aim* which states the endpoint that participants should achieve on completion of the activity. Also you will notice that each activity links to Bloom's Taxonomy in the Cognitive Domain which is one of the foundation theories used in the ID9® process for writing behavioral learning objectives. Each activity in **Training Activities that Work** states the level of Bloom's taxonomy that the activity strives to achieve. The benefit of including these two checkpoints is that firstly the activity goal is clearly stated, creating clarity on what the learning activity is to achieve, and also if you have been using Bloom's Taxonomy for training development you'll be able to confidently link learning activities from **Training Activities that Work** to achieve your prescribed learning objective level.

Step 2 – Instructional Design

The Instructional Design phase delivers the learning design and all physical materials required for the training program.

As stated above:

> *Instructional Design is the systematic development of training materials for both trainers and participants to ensure the quality of training delivery and achievement of learning objectives. Instructional Design is the entire process of analysis of learning needs and the development of a delivery system to meet those needs. It includes development of instructional materials and learner activities. The person who undertakes this work is the Instructional Designer.*

Training Activities that Work is focused on a core area of Instructional Design using the ID9® process: creating learning and review activities that build and measure learning before, during and after the training program.

Step 3 – Training Delivery

For many people they say "Oh, delivering training…that is the hardest part." For me delivering a training course is the easiest part. The hardest part for me is finding the needs, establishing the true gap and then writing the program to fill the gap. When I train, it's so easy; all I do is train what's been written and focus my attention not on what to train but the needs of the individual participants on that day!

Training delivery should not be confused with presentation skills. It is the task of a *Trainer* to impart skills and knowledge to participants so that they can implement the new skill or knowledge when they return to their workplace, thus, learning application. Training programs should be highly interactive two-way interactions between trainer and participants who learn new skills, practice them through learning activities and measure their learning during the training program during review activities.

By contrast, *Presenters* present information where there is no requirement for a change of behavior or learning application. Presentations are usually one-way meetings with the presenter using PowerPoint or another visual aid to help impart their message usually with very little or no participant interaction.

Training Activities that Work is focused on training, not presenting.

Step 4 - Measurement

There have been many books and training programs about measuring training. **Training Activities that Work** does not focus on traditional measurement of ROE or ROI *after* the training program, but rather measures learning *during* the training program by way of learning and review activities. Also, **Training Activities that Work** provides pre-course learning activities and post-course review activities to strengthen the learning process. Every activity in **Training Activities that Work** forms the basis of the measurement process.

Traditional learning measurement models include a two-step post-course measurement process asking two questions: (1) does the participant have the skill/knowledge? And (2) have they applied the skill/knowledge? Using the ID9® process the trainer knows that question (1) is answered 'yes' *during* the training, by way of participants completing learning and review activities which provides proof of participants' learning, leaving only question (2) to answer as the post-course measure.

The ID9® process also adds to many traditional measurement processes by establishing solid learning objectives *before* creating any training materials, up front, as the first step in the Instructional Design process. After the training has been conducted training professionals must be able to measure *against these solid learning objectives* otherwise the question must be asked, what are they measuring? By setting down a specific and clear training aim, establishing behavioral learning objectives that meet the aim and then writing the program targeted to these two elements, the post-course measurement data becomes targeted, realistic and meaningful.

By incorporating learning and review activities *during* the training program the trainer can be confident that by the time participants leave the training course they are ready and confident to apply their new skills and knowledge. Therefore, during the post-course measurement it is assured that participants *know what they are expected to apply* and only needs to check whether participants *have or have not chosen to apply their learning*.

This measurement process *begins in the Instructional Design phase* where the measures are designed by the Instructional Designer as an integral part of the process.

The benefits of measuring <u>during</u> the training program are that:

1. The **participant**, during the program…
   a. Has evidence of his or her learning which builds learning motivation
   b. Can be provided with positive and corrective feedback by the trainer which ensures the participant doesn't derail
   c. Builds confidence that propels and fuels the chance that participants will apply their learning after the course

2. The **trainer**, during the program...
   a. Has evidence that each of their participants has activated their learning
   b. Has evidence that each of their participants has reviewed each learning topic therefore providing further evidence and proof of learning achievement
   c. Reduces 'presentation' of materials and increases interaction with active and participative learning and review activities
   d. Can collect data to provide feedback to key stakeholders, as required, on each participant's progress and provide this feedback during or after the program
   e. Can further support participants with debriefing pre-course learning activities during the course which potentially reduces in-class time and or strengthens and deepens the learning content
   f. Can further support participants by providing post-course review activities further strengthening the learning (i.e. providing points of measurement on learning application) and or deepen the content trained

3. The **organization** (managers, key stakeholders, other key influencers) as a result...
   a. Receives feedback from the trainer on the progress and accomplishments of individual participants
   b. Can provide support to participants through targeted review activities post-course
   c. Is provided with high training value knowing that the training courses are:
      i. targeted to learning objectives
      ii. embedded with interactive learning and review activities providing participants with confidence and the skills required to embrace behavior change
      iii. designed so that their employees are returning from training ready to apply their learning
   d. all roles in training (internal performance consultants, instructional designers, trainers and other learning professionals) are targeted to deliver the course aim and objectives resulting in providing learning application and therefore behavior change to the organization.

Theoretical basis of ID9®

Overarching Influence for ID9®
ID9® is a constructivist approach to learning design that encourages collaborative experiential learning. The ID9® framework and process was developed by Catherine Mattiske in 1997.

ID9® is a process that builds on learning through the use of learning activities and confirms new knowledge through structured review activities.

The influences from theory on the design and development of instructional systems design which create the foundation to ID9® can be drawn from several areas of research including learning and psychological theory.

To enable further understanding of the 'learning theory' that has led toward our current knowledge on the application of learning and the need for aligning learning interventions to individual and corporate objectives, the following summary of researched authors is provided.

Major Influential ID9® Theorists:
The ID9® framework and process (Mattiske 1997) was influenced by Benjamin Bloom (1913 – 1999), John Dewey (1859 – 1952), Jerome Seymore Bruner (Born 1915), Robert Mills Gagne (1916 – 2002), Howard Earl Gardner (Born 1943), Hermann Ebbinghaus (1850 – 1909) and Marton and Saljo (Published 1976). The theories and models presented by these authors are major influences that form foundation for the ID9® framework and process.

- Benjamin Bloom: Bloom's Taxonomy – the use of verbs to describe learning objectives, content and outcomes
- John Dewey: Experiential learning
- Jerome Seymore Bruner: Constructivism and the role of structure in learning
- Robert Mills Gagne: The building block for ID9®'s step 5 'Topic Rotation'
- Howard Earl Gardner: The use of Multiple Intelligences in course design
- Hermann Ebbinghaus: Primacy and Recency - overarching influence over ID9® process
- Marton and Saljo: Deep Learning principles for ID9®

Supportive ID9® Theorists:
Further theories and models which are supportive influences to the ID9® framework and process are John Biggs (Born 1934), David Kolb (Born 1939), Jean Piaget (1896 – 1980), Burrhus Frederic Skinner (1904 – 1990), David A. (Anthony) Sousa, Roger Sperry (1913 – 1994), and Edward Thorndike (1874 – 1949).

- John Biggs: Constructive alignment of learning, surface and deep learning and the SOLO Taxonomy
- David Kolb: Experiential learning

- Jean Piaget: Constructivism, progressively building and constructing upon learning and the importance of learning activities

- Burrhus Frederic Skinner: Learning feedback, learning reinforcement and self-paced learning

- David A. (Anthony) Sousa: Importance of emotions, feedback, past experiences and meaning in adult learning.

- Roger Sperry: Left-Right brain and adult learning engagement methods and styles

- Edward Thorndike: Adult learning theory

Other ID9® Theoretical Influences:

The work of the following authors have also influenced or link to the ID9® framework and process (listed in order of approximate birth date): Socrates, Plato, Aristotle, Thomas Hobbs, Rene Descartes, John Locke, George Berkley, Thomas Reid, David Hume, Jean-Jacques Rousseau, Immanuel Kant, Franz-Joseph Gall, James Mill (father of John Stuart Mill), John Stuart Mill, Charles Robert Darwin, William James, Ivan Petrivich Pavlov, Mary Calkins, Edward Bradford Titchener, James Rowland Angell, Montessori, Carl Jung, John Broadus Watson, Kurt Lewin, Lev Vygotsky, Carl Rogers, Malcolm Shepherd Knowles, Donald Kirkpatrick, David Ausubel, George Miller, Albert Bandura, Allen Paivio, Eric Kandel, Edward de Bono, John Favell, Bernice McCarthy, Jay Cross, Robin Fogarty, Atkinson-Shiffrin Memory Model, Black & Wiliam, Honey & Mumford and Jean Lave.

Further Information

For further information on the theoretical research basis for ID9® please refer to **Appendix A: Theoretical Research Reference.**

ID9® Foundation Principles

There are several foundation principles that form the basis of ID9® taught to ID9® Certified Professionals during their training program. Four foundation principles are explained in this chapter and as a result are the underlying principles driving the contents of **Training Activities that Work**, being:

- ID9® Foundation Principle 1: It's not your course — it's *their* course

- ID9® Foundation Principle 2: Training = Behavior Change

- ID9® Foundation Principle 3: End goal = Learning Application

- ID9® Foundation Principle 4: There is plenty of time for learning and review activities

ID9® Foundation Principle 1: It's not your course — it's their course

After many years as a corporate training professional my most important belief remains: it's not your course — it's their course. It's not the trainer's course; **it's the participant's course**.

When I train professional trainers and say "it's not your course — it's their course" to them, usually the response is quite flippant. 'Oh yes,' they say, 'of course, it's *their* course.' Over the years some of these trainers have gone on to show me their hundreds of PowerPoint slides where they talk *at* participants for hours on end, with hardly a break and rarely a learning or review activity in sight. Their approach, sometimes called 'death by PowerPoint' is totally against this principle. Their approach is 'trainer focused' training not 'participant centered' training.

To move towards the notion of "it's not your course — it's their course" and to take this seriously is a huge step as a trainer, perhaps one of the most important steps a trainer will take, if they take it at all. It means that the trainer must have all care and all responsibility to ensure participants are fully equipped and ready to apply their learning to their workplace the moment each participant leaves the training program.

It means that the trainer must build their confidence to ensure that they are open to working outside their comfort zone and to accept change. The trainer should support participants when they succeed and more importantly when they don't. It means that the trainer must collect hard and soft data to support the claim that participants can indeed apply what has been taught to them (whether voiced to the trainer or others).

It means that the trainer may have to fight the bureaucracy and norms of their own corporate training environment that have been in place for perhaps decades and convince, or at least persuade others, that the trainer's ideas have merit.

What does this mean for the trainer?

In my experience, when a professional trainer takes this step, they will have one of two possible responses: give up or persist.

1. **Give up**

   The first response comes from the less confident or less competent trainer, who might give up and might even leave training forever because the notion of 'it's their course' is too hard to deal with.

   They choose not advance their own learning about how to achieve this, do not invest the time for preparation of training materials including participant centered learning and review activities and or won't put in the effort to create a participant centered training program and energy required to convince others that this approach has merit. Even though they know the possibility of outstanding success exists on achievement of this goal they give up.

To know that a new dimension of training exists and not adopt the new method is sometimes considered as personal failure. Often this feeling comes, not from others, but from the trainer themselves. To personally step out of and change their 'presentation' style of delivery and move out of their own comfort zone is too hard for them. If they do try and experiment with this new dimension of training, they will realize how easy the process really is, however complex it may have looked at first glance.

In my opinion, it is ironic that some trainers won't step out of their own comfort zone and change their own behavior while the same trainer expects their participants to accept what they are being taught and expect their participants to change *their* behavior. This defies intuition as it leads to seemingly irreconcilable contradictions between what trainers will or won't change themselves vs their expectation of their participants.

2. Persist

The second response comes from the professional trainer, who will persist, reflect and re-evaluate what they have been doing in their training and the effectiveness of their past and current training programs.

Over time such re-evaluation will result in an outstanding metamorphosis of who they are as a trainer. It also radically changes the training results that they get.

They may have even received sensational evaluation feedback before this radical departure from their old ways and may have thought "Why change? Everything is going well." However, using the ID9® process as their new strategy the professional trainer will find that they never again need to seek out accolades or 'blow their own trumpet'. This is because the success they foster before, during and after their training comes back to them tenfold.

The accolades will come to the trainer without their pushing or prodding. Every evaluation will be sensational, senior people will delight in having their staff well skilled and the personal demand for the trainer will rise, regardless of their internal of external position or capacity.

The professional trainer will look forward to and strive for the success of others and will be re-fuelled again and again to recreate this success every time they train. Success will be theirs mirrored from the success of others. The professional trainer knows that to employ this change in direction that

only minor adjustments need to be made to what they are doing to create major impact.

Therein lays the paradox. A minor adjustment of focus, like a slight shift of a compass on a map, will lead you to a totally new place.

"It's their course" link to Training Activities that Work

Every activity in **Training Activities that Work** is learner focused and puts the participant at the center of the learning experience. Each learning activity is designed for the participant to safely test drive their new skills or knowledge for the first time in a supportive learning environment where the trainer and other participants are on hand to provide feedback and support. Each review activity is designed to measure the learning progress of the participant, without pressure-testing or exams, in a supportive interactive way which builds learning motivation to fuel learning application.

ID9® Foundation Principle 2: Training = Behavior Change

The goal of training is to change behavior. Therefore quite simply: Training equals behavior change. It assumes that something different will be done as the result of the training. Presentations do not aim to change behavior.

To establish whether the program is training or a presentation I ask the question "What is the expected behavior change?" If the answer is 'nothing' then the program is not a training program, it's a presentation. Presenters should structure their session as a presentation with a beginning, middle and end and summarize each part and do a summary at the end. Simply: get them in and get them out and you're done.

I have very tough and pragmatic measure to training, which is *Training equals a change in behavior*. There is no middle ground. Participants either *did* or *did not* change their behavior. If participants tried to change and didn't, they *didn't* change their behavior. If no change in behavior happens then, in my opinion, no training has happened. In other words, if nothing results from the training by way of change of behavior because of the application of learning then the entire training process (including the needs analysis, instructional design, delivery and measurement processes) has resulted in a waste of time and waste of money.

"Training = Behavior Change" link to Training Activities that Work

Each learning and review activity in **Training Activities that Work** focuses on driving learning application that sets the stage for participants to be confident and knowledgeable to change their behavior.

ID9® Foundation Principle 3: There is plenty of time for learning and review activities

As far as time goes, review activities are self-accommodating. When participants are feeling confident about their new skills and knowledge, they will learn at a much faster rate than if they are feeling overwhelmed and mentally fatigued.

Learning activities are essential to test drive new skills and knowledge learned in the course. Learning activities must be included in the flow of the training, if not, participants will be expected to use their new skills and knowledge for the first time when they leave the training and when they do so (if they do!) they won't have the support of their trainer or other participants to support and remediate where necessary to ensure success.

Review activities are added to the training program to review material already learned and practiced. Using a variety of methods, many very quick (e.g. 1 - 5 minutes) trainers are able to measure *during* the program the new skills and knowledge participants have learned. In a review activity, skills and knowledge are measured during the training course, reassuring participants that they are learning, and trainers that they are successfully transferring skills and knowledge.

The *pace of learning is faster* when learning and review activities are added to the program because of:
1. the social proof being demonstrated in the training room,
2. the high level of confidence on the part of participants and
3. the usefulness or relevance of the material being learnt.

As a professional trainer, my goal by the end of my training courses is for my participants to know 100%, or close to it, of all the topics that I have trained. The only way I will know this is to see evidence of it for myself, and the outcome of review activities helps me to know they know. When I am behind schedule, I would rather ensure that my participants are confident and able to apply, say, 19 out of the 20 topics than risk putting in the twentieth topic and leaving them confused and without time to recover from that confusion.

You, the professional trainer, need to make that decision at the time of training. However, I would urge you not to risk a drop in your participants' confidence levels by cramming in more content, just so you can say you've delivered everything on your course outline.

Your role as a professional trainer is to ensure that participants are confident enough to apply their new skills and knowledge in practice.

I rarely drop a review, preferring to drop content and measure the learning, driving home key points in preference to adding

more content. I would prefer my participants to fully understand and feel confident about 80% of the material I planned to train, than have them lose much of their confidence and ability on 100%.

"There is plenty of time for learning and review activities" link to Training Activities that Work
Each learning and review activity in **Training Activities that Work** focuses on driving learning motivation which leads to learning application. The higher the learning motivation the faster your course will go!

ID9® Foundation Principle 4: End goal = Learning Application

As previously stated the end goal of training is to achieve the application of learning objectives by each attending participant. This is easy to say and most often difficult to achieve, yet it is achievable.

Some organizations have a 'get them through the training' model, which personally I disagree with. In this model participants are nominated for training, attend, receive a certificate or some form of acknowledgement that they have completed the training and that's the end of the process. In these organizations it is easy to understand why training departments often see budget cuts, lack of senior management support and training is not highly valued because in this 'model' the training department is not setting out with clear goals and measuring against those goals.

I've heard this approach called the 'sheep dip' approach (referring to sheep being dipped in insecticide through a trough – in one end, out the other). I've also heard it called the 'spray and pray' approach (where participants are 'sprayed' with information and trainer 'prays' that it sticks!)

Training delivery is simply one of the steps in the overall ID9® Framework. Analysis of *what* and *how* participants are or are not *applying their learning* is the important final step to the process.

High Performance Learning Model™
The High Performance Learning Model™ (Mattiske, 2006) was developed as a visual representation of the degrees of learning application by defining four types of learners. For training professionals, participant's managers and key stakeholders involved in the training process The High Performance Learning Model™ helps to determine the levels of learning support required and to raise learning motivation to reach the goals of learning programs.

The High Performance Learning Model™ (HPLM) is like a 'landing pad' where participants 'land' after the training has been completed. Each participant will 'land' in one of the four HPLM quadrants.

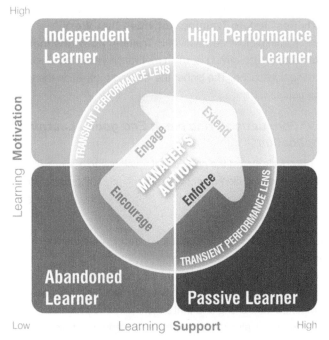

Figure 2 - High Performance Learning Model™
(Mattiske, 2006)

The High Performance Learning Model™ clearly places accountability for the success of learning with the participant (employee), trainer, participant's manager and other key influencers by forming a shared responsibility for the learning success with all of these roles throughout the training process partnered for learning success.

High Performance Learning Model™ Aim
The aim of the High Performance Learning Model™ is designed to help Managers and trainers increase the number of naturally occurring High Performance Learners by providing high Learning Support and encouraging high Learning Motivation.

Four Types of Learner Outcome
The High Performance Learning Model™ describes four types of learners *after* they have completed their learning and return to their workplace to apply what they have learned: The High Performance Learner, The Independent Learner, The Abandoned Learner and **The Passive Learner.**

The four Learner Types are not designed to 'box' people into one type or another. One employee may be simultaneously all four Learner Types, or just one, two, or three depending on the course he or she has attended.

The High Performance Learner
The High Performance Learner already displays high levels of motivation towards learning. Also the already apparent high levels of learning support fuel them to even greater learning achievement.

They have applied their learning on the job and are comfortable in their ability to do it well. High Performance Learners may have returned to their workplace and already be coaching others in the team formally or informally. Due to their high level of motivation, they may explore more in-depth knowledge of the subject autonomously.

The goal for Trainers and Managers is to **extend High Performance Learners** to achieve higher levels of performance.

The Independent Learner
The Independent Learner displays high levels of motivation, however requires Manager Learning Support in order to become a High Performance Learner.

Independent Learners may have applied their learning on the job and are comfortable in their ability to do it well, however have probably not shared their learning with others.

If they have not applied their learning on the job they may have completed the learning for their own personal benefit. In this regard, they have little or no intention of using their learning in their current role, and may have attended the learning for future roles within their current organization or to set themselves up to move to a new organization.

The goal for Trainers and Managers is to **engage Independent Learners** by coaching them to share their learning, apply their learning in their current role, and be a part of the team to achieve higher levels of performance.

The Abandoned Learner
The Abandoned Learner displays low levels of motivation, and has little to no external support. They require Trainer and Manager encouragement in order to become a High Performance Learner.

Abandoned Learners have not applied their learning on the job. In order to encourage an increase in their motivation to do so, first the Trainer and Manager should **support Abandoned Learners**.

The Passive Learner
The Passive Learner displays low levels of motivation despite having organizational and managerial support. They require counselling in order to become a High Performance Learner.

The Passive Learner has been given what is required by way of learning opportunity and support. Quite simply - they are not doing their job. Therefore, this issue is no longer a training issue, but a performance issue focused on their poor performance and lack of learning application.

The Manager may **counsel the Passive Learner** using a formal performance process provided by the organization or an informal first-step conversation to attempt to motivate them to change their behavior. The focus of the conversation should be on the positive implications of applying their learning, rather than a punishment that they have not yet applied what they have learned.

Transient Performance Lens

One person may transition from one Learner Type to another depending on the learning that have encountered or the learning they are participating in at the time.

They may even transition during a training program, entering the training program as one Learner Type (for example highly motivated and headed towards being a High Performance Learner), and then changing midstream (either positively or negatively) depending on what's happening during the training (for example becoming demotivated during the training and becoming a Passive Learner).

The reverse example can also happen where a participant begins a training program being an Abandoned Learner, thinking that they are undertaking the training as 'tick in the box' (e.g. compliance training) but during the training process realizes the support being provided for learning application and in turn becoming highly motivated, 'landing' after training as a High Performance Learner'.

The Action Arrow

The Action Arrow, the arrow in the center of the model, points to the High Performance Learner and provides the ways for trainers and managers to assist their employees to become High Performance Learners. The focus of the model is to *extend High Performance Learners* and for *all other Learner Types, support them, build their motivation and encourage them to transition to becoming a High Performance Learner*.

The High Performance Learning Model™ link to Training Activities that Work

As discussed all participants will make the personal adult choice to change their behavior as a result of training, or not. The High Performance Learning Model™ helps trainers and managers to diagnose who has and who has not applied their learning, that is changed their behavior. In the event that 100% of participants have not applied their learning the High Performance Learning

Model™ helps to prescribe activities to further support and motivate those who haven't to done so.

In **Training Activities that Work** Susan Giddens and Emma Lambert focus their chapters on providing support to managers and participants before and after training to increase learning support and build learning motivation to achieve learning application. All other co-authors focus their chapters on during the training to build motivation and display learning support thus encouraging learners every step of the process to become High Performance Learners.

Link to Adult Learning

Adult Learners: Individual Learning Preferences
Not everyone learns the same things in the same way. Not all participants in an adult learning environment need to learn the same materials in the same way, even when they are in the same training room or e-learning program. Given this, the suggestion to vary training activities would seem obvious, but too often even the best trainers can fall into habitual ways of training certain topics that don't work at an optimum level for *all* participants.

The reliance on just a few training approaches may be a combination of trainer 'comfort' and organizational expectations and norms. Often training has come to represent a specific method that is reminiscent of bygone school-days, for example mini-lectures and hands-on activities. When trainers challenge those notions and vary the structure of the learning environment and the methods they use to train, participants and organizations sometimes feel lost or become defensive of these 'new ways'. It's important for participants and organizations to stretch their idea of what it means to learn.

Some participants who enter corporate training programs are concerned about the formality of the learning environment, nervous that they may be 'tested', worried about other participants in their group, or have concerns about their own academic skills and abilities. By providing learning in many different formats building on what they already know will help participants see that their learning skills are already in place and will help them face the challenges of the new skills and knowledge with confidence.

At the heart of our learning philosophy is the question "who is responsible for learning, the trainer, the organization or the participant?" It has become widely accepted that for adult learning the responsibility should lie firmly with the participant and yet the behavior of the trainer in the classroom and managers before, during and after the course often mitigates against this. Trainers often spend more than half of their training time 'informing' participants (via mini-lectures) to the detriment of the participant's active involvement and effective learning.

Trainers without a formal training background or understanding of adult learning styles often believe that by contributing more themselves they are helping their participants to learn. However, participants retain more after the course and apply skills more effectively in the workplace if they have been actively, rather than passively, involved in the learning process. Clearly, regardless of the subject matter, it is a *balanced* approach to trainer/participant participation that will reap the greatest benefits.

It is the participant's responsibility to learn and the trainer's responsibility to create an environment in which learning can take place then it is the manager's responsibility to support the participant to create an environment where participants are able to apply what they have learned to their job.

Long before the training program begins it's the responsibility of the instructional designer to create a balanced training program that caters for the various adult learning styles to set participants up for learning success: that is, to have the motivation and ability to change their behavior.

Adult Learning Principles in Training Activities that Work

Within the ID9® process there are many adult learning principles taught throughout the ID9® Silver, Gold and Platinum levels of certification.

In **Training Activities that Work** each activity includes an **Adult Learning Checksheet** for introductory principles: Modalities (Visual, Auditory, and Kinesthetic), Global vs. Specific, Hemispheric Preference and Multiple Intelligences, which will assist the instructional designer to write the training course so that regardless of their adult learning style the course will cater for all participants. The instructional designer should incorporate a mix of all elements of these introductory principles for each training topic or training session.

Creating Balanced Learning

The instructional designer's goal is to write a balanced program that incorporates a good blend of training methods catering for all adult learners. If this balance is achieved, on the day of the training the trainer can deliver the program with the assurance that the theoretical balance is in place. This allows the trainer to concentrate on individual participant development and classroom management.

If the course is out of balance (e.g. all lecture - catering well to auditory learners but not the easiest learning approach for everyone else), the trainer may be forced to repeat sections, explain things in different ways, invent options 'on the fly' or manage struggling participants. All of these issues slow down the pace of the course and in the extreme may disengage participants or reduce their motivation to learn.

By using the activities in **Training Activities that Work** you will add to your knowledge about how adults learn and how you can refine your instructional design and or training methods to best meet participant's needs. Regardless of the complexity and difficulty of the training content, when a sound balance of all adult learning principles is struck participants may remark "I feel the course was written for me" , "the course was well presented and the content easy to learn", or "the trainer made a complex process simple". This is 'participant language' where they feel the program was trained to their preferred personal learning style, not necessarily realizing that all participants feel the same!

Conducting Learning and Review Activities

By Catherine Mattiske

In **Training Activities that Work** there are two types of activities presented: Learning Activities and Review Activities. The aim of this section is to define and explain the difference between the two as well as to define the last, and most crucial, step of the process: the Debrief.

Learning Activity vs. Review Activity

'Learning activity' versus 'Review activity'

Learning Activity Defined

Learning activities are usually conducted immediately after the trainer gives theoretical or practical information. During the activity learning is still taking place. It might be the first time that participants get to try out their new skills or learning. During learning activities the participant is usually undertaking a fully guided exercise with the trainer close at hand for feedback and remediation.

Review Activity Defined

A review activity is a way of measuring skills and knowledge during the training course. Review activities reassure participants that they are learning by providing 'proof of knowledge'. Review activities reassure trainers that they are successfully transferring skills and knowledge.

In the book Train for Results (Mattiske, 3rd Edition, 2013) this definition is explored and discussed in depth. To assist with the context of **Training Activities that Work** the following summary provides key points across the surface of this large topic.

Learning Activities presented in Training Activities that Work

The **learning activities** presented in **Training Activities that Work** are designed to accommodate different learning preferences and different types of content that is being presented prior to or during the program.

Learning activities will be chosen by the instructional designer according to the type of content, time of day, expertise of the participants in the subject and the overall learning balance of the program.

In **Training Activities that Work** learning activities are presented in Chapters 1 and 2 and all activities are focused on activating for the first time something that has been taught to participants. Chapter 1 focuses on pre-course activities which may prompt participants to reflect on what they already know, and how they'll build on their knowledge in the upcoming course, or to begin the learning of the course content prior to the course start to jump start the learning, thus saving in-class training time.

All of the learning activities presented are designed to engage different adult learning styles and allow the participant to be supported by their trainer and other participants to correct, remediate, answer questions and solidify their learning prior to moving on with further content.

Review Activities presented in Training Activities that Work

Just like learning activities, the **review activities** presented in **Training Activities that Work** are also designed to accommodate different learning preferences and different types of content that is being presented during or after the program.

In **Training Activities that Work** review activities are presented in Chapters 3 to 9 and all activities are focused on activating for the second or subsequent time something that has been taught to participants.

Review activities form an essential part of the ID9® process and ID9® Certified Professionals aim to include at least six review activities in a one-day training program, with the aim of 11 being ideal.

A training technique versus a continual process
The process of reviewing material learned throughout a training course is measured during the training. A review activity is conducted at least six times in each training day (but preferably 11 times a day) to check understanding and combat gaps and questions that bubble to the surface.

To evaluate the potential success of each participant is not a one-time technique; it is a continual process that requires the trainer to be dedicated to his or her ultimate goal. That is, to care for and share in the responsibility of the success of each participant.

This process is outlined in the chapters ahead and provide clear directions on what to do, and when, where and how to maximize your chances of success.

If reviews are in, then what's out?

I think of training courses like intricate structures — buildings of intertwined concepts and processes. Reviews do not take the place of any other training 'technique', rather they are added to the structure, like support beams in a building. They can be added into existing courses and the trainer's existing style and delivery technique.

A new trainer can also quickly adopt this process of adding review activities into their program and in doing so will be ahead of many of his or her seasoned colleagues.

Amazingly, review activities do not require any further training time; they allow you to change the pace of your training to accommodate them. They can even save you training time, a paradox which is a great 'secret' bonus to the professional trainer.

Regardless of whether you are a new trainer with a single story building of training experience, or have a skyscraper of training experience, you can successfully build on this process to create a new dimension of brilliance to every training course that you conduct.

What does a review activity do?

A review activity is conducted during the training course to measure skills and knowledge. A review activity reassures participants that they are learning, and it reassures trainers that they are successfully transferring skills and knowledge.

A review activity checks and measures the learning on a particular topic or group of topics while the participants are still in the training.

For example, in computer systems training course, a review activity might be conducted immediately after participants have learnt the parts of the desktop and the parts of a window. This topic might include the scroll bar, title bar, menus and toolbars.

- The review may take the form of a fill-in-the-blanks puzzle, where the trainer draws up a flip chart with a giant screen capture of a window on it or, easier still, prints it on a large format printer.
- Participants are given stick-on flags, each flag labelled with a part of the window, and they place their flags onto the flip chart pointing to the corresponding parts of the window.
- When all parts are identified, the trainer goes through each part and, with the group, checks for accuracy, asking in-depth questions along the way.
- The completed picture is posted on the training wall for the rest of the course as a learning prompt.

This example is a group activity, but it could easily be done as an individual exercise with a handout.

In this example, the whole process may take as little as five minutes; however, the benefit for the trainer is twofold.

- First, the trainer knows that the participants know the correct terminology.
- Second, for the rest of the course the trainer can confidently tell people to 'Click on minimize' and they know what it is!

If participants aren't familiar with this most basic of basic terminology, the trainer gets led down the disastrous path of saying things like, 'Click on minimize, no not that one. Now click here, here, here, okay, you're back to where you were — [sigh] — now click minimize. It's the button with the little line in the top right corner of the screen. That's it, good.' I used to find myself in situations where I sounded more like a broken record than a trainer!

This second benefit saves the trainer loads of frustration and ensures that the whole group is kept travelling at a much more even pace throughout the day, not to mention the huge time saving entailed by being able to give instructions once!

So, for a five-minute investment in the review activity, the benefits are endless — for both them and you!

What is the purpose of the review activity?

The purpose of a review activity is to ensure that you are meeting clearly established training goals and objectives.

The choice and placement of the review are both relatively straightforward however for an instructional designer is a skill which involves underlying complexities.

A trap for trainers who are starting out adding reviews to their courses is that sometimes 'the point' of the review gets muddied by the desire to produce exciting activities that not only enhance learning but breathe life into the course. In order to be truly successful and a true measure of learning, the review activity must have a set outcome for participants.

If the standard (in other words the training goal and learning objective) is not set then how will you know when your participants have met it?

Trainers can only measure the effectiveness of the training against the learning objective. Therefore having sound behavioral learning objectives is the key to success.

How many participants are involved in a review activity?

Review activities can be designed for individual participants, pairs, small groups or large groups. I have conducted review activities with one participant as effectively as with a group of 700 participants. A mix of different review activities provides variety for the participants and the trainer and, more important, different levels of participation help to support and provide for people's different learning styles. A mix of whole-group, team-based, pair-and-share, individual and metacognitive (or reflective) reviews should be in every training course, regardless of duration or participant job title and experience.

What form does a review activity take?

The review activity may be a handout, a card sort, a puzzle, a board game or a competition or a myriad of other training methods. Some review activities will take little or no preparation, while others will require more lead time.

A review activity may be as simple as 'squad challenge', where the trainer asks participants in small groups to write down questions to ask an opposing team of participants. This takes no preparation time on the trainer's part, but is an excellent way to review the content both for the questioning team and the answering team. The questioning team is reviewing the content when composing questions; the answering team is reviewing content by coming up with the answers.

An example of a review activity requiring preparation is a board game. Many commercially available games have boards that can easily be adapted for a training review. You need to write the questions, know the rules clearly and be able to facilitate the game or create your own. Preparation may take 30 minutes or several hours, but once the review activity is created, it can be used time and time again, making it a wise investment of preparation time.

Comparing reviews with other 'training techniques'

Review activities should not be compared with training games and review activities are *not* a technique to add 'fun' or gimmicks to training. Review activities focus only on material already taught and they are conducted at various intervals during the training course.

A training game can be used successfully or not, but mostly (unfortunately) they are just for 'fun'. These 'fun' activities are referred to by many as 'energizers'. In my opinion a learning or review activity *will* energize *and* add to the goal of achieving the learning objective. To conduct an activity as simply an energizer, without a point, just for fun, is a waste of time.

Link to Training Activities that Work

In **Training Activities that Work** each activity includes the heading **Essential Data** which will inform you on the type of course the activity is suited towards, the suggested group size, the time of day, the pace and the time, both to prepare the activity and to conduct the activity. This information is provided as a guide only and of course can be adapted to suit individual needs.

The Debrief Process

Following the learning or review activity, the trainer conducts a debriefing (known as a 'debrief'), in which further questions, comments and knowledge gaps of individual participants are fully explored.

Feedback and Debrief Feedback defined

To assist with clarification the definition of feedback and debrief, comparing and contrasting both, are provided as follows.

Feedback defined

As a participant seeks to improve his or her performance, feedback helps to make required adjustments. Feedback lets participants know if they are on track with their learning, or if they require further assistance. It also encourages and motivates participants providing the positive reinforcement needed to maintain a safe learning environment. Feedback occurs throughout the entire training program and is communicated mainly by the trainer to the participant.

Debrief defined

A debrief is conducted by the trainer as the final step to a learning or review activity. During the debrief the trainer checks the results of the activity, provides feedback, fills gaps in learning and ensures that participants are confident to move on to the next session of content.

The Value of Debrief

Why is debriefing a crucial step? Learning is evolutionary. Knowledge and learning is formed step by step over time. During a training session the participant should become proficient with each stage of the learning, gaining the confidence to progress to the next stage. The trainer mediates this process. If left to themselves, only truly self-motivated participants will link the learning to real life and persist with applying their learning to their day-to-day lives. A debrief gives the participants an opportunity to talk through their learning experience and then discuss how they will transfer their learning.

The value of prepared questions

The right questions are powerful tools for engaging participants so that they reflect on new knowledge and explore the ways in which they may apply their new learning in work and life. Generally there is a strong relationship between the amount of time spent preparing appropriate questions by the instructional designer and the effectiveness of the debrief. Preparing questions beforehand is the surest way of knowing your questions will lead your participants to reflect on the key points. Prepared questions should be open-ended and higher order questions that usually begin with the typical question words *what, where, which, why* and *how?*

Thoughtfully prepared questions can help the debrief flow so well it seems to lead itself!

Debrief Questions link to Training Activities that Work

In **Training Activities that Work** debrief questions have been written for every activity. The benefit of having these debrief questions already written is that each of the questions are constructed using the ID9® process of creating high-impact debrief questions and each strive to meet the prescribed level of Bloom's Taxonomy in the Cognitive Domain as stated in the activity.

Using Training Activities That Work

By Catherine Mattiske

Training Activities That Work is designed as a book that you can either read cover to cover or use as a reference guide to spark ideas for learning and review activities.

If you haven't already done so I suggest that you read the chapters **ID9® Overview** and **Conducting Learning and Review Activities** to provide context and foundation to the book.

Training Activities that Work - Structure

The book is divided into main sections – pre-course, during course, post-course and manager tracks. Each of the eight co-authors has focused on one of these areas of the learning process.

Pre-Course

Chapter 1 - Pre-Course Activities for Participants focuses on learning activities that set the stage for learning. Emma Lambert presents activities that can be prescribed to participants for completion before the training program and then debriefed either prior to or during the program.

During-Course

In **Chapter 2 - During Course: Learning Activities** Denise Gaul writes activities for activating new knowledge. Please refer to the definition of learning activities versus review activities. This chapter will generate ideas for new ways for participants to practice new skills and knowledge.

In **Chapter 3 - During Course: Mini Review Activities** Diana McLeod presents review activities which take very little time. These review activities (see definition stated previously) are ideal to conduct either before or after a break. There is no need for trainers to 'announce' the activity but rather 'just do it' and participants will benefit from the review activity without any emotional feeling of being tested in an examination environment.

Chapter 4 - During Course: Review Activities - Post-Lunch, Elizabeth Tighe presents new and creative ideas to refocus participants after lunch or a significant break. These activities run for an approximate duration of 15 minutes and are all targeted to reengage the learner by reviewing material presented in the previous session and building motivation to move on with further learning.

Melanie Barn presents in **Chapter 5 - During Course: Review Activities - End of Day / Start of Day** activities that are suited for multi-day or multi-session training programs. These activities finish the day/session or begin the day/session with the aim of filling any knowledge gaps that exist from previous sessions before moving on and building learner confidence and motivation.

In **Chapter 6 - During Course: Review Activities - End of Course** Aly Rumbelow presents activities that are suitable as 'Step 6 – Major Review' in the ID9® nine-step instructional design process. These review activities review the key learning points of the entire program and should be designed in accordance with the overall learning objectives of the entire program.

For training programs spanning several sessions over a period of days or weeks, Alison Asbury presents in **Chapter 7 - Bridging Tasks for Participants - Learning and Review Activities**. These activities are noted as either a learning activity or a review activity and provide a resource to keep learning alive in between sessions.

Post-Course

Emma Lambert, who wrote Chapter 1, also presents **Chapter 8 - Post-Course Tasks for Participants - Application of Learning Activities**. These activities are focused on supporting learners after the training program as they strive to apply what they have learned in the workplace.

Manager Track

In **Chapter 9 - Supporting the Learning - Activities for Managers and Trainers** Susan Giddens has focused on activities that the instructional designer can provide to trainers and managers for them to conduct with participants who are registered to or who have completed the course with the express aim of keeping support high which we know maximizes the chances that the participants will become High Performance Learners and apply what they have learned.

Adult Learning Base Processes

In all chapters the theory or training process which forms the foundation stone to the activity is stated in each activity under the heading Adult Learning Base Process. In **Chapter 10 Adult Learning Base Process** each of the base processes are listed with a brief definition. Each of these processes, and many more, are learned in detail during the ID9® Certification programs.

I hope that you will find that each of the chapters in **Training Activities that Work** like a Pandora's box of ways to spark new ideas, save instructional design and training time and create highly engaging learning that results in a high degree of learning application.

Enjoy!

Chapter 1:
Pre-Course Activities for Participants

Emma Lambert

About the Co-Author:

Emma Lambert

Emma Lambert discovered her love of teaching in 1995 when she qualified as a nurse and took a teaching qualification (C&G 7307 Further and Adult Education Teaching Certificate) to improve her chances of promotion in nursing. Little did she know then that she was opening a door to a whole new passion. Since then there have been a number other qualifications, including those in teaching and training which have taken her through a number of roles in the clinical setting and finally to the pharmaceutical industry where she has been in leadership and management roles all of which have involved teaching or training, including designing whole curricula, either formally or informally for her team. Currently Global Head Learning Operations and Quality at Novartis AG Switzerland Emma continues to build her knowledge of the science behind teaching and training and feed her passion for the speciality.

Chapter Introduction

Welcome to this chapter on pre-course activities. Before you turn the page and move on let me tell you why I think you should read this chapter! I can't promise that it will change your life but I do think it will give you some practical ideas that you can use.

As committed professionals, we trainers want to make the most of the window of opportunity that we have to influence our participants. Pre-course work acts to leverage to the time we have with our participants whether the training is conducted face to face in a traditional classroom setting or virtually where participants join their class via the internet in a meeting space. Certainly for me, assigning pre-course work is a learning opportunity that should not be missed.

Pre-course work can be used to set the expectation that training is an interactive journey not a passive ride and delivers the message "Hey, you need to take part" before the course begins. It can also be used as a tool to assist participants in examining why they are taking the training, asking them to really analyze why they are giving, or being told to give, time to the training program and what they want to get out of the training. Pre-course work may even hook them in and build on existing motivation or lighting a flame of motivation where there was none.

When we need to make sure that all our participants are in possession of similar knowledge so that we can move forward with new learning a pre-course activity can deliver this for us. Also, let's not forget that as well as providing this background information about the upcoming training program, we can also use a pre-course activity to reduce the actual time needed during the training program by delivering some of our content in advance. This way the learning begins well before participants arrive at the course.

As learning checkpoints make sure all pre-course activities you assign link to your learning objectives and that each pre-course activity is debriefed in some way during the training program with your participants, simple!

Whatever purpose you have in whatever content area that you are training I hope you will find something useful in the pages that follow.

1. Setting the Pace of Achievement

Learning outcome
Identifying key goals the participant has in attending this course.

Overview
This pre-course activity is used to assist the participant in examining their own skills or knowledge gap before the course and focusing in on what it is they really want to gain from attending it.

In my experience
The aim of a course can be appealing to the global learner who may then skim the objectives seeing only the big picture and not the steps involved in reaching the destination. Similarly the objectives can hold the attention of the specific learner without really linking to the overall view of what the course aims to achieve. This pre-course activity encourages participants to examine the aim and objective in detail and really think about the course content and their motivation for attending the course whether they have chosen it themselves or been nominated to attend. In doing this they begin to formulate their own expectations of the course and the work involved.

The hidden twist
Participants are channeled into thinking about what their attendance at the course means, what they want to get out of it but also what is expected of them when they have completed the course. This directs the thinking away from training as being an event that they attend for the duration to it being a step in a journey towards a different way of thinking or doing things. In doing this we increase the chance of learning transfer and application leading to the intended objectives by strengthening the message that this training has expected outcomes. It also has the added advantage that in examining the aim and objectives in detail the participant may reach the conclusion that this course is not the route they need to take to fill the gap in their skills thus preventing the waste of time and resource that results in participants attending training that they do not need.

Finally, this pre-course activity starts the process of linking attendance to the need to take action after the course further optimizing the chance of attendance leading to the results managers are looking for.

Essential data
Course Type – Any
Group Size – Individual
Time of day – This is a pre-course activity that should be completed prior to attendance. Ideally at least one week before the course
Pace – Slow and focused
Time to Create – 15 minutes
Time to run – Zero Trainer time – (debriefed in expectation and concerns if used)

Steps to create
- Create an e-mail to the participants detailing the course aim and objectives again and instructing them on what to do. Attach a template of your questions so that participants can write their answers.
- Write your aim and objectives on your template and then ask the questions
  - What do you want from this course?
  - What benefit will this bring you?
  - How will you know when you have got this?
  - How will someone else know when you have got it?
  - What is your first step to achieving the outcome you desire?
  - What will be the final step?
  - How long do you think it will take to achieve your desired outcome?
  - How does this fit in with your other goals?
  - Can you start this journey to your goal and sustain it?
  - What resources do you need e.g. time, money, manager support
  - How will you feel when you achieve your goal?

Steps to run
- Send your e-mail and template to the participants
- Explain the steps
  - Read the course aim and objectives carefully
  - Answer the questions on the attached sheet
  - Bring the sheet with you to the course as we will refer to it
  - If you have any questions please contact me

Suggested Debrief Strategy / Sample Questions

By using Expectations and Concerns as an activity to connect the participants to the course the trainer can ask participants to refer to the pre-course activity to define what they want to get from the course.

The trainer should check that the expectation will be facilitated by the course or explain if it won't.

Ask the participants if anybody identified a desired outcome that they hadn't realized they had.

When participants complete the pre-course work this can also be used by the trainer to initiate conversation before the official start of the course e.g. "What is your key personal objective in attending the course?"

Working example

This pre-course activity is particularly useful in a course that has post course outcomes which will be measured by defined indicators (e.g. a measurable increase in productivity) as it allows the participant to consider their personal motivation for attending while setting the expectation that there will be some change resulting from attendance at the course for which they, the participant, are responsible and accountable.

Tips, tricks and traps

- Make sure participants are aware that you will refer to pre-course work in class – they are more likely to do it
- Debrief in some way to ensure expectations and planned outcomes are appropriate to the course
- Give participants your contact details when you send the e-mail and invite them to contact you with questions – builds rapport and gives the participant permission to ask
- Beware of unrealistic expectations from the course
- Make sure you link the effort required by the participant to desired outcomes – they will not get what they want by attending the course alone.

Adult Learning Base Process – NLP – Pacer

Refer to **Adult Learning Base Process Reference Guide** for more information about this learning process.

Adult Learning Dashboard

This activity links participant's preferred style of learning. The following dashboard provides a quick reference to adult learning theorists and principles as part of the ID9® methodology.

This activity achieves the following level of Bloom's Taxonomy of the Cognitive Domain (Bloom et al 1956), shown with "X" in the following table.

Bloom's Taxonomy of the Cognitive Domain Level					
Knowledge	Comprehension	Application	Analysis	Synthesis	Evaluation
			X		

This activity also achieves a link, shown with "X" in the following table, to participant's naturally occurring learning preferences. Global/Specific, Learning Modalities, Hemispheric Preference (Sperry, 1981), and Multiple Intelligences (Gardner, 1983) are referenced in ID9® methodology and process. This is not a complete list of links that are covered within the ID9® process however this dashboard aims to provide a quick reference for trainers to use to balance instructional design to provide equality for participants' learning preferences.

Global/Specific Learners		Learning Modalities (Sensory Intake)			Hemispheric Preference	
Global	Specific	Visual	Auditory	Kinesthetic	Left Brain	Right Brain
X	X	X		X	X	X

Multiple Intelligences								
Visual	Intrapersonal	Interpersonal	Musical	Mathematical / Logical	Linguistic	Kinesthetic	Naturalist	Existential
X	X				X	X		X

2. Islands of Knowledge or Curiosity

Learning outcome
Identifying the level of knowledge the participant has prior to the course and focusing the participant on what they already know "islands of knowledge" and what they want to learn "islands of curiosity".

Overview
This pre-course activity is designed to draw out the knowledge of the subject to be taught so that the trainer can assess the level at which to pitch a course. It makes a change from the usual questionnaire format and is based loosely on the Rico Clusters principal developed by the late Gabriele Rico PH.D.

In My Experience
As trainers, we all know that sinking feeling when we dive in to delivering a course and suddenly see eyes glaze over as what we are saying sails over the heads of our participants or eyelids droop as our participants are lulled to sleep by something they already know. It is no fun for us as trainers and it is no fun for the participants either. This pre-course activity allows the trainer to assess the level of knowledge of the participant while engaging the global and specific learners, and our left and right brain learners. The global learners can go to town with the concepts and big picture while the specific learners can go through the process in an ordered and linear manner and the benefits it delivers are multifaceted as we will see in the hidden twist.

The Hidden Twist
Before the course begins, participants are asked about their knowledge of the subject which gets them thinking about what they know and also what they don't know. In turn this pre-course activity helps to focus a participant on why they are going to a course and what they want to learn and can optimize the chance of the reluctant attendee reaching the point of realizing what's in it for me in spending time on this course and motivate the already on-board or high performance learner (Mattiske) further by identifying knowledge and gaps. This helps the trainer to assess where to pitch the course to make sure they are on target by identifying the level of knowledge, the gaps and the areas where people really want input. It also does the following:

- Indicates to the trainer the ratio of global learners to specific learners in the class. You can identify these traits by looking at the way in which the participant has completed the activity. Of course your training will be well balanced so this isn't critical but knowing this in advance may lead you to amend your delivery to weight it more if needed.
- Gives the trainer pointers as to whether a participant has a left or right brain dominance. Again, of course your training is balanced for both of these but if you are putting together groups for activities you may want to avoid putting all your right brained and global learners together.
- It allows the trainer the luxury of some background knowledge of each participant so that, in the event that they are difficult to engage, you have an optimal chance of finding the hook that works for them by appealing to their preferences. An experienced trainer will pick these preferences up during the session but prior knowledge can be a great safety blanket for the new trainer.
- Indicates the experts in the room. The trainer can easily identify in advance the people in the room with a lot of knowledge. These people can be used to coach those with less knowledge thus helping to make sure that both get the best out of the session and stay engaged and motivated.
- Conversely it indicates the participants with weaker knowledge. The trainer can make sure that in putting groups together there is a balance of knowledge so that you avoid having a group that struggles to complete a task while another finishes in minutes and needs a stretch task to keep them interested

All of these advantages assist the trainer in potentially making the course as impactful as possible for all attendees, identifying what needs a lot of time and where content can be dropped if needed and making sure that the participant has had the opportunity to really think about why they are attending a course and what they want to get from it.

As a final advantage, you can use the results of the activity during the training to identify the participant expectations and really help to connect them to the session.

Essential data

Course Type – Any

Group Size – Any

Time of day – Pre-course

Pace – quick

Time to create – Thirty minutes

Time to run – Allow around five minutes per participant to review the answers and a further 30 minutes to assimilate the information and decide on any actions as a result.

Steps to Create

- In your email/communication about the pre-course activity ask participants to take two pieces of paper and on the top of one write "Things I know about ……" and at the top of the other write "Things I want to know about……"
- Below this write the subjects you want information on in individual circles placed randomly on the page. This could be one word for example "Communication" or content specific to their workplace such as "Use of Bayesian Statistics"
- Provide a sample of a Rico Cluster (see Adult Learning Base Process Reference Guide) and provide information on how to create a Rico Cluster. For example: start somewhere on the page with a central idea "Communication", then using unstructured branches write any words that come to mind about Communication to create a network of islands. Provide tips for success such as work quickly, don't edit, put down what comes immediately to mind and there are no incorrect answers.
- Send the pre-course work instructions to the participants up to two weeks before the training.

Steps to run

- As pre-course work, ask the participants to spend five minutes brainstorming each word or phrase (Island) and jotting down whatever comes to them around the island.
- When they have completed the "Things I know about …" page, ask them to do the same for the "Things I want to know about…" page
- Ask the participant to send a copy of the activity to you and to bring a copy to the training if you will be using it during the session.

Suggested Debrief Strategy / Sample Questions

Use the activity as the basis for an "expectations and concerns" activity in the training by asking the participant to refer to the activity and identify an expectation. Alternatively, you could do this as a pair and share activity and ask the participants to work in twos and find areas where one can teach the other about an area. You can even expand this to a "bingo" style ice breaker using selected facts and asking people to find somebody who wrote down that they know 'X' or would like to know 'Y'.

Working Example

This activity works particularly well for any kind of training as you tailor your islands to the objectives of the course. However, it is best suited to small groups of less than 10 participants due to the input required from the trainer and the issues around remembering all the information you have gleaned from the activity. It is also best used for short courses where you can collect meaningful data rather than long and complicated ones.

Tips Trick and Traps

- Choose the words or phrases in your islands carefully to ensure you really do focus people in the right place
- Make the islands as specific as needed as a general heading such as 'leadership' could invoke a tsunami of irrelevant information. Use your objectives to craft the island. For instance, if the objective is 'Identify the leadership model used in our organization' then use the island "The leadership model at xxxx" and so on.
- Read the responses and refer to them during the course, otherwise your participants will wonder why they had to make an effort and you will lose some credibility

Adult Learning Base Process – Rico Cluster

Refer to **Adult Learning Base Process Reference Guide** for more information about this learning process.

Adult Learning Dashboard
This activity links participant's preferred style of learning. The following dashboard provides a quick reference to adult learning theorists and principles as part of the ID9® methodology.

This activity achieves the following level of Bloom's Taxonomy of the Cognitive Domain (Bloom et al 1956), shown with "X" in the following table.

Bloom's Taxonomy of the Cognitive Domain Level					
Knowledge	Comprehension	Application	Analysis	Synthesis	Evaluation
X					

This activity also achieves a link, shown with "X" in the following table, to participant's naturally occurring learning preferences. Global/Specific, Learning Modalities, Hemispheric Preference (Sperry, 1981), and Multiple Intelligences (Gardner, 1983) are referenced in ID9® methodology and process. This is not a complete list of links that are covered within the ID9® process however this dashboard aims to provide a quick reference for trainers to use to balance instructional design to provide equality for participants' learning preferences.

Global/Specific Learners		Learning Modalities (Sensory Intake)			Hemispheric Preference	
Global	Specific	Visual	Auditory	Kinesthetic	Left Brain	Right Brain
X	X	X	X	X	X	X

Multiple Intelligences								
Visual	Intrapersonal	Interpersonal	Musical	Mathematical / Logical	Linguistic	Kinesthetic	Naturalist	Existential
X	X	X (in debrief)		X	X	X		X

3. Talking To Myself

Learning Outcome
Beginning the process of breaking down the barriers that participants have to learning before they attend a training session

Overview
Whether we realize it or not we all have potential barriers to learning which, when brought to the training session, slow us and our fellow participants down and can potentially result in training being a waste of resources for the participant, the trainer and the organization. By encouraging the participant to acknowledge and challenge the barriers before reaching the training we can increase the chance of resolving at least some of them and thus improve the chances of minimizing their impact on the day

In my experience
Acknowledging that barriers exist and are normal and encouraging the participant to rationalize them helps to lessen their impact and can open doors that participants were not even aware existed. I first saw this used this as a pre-course activity when introducing a new system which resulted in major changes and have since used it in similar situations. I have been constantly surprised by the positive reaction to the activity and to the number of participants who have reached out before the course for help.

The Hidden Twist
While they examine the barriers applicable to them and challenge their perception of them the participant is also learning a new technique for addressing other situations. In addition you are starting to acknowledge and address sources of resistance to making the change in behavior. If participants identify a major barrier with no strategy available to address it you have the opportunity to suggest they attend at a different time if possible

Essential Data
Course Type – Any
Group Size – Any
Time of day – Pre course
Pace – Intermediate
Time to Create – Approximately 60 minutes
Time to Run – No trainer time – Approximately 40 minutes

Steps to Create
- The trainer needs to create a scenario based on a case study of a participant invited to the particular training course. In the scenario the participant receives the invitation to the course and then experiences the nine most common barriers to learning. The scenario should map out what these are and why they exist
- Create an instruction sheet for the participant
- Create a question and answer template
- Create debrief page

Steps to run
- Send the package to the participant up to three weeks before the course
- Ask them to read the case study and highlight any situations they have found themselves in e.g. not wanting to attend a course because they doubt whether they can achieve what is required from it
- When they have completed this step ask them to write down any of the barriers that apply to them on receiving this invitation
- Next ask them to imagine that they are sitting opposite themselves and asking the question 'Why do you feel like this about this training?'
- Answer those questions
- Next imagine yourself asking the question 'What can I do to overcome these barriers?' and each time the answer is 'nothing' or 'I don't know' imagine a third person is challenging that and putting forward a suggestion
- Collate this information into the template and review it
- Identify one step you can take to reduce the size of the barrier
- Read the final page

Suggested Debrief/ Sample Questions
Include as a final page a personal message from you the trainer explaining that these barriers are normal and that everybody will experience at least one of them. Explain why you have asked them to do this activity and offer them the opportunity to contact you to discuss this further if they have concerns around the outcome

If you are using an expectations and concerns activity in your course you can refer to this activity here and ask people to share their concerns and coping strategies

Working Example

This is a really good pre-course activity to use when you are implementing a new process and are expecting a lot of resistance to it as the participant is encouraged to challenge himself and herself and this can lead to them really examining the root cause of their feelings.

Tips Tricks and Traps

- Make the case study believable, you are aiming for a situation people can identify with not a comic book scenario with extreme reactions
- Include your contact details and be prepared to coach people who contact you

Adult Learning Base Process – Case Study/ Perceptual Positions

Refer to **Adult Learning Base Process Reference Guide** for more information about this learning process.

Adult Learning Dashboard

This activity links participant's preferred style of learning. The following dashboard provides a quick reference to adult learning theorists and principles as part of the ID9® methodology.

This activity achieves the following level of Bloom's Taxonomy of the Cognitive Domain (Bloom et al 1956), shown with "X" in the following table.

Bloom's Taxonomy of the Cognitive Domain Level					
Knowledge	Comprehension	Application	Analysis	Synthesis	Evaluation
			X		

This activity also achieves a link, shown with "X" in the following table, to participant's naturally occurring learning preferences. Global/Specific, Learning Modalities, Hemispheric Preference (Sperry, 1981), and Multiple Intelligences (Gardner, 1983) are referenced in ID9® methodology and process. This is not a complete list of links that are covered within the ID9® process however this dashboard aims to provide a quick reference for trainers to use to balance instructional design to provide equality for participants' learning preferences.

Global/Specific Learners		Learning Modalities (Sensory Intake)			Hemispheric Preference	
Global	Specific	Visual	Auditory	Kinesthetic	Left Brain	Right Brain
X	X	X	X	X	X	X

Multiple Intelligences								
Visual	Intrapersonal	Interpersonal	Musical	Mathematical / Logical	Linguistic	Kinesthetic	Naturalist	Existential
X	X			X	X	X		X

4. Read All About It

Learning Outcome
Providing background reading on a topic to be covered in the course.

Overview
An aim in pre-course work is to start to identify benefits of learning to engage the participant in the learning process and also to establish base line knowledge from which to work. In addition we can use this time as an opportunity to provide background reading on a topic that is needed during the course but which will not be directly covered. This activity is used to provide that background or, where a participant has previously learned it, to refresh the learning.

In my experience
Background information can be provided just by sending out newspaper or magazine articles and asking the participant to read them but I find that mostly only the very dedicated are likely to do this. By linking the information to an activity we are not only increasing the chance of completion of the work but by using this case study approach we are demonstrating the application of the knowledge and by choosing the right case study increasing our chance to light the flame of interest in our participant and underline the benefit of taking part. The creation of the case study is the time consuming piece but once created you can use it for every course and there is no trainer time required to run

The hidden twist
Participants are directed to information that we want them to have and are asked to analyze and apply the learning rather than just skim it. In using this technique we can increase the content of the training without increasing the actual attendance time.

Essential Data
Course Type – Any
Group Size – Any
Time of day – Pre-course
Pace – Individual
Time to create – Approximately half a day
Time to run – No trainer time and participant time dependent on amount of information to be covered

Steps to Create
- Identify topic to be covered
- Identify newspaper article, journal article, book or book chapter to be used
- Write the case study
- Write the instructions to the participant

Steps to Run
- Send the case study, instructions and information/book/article to the participant

Suggested Debrief Strategy/Questions
Refer to the case study when you reach the part of the course it was the foundation for and check whether any of the participants have outstanding questions about it before moving on. You may want to check whether the subject was completely new to anybody so that you can keep an eye out to ensure that they have grasped the overall concept and are keeping up with people with prior knowledge.

Working Example
This is particularly useful in courses for managers and senior people where there is a tendency to assume that they will know the "basics" but the reality is that they may well have covered something some years ago, or perhaps not at all. It is also useful in providing updates to established information. With time being a constraint for trainers we do not want to spend time on the topic during the course that participants may already know but it is essential to other activities that they have prior knowledge. In providing a pre-course case study we have a vehicle for delivering extra content without increasing valuable in-session training time.

Tips, tricks and traps
- Make sure your case study is relevant to the course objectives, don't be tempted to just write anything to match the information
- Keep the length of the case study appropriate to the level and duration of the course
- If there are key points you want participants to retain then craft a key question around them to improve the chance of them reading and retaining that point
- Ensure that you do not breach any copyright or intellectual property rules in the use of the articles, books etc. Where necessary purchase copies of books to distribute with the pre-course work instructions.
- Make sure participants are aware that you will be referring to the pre-course activity during the course and so completing it will be to their advantage

Adult Learning Base Process – Case Study
Refer to **Adult Learning Base Process Reference Guide** for more information about this learning process.

Adult Learning Dashboard
This activity links participant's preferred style of learning. The following dashboard provides a quick reference to adult learning theorists and principles as part of the ID9® methodology.

This activity achieves the following level of Bloom's Taxonomy of the Cognitive Domain (Bloom et al 1956), shown with "X" in the following table.

Bloom's Taxonomy of the Cognitive Domain Level					
Knowledge	Comprehension	Application	Analysis	Synthesis	Evaluation
			X		

This activity also achieves a link, shown with "X" in the following table, to participant's naturally occurring learning preferences. Global/Specific, Learning Modalities, Hemispheric Preference (Sperry, 1981), and Multiple Intelligences (Gardner, 1983) are referenced in ID9® methodology and process. This is not a complete list of links that are covered within the ID9® process however this dashboard aims to provide a quick reference for trainers to use to balance instructional design to provide equality for participants' learning preferences.

Global/Specific Learners		Learning Modalities (Sensory Intake)			Hemispheric Preference	
Global	Specific	Visual	Auditory	Kinesthetic	Left Brain	Right Brain
X	X	X	X	X	X	X

Multiple Intelligences								
Visual	Intrapersonal	Interpersonal	Musical	Mathematical / Logical	Linguistic	Kinesthetic	Naturalist	Existential
X	X	X		X		X	X		X

5. Case in Point

Learning Outcome
Providing the participant with the opportunity to receive peer coaching during the course on a topic that has real relevance for them.

Overview
This pre-course activity is designed to allow the participant to examine a situation or challenge that is personal and current to them prior to the course and then to receive coaching and feedback from their peers during it.

In my experience
Case studies are a great way to share information and experience and learn from ourselves and our fellow participants. I find though that people really engage in them when the case study is really pertinent to their role and real life situation. I also find that participants really buy into a real life situation rather than a fictional scenario. They can identify with people, processes and politics amongst other things in the case study and often relish in helping a colleague to work through the study and come out with something tangible at the end of it that they can try back on the job.

The hidden twist
Prior to the course our participant is encouraged to analyze an aspect of their job, explore their feelings, actions, perceptions and plans and commit it to paper. There is an unspoken message here that this training is going to have an advantage for the participant because we are going to use this in class. For the trainer the advantage is that participants are creating your activities for you!

Essential Data
Course Type – Any course type, but particularly useful in leadership and change management courses
Group Size – Can be used from small to really large as you will split participants into smaller groups to work
Time of day – Prior to the course
Pace – Medium
Time to create – 20 minutes
Time to run – Zero time pre-course but debrief will depend upon size of group and desired outcomes

Steps to Create
- Create a message to the participants giving them the outline of the scenario you want them to write a case study on, e.g. giving feedback, coaching a team member
- Ask the participant to prepare the case study using a situation they are currently dealing with
- Tell them you will be using the case study during the course

Steps to Run
- Send the message to the participant at least four weeks prior to the course

Suggested Debrief Strategy/Questions
The case study will be used during the training as part of a small group activity and the debrief will depend upon the desired outcome of that activity. As a rule though make sure that you bring the group back together and ask some higher order questions such as "What questions has this activity raised?" to close the loop before moving on.

Working Example
This activity is great in leadership courses where you have a broad spectrum of experience in the room and want to encourage learning from each other and coaching skills. The fact that the case studies come from real life, current situations gives the activity credibility and relevance and the fact that it is prepared before the course allows the participant to really think through what they would like coaching on and so choose the right scenario.

Tips, tricks and traps
- Make sure the participants know that you will be using these case studies during the course so they are not taken by surprise with something they do not want to share with the group
- Brief the participants to use language that is generic for people outside their area to understand i.e. no highly technical or specialized words and acronyms!
- Advise participants not to choose a highly complex situation as there will be a time limit on the session
- Never spotlight participants during the course to 'perform' or 'act out' their case study

- Suggest the participant gives general background: your situation; the people involved; and the context, environment and current factors affecting your ability to handle the challenge
- Guide the participant to give key problems or issues: i.e. why the situation presents a challenge
- Remind participants that they need to maintain confidentiality so should not use actual names
- Encourage participants to use positive situations as well as negative

Adult Learning Dashboard

This activity links participant's preferred style of learning. The following dashboard provides a quick reference to adult learning theorists and principles as part of the ID9® methodology.

This activity achieves the following level of Bloom's Taxonomy of the Cognitive Domain (Bloom et al 1956), shown with "X" in the following table.

Bloom's Taxonomy of the Cognitive Domain Level					
Knowledge	Comprehension	Application	Analysis	Synthesis	Evaluation
			X		

This activity also achieves a link, shown with "X" in the following table, to participant's naturally occurring learning preferences. Global/Specific, Learning Modalities, Hemispheric Preference (Sperry, 1981), and Multiple Intelligences (Gardner, 1983) are referenced in ID9® methodology and process. This is not a complete list of links that are covered within the ID9® process however this dashboard aims to provide a quick reference for trainers to use to balance instructional design to provide equality for participants' learning preferences.

Global/Specific Learners		Learning Modalities (Sensory Intake)			Hemispheric Preference	
Global	Specific	Visual	Auditory	Kinesthetic	Left Brain	Right Brain
X	X	X	X	X	X	X

Multiple Intelligences								
Visual	Intrapersonal	Interpersonal	Musical	Mathematical / Logical	Linguistic	Kinesthetic	Naturalist	Existential
X	X	X		X	X	X		X

6. Go to jail!

Learning Outcome

Focus the participant on the importance of the training for them, their colleagues and the organization.

Overview

Use this pre-course activity when you really want to highlight the impact of not following process, regulations etc. It is particularly useful in preparing people for compliance training or process training where skepticism or lack of awareness of consequences can be high and participants may be tempted to think that they really don't need to do what is being asked of them. The idea behind the activity is to get participants to research cases such as law suits arising from breaches of policy or non-compliance. Seeing the consequence, for instance, of loss of life from not following a health and safety process and a subsequent case against an organization or individual brings the importance of process and policy into very sharp focus.

The Hidden Twist

Before the participant steps through the door or logs on to the session they know that what they are being taught is highly important and that the consequences of non-compliance are potentially far reaching and could be personal. As a trainer you have grabbed their attention already and have already started the process of linking what they will learn to the expectation of a behavior change

Essential Data

Course Type – Compliance and process training
Group Size – Any
Time of day – Any
Pace – Medium
Time to create – Fifteen minutes
Time to run – Zero trainer time

Steps to create

- Decide on the issue you want the participant to research
- Create a template for participants to list the cases they have found and answer the questions
- Create a message to the participant detailing what you want them to do
  - Introduce yourself and the course aim
  - Explain that you want the participant to research current and recent cases involving x – the subject of your training
  - Ask the participants to briefly outline the cases they found

  - Ask the participants to answer the following questions
    - What is the likelihood of this situation arising in my place of work
    - How might you be implicated
    - What thoughts or concerns have been raised by reading the cases
    - What were your first thoughts on being invited to this training
    - Have your thoughts been changed by your findings and if so why

Steps to run

- Send the message and the template to the participants
- Explain what to do
  - Using the internet and the intranet search for legal cases resulting from xxxxx
  - Using the template provided
    - Write a brief outline of the facts behind the case and the outcome
    - List the impact for the following people
      - The victim if there is one
      - The perpetrator/s
      - Any people found "guilty by association"
      - The organization
      - The reputation of the organization
- Using the template write up your findings
- Answer the questions listed
- Bring your findings to the course

Suggested Debrief Strategy/Simple Questions

In doing this the trainer is identifying the 'why' question which benefits the participant. As in, 'Why do I have to do this training?' and giving the participant a clear 'what's in it for me'. The WIIFM being the opportunity to make sure you are never caught up in such a scenario. You are also examining the 'what if' quadrant by focusing on what can happen if rules are not followed. Participants favoring the left brain will find the research and analysis side of this activity appealing while those favoring the right will be hooked by the opportunity to explore the human side of the cases in thoughts, feelings and intuition.

One way of debriefing this is to refer to it during the introduction to the course along the lines of "We are here today to minimize the possibility of people reading your name in such cases in the future." It can also be used as a connect activity to refocus the participants on why they are in the training.

Working Example

This activity has particular impact in training that has resulted from an audit finding or a "near miss" incident. I have found that getting participants to really think about what can happen when a process is not followed breaks down barriers that can arise if people think they are being sent on a training course as a punishment for their part in a near miss. It is also very effective in destroying the perception that processes are something we have to follow when we have time but in the real world we sometimes have to do things differently. While the vast majority would never breach a process with malicious intent there are many who would innocently do it thinking it was "with the best intent" or "to speed things up" or any number of the circumstances that lead to these situations. I have seen mindsets change completely on completion of this activity and had people almost clamoring to get into the training!

Tips, tricks and traps

- Define what you mean by 'recent' when you send out the task, state for instance the last five years, this year, this month, etc so you avoid people looking back centuries for examples
- Be clear about the topic you want them to research
- In debriefing the task make sure you allay any fears. You want participants to feel confident they can avoid situations and not be terrified of going to work
- Make sure you provide participants with details of where to get help if they feel there are breaches in their area
- Be aware of the issues that may arise for participants who have been involved in audit findings or similar and may feel threatened by this

Adult Learning Dashboard

This activity links participant's preferred style of learning. The following dashboard provides a quick reference to adult learning theorists and principles as part of the ID9® methodology.

This activity achieves the following level of Bloom's Taxonomy of the Cognitive Domain (Bloom et al 1956), shown with "X" in the following table.

Bloom's Taxonomy of the Cognitive Domain Level					
Knowledge	Comprehension	Application	Analysis	Synthesis	Evaluation
			X		

This activity also achieves a link, shown with "X" in the following table, to participant's naturally occurring learning preferences. Global/Specific, Learning Modalities, Hemispheric Preference (Sperry, 1981), and Multiple Intelligences (Gardner, 1983) are referenced in ID9® methodology and process. This is not a complete list of links that are covered within the ID9® process however this dashboard aims to provide a quick reference for trainers to use to balance instructional design to provide equality for participants' learning preferences.

Global/Specific Learners		Learning Modalities (Sensory Intake)			Hemispheric Preference	
Global	Specific	Visual	Auditory	Kinesthetic	Left Brain	Right Brain
X	X	X	X	X	X	X

Multiple Intelligences								
Visual	Intrapersonal	Interpersonal	Musical	Mathematical / Logical	Linguistic	Kinesthetic	Naturalist	Existential
X	X	X		X	X	X		X

7. How do you do

Learning Outcome
Build a rapport with your participants in advance of the course.

Overview
This pre-course activity is a simple way of making sure that participants know who you are before they reach the training. You will of course introduce yourself at the beginning of the course but this activity gives the trainer the opportunity to establish a relationship with the participants in advance and give them a point of contact for any questions.

In my experience
This is a really simple way of getting your participants to do a small task such as read the course outline.

The hidden twist
Use this opportunity to establish a rapport and give some background as to who you are thus building your credibility and easing some of the most common barriers to training before they become walls. The participant will feel that the trainer values the training and the participant, and you can use this opportunity to slip in any messages you want around why the training is taking place or what you expect from the participants in a friendly and non-threatening manner.

Additionally, this serves as a reminder to those who may not have the training in their calendar or who were planning to "forget" they had it.

Essential Data
Course Type – Any
Group Size – Any
Time of day – Pre course
Pace – Quick
Time to create – thirty minutes maximum
Time to run – Zero trainer time

Steps to create
- Decide what your key purpose is – e.g. have the participant read the course aim, objectives and course outline
- Create a template for use in future courses according to your need
- Write your letter including
  - Who you are
  - What your background is
  - Why you are facilitating the training
  - What you hope the participants will gain from the training
  - How much you are looking forward to the training
  - What you want the participant to do
  - Your contact details
  - Any other details or requests

Steps to Run
- Send your message with any supporting information

Suggested Debrief Strategy/Sample Questions
The beauty of this is that no real debrief is needed. The trainer should always assume that pre-course work has been done and refer to it during the training so participants are not left wondering why they wasted their time. If you are using an activity such as expectations and concerns the trainer can refer to the fact that participants have all read the course outline in opening this.

Working Example
Use this for any course as a simple means to put participants at ease before they come to the course. It is particularly useful if you know that there is some resistance to the course and you want to maximize your chances of getting people onboard by appealing to the human side.

Tips, Tricks and Traps
- Keep your introduction brief, they don't need your autobiography in full
- Make sure that you are clear in what you want them to do e.g. read the course outline
- Include the date, time and venue for reminder
- Include the information such as the course outline
- Be friendly!

Adult Learning Dashboard

This activity links participant's preferred style of learning. The following dashboard provides a quick reference to adult learning theorists and principles as part of the ID9® methodology.

This activity achieves the following level of Bloom's Taxonomy of the Cognitive Domain (Bloom et al 1956), shown with "X" in the following table.

Bloom's Taxonomy of the Cognitive Domain Level					
Knowledge	Comprehension	Application	Analysis	Synthesis	Evaluation
X					

This activity also achieves a link, shown with "X" in the following table, to participant's naturally occurring learning preferences. Global/Specific, Learning Modalities, Hemispheric Preference (Sperry, 1981), and Multiple Intelligences (Gardner, 1983) are referenced in ID9® methodology and process. This is not a complete list of links that are covered within the ID9® process however this dashboard aims to provide a quick reference for trainers to use to balance instructional design to provide equality for participants' learning preferences.

Global/Specific Learners		Learning Modalities (Sensory Intake)			Hemispheric Preference	
Global	Specific	Visual	Auditory	Kinesthetic	Left Brain	Right Brain
X	X	X			X	X

Multiple Intelligences								
Visual	Intrapersonal	Interpersonal	Musical	Mathematical / Logical	Linguistic	Kinesthetic	Naturalist	Existential
X		X			X			

8. In the News

Learning Outcome
Relating the training course to something actually happening in their area to reinforcing why they are attending.

Overview
This pre-course activity is used when you the trainer want to make sure that the participant is aware of the rationale for the training and the expected benefits for them and the organization but does not want to spend the time doing this in class. You will ask the participant to search the internal website for information about the subject of your training and get them to assimilate this with why they are attending.

The Hidden Twist
Training often results from organizational changes in strategy, initiatives or goals or from findings such as audits. The organization often believes that the employees are aware of these as there have been memos and newsletters etc. In reality the employee is too busy to read them and is blissfully unaware. This activity encourages the participant to research the reason for the training giving them the background information and the expected outcomes. It starts to deliver the message that there is an outcome expected from you that contributes to performance and as a final benefit to participant and organization, it helps to make sure that they are aware of what is going on in the organization. The trainer benefits from this by optimizing the number of people on the course who know why the training is taking place and so better understand why they are giving their time to it.

Essential Data
Course Type – Any
Group Size – Any
Time of day – Pre course
Pace – Medium
Time to create – 1 hour
Time to run – Zero trainer time

Steps to create
- Create a message to your participants
- Explain what you want them to do
  - Search the internal website and/or talk to colleagues to obtain information on xxxx (the subject of the training)
  - Answer the following questions
    - What is the key driver behind this training
    - Who is sponsoring this initiative
    - When was it announced
    - Why is this training important to the organization
    - What is the predicted outcome of the training
    - Why have you been selected to attend
- Create a template for the questions and answers

Steps to run
- Send your e-mail and template to the participant
- Explain the steps
  - Read the e-mail
  - Conduct a search of the internal website
  - Talk to colleagues
  - Answer the questions on the attached sheet
  - Bring them with you to the course
  - If you have any questions please contact me

Suggested Debrief / Sample Questions
You can use this pre-course activity as a link within the course introduction simply by asking the questions or as a connect activity by getting people to work in pairs to explain to their partner why they are attending and what their part in implementing what they learn will be. This helps to emphasize that the training is part of a bigger picture and not just an isolated idea and then brings in the specifics of what is expected of the individual.

Working Example
I used this as an activity before training on a new learning management system. There had been multiple messages about it as it was a company-wide roll out but there was still little awareness as to why we were changing from the old system and the training was seen as a waste of time because the old system was perfectly fine. Directing people to the messages about the rationale and perceived benefits helped to break down the resistance both to the training and the system and helped to ease the way forward. As an additional pay-off some participants reported that they would make sure they read the regular newsletters as they had not realized how much information was in them!

Tips, tricks and traps
- Make sure there really is information out there
- Provide a few key words for searches
- Have key communications or at least the links to them available in the training in case people did not find them all

Adult Learning Dashboard

This activity links participant's preferred style of learning. The following dashboard provides a quick reference to adult learning theorists and principles as part of the ID9® methodology.

This activity achieves the following level of Bloom's Taxonomy of the Cognitive Domain (Bloom et al 1956), shown with "X" in the following table.

Bloom's Taxonomy of the Cognitive Domain Level					
Knowledge	Comprehension	Application	Analysis	Synthesis	Evaluation
	X				

This activity also achieves a link, shown with "X" in the following table, to participant's naturally occurring learning preferences. Global/Specific, Learning Modalities, Hemispheric Preference (Sperry, 1981), and Multiple Intelligences (Gardner, 1983) are referenced in ID9® methodology and process. This is not a complete list of links that are covered within the ID9® process however this dashboard aims to provide a quick reference for trainers to use to balance instructional design to provide equality for participants' learning preferences.

Global/Specific Learners		Learning Modalities (Sensory Intake)			Hemispheric Preference	
Global	Specific	Visual	Auditory	Kinesthetic	Left Brain	Right Brain
X	X	X	X	X	X	X

Multiple Intelligences								
Visual	Intrapersonal	Interpersonal	Musical	Mathematical / Logical	Linguistic	Kinesthetic	Naturalist	Existential
X	X			X	X	X		X

9. A Message from Our Sponsor

Learning Outcome
Reinforce the purpose and importance of the training.

Overview
This is a simple, passive yet very effective way of making sure that the participant knows the rationale for the training, impact on the organization and expectations of them as participants and employees

In My Experience
There is nothing more powerful in underlining the importance of training than having a senior person in the organization deliver that message.

The Hidden Twist
The aim and objectives of the course are being delivered by somebody with high impact and credibility and the reason for the training is being delivered right on point. Participants know that this is serious and that in attending they are part of something important.

Essential Data
Course Type – Any
Group Size – Any
Time of day – Pre course
Pace – Passive
Time to create – Can be up to several weeks but it's worth it
Time to run – 5-10 Minutes

Steps to create
- Ask your sponsor to nominate as senior a person as possible to record a video message
- Have your sponsor contact that person through appropriate channels
- Contact your communications team (if you have one) and work with them to arrange filming and format for loading on the company website
- Write a script delivering the message and have it approved if necessary by the communications team
- Have the message recorded
- Have the message uploaded to the company website
- Create a message to the participants with a link to the video and instructions

Steps to run
- Send your message to the participants with the link to the video

Suggested Debrief / Sample Questions
There is nothing really needed here but the trainer can refer to it in the opening of the course to reinforce the message.

Working Example
This is great for major initiatives to support changes in strategy or any course where you really want to roll out the big guns!

Tips, Tricks and Traps
- Do not underestimate how much time it can take to create this activity especially if you want the input from a very senior person
- Do not be tempted to shoot a video yourself, unless you are a professional, as an amateur production will negate any impact
- Use the appropriate channels to approach leaders
- Check your link before you send it out
- Make sure all your participants have access to a computer

Adult Learning Dashboard

This activity links participant's preferred style of learning. The following dashboard provides a quick reference to adult learning theorists and principles as part of the ID9® methodology.

This activity achieves the following level of Bloom's Taxonomy of the Cognitive Domain (Bloom et al 1956), shown with "X" in the following table.

Bloom's Taxonomy of the Cognitive Domain Level					
Knowledge	Comprehension	Application	Analysis	Synthesis	Evaluation
X					

This activity also achieves a link, shown with "X" in the following table, to participant's naturally occurring learning preferences. Global/Specific, Learning Modalities, Hemispheric Preference (Sperry, 1981), and Multiple Intelligences (Gardner, 1983) are referenced in ID9® methodology and process. This is not a complete list of links that are covered within the ID9® process however this dashboard aims to provide a quick reference for trainers to use to balance instructional design to provide equality for participants' learning preferences.

Global/Specific Learners		Learning Modalities (Sensory Intake)			Hemispheric Preference	
Global	Specific	Visual	Auditory	Kinesthetic	Left Brain	Right Brain
X	X	X	X	X	X	X

Multiple Intelligences								
Visual	Intrapersonal	Interpersonal	Musical	Mathematical / Logical	Linguistic	Kinesthetic	Naturalist	Existential
X	X		X	X	X			X

10. Definition Match

Learning Outcome
Making sure that all your participants understand the specific vocabulary of the course

Overview
This pre-course activity serves to optimize the chances of all your participants knowing the definition of specific vocabulary you will use in the course thus avoiding any misunderstanding or putting participants in the awkward position of having to ask what something means. It involves providing the participant with a word or acronym on one side of a list and the definition on the other. The participant then has to match the word or acronym to the correct definition.

In my experience
It is easy to assume that people will be familiar with the terms we are going to use in a course but in reality this is not always the case. Although we are not encouraged to use acronyms many of us work in organizations that thrive on them and it is impossible to ignore them. What then do we do to make sure that our participants really do know what we mean and are not forced to sit in silence or face the embarrassment of asking? We give them this pre-course activity in advance!

The Hidden Twist
We are getting all our participants on a level playing field before we start and with clever selection of words that can provoke some thought around the topics to be covered.

Essential Data
Course Type – Any
Group Size – Any
Time of day – Pre course
Pace – Moderate
Time to create – 1 hour
Time to run – 15 Minutes

Steps to Create
- Decide on the words or acronyms you will use
- Using Microsoft Word create a table with two columns and enough rows for your words plus a heading
- In the top row of the left hand column write Word/Acronym
- In the top row of the right hand column write Definition
- Type each word or acronym into its own row on the left hand column
- Type the definition of the word or acronym into the right hand column
- Save the document as your answer sheet
- Save the document again under another name to suit yourself
- On this second document use copy and paste to jumble up the words so that they are not listed next to the correct definition
- Create a message for your participants that
  - Introduces you as their trainer
  - Welcomes them to the training
  - Explains what you want them to do
    - Read the list of words and definitions
    - Use a pen or highlighters to join the correct word to the correct definition
  - And why
    - To refresh your knowledge
    - Make sure that everybody is working from a common understanding
    - Give you the opportunity to look up anything you are unsure of

Steps to Run
- Send the message and the list to your participants
- Explain what you want them to do
  - Read the list of words and definitions
  - Use a pen or highlighters to join the correct word to the correct definition
- Ask participants to contact you if they have questions

Suggested Debrief
When the participant arrives at the training give/send them a copy of the answers and ask them to check their answers while they are waiting for the course to start. For an e-learning program this may be provided as a downloadable document. This will ensure that they are working from the correct information and if they did not do the pre-work at least they have the definitions now!

Working example

The beauty of this pre-course activity is that it really can be used for any content!

Tips, tricks and traps

- Make sure you get the definitions right!
- Use a maximum of 15 words – remember, you are not creating a dictionary
- Encourage even the most confident participant to check their answers

Adult Learning Dashboard

This activity links participant's preferred style of learning. The following dashboard provides a quick reference to adult learning theorists and principles as part of the ID9® methodology.

This activity achieves the following level of Bloom's Taxonomy of the Cognitive Domain (Bloom et al 1956), shown with "X" in the following table.

Bloom's Taxonomy of the Cognitive Domain Level					
Knowledge	Comprehension	Application	Analysis	Synthesis	Evaluation
	X				

This activity also achieves a link, shown with "X" in the following table, to participant's naturally occurring learning preferences. Global/Specific, Learning Modalities, Hemispheric Preference (Sperry, 1981), and Multiple Intelligences (Gardner, 1983) are referenced in ID9® methodology and process. This is not a complete list of links that are covered within the ID9® process however this dashboard aims to provide a quick reference for trainers to use to balance instructional design to provide equality for participants' learning preferences.

Global/Specific Learners		Learning Modalities (Sensory Intake)			Hemispheric Preference	
Global	Specific	Visual	Auditory	Kinesthetic	Left Brain	Right Brain
X	X	X	X	X	X	X

Multiple Intelligences								
Visual	Intrapersonal	Interpersonal	Musical	Mathematical / Logical	Linguistic	Kinesthetic	Naturalist	Existential
X	X				X	X		

Chapter 2:
During Course:
Learning Activities

Denise Gaul

About the Co-Author:

Denise Gaul

I came to the training profession as a subject matter expert (SME) turned default trainer. Through all my jobs, registered nurse, clinical research coordinator, clinical research associate, I loved training. I repeatedly found myself leading the training and orientation programs for every job I've ever had. So, I decided it was time to seek a position where training and development were a central focus of my work and not a side role.

My informal training experiences confirmed for me how very much I loved to facilitate learning and watch people develop into confident, competent employees. However, my lack of knowledge about good training methods and adult learning theory limited my effectiveness as a trainer and developer. I loved watching people learn, but my methods required learners to watch me lecture. Something had to change.

I began to study and take courses in adult learning, instructional design (ID9® is a game changer), and facilitation. My work now allows me to regularly apply the content of my studies and training to the courses I develop and deliver. Practice, trial and error and more practice are my greatest tools to refine skills and continue to develop competencies.

Every activity in this book is an opportunity to practice. Each activity is designed to help trainers implement effective training techniques founded on sound learning principles. Join me in bravely applying as many of these techniques as possible so that our courses inspire our participants to be their highest self.

My contribution to of this chapter would not have been possible without the generous contributions of my talented colleagues and teacher. Thank you Mel, Liz, Diana and Catherine.

Chapter Introduction

Interactive, engaging learning activities, well designed to appeal to a variety of learning preferences, are the secret sauce of instructional design. Learners get caught up in the activity and learning happens naturally. The more we (trainers and designers) move away from over reliance on lecturing and begin to make learning a series of well-orchestrated learning activities, the more our participants are able to connect with the content and apply their learning.

The learning activities in this chapter and every other chapter can be selected to best match the content, the participants and the facilitators. When you're developing a course, have wide selection of our activities in mind. Pitch your content and matching activity to a few test subjects to get instant feedback on your approach.

If you're preparing SMEs to deliver the content, the activity descriptions in this book can help SMEs understand the overall outcome and hidden twists of the learning activities in your course.

This chapter differs from the other chapters in **Training Activities that Work** because it focuses on learning activities, rather than review activities. Learning activities can best be defined as 'first time learning' where participants activate theory, methods, processes or whatever content they are learning for the first time. By contrast, review activities, which are covered by my co-authors in other chapters, can best be defined as 'second or subsequent learning' whereby participants review material they have learned and practiced before.

With this book in hand and a good instructional design method, your participants will never again be bored or checked out during a long lecture.

During a learning activity the trainer facilitates the activity taking the role of coach, observer, provider of feedback and facilitator. The trainer is NOT the silent bystander checked-out of the process while participants go it alone. Rather, the trainer is actively observing, ready to jump in to provide positive feedback or remediate to bring participants back on course. The participant test drives the new skills or knowledge for the first time and because of their achievement and successful outcome of completing the learning activity, they simultaneously build confidence and learning motivation. In my experience the "hidden twist" that happens when you design and facilitate a course using solid and highly participative learning activities is that the trainer does less work and the learner works constantly on learning. This is a surely a win-win for both participant and trainer.

11. Learner Teacher (Teach Back)

Learning outcome
Participants learn a topic, then create a presentation and present this to the whole group.

Overview
In teams of 2-3, participants research and discuss an assigned topic. Then they create a short presentation, which all team members must deliver to the whole group. The listening groups are designated assignments to provide specific feedback and comments at the end. For example, listening teams might be asked to make comments in agreement or disagreement with the topic. Or, they could be asked to question or summarize what they hear.

In My Experience
Giving participants the opportunity to learn, discuss and present a topic results in them gaining a greater depth of knowledge. When participants present or co-present a topic to the whole group, vigorous group discussion and engagement is activated.

Effective for an entire course or select sections depending on content and group characteristics. Particularly effective with experienced, competent groups.

The Hidden Twist
Whether presenting or listening, all participants are so engaged in fully describing and understanding a topic that they forget they are experiencing training.

In contrast to a traditional lecture, when the responsibility for teaching is on the participants, they become fully engaged in the topic. Because of the roles assigned to the listening group they also are actively engaged in the topic in order to fulfill their assigned role and contribution.

Essential Data

Course Type:	Instructor Lead Training either face to face or webinar/virtual classroom.
Group Size:	2-15
Time of Day:	Any time.
Pace:	Moderate
Time to Create:	1-2 hours, depending on time to assemble study materials
Time to Run:	30-45 minutes study time and 10-15 minutes per topic presented

Steps to Create:
1. Select course training topics to designate as Learner Teacher topics
2. Assemble or create study materials
3. Create Teach Back aids (series of Questions, Flip Charts, Slide templates, hand-outs)
4. Create Activity Instructions for each team
5. Create debrief material

Steps to Run:
1. List topics and assigned teams on slide or flipchart
2. Hand out to teams and explain instructions for learning and presenting topic back to whole group (can be structured or unstructured teach back)
3. Specify time limits for learning and presenting (example: 45 minutes to study, 10 minutes to present)
4. Teams work together to research material and create presentation.
5. As groups prepare play music quietly in the background.
6. When team learning/planning time is complete, regroup to whole group
7. Explain assignments to listening group and provide any hand outs
8. Presentations begin (in random order if possible)
9. Debrief each presentation

Suggested Debrief Strategy/Sample Questions
When a team is presenting their topic, the remaining teams who are listening are assigned specific roles to give feedback and comments. Suggested listening group assignments include an agreeing group, a disagreeing group, a questioning group and summarizing group.

The agreeing group will state what parts of the presentation they agree with or not. The disagreeing group will state whether there are any parts of the presentation they disagree with or refute. The questioning group will ask questions about the topic. And the summarizing group will give a final summary of the topic. Each listening team is given 2-3 minutes to share their feedback and comments.

When each topic presentation is complete, give the presenting team 5 minutes for a journal reflection on the process. Suggested questions for journal reflection are:
- What happened when you and your team were learning and preparing your presentation?
- What was it like to prepare and present a topic that is new to you?
- What did the feedback and comments from the others teach you?
- Now that your presentation is complete, what is one key learning?

Working Example
For a sales and marketing team, use this approach to facilitate in-depth understanding of a clinical paper (by sections) or multiple clinical papers. Divide the clinical

paper (or other reference material) into sections and assign one section per group. Each group creates their presentation to teach back to the whole group.

Tips, Tricks and Traps

Trap: Without well-defined roles for the listening groups, they may disengage and focus on their upcoming presentation.

Tip: Offer a tool for structured note taking for the listening group/s.

Trap: People need time to consolidate their thoughts before going to the listening group feedback. Give listening groups time to gather their thoughts before they provide their feedback.

Trick: If you, the instructional designer, are not the subject matter expert on the content, this is an excellent activity to use to get the subject matter experts (SMEs) in the room to deliver the content.

Trick: The need to develop materials can be minimized if participants are able to use freely available resources (internet, interview, book or article)

Tip: For larger groups assign small groups more varied roles: "the listening group", "the questioning group" (where they have to formulate a number of questions at the end of each teach-back to ask the presenters or the listening group), the "black hat group" (DeBono, 6 Thinking Hats) where they provide potential challenges, business roadblocks, barriers to what has been presented (not in a criticizing way but in a logical way) and other roles that would suit the content.

Tip: Playing music while groups are preparing 'fills the space'. Faster music can increase the pace of learning and support a competitive environment (i.e. faster than heart rate).
Or
Slower music can decrease the pace of learning and support a quiet reflective environment where participants quietly (or individually) prepare.

Adult Learning Base Process: Teach Back
Refer to **Adult Learning Base Process Reference Guide** for more information about this learning process.

Adult Learning Dashboard
This activity links participant's preferred style of learning. The following dashboard provides a quick reference to adult learning theorists and principles as part of the ID9® methodology.

This activity achieves the following level of Bloom's Taxonomy of the Cognitive Domain (Bloom et al 1956), shown with "X" in the following table.

Bloom's Taxonomy of the Cognitive Domain Level					
Knowledge	Comprehension	Application	Analysis	Synthesis	Evaluation
				X	

This activity also achieves a link, shown with "X" in the following table, to participant's naturally occurring learning preferences. Global/Specific, Learning Modalities, Hemispheric Preference (Sperry, 1981), and Multiple Intelligences (Gardner, 1983) are referenced in ID9® methodology and process. This is not a complete list of links that are covered within the ID9® process however this dashboard aims to provide a quick reference for trainers to use to balance instructional design to provide equality for participants' learning preferences.

Global/Specific Learners		Learning Modalities (Sensory Intake)			Hemispheric Preference	
Global	Specific	Visual	Auditory	Kinesthetic	Left Brain	Right Brain
X	X	X	X	X	X	X

Multiple Intelligences								
Visual	Intrapersonal	Interpersonal	Musical	Mathematical / Logical	Linguistic	Kinesthetic	Naturalist	Existential
X	X	X	X	X	X	X		

12. Rapid Returns

Learning Outcome
Participants summarize (or state in their own words) key concepts about an assigned topic.

Overview
To quickly present a list of topics, concepts or definitions, assign each participant to read about a short topic and summarize it back to the whole group.

In My Experience
This method is an excellent way to engage learners to quickly review and comprehend a list of related concepts or definitions. They gain a rapid overview of information-packed topics.

The Hidden Twist
Allows participants to actively engage with the content. Asking participants to summarize and restate information in their own words ensures a deeper level of comprehension.

Essential Data
Course Type:	Any
Group Size:	6-12 Even larger groups if it is not important that everyone has an assignment
Time of Day:	Anytime.
Pace:	Moderate with quick summary presentations
Time to Create:	30 minutes
Time to Run:	5-15 minutes (depends on number of topics involved)

Steps to Create
1. Develop topic descriptions or definitions on slides, a hand-out or in a participant guide
2. When participants are known ahead of time, pre-assign participants to topics before the start of the course or perhaps on day 1 of a multi-day course
3. Develop concise written instructions

Steps to Run
1. Introduce series of topics
2. Assign a topic to each individual
3. Explain instructions (3-5 minutes to read and prepare, 1-2 minutes to present summary)
4. Display assignments (with page numbers if applicable) while participants are reading their topic
5. Regroup to whole group
6. Ask participants to present topics

Suggested Debrief Strategy/Sample Questions
After all presentations are complete, ask participants to share their responses to one or two of the following sample questions.

What did you learn?
What is your favorite "hot tip" from what you learned?
What topic would you like to research further after the course?

Working Example
To instruct a group on Neuro Linguistic Programming (NLP) processes, each process was assigned to a participant. Participants reviewed provided material describing the assigned NLP process. After a time to review and understand the assigned material, each participant presented their assigned process to the whole group.

Tips, Tricks and Traps
Keep the activity moving quickly. If someone stumbles, move on to the next person and come back to them at the end of the activity. If someone delivers incorrect information, be ready to jump in and offer support and the correct definition. Keep it moving.

Adult Learning Base Process - Teach Back
Refer to **Adult Learning Base Process Reference Guide** for more information about this learning process.

Adult Learning Dashboard
This activity links participant's preferred style of learning. The following dashboard provides a quick reference to adult learning theorists and principles as part of the ID9® methodology.

This activity achieves the following level of Bloom's Taxonomy of the Cognitive Domain (Bloom et al 1956), shown with "X" in the following table.

Bloom's Taxonomy of the Cognitive Domain Level					
Knowledge	Comprehension	Application	Analysis	Synthesis	Evaluation
	X				

This activity also achieves a link, shown with "X" in the following table, to participant's naturally occurring learning preferences. Global/Specific, Learning Modalities, Hemispheric Preference (Sperry, 1981), and Multiple Intelligences (Gardner, 1983) are referenced in ID9® methodology and process. This is not a complete list of links that are covered within the ID9® process however this dashboard aims to provide a quick reference for trainers to use to balance instructional design to provide equality for participants' learning preferences.

Global/Specific Learners		Learning Modalities (Sensory Intake)			Hemispheric Preference	
Global	Specific	Visual	Auditory	Kinesthetic	Left Brain	Right Brain
X	X	X	X		X	

Multiple Intelligences								
Visual	Intrapersonal	Interpersonal	Musical	Mathematical / Logical	Linguistic	Kinesthetic	Naturalist	Existential
X		X		X	X			

13. Why Me, Why You, Why Them?

Learning outcome
Participants will identify the significance of a topic from various points of view, such as from the point of view of: self, another specific role and the larger organization.

Overview
After introducing a topic (or agenda) ask the participants to reflect on why/how/when the topic is important to them, why/how/when it may be important to specific colleagues and why/how/when it is important to the larger organization.

In My Experience
This learning activity allows the participants to identify, in their own words, how a given subject impacts different roles, departments and stakeholders. By analyzing a topic from different perspectives, individuals gain an appreciation for the many important facets of a topic.

Often when a new program or change is introduced to an organization, many may not see the importance of the change across functions. Particularly when participant's direct involvement and personal commitment to a topic or change initiative may be particularly low, this simple activity can create a greater shared since of importance and engagement.

The Hidden Twist
When participants identify the significance of a topic or program from several different perspectives, they gain a broader understanding of how their role and responsibility influences others and the wider organization. This expanded connection to a subject can result in participants who are more engaged in related learning activities.

Essential Data

Course Type:	Any
Group Size:	Any
Time of Day:	Early in the training session to create connection and meaning
Pace:	Moderate
Time to Create:	5-10 minutes
Time to Run:	10-15 minutes including debrief

Steps to Create
1. Prepare to present a high level overview of a topic or program
2. On a slide or flip chart, prepare reflection questions (use SmartArt or a graphic to add visual impact)
- Why is (insert topic) important to me?
- Why is (insert topic) important to (name a specific role other than participants role)?
- Why is (insert topic) topic important to the organization?
- What can I do to influence the success of this topic?

Steps to Run
1. Present overview of topic
2. For groups larger than 5, divide the group into table groups of 5-6
3. Provide the reflection questions on a slide or flip chart
4. Instruct participants to reflect on the topic and as a table group, write their responses on a flip chart or worksheet.
5. As groups prepare play music quietly in the background.
6. Participants share their written responses with the table group.

Suggested Debrief Strategy/Sample Questions
Debrief the activity by asking a few of the following questions.
- What common themes emerged from your group responses?
- Did you gain a new perspective from the responses of others in your group?
- What can you do to influence the success of this topic?

Working Example
Training for a new role/ responsibility, e.g. a group of department mentors: The participants are the staff members who are conducting the new role. The training is on how to conduct their role. Early on in the course they conduct this learning activity. They consider the importance of their role for them, for colleagues they will be supporting directly, and for the department. They write one benefit for each onto a post-it note and stick onto the wall as directed.

Tips, Tricks and Traps

The activity can work equally well as a personal reflection, pair and share, or small group reflection.

If representatives of each reflection role are present in the course, have one person from each role share why the topic is important to them.

Add visual impact by using SmartArt or an image which has 3 distinct but linked parts for participants to write their responses to the reflection questions.

Add creative impact by asking participants to create a mindmap with 3 branches for the 3 different perspectives.

Playing music while groups are preparing 'fills the space'.

Faster music can increase the pace of learning and support a competitive environment (i.e. faster than heart rate).
Or
Slower music can decrease the pace of learning and support a quiet reflective environment where participants quietly (or individually) prepare.

Adult Learning Base Process: Neuro Linguistic Programing – Perceptual Positions
Refer to **Adult Learning Base Process Reference Guide** for more information about this learning process.

Adult Learning Dashboard

This activity links participant's preferred style of learning. The following dashboard provides a quick reference to adult learning theorists and principles as part of the ID9® methodology.

This activity achieves the following level of Bloom's Taxonomy of the Cognitive Domain (Bloom et al 1956), shown with "X" in the following table.

Bloom's Taxonomy of the Cognitive Domain Level					
Knowledge	Comprehension	Application	Analysis	Synthesis	Evaluation
			X		

This activity also achieves a link, shown with "X" in the following table, to participant's naturally occurring learning preferences. Global/Specific, Learning Modalities, Hemispheric Preference (Sperry, 1981), and Multiple Intelligences (Gardner, 1983) are referenced in ID9® methodology and process. This is not a complete list of links that are covered within the ID9® process however this dashboard aims to provide a quick reference for trainers to use to balance instructional design to provide equality for participants' learning preferences.

Global/Specific Learners		Learning Modalities (Sensory Intake)			Hemispheric Preference	
Global	Specific	Visual	Auditory	Kinesthetic	Left Brain	Right Brain
X		X	X	X	X	X

Multiple Intelligences								
Visual	Intrapersonal	Interpersonal	Musical	Mathematical / Logical	Linguistic	Kinesthetic	Naturalist	Existential
X	X	X	X		X	X		

14. Poster Train

Learning outcome

Process Poster Train: Participants will analyze information and answer detailed questions about the poster station content.

Conceptual Poster Train: Participants will reflect on concepts presented and practice applying concepts.

Overview

In small groups, participants rotate through a series of poster stations. At each station, the poster content is presented to participants by a poster station host.

Participants complete poster station assignment (written questions, perform an activity, role play, etc.) before the group moves on to the next poster station to repeat the process until all stations have been visited.

In My Experience

Poster stations can either be information centers or experience centers based on whether you are training a process and technical information (for example systems training, computer training or step-by-step information) or training more conceptual ideas (for example topics such as leadership, change, customer service, motivation, and delegation where processes may be involved but the content mainly centers around conceptual ideas and theories).

The Hidden Twist

By completing short assignments at each poster station, participants are actively learning a variety of content in a practical as well as a highly visual and kinesthetic way. Using subject matter experts (SME) as 'poster station hosts' gives participants an opportunity to interact though Q&A with the SMEs.

Essential Data

Course Type: Process, Technical and Conceptual
Group Size: 3-5 participants per poster station
Time of Day: Any
Pace: Depends on content, from fast to slow
Time to Create: 1-3 hours per poster station (hint: get your SMEs to help create the content)
Time to Run: Depends on content

Steps to Create

1. Determine poster station topics
2. Design station content and participant activities
3. Develop poster and station materials (SMEs are a good resource)
4. If stations require a facilitator, orient facilitators to the station content and activities

Steps to Run

1. Set up stations in the room or multiple rooms
2. Divide participants into equal groups. Number of groups = number of poster stations.
3. Give instructions:
   a. Visit every station as a whole group
   b. Complete station assignment
   c. Time allowed per station
   d. Time keeper will tell groups when it is time to rotate to the next station (give a 5 minute warning)

Suggested Debrief Strategy/Sample

Debrief the learning activity by doing a gallery walk. At each station, ask a couple of the following questions.

- What happened during the activity?
- What did you do well?
- How did completing this activity help you to learn about/ apply (insert topic)?
- How could you summarize your learning about this poster in one sentence?
- What questions are raised by this activity?
- What is your next action related to the poster station content?

Working Example

To deliver Health and Safety (H&S) training: each station contains a poster about a practical Health & Safety rules – e.g. lifting, confined spaces, high visibility workwear etc. Participants have to rotate around the three stations, then complete an activity at each station. At the 'lifting station' they might observe some images and spot the H&S lifting errors. At the 'confined spaces station' they may have to fill in blanks within the correct process for entering confined spaces. At the 'high visibility workwear station' they may need to match the suitability of high visibility workwear with different tasks presented. A fourth station might contain information about working at a desk – how to adjust chair, etc. and rules, tips, common errors – participants have to write down a list of tips. The next station may contain information about how to report workplace injuries (the assignment is to report an injury). This highly kinesthetic activity has individuals, pairs or small groups on a 'train' visiting each station in a highly engaging way to learn new training content.

Tips, Tricks and Traps
- Keep station activities brief and simple and keep station questions concise.
- Poster stations don't require a host, however, for more complex subjects; a poster station facilitator can really help! You might call this person the 'station master' to keep the train theme alive.
- Once the posters are developed they can be used for other related courses too
- Print the posters as a hand-out/job aid for participants to take away
- Put a poster outside or in another location related to the content.
- Explore whether using background music will enhance the poster station time.

Adult Learning Base Process: Gallery Walk
Refer to **Adult Learning Base Process Reference Guide** for more information about this learning process.

Adult Learning Dashboard
This activity links participant's preferred style of learning. The following dashboard provides a quick reference to adult learning theorists and principles as part of the ID9® methodology.

This activity achieves the following level of Bloom's Taxonomy of the Cognitive Domain (Bloom et al 1956), shown with "X" in the following table.

Bloom's Taxonomy of the Cognitive Domain Level					
Knowledge	Comprehension	Application	Analysis	Synthesis	Evaluation
			X		

This activity also achieves a link, shown with "X" in the following table, to participant's naturally occurring learning preferences. Global/Specific, Learning Modalities, Hemispheric Preference (Sperry, 1981), and Multiple Intelligences (Gardner, 1983) are referenced in ID9® methodology and process. This is not a complete list of links that are covered within the ID9® process however this dashboard aims to provide a quick reference for trainers to use to balance instructional design to provide equality for participants' learning preferences.

Global/Specific Learners		Learning Modalities (Sensory Intake)			Hemispheric Preference	
Global	Specific	Visual	Auditory	Kinesthetic	Left Brain	Right Brain
X	X	X	X	X	X	X

Multiple Intelligences								
Visual	Intrapersonal	Interpersonal	Musical	Mathematical / Logical	Linguistic	Kinesthetic	Naturalist	Existential
X	X	X	X	X	X	X	X	

15. Now What?

Learning outcome

Participants identify and manage risk scenarios. Through feedback, skills are enhanced and learning needs are identified.

Overview

Present single or pairs of participants with an "in-box" of potential business risk scenarios. Ask participants to identify the necessary next steps to adequately manage the scenario. Give participants 1-2 minutes to record necessary actions. Include some scenarios that require no immediate action.

In My Experience

This is an excellent approach to practice and improve issue and risk management skills and decision making. Application of learning concepts to day-to-day scenarios during a course increases the rate of learning transfer post course. Practice may not "make perfect", but it certainly builds confidence and competence. Make sure to include a range of simple to complex scenarios to build confidence and stretch skills. Feedback can come from peers and the facilitator.

The Hidden Twist

Providing participants with a series of scenarios to work through enables them to practice managing a wide range of practical risks/issues in a short space of time.

Essential Data

Course Type:	Any, but particularly good for risk management and customer service interactions
Group Size:	Any
Time of Day:	Before lunch or post lunch practice if previously introduced content
Pace:	Rapid to moderate depending on complexity of scenarios
Time to Create:	1-1.5 hours – time to collect and write up scenarios
Time to Run:	15-45 minutes

Steps to Create

1. Collect example scenarios, issues or risks
2. Write scenarios on cards or produce on printed hand outs
3. Create physical or email inbox (if participants are using laptops)
4. Create structured triage form for participant to write: risk/issue identified, proposed next action, escalation plan (if needed), and resolution.
5. Customize triage form for your content.

6. Prepare completed triage form as hand-out for end of activity

Steps to Run

1. Give each participant their assigned issues (email or paper)
2. Participants work individually or in pairs to review each scenario and document issue/risk management plan on triage form.
3. As groups prepare play music quietly in the background.
4. When all scenarios have been addressed, give the participants a hand-out of correctly completed triage forms for each scenario.
5. Participants take time to check their own work before moving on to debrief.

Suggested Debrief Strategy/Sample Questions

Ask participants to share one scenario for which they would like recommendations from the whole group. For very large groups, the sharing can occur at table groups. Participants will share scenario, how they managed the scenario and ask the group to add triage recommendations.

- What management plan ideas does the group agree with or confirm?
- What additional recommendations can the group add?
- How can the risk or issue be resolved?

Working Example

Clinical Trial Monitoring & Site Issue Management. The issues and scenarios are all trial site data and communications regarding trial activities. The issues include common scenarios such as drug shipment issues, inclusion/exclusion criteria, site staff changes, safety information, or medication administration questions. Participants process the questions identifying the level of risk presented and the best issue management plan.

Customer Service

A series of brief customer service issues can be prepared and delivered to individuals, pairs or small groups of participants to solve. These might mirror actual customer complaints, service issues, questions, product enquiries that may be encountered by the customer service representative. If speed of resolution is a part of the customer service representative's job (for example if they receive these types of customer service via incoming phone calls where they need to think on their feet and provide instant answers) then consider putting a time limit on the activity.

Tips, Tricks and Traps
- Mix it up with low, medium and high risk scenarios
- Allow time for discussion and debrief so that participants learn how others have rated and managed issues.
- Put some time pressure on the activity – 10 minutes to triage all assigned issues.
- Encourage debrief as a lively exchange of suggested issue management ideas from the participants.
- Playing music while groups are preparing 'fills the space'.
- Faster music can increase the pace of learning and support a competitive environment (i.e. faster than heart rate).
Or
Slower music can decrease the pace of learning and support a quiet reflective environment where participants quietly (or individually) prepare.

 Adult Learning Base Process: Case Study (in-tray diagnosis)
Refer to **Adult Learning Base Process Reference Guide** for more information about this learning process.

 Adult Learning Dashboard
This activity links participant's preferred style of learning. The following dashboard provides a quick reference to adult learning theorists and principles as part of the ID9® methodology.

This activity achieves the following level of Bloom's Taxonomy of the Cognitive Domain (Bloom et al 1956), shown with "X" in the following table.

Bloom's Taxonomy of the Cognitive Domain Level					
Knowledge	Comprehension	Application	Analysis	Synthesis	Evaluation
			X		

This activity also achieves a link, shown with "X" in the following table, to participant's naturally occurring learning preferences. Global/Specific, Learning Modalities, Hemispheric Preference (Sperry, 1981), and Multiple Intelligences (Gardner, 1983) are referenced in ID9® methodology and process. This is not a complete list of links that are covered within the ID9® process however this dashboard aims to provide a quick reference for trainers to use to balance instructional design to provide equality for participants' learning preferences.

Global/Specific Learners		Learning Modalities (Sensory Intake)			Hemispheric Preference	
Global	Specific	Visual	Auditory	Kinesthetic	Left Brain	Right Brain
X	X	X	X		X	X

Multiple Intelligences								
Visual	Intrapersonal	Interpersonal	Musical	Mathematical / Logical	Linguistic	Kinesthetic	Naturalist	Existential
X	X	X	X	X	X	X		

16. Changing Hats

Learning outcome
Participants practice applying desired processes to manage common real life scenarios.

Overview
Participants take on the role of specified team members while managing an assigned scenario according to the prescribed process. Participants switch roles throughout the activity so that they apply the process from different perspectives.

In My Experience
This activity allows participants to practice new skills while managing a real life scenario. It also gives them working knowledge of how a process is implemented from end to end.

The Hidden Twist
Participants are so involved taking on various roles and perspectives that they don't realize they are expanding their understanding of the topic. They also gain new ideas on how to manage common or complex scenarios.

Essential Data
Course Type: Process or conceptual
Group Size: Any
Time of Day: Mid-course or late in the day
Pace: Moderate to brisk
Time to Create: 30-60 minutes
Time to Run: 15-30 minutes

Steps to Create
1. Create brief written description of the roles (hats)
2. Create a written scenario(s) (1 copy for each group)
3. Create hats or other image to be worn to represent the role a person is currently holding (one set for each small group)

Steps to Run
1. Divide participants into small groups – small group size will match the number of roles to practice: small group size of 4 for 4 roles to practice
2. Participants select hat (role) to begin activity
3. Participants review scenario and take appropriate action based on current role assumed
4. Participants switch hats and repeat activity until each participant in the group has performed all roles.

Suggested Debrief Strategy/Sample Questions
I suggest keeping the participants in their small groups and asking a series of questions:
- What happened during the scenario?
- What parts of the activity were successful?
- If you could do the activity again, what parts would you improve?
- What were your key learnings from the activity

Have the small groups share their key learnings with the whole group.

Working Example
Safety report management:
The roles are: Principal Investigator, Safety Desk, Clinical Trial Manager, Safety Manager, and Regulatory Authority. Participants read a scenario describing a reportable safety event and then implement the steps of the safety report process based on the hat they are currently wearing. If possible, give participants the opportunity to process the safety report in each role.

Tips, Tricks and Traps
Use actual hats or images of hats to visually represent each role. This theme adds visual impact.

Keep the scenario activities moving from one role to the next so that all roles take appropriate action per the process being implemented.

Adult Learning Base Process: Role Play
Refer to **Adult Learning Base Process Reference Guide** for more information about this learning process.

Adult Learning Dashboard

This activity links participant's preferred style of learning. The following dashboard provides a quick reference to adult learning theorists and principles as part of the ID9® methodology.

This activity achieves the following level of Bloom's Taxonomy of the Cognitive Domain (Bloom et al 1956), shown with "X" in the following table.

Bloom's Taxonomy of the Cognitive Domain Level					
Knowledge	Comprehension	Application	Analysis	Synthesis	Evaluation
		X			

This activity also achieves a link, shown with "X" in the following table, to participant's naturally occurring learning preferences. Global/Specific, Learning Modalities, Hemispheric Preference (Sperry, 1981), and Multiple Intelligences (Gardner, 1983) are referenced in ID9® methodology and process. This is not a complete list of links that are covered within the ID9® process however this dashboard aims to provide a quick reference for trainers to use to balance instructional design to provide equality for participants' learning preferences.

Global/Specific Learners		Learning Modalities (Sensory Intake)			Hemispheric Preference	
Global	Specific	Visual	Auditory	Kinesthetic	Left Brain	Right Brain
X	X	X	X	X	X	X

Multiple Intelligences								
Visual	Intrapersonal	Interpersonal	Musical	Mathematical / Logical	Linguistic	Kinesthetic	Naturalist	Existential
X	X	X		X	X	X		

17. What Do You Need? – Job Aid

Learning outcome
Participants create a personalized job aid of resources and reminders that are critical to maximize learning transfer and application.

Overview
Participants identify what it would take for them to be 100% effective with the new process or skill. Then they use course content and creative materials to create a job aid that will help them implement the new knowledge and/or skill back on the job.

In My Experience
In order to become "High performance learners" and successfully apply learning from a course, participants need two key things: 1. To be highly motivated; 2. A high level of support (Mattiske's **High Performance Learning Model**). This activity gets participants thinking ahead and working out their personal strategy and needs to take their learning to the next level.

The Hidden Twist
By creating a custom job aid of resources and reminders, participants are thinking ahead and already identifying the supports they need to effectively transfer their learning back on the job. A job aid, created by the participant, is personalized to their particular needs and therefore more likely to be retained and used after the course.

Essential Data
Course Type: Any
Group Size: Any
Time of Day: Mid-Morning or Mid After-noon
Pace: Slow to Moderate
Time to Create: 60 minutes or less
Time to Run: 15 minutes

Steps to Create
1. Create 2-3 job aid templates in varying formats with prompting titles (see tips)
2. Print templates in color and also have them available in electronic format
3. Create a mockup slide of each template with sample job aid information inserted
4. Create "AIM" poster. AIM = Create a tool that will make you wildly successful with this process/skill back on the job.

Steps to Run
1. Provide job aid templates
2. Provide creative tools (markers, stickers, hole punch, etc.)
3. Provide electronic version of template
4. Participants use available resources and materials to create personal job aid

Suggested Debrief Strategy/Sample Questions
Ask participants to exchange and read each other's job aids at their table group. After they have read each other's job aids, ask the group a few of the following questions.
- What common resources were listed on your job aids?
- Do you want to add anything to your job aid now that you've read others?
- How will you use your job aid?
- Where will you post it to capture your attention?
- How can your share your job aid with others back at the office?

Working Example
This activity is really versatile and could apply to many courses! Think of a skills course you've been on. Or go back to our old friend "Process training". How about computer training or appraisal process training?

Communication skills 101 – participants create a job aid of communication barriers and how to overcome them. Or create a job aid of the communication process and 3 topics covered– active listening, questioning and body language.

Tips, Tricks and Traps
- Ensure job aid includes prompting titles such as: supports, enforcers, tools, resources and practice opportunities
- Prompt participants to add visuals and images to enhance the effect of their job aid
- If participants struggle with creativity, simply ask them to design a 'mini-poster' which helps them to remember all of the key points, resources and reminders from the topic(s) covered.
- If participants want to work electronically, have a printer available to print the job aid or instruct participant to email the document to themselves for printing.

Adult Learning Base Process: Job Aid
Refer to **Adult Learning Base Process Reference Guide** for more information about this learning process.

Adult Learning Dashboard

This activity links participant's preferred style of learning. The following dashboard provides a quick reference to adult learning theorists and principles as part of the ID9® methodology.

This activity achieves the following level of Bloom's Taxonomy of the Cognitive Domain (Bloom et al 1956), shown with "X" in the following table.

Bloom's Taxonomy of the Cognitive Domain Level					
Knowledge	Comprehension	Application	Analysis	Synthesis	Evaluation
				X	

This activity also achieves a link, shown with "X" in the following table, to participant's naturally occurring learning preferences. Global/Specific, Learning Modalities, Hemispheric Preference (Sperry, 1981), and Multiple Intelligences (Gardner, 1983) are referenced in ID9® methodology and process. This is not a complete list of links that are covered within the ID9® process however this dashboard aims to provide a quick reference for trainers to use to balance instructional design to provide equality for participants' learning preferences.

Global/Specific Learners		Learning Modalities (Sensory Intake)			Hemispheric Preference	
Global	Specific	Visual	Auditory	Kinesthetic	Left Brain	Right Brain
	X	X	X	X	X	X

Multiple Intelligences								
Visual	Intrapersonal	Interpersonal	Musical	Mathematical / Logical	Linguistic	Kinesthetic	Naturalist	Existential
X	X	X		X	X	X		

18. Solve My Problem

Learning outcome
Participants analyze complex scenarios and formulate action plans to facilitate necessary change.

Overview
Participants share from their experience, a real life "tough case" related to the topic being presented. Use 3 Rico Cluster activities to get the participants to analyze the tough case and identify necessary steps to move the tough case forward. 3 Rico Cluster assignments are "what is the challenge/root cause of challenge", "what outcome is desired" and "steps to achieve desired outcome".

In My Experience
Participants identify their own highly relevant and practical cases and then work on strategies for solving them. The power of the group provides different ideas and perspectives and generates more varied action plans. This activity works well with a diverse group of participants who have varied experiences. It is extremely useful for problem solving or handling complex situations.

The Hidden Twist
While working together and sharing solutions to solve a current challenge, the group is also using a problem solving technique that is an effective way to approach future challenges.

Essential Data
Course Type: Any, works well for conceptual course content
Group Size: 5-20
Time of Day: Mid-Morning or Mid after-noon
Pace: Fast to Moderate
Time to Create: 15-30 minutes
Time to Run: 30 minutes

Steps to Create
1. Familiarize with Rico Clusters (Gabriele Rico)
2. Create a template for participants to record their "tough case". Template sections: background, problem statement, key characters, resources available
3. Provide paper, colored pens/pencils/markers
4. Prepare slide(s) describing Rico Cluster brainstorm activity

Steps to Run
1. Participants will work in pairs
2. Each participant writes their tough case on the provided template
3. Exchange tough case with partner
4. Participants use 3 Rico Clusters to problem solve the tough case.
   a. Root cause of problem
   b. Desired outcome
   c. Steps to achieve desired outcome
5. Pairs share and explain themes and clusters identified from activity

Suggested Debrief Strategy/Sample Questions
Ask participants to respond out loud to several of the suggested debrief questions.
- What insights did you gain when reviewing your partners Rico Cluster information regarding your tough case?
- How did using Rico Clusters influence your thinking about the problem; the solution?
- How might you use Rico Clusters in the future?

Working Example
Use this technique for a management course on coaching techniques improving the performance of poor or underperforming staff. Managers use the Rico Cluster activity to better comprehend employee performance issues, clarify specifics of the desired outcome, and plan detailed action steps to promote improved performance.

Tips, Tricks and Traps
- Use pre-course assignment to prepare the activity and collect real life scenarios.
- Mindmapping could be used instead of Rico Clusters.
- Keep the Rico Cluster writing quick and free flowing.
- Play music that promotes concentration during cluster writing.

Adult Learning Base Process: Case Study with Rico Cluster
Refer to **Adult Learning Base Process Reference Guide** for more information about this learning process.

Adult Learning Dashboard

This activity links participant's preferred style of learning. The following dashboard provides a quick reference to adult learning theorists and principles as part of the ID9® methodology.

This activity achieves the following level of Bloom's Taxonomy of the Cognitive Domain (Bloom et al 1956), shown with "X" in the following table.

Bloom's Taxonomy of the Cognitive Domain Level					
Knowledge	Comprehension	Application	Analysis	Synthesis	Evaluation
			X		

This activity also achieves a link, shown with "X" in the following table, to participant's naturally occurring learning preferences. Global/Specific, Learning Modalities, Hemispheric Preference (Sperry, 1981), and Multiple Intelligences (Gardner, 1983) are referenced in ID9® methodology and process. This is not a complete list of links that are covered within the ID9® process however this dashboard aims to provide a quick reference for trainers to use to balance instructional design to provide equality for participants' learning preferences.

Global/Specific Learners		Learning Modalities (Sensory Intake)			Hemispheric Preference	
Global	Specific	Visual	Auditory	Kinesthetic	Left Brain	Right Brain
X	X	X	X	X	X	X

Multiple Intelligences								
Visual	Intrapersonal	Interpersonal	Musical	Mathematical / Logical	Linguistic	Kinesthetic	Naturalist	Existential
X	X	X	X	X	X	X		X

19. Novice, Competent, Expert (mentor, coach)

Learning outcome

Participants create their personal development plan to advance them towards learning transfer and application.

Overview

Learners identify their current level of competence with the course content and their desired level of competence. Then learners create a process map taking them from their current state to the desired state, or next level of competence.

In My Experience

When participants identify their current and desired state of competence on a topic or skill, this helps the participant and trainer direct during-course and post-course learning and next actions. Participants are supported to create short and mid-term development plans that will facilitate their growth and competence with the course content.

The Hidden Twist

While identifying current and desired state, participants are activating a personal vested interest in the future desired state. This activity helps the trainer direct instruction to the correct level for the experience present in the course.

Essential Data

Course Type:	Soft Skills, Tech Skills, Conceptual
Group Size:	Any
Time of Day:	Early
Pace:	Quick
Time to Create	15 minutes
Time to Run:	2-5 minutes or less

Steps to Create

1. Develop a self-assessment worksheet and include a behavioral definition of competence levels
2. Create a development plan template – include icons/images for competence levels

Steps to Run

1. Give participants the competency self-assessment worksheet and development plan template (or include it in the participant guide)
2. After an introduction to the topic, ask participants to reflect on and rate their current competence level on the provided worksheet
3. Describe characteristics of each competence level
4. Then ask participants to indicate where they would like their competence level to be at the end of the course, the end of the month and the end of the year.
5. Give participants time to complete their development action plan for growing their competency.
6. Ask participants to share their top two action plans either at their table group or with the whole group

Suggested Debrief Strategy/Sample Questions

Debrief by asking the group to identify similar competency partners and potential mentors in the room. When action plans were shared, what common actions were mentioned? What new actions might you add to your development plan now that you've heard from your colleagues? How will growing your competency for this topic affect you?

Working Example
Conflict Resolution Training.

During the introduction of conflict resolution training, participants are asked to rate their current comfort and self-assessment of competence with managing conflict. Once current competence is assessed, participants then write what competence level they would like to have and why. How would a higher level of competence benefit them? How will you implement your development plan when you return to work?

After more of the topic and strategies are presented, participants are asked to spend time writing action steps for a Conflict Resolution personal development plan.

Tips, Tricks and Traps

For those who identify as expert, coach and mentor are the suggested next steps for their development.

If there are novice and experts in the room, the facilitator should encourage knowledge sharing and a supportive learning environment between all skill levels.

If managers and direct reports are in the room, this may not be a suitable activity depending on the organizational culture.

When topic or course is complete, encourage participants to revisit their action plan and competency assessment. What has changed and what would they add to their plan?

I've seen this done using flip chart stations for the various competence levels. Participants walk to the flip chart that best represents their current competence level. They discuss the reasons for their selection with others at the same flip chart. The facilitator asks each group to have a representative discuss common experiences represented at each station.

Adult Learning Base Process: NLP Future Pacing
Refer to **Adult Learning Base Process Reference Guide** for more information about this learning process.

Adult Learning Dashboard
This activity links participant's preferred style of learning. The following dashboard provides a quick reference to adult learning theorists and principles as part of the ID9® methodology.

This activity achieves the following level of Bloom's Taxonomy of the Cognitive Domain (Bloom et al 1956), shown with "X" in the following table.

Bloom's Taxonomy of the Cognitive Domain Level					
Knowledge	Comprehension	Application	Analysis	Synthesis	Evaluation
					X

This activity also achieves a link, shown with "X" in the following table, to participant's naturally occurring learning preferences. Global/Specific, Learning Modalities, Hemispheric Preference (Sperry, 1981), and Multiple Intelligences (Gardner, 1983) are referenced in ID9® methodology and process. This is not a complete list of links that are covered within the ID9® process however this dashboard aims to provide a quick reference for trainers to use to balance instructional design to provide equality for participants' learning preferences.

Global/Specific Learners		Learning Modalities (Sensory Intake)			Hemispheric Preference	
Global	Specific	Visual	Auditory	Kinesthetic	Left Brain	Right Brain
	X	X	X	X	X	X

Multiple Intelligences								
Visual	Intrapersonal	Interpersonal	Musical	Mathematical / Logical	Linguistic	Kinesthetic	Naturalist	Existential
X	X	X		X	X			X

20. Flip it

Learning outcome
Participants will plan and practice new skills.

Overview
Key concepts are delivered prior to the training via recorded lecture, eLearning or reading written materials. During the live training, participants work together to plan and practice new skills in simulated or real life activities.

In My Experience
Flipping is an excellent way to present technical concepts that require considerable practice in order to develop proficiency.

The Hidden Twist
Concepts learned prior to the live session are planned and practiced during the live training session. Participants receive one-on-one assistance, direct feedback, and learn from other participants during the course. The result is that participants leave the course with considerable practice and advanced competence with the new skill.

Essential Data
Course Type:	Any
Group Size:	5-25
Time of Day:	Any
Pace:	Moderate to slow
Time to Create	1 day – longer if you have to develop pre-course learning modules
Time to Run:	half day to full day course

Steps to Create
1. Identify available or create new independent learning activities (eLearning, Tutorials, Reading with Workbooks Activities, Recorded Presentations, etc.)
2. Create practice scenarios for in-class work or
3. Instruct participants to prepare an outline of a real project to work on as the in-class learning activity. (Alternatively, provide mock projects for development)
4. Develop participant instructions for pre-class learning
5. Write participant guide for in-class work
6. Identify adequate facilitator resource to provide instructional support for planned in-class learning activities. (Could be one or more facilitators needed. Use SMEs for one-on-one support)
7. Plan agenda to provide structure for in-class hands-on learning activities.

Steps to Run
1. Send course instructions to participants
2. Assign/deliver pre-class learning materials
3. Facilitate in-class practical application learning activities
4. Participants either work independently or in pairs on in-class practical application learning activities.

Suggested Debrief Strategy/Sample Questions
Begin the day by debriefing the pre-class learning activities. Suggested questions include:
- What do you recall from your pre-class assignments?
- What questions do you have about the pre-work assignment?
- Now that you've completed the pre-work, what do you expect to learn or do today in class?

Debrief the in-class learning activities by asking summary questions such as:
- How did it go for you today?
- What benefits did you gain from today's learning activities?
- What is your one key learning from today?
- Did you gain any confidences today?

Working Example
Articulate Storyline Training (eLearning software)

Participants complete a series of online tutorials one week prior to attending the face to face training.

On the day of the classroom portion of the training, participants work independently or in pairs to develop a simple eLearning module. The eLearning module to be developed is described, step by step, in a participant guide.

The in-class training day begins with a debrief of the pre-class learning activities. Participants are then given their assignments and choose a training partner. The remainder of the in-class learning time is spent alternating between facilitator demonstration of how to develop a section of the assigned eLearning and then the participants practice performing the demonstrated techniques. Participant support is constantly available from facilitators, the learning partner and the participant manual.

The course ends by each participant demonstrating their completed eLearning module.

Tips, Tricks and Traps
- Quality of pre-class instruction is essential
- Participants must carefully attend to pre-class instruction
- Inform participants how the skills will be practiced during the course
- For more experienced practitioners, participants can develop a personal, real life project rather than using the mock project for the in-class learning activity.
- Find time to use background music during learning activities. Match the energy of the music to the energy of the assigned activity.

Adult Learning Base Process: Socratic Method
Refer to **Adult Learning Base Process Reference Guide** for more information about this learning process.

Adult Learning Dashboard
This activity links participant's preferred style of learning. The following dashboard provides a quick reference to adult learning theorists and principles as part of the ID9® methodology.

This activity achieves the following level of Bloom's Taxonomy of the Cognitive Domain (Bloom et al 1956), shown with "X" in the following table.

Bloom's Taxonomy of the Cognitive Domain Level					
Knowledge	Comprehension	Application	Analysis	Synthesis	Evaluation
				X	

This activity also achieves a link, shown with "X" in the following table, to participant's naturally occurring learning preferences. Global/Specific, Learning Modalities, Hemispheric Preference (Sperry, 1981), and Multiple Intelligences (Gardner, 1983) are referenced in ID9® methodology and process. This is not a complete list of links that are covered within the ID9® process however this dashboard aims to provide a quick reference for trainers to use to balance instructional design to provide equality for participants' learning preferences.

Global/Specific Learners		Learning Modalities (Sensory Intake)			Hemispheric Preference	
Global	Specific	Visual	Auditory	Kinesthetic	Left Brain	Right Brain
X	X	X	X	X	X	X

Multiple Intelligences								
Visual	Intrapersonal	Interpersonal	Musical	Mathematical / Logical	Linguistic	Kinesthetic	Naturalist	Existential
X		X	X	X	X	X		

21. Read, Analyze, Do

Learning outcome
A learning activity for systems or computer training (or other linear or systematic content) to provide an opportunity to practice what was just learned.

Overview
This learning activity is created in a participant guide and provides real-life scenarios and questions for a participant to read, analyze and then determine the appropriate course of action in the system.

In My Experience
This is an excellent learning activity after teaching steps in a system or computer class. After teaching 1-3 major steps, provide a real-life scenario and questions for a participant to practice, ask questions, and hear feedback. This will help build their confidence when they use the system back at their desk. This also provides the instructor with an easy assessment of those who may need a little more explanation or practice before gaining full understanding of a step/process.

The Hidden Twist
This also acts as a review when they are back on the job, because they will have the participant guide as a resource to reference if they forget what to do in certain situations, or if they just want to practice.

Essential Data

Course Type:	Systems or Computer Training
Group Size:	3-20 (optimal) 1-2 or 20+ is possible
Time of Day:	Any time.
Pace:	Moderate
Time to Create:	~3 days (depends on the schedule of the subject-matter expert and IT)
Time to Run:	20-45 minutes per 1-3 major steps

Steps to Create
1. Work with the subject-matter expert (SME) to create the real-life scenarios, questions to ask about the scenarios and answers for the major steps.
2. Work with the IT team to set-up the system's learning environment in order for the activities to work properly.
3. Practice answering the scenario questions to verify functionality and accuracy.
4. Ask a contact in the business to go through all of the activities to verify functionality and accuracy. They may catch things that you don't.

5. Transfer the scenarios and questions to a participant guide.
6. Transfer the scenarios, questions, and answers to the Leader's Guide.

Steps to Run
1. After teaching 1-3 major steps, give participants a chance to practice what they just learned.
2. Instruct them how to navigate back to the beginning screen in order to start the activities.
3. Explain they will have a real-life scenario to read and then questions to answer regarding that scenario.
4. Participants work in pairs or alone.
5. Distribute scenarios (e.g. cards, hand-outs or participant guide). Each scenario has 2-3 questions for participants to answer.
6. Tell them they have XX time to complete the scenario with questions and then get ready to discuss the answers.
7. Explain that you are available and the subject-matter expert(s) are available to help guide them if they have questions.

Suggested Debrief Strategy/Sample Questions
- The instructor needs to be aware of the scenarios with questions that may cause the most difficulty.
- Read a scenario and questions.
- Ask a participant to answer the question.
- Ask the participant how they got to that answer.
- Ask if anyone else got a different answer and how they got their answer.

Working Example
Supply Chain System Training
Your Merchants informed you via email about a variance between your stock report and what's actually in the warehouse for PRODUCT X. You need to assess the implications to your plan and determine an updated strategic forecast using the Receipt Plan Comparison Report in ABC system to answer the questions below.
- How would you use the Receipt Plan Comparison report in the Pre-Release Forecasting timeframe?
- Use the Receipt Plan Comparison Report to recap the receipt plan for the PRODUCT X.
- What actions would you take? Which worksheet in the system do you use? What's different if the enquiry date is today, or last month? What cross-functional conversations would you have based on each of those actions?

Tips, Tricks and Traps
- Real-life scenarios will help participants relate and make a connection.
- Fictional scenarios could also be used; however, the connection to their day-to-day tasks may not be as strong.
- Test the system the day prior to validate functionality.
- Ask 1-3 subject matter experts (depends on the size of the class) to be available during the activities to walk around and guide participants if they have questions.

Adult Learning Base Process: In-Tray Diagnosis Case Study
Refer to **Adult Learning Base Process Reference Guide** for more information about this learning process.

Adult Learning Dashboard
This activity links participant's preferred style of learning. The following dashboard provides a quick reference to adult learning theorists and principles as part of the ID9® methodology.

This activity achieves the following level of Bloom's Taxonomy of the Cognitive Domain (Bloom et al 1956), shown with "X" in the following table.

Bloom's Taxonomy of the Cognitive Domain Level					
Knowledge	Comprehension	Application	Analysis	Synthesis	Evaluation
		X			

This activity also achieves a link, shown with "X" in the following table, to participant's naturally occurring learning preferences. Global/Specific, Learning Modalities, Hemispheric Preference (Sperry, 1981), and Multiple Intelligences (Gardner, 1983) are referenced in ID9® methodology and process. This is not a complete list of links that are covered within the ID9® process however this dashboard aims to provide a quick reference for trainers to use to balance instructional design to provide equality for participants' learning preferences.

Global/Specific Learners		Learning Modalities (Sensory Intake)			Hemispheric Preference	
Global	Specific	Visual	Auditory	Kinesthetic	Left Brain	Right Brain
	X	X	X	X	X	

Multiple Intelligences								
Visual	Intrapersonal	Interpersonal	Musical	Mathematical / Logical	Linguistic	Kinesthetic	Naturalist	Existential
X	X	X		X	X	X		

22. Communication Constructions

Learning outcome
Individuals recognize what is involved when communicating messages so that the messages are understood correctly.

Overview
This learning activity is a way of experiencing just how strange some communication can get. It illustrates how careful we have to be with what we say and how we say it, especially when no body language is visible.

In My Experience
In the game "Chinese Whispers" or "Telephone" children sit in a circle and one child would begin by whispering a sentence to the next child in the circle. Then, that child would repeat what was said to the next and so on until the message had been passed around the circle. Then, the last child would tell the whole group what he/she heard. Usually, the message was totally different to what was started. A stark reminder of the reality of this childhood game motivates people to examine their communication methods and remediate them according to some concrete guidelines. In corporate communication where messages get diluted, confused, mixed up or changed as they pass through the organization this learning activity brings to life the potential downstream impact of not communicating clearly from the outset. This activity is suited to any type of communication training course but also is of value for Corporate marketing or during leadership training when discussing how to communicate the business vision/mission to the organization and how communication can potentially be changed.

The Hidden Twist
People experience what is going wrong and itch to intervene and correct miscomprehension – they kick start the remediation themselves (before being given guidelines and this makes them more receptive when they receive the guidelines – the guidelines resonate with them when they recognize them from their own experience)

Essential Data

Course type:	Course where good communication is essential
Group size:	4 -20 (4 groups of 5 participants)
Time of day:	Particularly effective after lunch or mid-afternoon to reenergize the group while still 'making a point'
Pace:	Fast
Time to Create:	30 minutes
Activity Duration:	30 minutes

Steps to Create
1. Buy (or borrow from children) LEGO ®
2. Get shapes built (examples: Airplane, house, tower, bridge, anything recognizable)
3. Bring to training room incognito and Keep hidden
4. Obtain Screens, flipcharts and coloring pens

Steps to Run
1. Position screens to separate the various groups
2. Split into four groups: (a) those who see the construction and are 'describers'; (b) those who are 'intermediaries'; (c) "end users" and finally (d) 'observers'
3. Explain the rules
   * "Describers" must tell the "intermediaries" what they see (not the actual item) but the main aspects of the item
   * "Intermediaries" must remember what they are told and at the end of the description relay all to the "end users"
   * "End Users" must draw on the flipchart what they understand the object to resemble colors and all
   * Observers must compare the result drawn by "end users" with the reality seen by the "describers"

Suggested Debrief Strategy / Sample Questions
* The trainer should collect observations from the behavior of the participants
* If what is drawn resembles what was seen then list what made that communication successful
* If what is drawn does not match what was seen then list what makes communication unsuccessful
* List agreed communications guidelines for the group given their experience
* Offer to laminate for them keep at their desk
* Link what they have done with the Lego to their 'real world' by discussing real life situations where miscommunication is at high risk.

Working Example
Communication for Scientists: A group of people who are not trained to communicate, e.g., scientists find that they have to do just that when they work in the real world and find it difficult to concentrate and learn the perceived "fluffy" rules about communication methods and techniques. This learning activity focused their attention on what works and what does not work in a scientific way (construction, remembering and drawing) and they make the rules themselves from their experience and so take ownership. There is, therefore,

a high chance of them implementing their own rules (which will match general guidelines given their collaboration with the trainer!) about communications.

Leadership: Build the lego. Split group into four (Describers, Intermediaries, End Users, Observers). Conduct the activity. In the debrief link what they have done to how they will communicate the company vision, mission statement, key strategies, future plans and what they need to consider to minimize the risk of miscommunication and changing the message.

Tips, Tricks and Traps
- The LEGO® constructions must be colorful, complex and real: not gray, complicated or abstract
- The Describer Group must not name the structure, e.g., car; house – they must describe it. As a backup have another structure ready in the event that this rule is broken.

- If the communications works perfectly and nothing is misinterpreted this is not a problem – the list will be about "why did it work so well"
- If the communications does not work at all and nothing is interpreted well this is not a problem either – the list will be about "how could we make communications work?"
- Ensure that participants have enough time to reflect on their thinking transferring the Lego activity into their real world.

Adult Learning Base Process: Simile and Metacognitive Reflection
Refer to **Adult Learning Base Process Reference Guide** for more information about this learning process.

Adult Learning Dashboard
This activity links participant's preferred style of learning. The following dashboard provides a quick reference to adult learning theorists and principles as part of the ID9® methodology.

This activity achieves the following level of Bloom's Taxonomy of the Cognitive Domain (Bloom et al 1956), shown with "X" in the following table.

Bloom's Taxonomy of the Cognitive Domain Level					
Knowledge	Comprehension	Application	Analysis	Synthesis	Evaluation
				X	

This activity also achieves a link, shown with "X" in the following table, to participant's naturally occurring learning preferences. Global/Specific, Learning Modalities, Hemispheric Preference (Sperry, 1981), and Multiple Intelligences (Gardner, 1983) are referenced in ID9® methodology and process. This is not a complete list of links that are covered within the ID9® process however this dashboard aims to provide a quick reference for trainers to use to balance instructional design to provide equality for participants' learning preferences.

Global/Specific Learners		Learning Modalities (Sensory Intake)			Hemispheric Preference	
Global	Specific	Visual	Auditory	Kinesthetic	Left Brain	Right Brain
X	X	X	X	X	X	X

Multiple Intelligences								
Visual	Intrapersonal	Interpersonal	Musical	Mathematical / Logical	Linguistic	Kinesthetic	Naturalist	Existential
X	X	X		X	X	X		X

23. Debate

Learning outcome
Teams debate the merits of assigned topics.

Overview
Teams are assigned a topic and position to defend during a debate.

In My Experience
Preparing for and delivering arguments for a debate requires participants to analyze both sides of the assigned topics and positions. Participants develop a working knowledge of the critical information that supports and refutes both sides of the debate arguments. In order to present the debate argument, participants must synthesis their research and anticipate counter arguments.

The Hidden Twist
Preparing for a debate requires the participants to acquire a considerable depth of knowledge about the assigned topic(s). As participants present arguments and respond to opposing views, they practice and plan arguments from a variety of viewpoints. The debate preparations and debate activities create a rich and demanding learning environment resulting in engaged, motivated learners.

Essential Data
Course type: Conceptual, Process or Technical
Group size: 8-15
Time of day: Early to mid-morning
Pace: Fast
Time to Create: 1-2 hours (less if the research resources are web-based and can be accessed from participant computers via hyperlinks or search engines)

Activity Duration: 30 minutes

Steps to Create
1. Set the topic
2. Develop the debate position which the teams will defend or refute through debate
3. Provide research material or web resources
4. Prepare detailed debate preparation instructions (see working example)
5. Debaters will be given 1-2 minutes to present their arguments. Develop slides, flip charts or posters to frame the debate (add visual interest and background)

Steps to Run
(Note: Ideally, debate research is assigned as pre-work before the training session or as a bridging task between sessions.)
1. Introduce the beginning of the debate.
2. If debate research was not done prior to the training session, give time for teams to research and plan during the course. Then after research and planning is complete, move on to step 3.
3. Give all participants 2 minutes to collect their thoughts and notes.
4. Beginning with the first affirmative argument, each debater will have 1-2 minutes to present their position. (Keep a timer)
5. The first negative debater follows first affirmative and presents their position.
6. Debate teams members alternate presentations until all positions are presented.
7. The debate moderator keeps score and announces the debate winner.
   See working example for suggested debate assignments for affirmative and negative team members.

Suggested Debrief Strategy/Sample Questions
There must be an open discussion following the debate – debates often miss the middle-ground surrounding an issue because they focus on the two ends of the spectrum. Questions to facilitate an open discussion are:
- What new insights did you gain about (topic) during the debate process?
- Do you agree with the debate outcome, why or why not?
- How does (insert topic) relate to your current work?
- What new questions do you have about (insert topic)?

New questions raised by participants can direct the discussion toward aspects of the topic not covered during the debate.

Working Example
In a sales program two teams debate "Our product 'Handy Glue' is superior to our competitors 'Zippy Glue'". The affirmative team, agrees with the statement and presents all of the positives for 'Handy Glue' while the negative team provide all of the positives of 'Zippy Glue' and the pitfalls of 'Handy Glue'. A third team could be assigned as the 'adjudicating panel'. The structure of the debate is:

1st Affirmative must:

- define the topic.
- present the affirmative's team line.
- outline briefly what each speaker in their team will talk about.
- present the first half of the affirmative case

>**1st Negative must:**
>
>- accept or reject the definition. If you don't do this it is assumed that you accept the definition.
>- present the negative team line.
>- outline briefly what each of the negative speakers will say.
>- rebut a few of the main points of the first affirmative
>- the 1st negative should spend about one quarter of their time rebutting.
>- present the first half of the negative team's case.

2nd Affirmative must:

- reaffirm the affirmative's team line.
- rebut the main points presented by the 1st negative.
- the 2nd affirmative should spend about one third of their time rebutting.
- present the second half of the affirmative's case.

>**2nd Negative must:**
>
>- reaffirm the negative's team line.
>- rebut some of the main points of the affirmative's case.
>- the 2nd negative should spend about one third of their time rebutting.
>- present the second half of the negative's case.

3rd Affirmative must:

- reaffirm the affirmative's team line.
- rebut all the remaining points of the negative's case.
- the 3rd affirmative should spend about two thirds to
- three quarters of their time rebutting.
- present a summary of the affirmative's case.
- round off the debate for the affirmative.

>**3rd Negative must:**
>
>- reaffirm the negative's team line.
>- rebut all the remaining points of the affirmative's case.
>- the 3rd negative should spend about two thirds
>- to three quarters of their time rebutting.
>- present a summary of the negative's case.
>- round off the debate for the negative.

Tips, Tricks & Traps

- Participants need pre-teaching on debate skills and how to successfully conduct a debate
- Participants need time to prepare for each debate - at least some of this time should be provided in class.
- Participants need pre-requisite knowledge on the topics – either in this course prior to the debate planning or from previous courses.
- All participants need a role in every debate – this may include being judges or being responsible for the debrief.
- Place participants into their roles of for or against an issue (affirmative, negative, adjudicating team). I would suggest that you do not allow them to choose their teams and suggest that perhaps a fishbowl (see next learning activity in this chapter) of random role cards be drawn by each participant therefore creating randomization in the allocation of teams. This allows for greater growth and new learning

Adult Learning Base Process: Debate
Refer to **Adult Learning Base Process Reference Guide** for more information about this learning process.

Adult Learning Dashboard

This activity links participant's preferred style of learning. The following dashboard provides a quick reference to adult learning theorists and principles as part of the ID9® methodology.

This activity achieves the following level of Bloom's Taxonomy of the Cognitive Domain (Bloom et al 1956), shown with "X" in the following table.

Bloom's Taxonomy of the Cognitive Domain Level					
Knowledge	Comprehension	Application	Analysis	Synthesis	Evaluation
				X	

This activity also achieves a link, shown with "X" in the following table, to participant's naturally occurring learning preferences. Global/Specific, Learning Modalities, Hemispheric Preference (Sperry, 1981), and Multiple Intelligences (Gardner, 1983) are referenced in ID9® methodology and process. This is not a complete list of links that are covered within the ID9® process however this dashboard aims to provide a quick reference for trainers to use to balance instructional design to provide equality for participants' learning preferences.

Global/Specific Learners		Learning Modalities (Sensory Intake)			Hemispheric Preference	
Global	Specific	Visual	Auditory	Kinesthetic	Left Brain	Right Brain
X	X	X	X	X	X	X

Multiple Intelligences								
Visual	Intrapersonal	Interpersonal	Musical	Mathematical / Logical	Linguistic	Kinesthetic	Naturalist	Existential
X		X	X	X	X	X		X

24. Process Mapping Fishbowl

Learning outcome
Participants assemble process steps in order

Overview
Participants work together in a team competition to correctly assemble the steps of a newly learned process.

In My Experience
Sometimes static and dry material, such as process maps and operating procedures, step-by-step information, or linear content require a dose of fun, memorable learning activities to ensure learning is retained.

The Hidden Twist
Driven by play and competition, participants turn sometimes dry static process maps into a lively, engaging and MEMORABLE learning activity.

Essential Data
Course type: Procedure
Group size: 10-30
Time of day: After Lunch or End of Day
Pace: Rapid and competitive
Time to Create: 30- 60 minutes
Activity Duration: 15-30 minutes

Steps to Create
1. Create the skeleton or structure lines of the process map on a large poster/wall chart (you'll need at least 2 posters)
2. Write each process step on a 3X5 card (you'll need 2 sets of process step cards)
3. Create or obtain a printed version of the complete process map (answer key)
4. Obtain fishbowl (or hat or bag) to put the process step cards into

Steps to Run
1. Divide the class into two equal teams, and each team forms a single line
2. Each team has a blank map and a fish bowl
3. Place the blank process map diagram on the wall or flip chart
4. One at a time, each team member selects a card from the fishbowl and places it in the appropriate location on the process map poster
5. Team members can help, but be careful, the other team is listening!
6. If the process map is incorrectly assembled, the team continues by rearranging steps until the map is correct.

7. The first team to correctly complete the process map wins.
8. Give everyone a printed copy of the correct process map.

Suggested Debrief Strategy/Sample Questions
Suggested questions to ask the whole group to debrief this activity include:
- What steps were the easiest to place correctly?
- Which process steps took you the longest to place correctly?
- What process steps do you need to review to solidify your knowledge of the process?
- How will you remember the process in the future?

Working Example
Standard Operating Procedure (SOP) Training – especially for complex, cross functional processes.

After listening to the presentation of a new, complex SOP, the participants work together to assemble the SOP process map in the correct order.

Tips, Tricks & Traps
- For a larger groups, use more than 2 teams.
- For larger groups, make sure you have a knowledgeable facilitator to help check correctness of posters.
- Give the teams hints by pre-placing several of the process steps on the poster prior to beginning the competition.
- Make the process steps and process map as colorful and graphic as possible to trigger visual learning.
- Play lively game music for competition. Stop the music when checking a team's map for correctness.

Adult Learning Base Process: Fishbowl
Refer to **Adult Learning Base Process Reference Guide** for more information about this learning process.

Adult Learning Dashboard
This activity links participant's preferred style of learning. The following dashboard provides a quick reference to adult learning theorists and principles as part of the ID9® methodology.

This activity achieves the following level of Bloom's Taxonomy of the Cognitive Domain (Bloom et al 1956), shown with "X" in the following table.

Bloom's Taxonomy of the Cognitive Domain Level					
Knowledge	Comprehension	Application	Analysis	Synthesis	Evaluation
				X	

This activity also achieves a link, shown with "X" in the following table, to participant's naturally occurring learning preferences. Global/Specific, Learning Modalities, Hemispheric Preference (Sperry, 1981), and Multiple Intelligences (Gardner, 1983) are referenced in ID9® methodology and process. This is not a complete list of links that are covered within the ID9® process however this dashboard aims to provide a quick reference for trainers to use to balance instructional design to provide equality for participants' learning preferences.

Global/Specific Learners		Learning Modalities (Sensory Intake)			Hemispheric Preference	
Global	Specific	Visual	Auditory	Kinesthetic	Left Brain	Right Brain
X	X	X	X	X	X	

Multiple Intelligences								
Visual	Intrapersonal	Interpersonal	Musical	Mathematical / Logical	Linguistic	Kinesthetic	Naturalist	Existential
X		X	X	X	X	X		

Chapter 3:
During Course:
Mini Review Activities

Start / End Session, Mini Reviews for Topic Rotations

Diana McLeod

About the Co-Author:

Diana McLeod

Diana McLeod has over ten years of instructional design experience spanning multiple industries including utilities, retail, educational services, biotechnology and biopharmaceutical. She has a strong background in designing and developing instructor-led and eLearning programs. Diana holds both Master's and Bachelor's degrees in education, with her Master's focused on Instructional Technologies. She has achieved the Certified ID9® Professional – level 3 (Platinum) of Catherine Mattiske's ID9® process.

In her spare time, she loves to travel, snowboard, hike and run. If she is not on the slopes in Tahoe she is probably traveling. She has traveled to 36 (and counting) countries and six continents and hopes to hit Antarctica soon.

Chapter Introduction

YAY, for mini-reviews! These quick and to-the-point activities are a powerful tool to determine if learning goals and objectives are being achieved. The purpose of mini-reviews is to provide continuous review throughout the entire program. The time spent running mini-reviews can range from one to ten minutes.

Mini-review activities do differ from learning activities. Learning activities are usually conducted immediately following a segment of content while learning is still taking place during the session, in other words, 'first time learning'. Learning activities are more orchestrated, controlled and directed by the trainer. In general, review activities can be thought of as 'second or subsequent time learning' where participants have already learned and practiced new skills or information and the review activity serves to check learning and confidence. Mini-review activities are short activities which are conducted regularly throughout the program to check the learners' understanding of the material just presented.

Mini-review activities offer a great deal of benefit for the participant as well as the trainer. The participants gain confidence as they practice a new skill in an environment that encourages active participation by removing the barrier of embarrassment. The trainer benefits by having the opportunity to observe, listening to participants as they work, and providing them immediate feedback of the participants' understanding of the topic just presented. Mini-reviews combined with the activity debrief help a trainer identify gaps in learning and provide an opportunity to clear up any misunderstanding before moving onto the next topic of new content.

The placement of mini-reviews is important. Using ID9® mini reviews is important and they may take as little as 1 minute of training time and can be easily placed either side of a break. The End of Session review falls just prior to the break and the Start of Session review is completed as soon as participants return from their break and before the next section of learning. It may seem overdone to have all of these review activities, however this one of the secrets of success in the ID9® process. Participants, through constant opportunities to activate their knowledge within a topic, via learning activities, and then followed by mini reviews constantly check their retention of their new learning, thereby increasing their motivation and maximizing learning transfer and application.

Throughout the chapter I refer to the ID9® term 'session' which can be best defined as 'any period of time between two breaks'. Ideally the duration of a session should be 50 minutes, and shouldn't exceed 90 minutes.

Remember, it's not the trainer summarizing the learning in a mini-lecture that forms a mini-review. It's the participants actively participating in an activity to 'show they know', seek assistance from the trainer if needed, and then move on with the training course with confidence.

The reviews that I've created within this chapter are quick, easy to facilitate and achieve the 'learning check' that both trainers and participants need to keep the learning pace and motivation high. Most of the activities in this chapter are equally suited for in-class face-to-face training as well as virtual training and many can be used as written, or be easily adapted, for eLearning.

25. Write it, Try it!

Learning outcome
To help participants develop well-defined goals for their learning.

Overview
This is a mini-review at the end of a session that gives learners an opportunity to set goals using the Positive, Achievement, Context, Ecology and Resources (PACER) model, which is a Neuro Linguistic Programming (NLP) tool. This goal writing technique consists of answering questions for each of the PACER categories using positive language. The theory behind this is that the mind is unable to process the word 'not' at an unconscious level. If the outcome is set as a negative such as, "I am NOT going to eat fried food" your mind may think "I AM going to eat fried food". The goal needs to be developed using positive language rather than something that should be avoided. For example, "Lose weight" should be worded with a positive connotation, "I want to be healthier".

In My Experience
It is an excellent activity to help participants set achievable goals using a specific framework (PACER). It's a different way for participants to explore goal setting using positive vocabulary. Writing meaningful goals and discussing them with someone else increases the likelihood the participants will be committed to following through to achieve their goals.

The Hidden Twist
This PACER goal setting model can be used in all aspects of a participant's life. The model can be used as a journal that the participant can use as a reference to check goal achievement.

Essential Data
Course Type: Any
Group Size: 1-50
Time of Day: Any time
Pace: Moderate
Trainer Preparation Time: 30 minutes
Activity Duration: 10 minutes

Steps to Create
1. Write instructions for developing a goal using the PACER model. This can be added to an individual handout or on a page in the participant guide.
   - Instructions: Reflect on the topic just presented and describe an action you will take to help you implement the mechanics of that topic. Read each question and using positive language write a short answer in the space provided. After your write it, try it!
2. Now create a table with the PACER acronym running down the left side and the corresponding question next to it (see example).

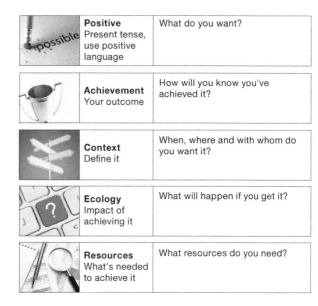

	Positive Present tense, use positive language	What do you want?
	Achievement Your outcome	How will you know you've achieved it?
	Context Define it	When, where and with whom do you want it?
	Ecology Impact of achieving it	What will happen if you get it?
	Resources What's needed to achieve it	What resources do you need?

Steps to Run
1. After a session topic, distribute the instructions and PACER table.
2. Have each participant write one topic related goal using the PACER model.
3. Explain to participants that PACER is an acronym for:
   - Positive – use positive language in the present tense to write a goal
   - Achievement – outcome of the goal
   - Context – define the goal
   - Ecology – impact of achieving the goal
   - Resources – resources needed to achieve the goal

4. Ask participants to reflect on the material just covered and a topic related goal they have for themselves.

5. Instruct them to review the PACER table and to provide a short answer for each question.

6. As participants work, play music quietly in the background.

7. After they write their goal, instruct participants to pair up with a partner at their table and share the goal they developed. Give each partner 1 minute to share their goal. (1 minute for each partner – 2 minutes total).

Suggested Debrief Strategy/Sample Questions

Ask participants to share a goal they set and ask them these follow-up questions (as applicable).

- How does that goal relate to the session topic?
- Why did you choose that goal?
- How do you plan to accomplish that goal after this class?
- What will happen when you achieve the goal?
- How will you feel after you achieve the goal?
- What does achieving the goal contribute to your organization or to yourself?

Working Example
Manage, Lead and Develop People.

During a three day management course the PACER technique can be used as a continuous review activity, meaning that participants update their PACER handout several times a day for each day of the course. Ideally, this would be done at the end of a session, prior to a break. Participants create one or two 'positives' at the end of a session (for example, leading and motivating individuals, identifying development needs, applying leadership skills and evaluating performance) and then work through each of the 'positives' with the remainder of the PACER technique. At the end of the program, participants in their final end of session review (or as the major review) consolidate their PACER handout to create an action plan. The benefit of the PACER technique when used in this way is that it focuses on goal setting (i.e. application of learning) throughout the program and also chunks down the often 'left until the last minute of training' action planning process which can be burdensome to participants if left in its entirety until the end of a long training program.

Tips, Tricks and Traps

- Throughout the session topic, ask the class questions about how they might accomplish this task/process when they leave the class. The idea is to get them thinking about their goals during the topic review and better prepare them for the upcoming review activity.
- Add corresponding images to the PACER table for visual learners.
- Playing music while participants are working 'fills the space'.
  - Faster music can increase the pace of learning and support a competitive environment (i.e. faster than heart rate)
  - Slower music can decrease the pace of learning and support a quiet reflective environment
- Additional PACER questions:
  - Positive:
    - What will this bring you?
  - Achievement:
    - How will you know you are succeeding?
    - How will you know when you have got it?
    - What will you see, hear and feel?
    - How will someone else know when you have got it?
    - What will it add to your organization of yourself?
    - What is the first step?
    - What is the last step?
  - Context
    - When, where and with whom do you not want it?
  - Ecology
    - How long will it take to achieve this outcome?
    - Who else is affected and how will they feel?
    - How does it fit in with your other outcomes?
    - How does it increase your choices?
    - What will not happen if you get it?
    - What will happen if you do not get it?
    - What will not happen if you do not get it?
  - Resources
    - Can you implement and maintain it?
    - What resources have you already got (i.e. skills, people, money, objects, etc.)?
    - Who has already succeeded in achieving this outcome?

Adult Learning Base Process: NLP Activity – Pacer Technique

Refer to **Adult Learning Base Process Reference Guide** for more information about this learning process.

Adult Learning Dashboard

This activity links participant's preferred style of learning. The following dashboard provides a quick reference to adult learning theorists and principles as part of the ID9® methodology.

This activity achieves the following level of Bloom's Taxonomy of the Cognitive Domain (Bloom et al 1956), shown with "X" in the following table.

Bloom's Taxonomy of the Cognitive Domain Level					
Knowledge	Comprehension	Application	Analysis	Synthesis	Evaluation
			X		

This activity also achieves a link, shown with "X" in the following table, to participant's naturally occurring learning preferences. Global/Specific, Learning Modalities, Hemispheric Preference (Sperry, 1981), and Multiple Intelligences (Gardner, 1983) are referenced in ID9® methodology and process. This is not a complete list of links that are covered within the ID9® process however this dashboard aims to provide a quick reference for trainers to use to balance instructional design to provide equality for participants' learning preferences.

Global/Specific Learners		Learning Modalities (Sensory Intake)			Hemispheric Preference	
Global	Specific	Visual	Auditory	Kinesthetic	Left Brain	Right Brain
X	X	X	X	X		X

Multiple Intelligences								
Visual	Intrapersonal	Interpersonal	Musical	Mathematical / Logical	Linguistic	Kinesthetic	Naturalist	Existential
X	X		X	X	X			

26. Aha!

Learning outcome

To help participants recognize learning accomplishments.

Overview

A mini-review to use at the end of a session that provides participants with an opportunity to reflect on the topic just covered and key learning(s) from that topic.

Start of Session Mini-Review	End of Session Mini-Review
	X

In My Experience

It is beneficial to slow the class down and take a couple of minutes to reflect on what was just learned. It helps participants to absorb the material and think about what it means to them and how they will use it.

The Hidden Twist

This review activity can be used throughout the day at the end of each session allowing participants to record, in their own words, what they learned during the session. It also acts as a helpful reminder to reflect on "Aha" moments when they leave the class.

Essential Data

Course Type: Any
Group Size: 1-50
Time of Day: Any time
Pace: Moderate
Trainer Preparation Time: 5 minutes
Activity Duration: 5-10 minutes

Steps to Create

1. Create a place for a journal entry (e.g. on an individual handout or on a page in the participant guide) that includes these instructions:
   - Reflect on the topic we just reviewed. Write an "Aha" moment you had when you suddenly gained insight or realization. Now visualize how you will use it.

Instructions: Reflect on the topic we just reviewed. Write an 'Aha' moment you had when you suddenly gained insight or realization. Now utilize how you will use it.

Steps to Run

1. After a topic, as an end of session mini-review, distribute the journal entry (e.g. handout or participant guide) to each participant.
2. Ask participants to reflect on what they just learned; record an "Aha" moment in their journal and then visualize doing it.
3. As participants work, play music quietly in the background.
4. Ask them to share their "Aha" moment with the person sitting next to them or debrief as a whole group.

Suggested Debrief Strategy/Sample Questions

Ask participants to share their "Aha" moments and then follow-up with these questions (as applicable).

- What in particular made this an "Aha" moment for you?
- How will you apply it after this class?
- Who else can you teach this new insight to?
- How does your Aha! add meaning to you and others.

Working Example

Implementing Change

During this 4 hour program the "Aha" moment handout is used as a start of session mini-review. Participants return from their break and before going on with the next stop they reflect on what they have covered so far and note it in their participant guide or "Aha" moment handout. Participants might remark that their "Aha" moment was how they can impact change on the organization and their team, the phases of change, how change development plans can reduce stress, and so on. This boosts energy and motivation and the training continues with everyone on the 'same page'.

Tips, Tricks and Traps

- At the end of the session, ask participants what stood out, what made the light bulb go on inside their head.
- As a start of session mini-review, ask participants to reflect on the previous session before the break. Perhaps ask them to go back over their notes and then complete their 'Aha moment' handout.
- Seeking social proof (Cialdini) is an important for participants to share their "Aha" moments either with a partner, their small table group, or the whole group. This allows for everyone else to know that all participants are 'on board' with the learning and learn from each other's "Aha" moments building confidence for all participants.
- Playing music while participants are working 'fills the space'.
  - Faster music can increase the pace of learning and support a competitive environment (i.e. faster than heart rate)
  - Slower music can decrease the pace of learning and support a quiet reflective environment

Adult Learning Base Process: Eureka Effect

Refer to **Adult Learning Base Process Reference Guide** for more information about this learning process.

Adult Learning Dashboard

This activity links participant's preferred style of learning. The following dashboard provides a quick reference to adult learning theorists and principles as part of the ID9® methodology.

This activity achieves the following level of Bloom's Taxonomy of the Cognitive Domain (Bloom et al 1956), shown with "X" in the following table.

Bloom's Taxonomy of the Cognitive Domain Level					
Knowledge	Comprehension	Application	Analysis	Synthesis	Evaluation
			X		

This activity also achieves a link, shown with "X" in the following table, to participant's naturally occurring learning preferences. Global/Specific, Learning Modalities, Hemispheric Preference (Sperry, 1981), and Multiple Intelligences (Gardner, 1983) are referenced in ID9® methodology and process. This is not a complete list of links that are covered within the ID9® process however this dashboard aims to provide a quick reference for trainers to use to balance instructional design to provide equality for participants' learning preferences.

Global/Specific Learners		Learning Modalities (Sensory Intake)			Hemispheric Preference	
Global	Specific	Visual	Auditory	Kinesthetic	Left Brain	Right Brain
X		X	X	X		X

Multiple Intelligences								
Visual	Intrapersonal	Interpersonal	Musical	Mathematical / Logical	Linguistic	Kinesthetic	Naturalist	Existential
X	X		X		X	X		X

27. What Would You Do? (Part 1)

Learning outcome
To challenge participants to watch, listen and analyze a situation related to the session topic.

Overview
This is a mini-review to use at the start of a session. This is a two-part activity. Conduct Part 1 at the beginning of the session and Part 2 at the end of the session. This is a structured role play that provides participants with an opportunity to watch a scenario, analyze it and then determine how they would approach the situation differently.

Start of Session Mini-Review	End of Session Mini-Review
X	

In My Experience
This activity is a great lead-in to a topic that provides participants with an opportunity for movement and helps to put the topic in context. It's helpful to bring up aspects of the scenario before you present the topic. This will keep participants thinking about how to better handle the situation throughout the topic session.

The Hidden Twist
Giving participants an experiential experience increases their interest in the topic.

Essential Data
Course Type: Any
Group Size: 4-20
Time of Day: Any time
Pace: Moderate
Trainer Preparation Time: 30 minutes
Activity Duration: 10 minutes

Steps to Create
1. Create a simple, structured scene for 1-4 people to re-enact (how many people involved depends on the scene you create and the size of the class).
2. Write a short script, related to the topic, for each "actor" on index cards or type it and provide each actor with their printed copies.
3. Highlight each character's part in the script so each actor can easily identify their part of the script.
4. Create a nametag for each actor to wear in order to identify the character they are playing.
5. Create a presentation slide or write on a flip cart, "I just watched a scene related to [insert topic] and I would do the following things differently."
6. Create a space for participants to write this statement on and their answer(s). This can be in an individual handout or a page in the participant guide.

Steps to Run
1. Explain to participants that they are about to watch a short scenario and while watching it they need to think about how they would handle it differently.
2. Ask for volunteers to act out the scene.
   - State that if you don't get volunteers you will have to randomly pick people.
3. Give each volunteer a character to play, their script, and a nametag to wear with their character's name on it.
4. Give the volunteers 2 minutes to read over their short script.
5. While the volunteers read over their part, show the presentation slide or reveal the flip chart page (see step 5 in Steps to Create above) and ask the rest of the class to write this sentence in the individual handout or a page in the participant guide, "I just watched a scene related to [insert topic] and I would do the following things differently."
6. Have the volunteers act out the scene. (1 minute)
7. Give everyone 2 minutes to write what they would have done differently, if anything at all.

Suggested Debrief Strategy/Sample Questions
- Ask participants these questions all under the umbrella of "What would you do?":
   ○ What did the two employees do well?
   ○ If you could create a 'new' way, what you would have done differently?
   ○ Why would you do it your 'new' way?
   ○ What would the result be for doing it your 'new' way?
   ○ What would the results be if it is not done your 'new' way?
- After asking participants the above questions, explain that this scene leads us into our discussion on the upcoming topic and as we review the topic to keep this scene in mind, what they said they would do differently, and at the end of the topic session if they would revise their recommendations for handling the scene. (1 minute)

Working Example
Informed Consent Training
During this start of session mini review two participants play the role of employees in a simple dialog about the process of using the Informed Consent Form.

The dialog is placed on two role cards. Participants complete the activity in pairs. Therefore each participant in the training is playing one of the roles. (It is not demonstrated in front of the class as this spotlights participants which isn't recommended).

Actor 1 (Employee 1): I need to develop the Informed Consent Form (ICF) for my study, but I'm not sure where to start.

Actor 2: (Employee 2): I used that investigator site for one of my studies. Just use the ICF I developed and change some of the areas to reflect your study.

Actor 1 (Employee 1): Thanks! That will save me so much time. When did you create this ICF?

Actor 2 (Employee 2): About 2 years ago, but it should still be about the same.

Actor 1 (Employee 1): Yeah, probably not too many changes have been made. Will you send me the ICF you used?

Actor 2 (Employee 2): Sure!

After all paired groups have completed the trainer debriefs the activity (as suggested above).

Tips, Tricks and Traps

- Ensure all participants are actively involved in the activity rather than spotlighting two participants to role play in front of the group.
- Do not provide validation or input to participant comments during the debrief. The trainer's goal is to guide them through the discussion to prepare them for Part 2 of this activity.

Adult Learning Base Process: Role Play
Refer to **Adult Learning Base Process Reference Guide** for more information about this learning process.

Adult Learning Dashboard
This activity links participant's preferred style of learning. The following dashboard provides a quick reference to adult learning theorists and principles as part of the ID9® methodology.

This activity achieves the following level of Bloom's Taxonomy of the Cognitive Domain (Bloom et al 1956), shown with "X" in the following table.

Bloom's Taxonomy of the Cognitive Domain Level					
Knowledge	Comprehension	Application	Analysis	Synthesis	Evaluation
					X

This activity also achieves a link, shown with "X" in the following table, to participant's naturally occurring learning preferences. Global/Specific, Learning Modalities, Hemispheric Preference (Sperry, 1981), and Multiple Intelligences (Gardner, 1983) are referenced in ID9® methodology and process. This is not a complete list of links that are covered within the ID9® process however this dashboard aims to provide a quick reference for trainers to use to balance instructional design to provide equality for participants' learning preferences.

Global/Specific Learners		Learning Modalities (Sensory Intake)			Hemispheric Preference	
Global	Specific	Visual	Auditory	Kinesthetic	Left Brain	Right Brain
X	X	X	X	X	X	X

Multiple Intelligences								
Visual	Intrapersonal	Interpersonal	Musical	Mathematical / Logical	Linguistic	Kinesthetic	Naturalist	Existential
X	X	X		X	X	X		

28. What Would You Do? (Part 2)

Learning outcome
To encourage participants to actively reflect on the topic they just learned.

Overview
This mini-review should be used after conducting Part 1 of this activity. In Part 1, participants have not yet been taught a new process, skill or new content area and are determining their answer based on their current knowledge (i.e. before they are taught the new or enhanced methodology). Part 2 of the activity asks participants to reflect on what they just learned and if it differs from their previous experience.

Start of Session Mini-Review	End of Session Mini-Review
	X

In My Experience
This activity provides an upbeat wrap-up to a session topic. In Part 1 of the activity, most participants are probably making an educated guess on what they would consider a better 'new' way. I found that most participants remain very alert and motivated during the session topic because they want to know if their answer from Part 1 is correct. This activity needs to be conducted in a non-threatening manner because, as the trainer, you are not expecting everyone to have the correct outcome and they need to know that is perfectly acceptable.

The Hidden Twist
Giving participants an experiential experience increases interest in the topic. Also, there is higher retention of the topic when participants are given a real-life situation, the opportunity to try, allow the trainer to correct and remediate their learning if they are off-track, and learn from it.

Essential Data
Course Type: Any
Group Size: 4-20
Time of Day: Any time
Pace: Moderate
Trainer Preparation Time: 5 minutes
Activity Duration: 5-10 minutes

Steps to Create
Use the same individual handout or page in the participant guide that was used for Part 1 of this activity. Each has the sentence, "I just watched a scene related to [insert topic] and I would do the following things differently."

Steps to Run
1. Inform participants by stating, "Now that we've finished the session topic, review the list you created in the activity at the beginning of this session and decide if you would adjust your list knowing what you have just learned during this session."
2. Give participants 2 minutes to revise their list based on the information they just learned.

Suggested Debrief Strategy/Sample Questions
Ask participants these questions:
- How did your outcome change after learning more about this topic?
- Why did you adjust your list?

Working Example
Informed Consent Training
During this end of session mini review participants reflect on their previous answers related to the Informed Consent Form role play.

They repeat the role play (in this case as the role play dialog is very short) or review it without actually re-running the activity (if it's lengthy).

In their participant guide they complete their notes answering the open ended question: I just watched a scene related to ICF development and I would do the following things differently.

I just watched a scene related to ICF development and I would do the following things differently.

Do not use a colleague's ICF as a template.

Always use the ICF template saved in SharePoint.

Tips, Tricks and Traps
- It is okay if you have some participants that do not need to make any revisions to their list.
- Make it a safe and respectful environment to encourage participation.

Adult Learning Base Process: Role Play
Refer to **Adult Learning Base Process Reference Guide** for more information about this learning process.

Adult Learning Dashboard
This activity links participant's preferred style of learning. The following dashboard provides a quick reference to adult learning theorists and principles as part of the ID9® methodology.

This activity achieves the following level of Bloom's Taxonomy of the Cognitive Domain (Bloom et al 1956), shown with "X" in the following table.

Bloom's Taxonomy of the Cognitive Domain Level					
Knowledge	Comprehension	Application	Analysis	Synthesis	Evaluation
					X

This activity also achieves a link, shown with "X" in the following table, to participant's naturally occurring learning preferences. Global/Specific, Learning Modalities, Hemispheric Preference (Sperry, 1981), and Multiple Intelligences (Gardner, 1983) are referenced in ID9® methodology and process. This is not a complete list of links that are covered within the ID9® process however this dashboard aims to provide a quick reference for trainers to use to balance instructional design to provide equality for participants' learning preferences.

Global/Specific Learners		Learning Modalities (Sensory Intake)			Hemispheric Preference	
Global	Specific	Visual	Auditory	Kinesthetic	Left Brain	Right Brain
X	X	X	X	X	X	

Multiple Intelligences								
Visual	Intrapersonal	Interpersonal	Musical	Mathematical / Logical	Linguistic	Kinesthetic	Naturalist	Existential
X	X			X	X	X		

29. Think about It

Learning outcome
To encourage participants to apply what they learned by mimicking a real-life situation related to the session topic.

Overview
Activities that reflect situations participants might actually encounter can help make the correlation between the topic learned and how to apply it back on the job. This is a great mini-review to use at the end of each session.

Start of Session Mini-Review	End of Session Mini-Review
	X

In My Experience
Any opportunity to tie in real life scenarios makes the experience a richer one for participants. Behavioral changes are more likely to occur after training when a participant can make the connection to the material learned during class and how they can apply it in real-life on-the-job. This is a particularly good activity for systems training.

The Hidden Twist
An experiential experience increases interest in the topic. This is also a quick gauge for the trainer to determine if any knowledge gaps exist and to be able to address those gaps immediately.

Essential Data
Course Type: Any
Group Size: 1-25
Time of Day: Any time
Pace: Moderate
Trainer Preparation Time: 10 minutes
Activity Duration: 5-10 minutes

Steps to Create
Write a real-life scenario based on content from the session topic. It can be written on an individual handout or on a page in the participant guide.

Steps to Run
Ask participants to read the real-life scenario and then record how they would handle that situation.

Suggested Debrief Strategy/Sample Questions
Ask participants these questions:
- What are your next steps?
- How did you determine what those next steps would be?
  - Write their answers on a flip chart or white board.

Working Example
Retail Sales Training
In a two-day retail sales training program participants practice a number of short scenarios based on real-life customer service encounters. The following is one of the scenarios presented to participants showing a copy of an email from a merchant to the customer service representative. Participants, either individually, in pairs or small groups, read the scenario (in this case, the email) and decide how they would react to resolve the issue.

You just received this email from your Merchant. What are your next steps to resolve the issue? Write your steps in the space below.

Variance for Red Pant - Message

To... Jan Smith
Subject: Variance for Red Pant

Hi Jan,

I noticed a variance between your DC U Rcpts OP for Style 383732CF Red Pant and what actually stocked In-DC. Please advice.

Thanks,
Tom

What are your next steps to resolve the issue?

Tips, Tricks and Traps
- Create a scenario that a participant would encounter on the job. Real-life scenarios will help participants relate and make a connection to the topic.
- Ask a subject-matter expert to help write the scenario to ensure relevance and accuracy.
- Depending on the complexity of the scenarios several could be presented to participants in one end of session mini-review.

Adult Learning Base Process: In-Tray Diagnosis
Refer to **Adult Learning Base Process Reference Guide** for more information about this learning process.

Adult Learning Dashboard
This activity links participant's preferred style of learning. The following dashboard provides a quick reference to adult learning theorists and principles as part of the ID9® methodology.

This activity achieves the following level of Bloom's Taxonomy of the Cognitive Domain (Bloom et al 1956), shown with "X" in the following table.

Bloom's Taxonomy of the Cognitive Domain Level					
Knowledge	Comprehension	Application	Analysis	Synthesis	Evaluation
					X

This activity also achieves a link, shown with "X" in the following table, to participant's naturally occurring learning preferences. Global/Specific, Learning Modalities, Hemispheric Preference (Sperry, 1981), and Multiple Intelligences (Gardner, 1983) are referenced in ID9® methodology and process. This is not a complete list of links that are covered within the ID9® process however this dashboard aims to provide a quick reference for trainers to use to balance instructional design to provide equality for participants' learning preferences.

Global/Specific Learners		Learning Modalities (Sensory Intake)			Hemispheric Preference	
Global	Specific	Visual	Auditory	Kinesthetic	Left Brain	Right Brain
X	X	X	X	X	X	

Multiple Intelligences								
Visual	Intrapersonal	Interpersonal	Musical	Mathematical / Logical	Linguistic	Kinesthetic	Naturalist	Existential
X				X	X	X		

30. I Know, I Don't Know (Part 1)

Learning outcome
To help participants reflect on what they already know about a topic and what they want to learn about the topic.

Overview
This activity helps participants identify what they know about a topic and highlights what they want to learn about the topic. This is a two part activity. Part 1 should be used as a start of session mini review.

Start of Session Mini-Review	End of Session Mini-Review
X	

In My Experience
This is a great activity to gauge participants' prior knowledge level on a topic and to discover what they would like to learn about the topic.

The Hidden Twist
As you move through the material, focusing on each topic and how it matches an area of interest for a participant will keep the participants engaged because it is something they are interested in learning.

Essential Data
Course Type: Any
Group Size: 1-50
Time of Day: Any time
Pace: Moderate
Trainer Preparation Time: 5 minutes
Activity Duration: 5-10 minutes

Steps to Create
Create a page that contains this sentence at the top of it, "What I already know about [insert topic]…" and has this sentence in the middle of the page, "What I want to learn about [insert topic]…". This can be written on an individual handout or a page in the participant guide.

What I know about [insert topic]...

What I want to learn about [insert topic]...

Steps to Run
Ask participants to read the partial statements and complete them.

Suggested Debrief Strategy/Sample Questions
- Ask these questions and write the responses on a flip chart or on a white board.
  - What are things you already know about this topic?
  - What are things you would like to learn about this topic?
    - Let participants know which of those listed will covered in the session.
- As you move through the topic, put a check mark next to the topic that is listed on the flip chart or white board that was just covered.

Working Example
Contract Law for Managers
The pre-requisite for this course is an undergraduate degree or at least five years of relevant management experience, therefore some participants come into the class with a both theoretical and practical experience however it's often inconsistent across the group with some participants knowing a lot about one topic, and others knowing little. This variance in participant experience is brought out by using this deceptively simple start of session mini review. Before starting a topic, for example, legislative requirements and organizational policies, participants complete the handout (see above). Then, they share their knowledge levels with their table groups before consolidating their thoughts on a group flipchart or having the trainer write it on a whole group flipchart or whiteboard. The mini review ends with clarity for trainer and participant on the level of previous knowledge by the group and allows the trainer to then 'pitch' the upcoming session of learning based on the needs of the group. This is equally effective in virtual training because the 'whiteboard' and the 'chat' feature can be used to facilitate this start-of-session mini review.

Tips, Tricks and Traps
It's totally acceptable if a participant doesn't know anything or very little about the topic (remember to reassure them that that's why they are taking this course).

Adult Learning Base Process: Metacognitive Reflection
Refer to **Adult Learning Base Process Reference Guide** for more information about this learning process.

Adult Learning Dashboard

This activity links participant's preferred style of learning. The following dashboard provides a quick reference to adult learning theorists and principles as part of the ID9® methodology.

This activity achieves the following level of Bloom's Taxonomy of the Cognitive Domain (Bloom et al 1956), shown with "X" in the following table.

Bloom's Taxonomy of the Cognitive Domain Level					
Knowledge	Comprehension	Application	Analysis	Synthesis	Evaluation
X					

This activity also achieves a link, shown with "X" in the following table, to participant's naturally occurring learning preferences. Global/Specific, Learning Modalities, Hemispheric Preference (Sperry, 1981), and Multiple Intelligences (Gardner, 1983) are referenced in ID9® methodology and process. This is not a complete list of links that are covered within the ID9® process however this dashboard aims to provide a quick reference for trainers to use to balance instructional design to provide equality for participants' learning preferences.

Global/Specific Learners		Learning Modalities (Sensory Intake)			Hemispheric Preference	
Global	Specific	Visual	Auditory	Kinesthetic	Left Brain	Right Brain
X	X	X	X	X	X	

Multiple Intelligences								
Visual	Intrapersonal	Interpersonal	Musical	Mathematical / Logical	Linguistic	Kinesthetic	Naturalist	Existential
X	X			X	X	X		

31. I Know, I Don't Know (Part 2)

Learning outcome
To help participants reflect on the topic they just learned.

Overview
Participants will reflect and identify the things they just learned. This is a two part activity and Part 2 should be used at the end of each session.

Start of Session Mini-Review	End of Session Mini-Review
	X

In My Experience
This is a great reflection activity. Asking participants to process and record what they just learned helps them to reinforce their learning.

The Hidden Twist
This activity can also act as a mini journal for participants to reference after class or to update regularly throughout the class and consolidate into an action plan as a final activity.

Essential Data
Course Type: Any
Group Size: 1-50
Time of Day: Any time
Pace: Moderate
Trainer Preparation Time: 5 minutes
Activity Duration: 5-10 minutes

Steps to Create
Use the same individual handout or page in the participant guide that you used for Part 1 of this activity (see previous activity in this chapter).

Steps to Run
1. Ask participants to review their list of things they wanted to learn about the topic.
2. As you call out the topics covered, instruct them to scan their list and put a check mark next to the topics that were reviewed during the session.
3. Ask the class if you missed any of the topics.
4. Instruct them to write any additional things they learned that wasn't on their initial list.

Suggested Debrief Strategy/Sample Questions
- Ask participants these questions.
  - What did you add to your list?
  - What were you hoping would be covered but wasn't?
    - Write their comments on a flip chart or whiteboard
  - What will you do to learn about that topic?
- Challenge participants to find information about those topics that weren't covered during this class.

Working Example
Contract Law for Managers
At the end of the session legislative requirements and organizational policies participants reflect on their new learning and then complete their lists again and share it with a partner, small group or the whole group.

Tips, Tricks and Traps
If there was a topic a participant wanted to learn more about that wasn't covered in that section and if it's in the scope of the course objectives, try to find the answer and/or provide the information to that individual during a break.

Adult Learning Base Process: Metacognitive Reflection
Refer to **Adult Learning Base Process Reference Guide** for more information about this learning process.

Adult Learning Dashboard

This activity links participant's preferred style of learning. The following dashboard provides a quick reference to adult learning theorists and principles as part of the ID9® methodology.

This activity achieves the following level of Bloom's Taxonomy of the Cognitive Domain (Bloom et al 1956), shown with "X" in the following table.

Bloom's Taxonomy of the Cognitive Domain Level					
Knowledge	Comprehension	Application	Analysis	Synthesis	Evaluation
	X				

This activity also achieves a link, shown with "X" in the following table, to participant's naturally occurring learning preferences. Global/Specific, Learning Modalities, Hemispheric Preference (Sperry, 1981), and Multiple Intelligences (Gardner, 1983) are referenced in ID9® methodology and process. This is not a complete list of links that are covered within the ID9® process however this dashboard aims to provide a quick reference for trainers to use to balance instructional design to provide equality for participants' learning preferences.

Global/Specific Learners		Learning Modalities (Sensory Intake)			Hemispheric Preference	
Global	Specific	Visual	Auditory	Kinesthetic	Left Brain	Right Brain
X	X	X	X	X	X	

Multiple Intelligences								
Visual	Intrapersonal	Interpersonal	Musical	Mathematical / Logical	Linguistic	Kinesthetic	Naturalist	Existential
X	X			X	X	X		

32. Find It

Learning outcome
To encourage participants to find supporting data and documentation on the topic.

Overview
This activity provides the participants with an opportunity to share some of the supporting data and documentation they found on a topic. This activity should be used at the end of a session.

Start of Session Mini-Review	End of Session Mini-Review
	X

In My Experience
Participants really enjoy this activity because they get the opportunity to find information and share it with the class. They get so excited that often times I'm surprised with how many quality resources they were able to find in such a short time period.

The Hidden Twist
An extra bonus about this activity is that sometimes you'll learn about a new resource that supports the topic.

Essential Data
Course Type: Any
Group Size: 1-15
Time of Day: Any time
Pace: Moderate
Trainer Preparation Time: 5 minutes
Activity Duration: 10 minutes

Steps to Create
Create an individual handout or a page in the participant guide for participants to create their list of supporting data and documentation about a topic.

Steps to Run
1. Ask participants to use their laptops to search the internet to find at least one resource that supports the topic (e.g. book, article, news clip, video clip, etc.).
2. Instruct them to write the resource(s) on the individual handout or on the page in their participant guide.
3. Explain that you will compile a list of the resources they find and will email it to each of them.
4. As participants work, play music quietly in the background.

Suggested Debrief Strategy/Sample Questions
- Ask participants these questions:
  - What resources did you find?
  - What key words did you search?
  - How will you use these resources?
- Write their answers on a flip chart or white board.
- Compile the list and create a handy tip sheet.
- Email the tip sheet to everyone that attended the session.
- Encourage participants to explore one or more resource(s) further on their own after this class to increase their knowledge on the topic

Working Example
Project Management
In the topic of stakeholder management participants look for articles and books about the topic specifically in the area of gaining stakeholder support and communicating appropriately with stakeholders. They search the internet for newspaper or journal articles, books from online book sellers or other websites related to the topic. They create a list of website links (URL) for the Videos, Books or Articles and email it to the trainer. Then, the trainer consolidates the list and provides it to all participants as a reference list.

Tips, Tricks and Traps
- Verify internet service is working in the training room.
- Ensure the training room has laptops or participants know beforehand they need to bring their laptops to class.
- Playing music while participants are working 'fills the space'.
  - Faster music can increase the pace of learning and support a competitive environment (i.e. faster than heart rate)
  - Slower music can decrease the pace of learning and support a quiet reflective environment

Adult Learning Base Process: Supporting Data and Documents
Refer to **Adult Learning Base Process Reference Guide** for more information about this learning process.

Adult Learning Dashboard

This activity links participant's preferred style of learning. The following dashboard provides a quick reference to adult learning theorists and principles as part of the ID9® methodology.

This activity achieves the following level of Bloom's Taxonomy of the Cognitive Domain (Bloom et al 1956), shown with "X" in the following table.

Bloom's Taxonomy of the Cognitive Domain Level					
Knowledge	Comprehension	Application	Analysis	Synthesis	Evaluation
	X				

This activity also achieves a link, shown with "X" in the following table, to participant's naturally occurring learning preferences. Global/Specific, Learning Modalities, Hemispheric Preference (Sperry, 1981), and Multiple Intelligences (Gardner, 1983) are referenced in ID9® methodology and process. This is not a complete list of links that are covered within the ID9® process however this dashboard aims to provide a quick reference for trainers to use to balance instructional design to provide equality for participants' learning preferences.

Global/Specific Learners		Learning Modalities (Sensory Intake)			Hemispheric Preference	
Global	Specific	Visual	Auditory	Kinesthetic	Left Brain	Right Brain
X	X	X	X	X	X	

Multiple Intelligences								
Visual	Intrapersonal	Interpersonal	Musical	Mathematical / Logical	Linguistic	Kinesthetic	Naturalist	Existential
X		X	X	X	X	X		

33. Acronym Hunt

Learning outcome
To have participants define topic related acronyms.

Overview
A topic related acronym is written on an index card and put into a big bowl. Participants will select one index card and are responsible for finding the acronym's meaning.

Start of Session Mini-Review	End of Session Mini-Review
X	X

In My Experience
This is an easy, fast way to review important acronyms that can be conducted either as a start of session or an end of session mini review.

The Hidden Twist
It gives each participant the responsibility of finding the meaning of an acronym and teaching it to the class.

Essential Data
Course Type: Any
Group Size: 1-16
Time of Day: Any time
Pace: Moderate
Trainer Preparation Time: 5 minutes
Activity Duration: 8 minutes

Steps to Create
1. Write a list of topic related acronyms and their meaning. This will be given to participants at the end of the session.
2. Write each acronym on an index card (one acronym per index card).
3. Put the index cards into a bowl.

Steps to Run
1. Ask each participant to pick one index card from the bowl.
   - The participants can also work with a partner.
2. Explain they are responsible for finding (hunting) the meaning of the acronym written on their index card and will share it with the class. They can use their participant materials and any other resources provided to find the answer.

Suggested Debrief Strategy/Sample Questions
- Ask each participant to share their acronym and meaning.
- Ask participants the following questions:
  - How did you find the meaning of your acronym?
- After defining the acronyms (stretch activity):
  - Put the acronyms into a logical order based on a set criteria (for example, put acronyms in the order where they are found in the process, or according to the project timeline)
- At the conclusion, give each participant the list of all acronyms and its meaning.

Working Example
Workplace Safety
We found in our company that people knew acronyms, used them in everyday business conversations, but had no idea what it stood for! In this occupational health and safety program there are a plethora of acronyms used which can often be overwhelming for participants, especially people new to the organization. This activity is conducted either as an end of session or start of session mini-review early in the program. The participants draw an acronym card from the bowl, define what each letter of the acronym stands for and writes the answer on the card. Cards are then posted on the wall creating an 'acronym wall' as a reference throughout the entire program. This allows participants to not only learn the acronyms (which they'll use in their day-to-day roles) but also embeds the meaning of what the acronyms stand for.

Tips, Tricks and Traps
It's important to create a tip sheet that includes all of the acronyms and their meanings and give it to participants to refer to when they are on-the-job. This is an easy job aid to create.

Adult Learning Base Process: Fishbowl
Refer to **Adult Learning Base Process Reference Guide** for more information about this learning process.

Adult Learning Dashboard

This activity links participant's preferred style of learning. The following dashboard provides a quick reference to adult learning theorists and principles as part of the ID9® methodology.

This activity achieves the following level of Bloom's Taxonomy of the Cognitive Domain (Bloom et al 1956), shown with "X" in the following table.

Bloom's Taxonomy of the Cognitive Domain Level					
Knowledge	Comprehension	Application	Analysis	Synthesis	Evaluation
	X				

This activity also achieves a link, shown with "X" in the following table, to participant's naturally occurring learning preferences. Global/Specific, Learning Modalities, Hemispheric Preference (Sperry, 1981), and Multiple Intelligences (Gardner, 1983) are referenced in ID9® methodology and process. This is not a complete list of links that are covered within the ID9® process however this dashboard aims to provide a quick reference for trainers to use to balance instructional design to provide equality for participants' learning preferences.

Global/Specific Learners		Learning Modalities (Sensory Intake)			Hemispheric Preference	
Global	Specific	Visual	Auditory	Kinesthetic	Left Brain	Right Brain
	X	X	X	X	X	

Multiple Intelligences								
Visual	Intrapersonal	Interpersonal	Musical	Mathematical / Logical	Linguistic	Kinesthetic	Naturalist	Existential
X				X	X	X	X	

34. Idea Toss

Learning outcome

To have participants reflect on what they learned during the session.

Overview

This activity should be used at the end of a session to give participants an opportunity to write something they learned and share it with the group.

Start of Session Mini-Review	End of Session Mini-Review
	X

In My Experience

This is a quick mini review activity that gives participants a chance to learn from someone else's point-of-view. It's a highly kinesthetic activity that gets participants up and moving. It's interesting to watch how many people run for the crumpled pieces of paper like it's a competition. It brings liveliness and energy to the room. The activity is best run at the end of a session immediately followed by a break.

The Hidden Twist

Gives the instructor an opportunity to gauge what and how much participants learned. This also provides participants a chance to get up and move around before the break.

Essential Data

Course Type: Any
Group Size: 1-25
Time of Day: Any time
Pace: Fast
Trainer Preparation Time: 1 minute
Activity Duration: 5-10 minutes

Steps to Create

Have Post-It notes for each participant.

Steps to Run

1. Ask each participant to take a blank Post-it note or small piece of paper and write on it something they learned today.
2. Place a stack of Post-It notes or small pieces of paper in the center of each table before the session starts.

3. When they are finished writing ask participants to stand, crumple the paper into a ball and toss it into a pile at the front of the room.
   - If a larger room, instruct participants sitting in the back to walk to the front and then toss their crumpled paper into the pile.
4. When all participants have tossed all their key learnings into the pile, tell them when you say "GO!" they need to pick one crumpled Post-it from the pile and return to their seat or stand in an area of the training room where no one else is standing.
5. Shout "Go!"

Suggested Debrief Strategy/Sample Questions

- Ask participants to share the message on the Post-it they selected.
- Ask participants this question:
  - How was this comment different from the one you wrote?

Working Example
Managing for Innovation

This one day program is packed with ideas and this end-of-session mini review allows participants to share their key learnings and hear the key learnings from their fellow participants. We call this activity "innovation idea toss". Participants write their key learning on small pieces of paper, such as the definition of innovation, innovation vs. creativity, how I influence the business culture through my level of innovation, my role in role modeling innovation, and so on. Participants then continue with the activity gaining value out of hearing everyone's key learning from the course so far. It's a great way to wrap up a session and provides a kinesthetic boost ready to go to the break and return to the next session energized.

Tips, Tricks and Traps

This is a fast paced timed activity so make sure you keep participants on track by providing time warnings so they know how much time they have to finish writing.

Adult Learning Base Process: Metacognitive Reflection

Refer to **Adult Learning Base Process Reference Guide** for more information about this learning process.

Adult Learning Dashboard

This activity links participant's preferred style of learning. The following dashboard provides a quick reference to adult learning theorists and principles as part of the ID9® methodology.

This activity achieves the following level of Bloom's Taxonomy of the Cognitive Domain (Bloom et al 1956), shown with "X" in the following table.

Bloom's Taxonomy of the Cognitive Domain Level					
Knowledge	Comprehension	Application	Analysis	Synthesis	Evaluation
X					

This activity also achieves a link, shown with "X" in the following table, to participant's naturally occurring learning preferences. Global/Specific, Learning Modalities, Hemispheric Preference (Sperry, 1981), and Multiple Intelligences (Gardner, 1983) are referenced in ID9® methodology and process. This is not a complete list of links that are covered within the ID9® process however this dashboard aims to provide a quick reference for trainers to use to balance instructional design to provide equality for participants' learning preferences.

Global/Specific Learners		Learning Modalities (Sensory Intake)			Hemispheric Preference	
Global	Specific	Visual	Auditory	Kinesthetic	Left Brain	Right Brain
X	X	X	X	X	X	

Multiple Intelligences								
Visual	Intrapersonal	Interpersonal	Musical	Mathematical / Logical	Linguistic	Kinesthetic	Naturalist	Existential
X	X	X		X	X	X		

35. Your Turn - Teach

Learning outcome
To give participants the responsibility of reviewing a topic to the class via a re-teaching method.

Overview
This activity heightens participant awareness of the topic because they are responsible for paying attention to a specific item and teaching back to the group.

Start of Session Mini-Review	End of Session Mini-Review
	X

In My Experience
This is a highly engaging activity that keeps the participants engaged because they have ownership of providing a review of their topic. Some participants get nervous they are going to miss a critical piece of information that they need. It helps to call the topic out to them when you're about to cover it.

The Hidden Twist
When told prior to a session of learning content that participants will be asked after the session to review the material and provide a teach back to the class participant attention throughout the entire session is heightened. This has the dual benefit because the learning part of the session is more effective as is the end of session mini-review.

Essential Data
Course Type: Any
Group Size: 1-16
Time of Day: Any time
Pace: Slow
Trainer Preparation Time: 30 minutes
Activity Duration: 10 minutes

Steps to Create
1. Write a single area of focus for each participant on an index card from topics or subtopics that are about to be presented.
   - Depending on the size of the class you may want to make this a partner or small group activity.
2. Put the index cards for each table inside an envelope.
   - The number of index cards and envelopes will depend on how many people are sitting at each table. The envelope should have one index card for each participant sitting at that table or one index card per partner or small group.
3. Create a poster with each single area of focus listed on it and display it at the front of the room.

Steps to Run
1. Ask someone at each table to open their envelope and pass one index card to each person (or each team of partners).
2. When everyone has their card, ask each person in turn to read their index card aloud.
3. As each person reads their area of focus, write their name next to that area of focus listed on the poster at the front of the room.
4. Explain that each individual will need to pay attention during the session for their assigned area of focus because they will be responsible for giving a very brief recap of it at the end of the topic session.

Suggested Debrief Strategy/Sample Questions
- One-by-one ask each participant to read the area of focus on their index card and give a 30 second recap of it.
- Provide guidance on the topic if it's needed.
- Provide additional topic input if it's needed.

Working Example
Communicate with Influence
This activity is conducted after the topic on connecting with different types of people. Examples of areas of focus for the index cards include the meaning of an acronym, definition of a term along with an example of when/how it is used, and list the different behavioral styles presented. Participants are focused on the entire session to firstly note the related content to what's on their card, and then teach back in a mini review.

Tips, Tricks and Traps
- During the session, when you are covering an area of focus give the participant responsible for recapping that section a hint to pay attention.
- This works especially well during a systems training course.

Adult Learning Base Process: Teach Back
Refer to **Adult Learning Base Process Reference Guide** for more information about this learning process.

Adult Learning Dashboard

This activity links participant's preferred style of learning. The following dashboard provides a quick reference to adult learning theorists and principles as part of the ID9® methodology.

This activity achieves the following level of Bloom's Taxonomy of the Cognitive Domain (Bloom et al 1956), shown with "X" in the following table.

Bloom's Taxonomy of the Cognitive Domain Level					
Knowledge	Comprehension	Application	Analysis	Synthesis	Evaluation
				X	

This activity also achieves a link, shown with "X" in the following table, to participant's naturally occurring learning preferences. Global/Specific, Learning Modalities, Hemispheric Preference (Sperry, 1981), and Multiple Intelligences (Gardner, 1983) are referenced in ID9® methodology and process. This is not a complete list of links that are covered within the ID9® process however this dashboard aims to provide a quick reference for trainers to use to balance instructional design to provide equality for participants' learning preferences.

Global/Specific Learners		Learning Modalities (Sensory Intake)			Hemispheric Preference	
Global	Specific	Visual	Auditory	Kinesthetic	Left Brain	Right Brain
	X	X	X	X	X	

Multiple Intelligences								
Visual	Intrapersonal	Interpersonal	Musical	Mathematical / Logical	Linguistic	Kinesthetic	Naturalist	Existential
X		X		X	X	X		

36. What to Do?

Learning outcome

To encourage participants to think about a problem and how to best solve it.

Overview

This activity should be used at the end of a session topic to provide participants with an open-ended problem that requires them to provide their best solution. The activity can also be used as a start-of-session mini review to pose a problem that relates to the previous session's content which participants will solve prior to moving onto their next topic.

Start of Session Mini-Review	End of Session Mini-Review
X	X

In My Experience

This is a quick activity that challenges participants to analyze what they learned and suggest a viable solution. This also helps the trainer gauge if participants are able to suggest a realistic solution. If the suggested solution is not realistic, the trainer can provide some quick coaching.

The Hidden Twist

Participants sometimes suggest a clever solution that may be new to the trainer. As a trainer ensure that you are open to new and innovative solutions rewarding participants for their new idea. Make sure you write it down so you have it as reference to research for future sessions.

Essential Data

Course Type: Any
Group Size: 1-16
Time of Day: Any time
Pace: Moderate
Trainer Preparation Time: 10 minutes
Activity Duration: 10 minutes

Steps to Create

Create an individual handout or a page in the participant guide with an open-ended problem related to the session topic.

Steps to Run

Instruct participants to read their open-ended problem and to write a realistic solution for it based on what they just learned.

- Depending on the size of the class you can have two or more people pair up and work together.

Suggested Debrief Strategy/Sample Questions

- Ask participants to read their open-ended problem aloud to the class.
- Ask participants these questions:
- What was your solution?
  - If the solution is not feasible, guide them to figure out why it's not feasible and see if they can suggest a different, more realistic solution.
- How did you determine your solution?
- What tools (resources), if any, are needed to make your solution work?

Working Example
Vendor management

In this class there is a topic covering fixed price contracts. On the 'problem card' the scenario is provided: "You have been instructed by your manager to send all vendors supplying computer equipment an email stating that your organization would like to change their contracts from a fixed price to a fixed discount approach to encourage more competition. It is your manager's expectation that each vendor will come back to you with a fixed discount percentage for all future proposals for computer equipment. You have also been asked to create a panel of vendors who are willing to change to this fixed discount approach and make them preferred suppliers for your organization." Participants then answer question the question: "What would you do?" and engage in a group discussion in class (see questions listed above in the debrief) to discuss the situation as a group.

Tricks and Traps

- Make the open-ended problem a real-life issue a participant may really experience.
- Work with a subject-matter expert to develop the open-ended problem to ensure its relevancy and accuracy.
- As a trainer be open to new ways of solving the issue.
- If there isn't a clear solution then ask participants 'what would you do first?' or 'what would you do next?'

Adult Learning Base Process: Open-ended Problem

Refer to **Adult Learning Base Process Reference Guide** for more information about this learning process.

Adult Learning Dashboard

This activity links participant's preferred style of learning. The following dashboard provides a quick reference to adult learning theorists and principles as part of the ID9® methodology.

This activity achieves the following level of Bloom's Taxonomy of the Cognitive Domain (Bloom et al 1956), shown with "X" in the following table.

Bloom's Taxonomy of the Cognitive Domain Level					
Knowledge	Comprehension	Application	Analysis	Synthesis	Evaluation
			X		

This activity also achieves a link, shown with "X" in the following table, to participant's naturally occurring learning preferences. Global/Specific, Learning Modalities, Hemispheric Preference (Sperry, 1981), and Multiple Intelligences (Gardner, 1983) are referenced in ID9® methodology and process. This is not a complete list of links that are covered within the ID9® process however this dashboard aims to provide a quick reference for trainers to use to balance instructional design to provide equality for participants' learning preferences.

Global/Specific Learners		Learning Modalities (Sensory Intake)			Hemispheric Preference	
Global	Specific	Visual	Auditory	Kinesthetic	Left Brain	Right Brain
X	X	X	X	X	X	X

Multiple Intelligences								
Visual	Intrapersonal	Interpersonal	Musical	Mathematical / Logical	Linguistic	Kinesthetic	Naturalist	Existential
X	X	X		X	X	X		

37. Truth or Trick

Learning outcome
To have participants listen to statements and determine if it is true or false (a trick).

Overview
This is a mini-review to use at the end of a session. It's a simple and quick activity incorporating Visual, Auditory and Kinesthetic modalities. True/False review combines individual reflection with group interaction and discussion. Learning is reinforced through a simple yet powerful debrief of the answers.

Start of Session Mini-Review	End of Session Mini-Review
	X

In My Experience
This is a quick mini review activity requiring participants to determine if a statement is true or false. Very little preparation is required and provides participants with a speedy review on major topics.

The Hidden Twist
A trainer is able to review quite a bit of information in a very short time span.

Essential Data
Course Type: Any
Group Size: 1-50
Time of Day: Any time
Pace: Moderate
Trainer Preparation Time: 30 minutes
Activity Duration: 5 minutes

Steps to Create
Write statements related to the session topic that is either true or false.

- Type one statement per slide in a PowerPoint presentation.
- On the next slide, retype the statement and in big colorful font type 'Truth' or 'Trickery' (depending on the correct answer to the statement)

Steps to Run
1. Display a statement on a screen by using an overhead projector (connect your laptop to the overhead projector).
2. Read the statement aloud to the class.
3. Ask participants to shout out if the statement is Truth (true) or Trickery (false).
4. Display the slide with the statement and the answer.

Suggested Debrief Strategy/Sample Questions
- Ask participants these questions:
  - What makes this statement true?
  - What would make this statement true?
  - Why is this statement important?
  - What makes this statement different from _____?
  - How can you apply this when you return to your job?
  - [for a false statement] What would happen if you did this?

Working Example
This activity is useful in any type of class (i.e. systems, process).

Tips, Tricks and Traps
- Ensure the training room has an overhead projector.
- It is important to handle the false answers well because there is no learning for participants in just a false answer. Explain why the statement is false and how to make it true.
  - In a review activity, it is important to embed the true answer in the participant's mind, not the false ones.
  - Always ask 'what would make this statement true?' to ensure that participants know the correct approach.

Adult Learning Base Process: True or False
Refer to **Adult Learning Base Process Reference Guide** for more information about this learning process.

Adult Learning Dashboard

This activity links participant's preferred style of learning. The following dashboard provides a quick reference to adult learning theorists and principles as part of the ID9® methodology.

This activity achieves the following level of Bloom's Taxonomy of the Cognitive Domain (Bloom et al 1956), shown with "X" in the following table.

Bloom's Taxonomy of the Cognitive Domain Level					
Knowledge	Comprehension	Application	Analysis	Synthesis	Evaluation
X					

This activity also achieves a link, shown with "X" in the following table, to participant's naturally occurring learning preferences. Global/Specific, Learning Modalities, Hemispheric Preference (Sperry, 1981), and Multiple Intelligences (Gardner, 1983) are referenced in ID9® methodology and process. This is not a complete list of links that are covered within the ID9® process however this dashboard aims to provide a quick reference for trainers to use to balance instructional design to provide equality for participants' learning preferences.

Global/Specific Learners		Learning Modalities (Sensory Intake)			Hemispheric Preference	
Global	Specific	Visual	Auditory	Kinesthetic	Left Brain	Right Brain
X	X	X	X	X	X	

Multiple Intelligences								
Visual	Intrapersonal	Interpersonal	Musical	Mathematical / Logical	Linguistic	Kinesthetic	Naturalist	Existential
X				X	X	X		

38. The Search is On

Learning outcome
To have the participants review topic content.

Overview
This is a crossword race and is a high-energy, fast and competitive activity that can be used for review of a session topic. This is simply a disguised set of review questions, which are presented in a visual and engaging way either at the end of a session or as a start of session mini review.

Start of Session Mini-Review	End of Session Mini-Review
X	X

In My Experience
It's a highly visual and participative activity, which encourages team work and gets participants moving and working faster than before. This is a great activity for adding energy during the afternoon of a full day session. Create a short activity using 6-8 questions, or a longer review activity for up to 30 or even 40 questions!

The Hidden Twist
Teams are so intensely focused on the competitive nature of the activity that they forget that all they are doing is really answering review questions!

Essential Data
Course Type: Any
Group Size: 4-25
Time of Day: Any time
Pace: Fast and competitive
Trainer Preparation Time: 60-90 minutes
Activity Duration: 10 minutes

Steps to Create
1. Purchase or find a free crossword maker (online).
2. Key in the answers and clues in the blank crossword.
3. Generate the crossword by following the instructions.
4. Print the following:
   • Blank crossword grid (enlarge to poster size)
   • Clue sheets – 1 per participant
   • Answer sheet for the trainer
   • Completed crossword grid as handout for participants at the conclusion of the activity.

Steps to Run
1. Trainer places crossword grid posters onto the wall at appropriate places (allow space for team gathering).
2. Put participants into teams.
3. Assign each group to a crossword grid poster.
4. Explain the rules:
   • Work as a team to complete the crossword
   • Use any resource materials available to help you
   • When your team has finished shout out "Finished"
5. Hand out crossword clue sheets to participants.
6. Shout "Go" to start the race.
7. As participants work, play lively music quietly in the background.
8. When the first team shouts "Finished", stop the race.

Suggested Debrief Strategy/Sample Questions
With the whole group assembled, have the team that finished first tell the group all of the answers.
• If all answers are correct, award the winning prizes.
• If an answer is incorrect, restart the race until a team correctly answers all the questions.
• The trainer should be aware of questions that are causing difficulty.
• After the race has finished, the trainer should ask 'why' and 'what if' questions to add depth to the learning and ensure that any 'sticking points' are overcome.

Working Example
Time Management
A whole group Crossword activity is conducted mid-afternoon just before the break as an end of session mini review. Poster size crosswords headed "the search is on" are placed around the training room walls and groups race to complete their crossword. The time management course is filled with lengthy words (concentration, reorganization, workload, delegation, assertiveness, procrastination, perfectionism etc) making these terms ideal for crosswords.

Tips, Tricks and Traps
- Playing music while participants are working 'fills the space'.
  - Faster music can increase the pace of learning and support a competitive environment (i.e. faster than heart rate)
  - Slower music can decrease the pace of learning and support a quiet reflective environment
- If you are conducting this activity as a race play fast music to heighten the pace and competitive element

Creation Tricks:
- Make the questions specific.
- Make the clues as short as possible.
- Make the answers one word
- Make the clues short – no more than 10 words.
- The Clue Sheet should fit on one page.

Trainer Facilitation Tips:
- Keep the groups moving
- Ensure you check in on each team's progress and observe any difficulties
- Give hints as necessary (e.g. give one letter to help them – write it into their grid)

Adult Learning Base Process: Crossword
Refer to **Adult Learning Base Process Reference Guide** for more information about this learning process.

Adult Learning Dashboard
This activity links participant's preferred style of learning. The following dashboard provides a quick reference to adult learning theorists and principles as part of the ID9® methodology.

This activity achieves the following level of Bloom's Taxonomy of the Cognitive Domain (Bloom et al 1956), shown with "X" in the following table.

Bloom's Taxonomy of the Cognitive Domain Level					
Knowledge	Comprehension	Application	Analysis	Synthesis	Evaluation
	X				

This activity also achieves a link, shown with "X" in the following table, to participant's naturally occurring learning preferences. Global/Specific, Learning Modalities, Hemispheric Preference (Sperry, 1981), and Multiple Intelligences (Gardner, 1983) are referenced in ID9® methodology and process. This is not a complete list of links that are covered within the ID9® process however this dashboard aims to provide a quick reference for trainers to use to balance instructional design to provide equality for participants' learning preferences.

Global/Specific Learners		Learning Modalities (Sensory Intake)			Hemispheric Preference	
Global	Specific	Visual	Auditory	Kinesthetic	Left Brain	Right Brain
	X	X	X	X	X	X

Multiple Intelligences								
Visual	Intrapersonal	Interpersonal	Musical	Mathematical / Logical	Linguistic	Kinesthetic	Naturalist	Existential
X			X	X	X	X		

39. What's the Order?

Learning outcome
To have the participant review a step-by-step process.

Overview
Participants are given individual cards, each bearing a single step of a process. They place their cards on the training room wall (or on a table) to recreate the process in the correct order. This is equally effective as a start of session or end of session mini review.

Start of Session Mini-Review	End of Session Mini-Review
X	X

In My Experience
It's a simple, adaptable, easy-to-create and easy-to-run mini-review activity, which readily incorporates Visual, Auditory and Kinesthetic modalities. It's a great way to add variety, interest and action to what may otherwise be perceived as a "dry and dull" topic. The value of this review is twofold — 1) the review itself and 2) the opportunity for a powerful debrief of learning, based on 'why' and 'what if' questions.

The Hidden Twist
To add depth to the review, two or more step-by-step processes can be jumbled up together, or "dummy" cards can be added so that participants have to select the correct cards for the process they are reviewing/learning. The trainer then has the opportunity of asking 'why' and 'what if' questions about the sequence. As with all review activities, the debrief adds depth to the learning and is the key to success!

Essential Data
Course Type: Any
Group Size: 1-30
Time of Day: Any time
Pace: Moderate
Trainer Preparation Time: 10-30 minutes
Activity Duration: 5-10 minutes

Steps to Create
Write each step of a process on separate sheets or card (approximately letter size card).
- OPTIONAL: Add a relevant picture or image to each card, to boost the visual power of this activity.

Steps to Run
1. Explain that you are passing out cards and that each card contains one step of the process.
2. Hand out the cards to participants.
   - Give each participant 1-2 cards each (until all cards are used).
3. Have participants form the step-by-step process by placing their cards in order.
4. Hang the cards on the wall using tape or Blu-Tac.
   - Use heading cards if appropriate (e.g. when working on two processes simultaneously) or arrange cards on a table if working in small groups.

Suggested Debrief Strategy/Sample Questions
- When all participants have finished, go through the process and check the correct order/sequence
- Ask participants the following questions:
  - What would happen if we removed this step?
  - What other topics/processes/procedures are related to this step-by-step procedure?
  - Why is this step important?
  - What makes this step different from _____?
  - How can you apply this when you return to your job?
  - Selecting an incorrect card: What would happen if we added this step?

Working Example
This activity works in any industry for any process.

Tips, Tricks and Traps
Participant Grouping Variations:
- Activity can be completed as a whole group (as described above).
- For larger numbers of participants, divide into small groups of 4-5 and provide each group with a set of cards to sort.
- For a short process of only 3-5 steps, this works best as a small group or partner activity.

Variations/stretch for Activity:
- OPTIONAL: Include some incorrect (or "dummy") cards so that participants have to identify the correct steps, as well as organize them in order
- OPTIONAL: Two or more processes can be mixed together and then sorted correctly: create heading cards for each process.

Adult Learning Base Process: Step Mix
Refer to **Adult Learning Base Process Reference Guide** for more information about this learning process.

Adult Learning Dashboard

This activity links participant's preferred style of learning. The following dashboard provides a quick reference to adult learning theorists and principles as part of the ID9® methodology.

This activity achieves the following level of Bloom's Taxonomy of the Cognitive Domain (Bloom et al 1956), shown with "X" in the following table.

Bloom's Taxonomy of the Cognitive Domain Level					
Knowledge	Comprehension	Application	Analysis	Synthesis	Evaluation
			X		

This activity also achieves a link, shown with "X" in the following table, to participant's naturally occurring learning preferences. Global/Specific, Learning Modalities, Hemispheric Preference (Sperry, 1981), and Multiple Intelligences (Gardner, 1983) are referenced in ID9® methodology and process. This is not a complete list of links that are covered within the ID9® process however this dashboard aims to provide a quick reference for trainers to use to balance instructional design to provide equality for participants' learning preferences.

Global/Specific Learners		Learning Modalities (Sensory Intake)			Hemispheric Preference	
Global	Specific	Visual	Auditory	Kinesthetic	Left Brain	Right Brain
X	X	X	X	X	X	

Multiple Intelligences								
Visual	Intrapersonal	Interpersonal	Musical	Mathematical / Logical	Linguistic	Kinesthetic	Naturalist	Existential
X				X	X	X		

40. Find It!

Learning outcome
To ensure participants know key terms/definitions from the topic just presented.

Overview
Create a word search of key terms and their definitions from the session topic. A word search is where participants need to find the word within a panel of letters. Words can run forwards, backwards, diagonally or vertically. Some word search puzzles also have a single key word that is created after all of the clues are found. This activity is effective as a start of session or end of session mini review.

Start of Session Mini-Review	End of Session Mini-Review
X	X

In My Experience
It's an easy-to-create and easy-to-run mini-review activity that gives participants the opportunity to review key terms/definitions in an engaging and interactive way.

The Hidden Twist
It's an opportunity to embed technical terms or business specific terms.

Essential Data
Course Type: Any
Group Size: 1-100
Time of Day: Any time
Pace: Moderate
Trainer Preparation Time: 30 minutes
Activity Duration: 5-10 minutes

Steps to Create
1. Write a list of key terms and definitions of each key term from the session topic.
   - The key terms will be hidden in the word search puzzle.
   - The definition for each key term will be the clue to the key term that needs to be found in the word search puzzle.
2. Using a computer software package, create the word search puzzle.
3. Print as a handout for each participant.
4. Print the answer sheet for the trainer.

Steps to Run
1. Distribute the word search puzzle to each participant.
2. Explain that the definitions to key terms are listed below the word search puzzle. Participants must read the definition and determine its key term, then write the key term in the blank space next to the definition and finally circle the key term in the word search puzzle.
3. Explain that the key terms hidden in the puzzle may run horizontally, vertically, backwards and forwards.
4. The trainer needs to give a time limit to complete the word search puzzle.

Suggested Debrief Strategy/Sample Questions
- Ask participants the following questions:
  - Why are these terms important?
  - How will these terms be used on-the-job?
    - Give me an example.

Working Example
Therapeutic Area Training
Medical terminology not only needs to be recalled but spelled correctly by participants as they apply their learning. By creating a word search puzzle and conducting the 'find it' mini review participants focus on the term and in the process of finding it in the puzzle are embedding the spelling of the term which is a double benefit.

Tips, Tricks and Traps
Only focus on key terms because this is a fast activity and you won't have time to include a lot of terms/definitions.

Adult Learning Dashboard
This activity links participant's preferred style of learning. The following dashboard provides a quick reference to adult learning theorists and principles as part of the ID9® methodology.

This activity achieves the following level of Bloom's Taxonomy of the Cognitive Domain (Bloom et al 1956), shown with "X" in the following table.

Bloom's Taxonomy of the Cognitive Domain Level					
Knowledge	Comprehension	Application	Analysis	Synthesis	Evaluation
	X				

This activity also achieves a link, shown with "X" in the following table, to participant's naturally occurring learning preferences. Global/Specific, Learning Modalities, Hemispheric Preference (Sperry, 1981), and Multiple Intelligences (Gardner, 1983) are referenced in ID9® methodology and process. This is not a complete list of links that are covered within the ID9® process however this dashboard aims to provide a quick reference for trainers to use to balance instructional design to provide equality for participants' learning preferences.

Global/Specific Learners		Learning Modalities (Sensory Intake)			Hemispheric Preference	
Global	Specific	Visual	Auditory	Kinesthetic	Left Brain	Right Brain
X	X	X	X	X	X	

Multiple Intelligences								
Visual	Intrapersonal	Interpersonal	Musical	Mathematical / Logical	Linguistic	Kinesthetic	Naturalist	Existential
X				X	X	X		

Chapter 4:
During Course:
Review Activities - Post-Lunch

Elizabeth Tighe

About the Co-Author:

Elizabeth Tighe

Elizabeth is Irish but has lived in Basel, Switzerland since 1995. Nowadays she works as a training professional because one of her abiding passions is training people so that they can work more effectively. She started her career in the pharmaceutical industry in 1990. It was a case of from Farm to Pharma because she holds a master's degree in Agricultural Science from the University College Dublin.

Elizabeth is a Loyal Skeptic: she questions everything. So when she was developing material for the Post-Lunch activities chapter she questioned and re-questioned the validity of the activities until she was certain they really would be of use to fellow training professionals. As part of this quest for excellence she asked several people to road-test the ideas and report back. Thank you – you know who you are!

To date Elizabeth has enjoyed working in many different roles with various (sometimes intriguing) responsibilities. She has been steadfast in her passion for capability building - working to make complex messages accessible so that everyone can fulfill their potential and enjoy their work.

Currently she is busy working with a global team of training professionals. Their aim is to make the elements of ID9® normal working practice. And how did this journey into the world of education and development start? Many years ago she was working with a pair of school friends (twins) and concentrating on working out the key messages and learning points in a piece of geography homework when the mother of the twins said: "I think that you would be a good teacher" and so the idea took root to flower years later. After qualifying and working as a scientist again and again it happened that Elizabeth would be drawn into situations that called for messages to be clarified so that work could progress. Finally she took the plunge and dedicated her working life to being a full time and fully qualified training professional.

Elizabeth uses the types of activities described in Training Activities that Work at every training program she organizes.

Chapter Introduction

Lunch is an incredibly important point in the training day. The best lunches are nutritious and convivial. The time just after lunch has the potential to be daunting. Participants are unsettled after networking and moving around and, at the same time, are prone to a post-prandial slump.

Affectionately daubed the graveyard slot it is the training time that I used to fear the most. This is why I chose to work on this very chapter because ... those days are gone!

The advice, to feel the fear and do it anyway, has led me to employ many activities designed to settle and engage – almost contradictory requirements – at this time of the training day with a considerable degree of success.

The following 24 activities have been tried and tested by me and by some seriously admired professional trainers. The post-lunch slot is now one to which I look forward with confidence. It is a time when we can ensure, as a group that we have internalized the key learning points from the morning sessions and so take a deep breath and continue with courage on our voyage of discovery for the rest of the day. I have organized the activities with those requiring the least preparation time first graduating finally to those that are most labor and time intensive to organize. Also within each time grouping there is a graduation from participants demonstrating knowledge right through to participants exhibiting the ability to evaluate on the basis of what they have already learned. I wish you and your participants many wonderful lunches and many rewarding post-lunch review sessions - bon appetite!

41. I Know What I Don't Know

Learning outcome
During this post-lunch review participants assess what they have learned during the last session or even during all the whole morning sessions put together. They use a Metacognitive Process to identify what they know and what they don't know.

Overview
Participants review what they know already about the topic under consideration and list the areas where they are still missing information.

In My Experience
By requesting recall of what participants do know in a very structured way it forces them to focus again on the topic and gives them a doorway through which they must pass into the world of new discoveries which will be the afternoon sessions – and they are now stating and committing to participate because of listing that which they do not yet know.

The Hidden Twist
This is a nice reprise of the connect activity that might have been used at the beginning of the course "Expectations and Concerns". It will be more targeted and it is a subliminal activity in self-motivation.

Essential Data
Course type: Any
Group size: 4 to 20
Time of day: Post-lunch
Pace: Medium
Trainer Preparation Time: 1 minute
Activity Duration: 15 minutes

Steps to Create
Write at the top of a flipchart the word KNOWN and at the top of another one the word UNKNOWN.

Steps to Run
1. Play suitable background music quietly
2. As participants come into the room after lunch ask them to take self-adhesive cards and start writing on them words or sentences or drawing icons about what they now know about the topic given the sessions during the morning that they attended
3. When they are sitting and have ceased to write ask them to turn their attention to writing what they do not know in relation to the topic under consideration
4. After 7 minutes of writing ask them to attach their cards to the prepared flipchart pages while saying out loud first what they know and then what they do not know

Suggested Debrief Strategy / Sample Questions
The trainer needs to be alert and to summarize that which is known and that which is yet to be illuminated and learned. This is an opportunity to confirm what has been done, what is going to be done and what is out of scope.

Working Example
By looking at the topic that they are studying and by acknowledging what they already know and identifying what they are lacking they become aware and are more likely to be able to identify key indicators of the success of the implementation of their learning. This is very good when management observe that processes are not being followed and they need the buy-in of staff and this in turn needs staff to be very clear about what they know and what they do not know so that trainers and the allied Subject Matter Experts (SMEs) can ensure that the necessary tools are in staff hands to enable procedural compliance.

This is a good activity if the trainer would like to assess the way the course is going. Open questions and knowledge gaps might appear that the trainer did not realize exist. Good for making the course as efficient as possible and tending to the personal needs of the participants. Also the participants see what the others are thinking and this might spark spontaneous discussion with the participants being able to explain to each other the answers to the questions.

Tips, Tricks & Traps
Make sure that the saying out loud of the messages is done in a deliberate manner so that all hear everything.

Remain focused to summarize and be able to call on SMEs if there are important items identified during this activity that need to be addressed but might not be in the original course materials. If not there then there needs to be a reference to where they may be obtained.

Adult Learning Base Process: Metacognitive Reflection
Refer to **Adult Learning Base Process Reference Guide** for more information about this learning process.

Adult Learning Dashboard

This activity links participant's preferred style of learning. The following dashboard provides a quick reference to adult learning theorists and principles as part of the ID9® methodology.

This activity achieves the following level of Bloom's Taxonomy of the Cognitive Domain (Bloom et al 1956), shown with "X" in the following table.

Bloom's Taxonomy of the Cognitive Domain Level					
Knowledge	Comprehension	Application	Analysis	Synthesis	Evaluation
X					

This activity also achieves a link, shown with "X" in the following table, to participant's naturally occurring learning preferences. Global/Specific, Learning Modalities, Hemispheric Preference (Sperry, 1981), and Multiple Intelligences (Gardner, 1983) are referenced in ID9® methodology and process. This is not a complete list of links that are covered within the ID9® process however this dashboard aims to provide a quick reference for trainers to use to balance instructional design to provide equality for participants' learning preferences.

Global/Specific Learners		Learning Modalities (Sensory Intake)			Hemispheric Preference	
Global	Specific	Visual	Auditory	Kinesthetic	Left Brain	Right Brain
X	X	X	X	X	X	X

Multiple Intelligences								
Visual	Intrapersonal	Interpersonal	Musical	Mathematical / Logical	Linguistic	Kinesthetic	Naturalist	Existential
X	X	X	X	X	X	X		X

42. Glossary Work

Learning outcome
Empower participants by making them conscious that they now possess and can use the right vocabulary.

Overview
The session that has been experienced will have been full of appropriate language and vocabulary. During this post-lunch review support participants to recall this new vocabulary from the morning session using the phrase: "I remember from the morning something beginning with . . ." someone shouts out a word, inserts the last letter of this word into the phrase "I remember from the morning something beginning with . . ." and another participant states another word from the morning session beginning with this letter. And so on.

In My Experience
When participants return to the work environment and have mastered a new vocabulary it empowers them when they are in the implementation phase. It also engenders the basis for networking: professionals who speak the same language enjoy enhanced communication.

The Hidden Twist
This review activity is very like the "I Spy" game from childhood and can be explained quickly using this analogy.

Essential Data
Course type: Any
Group size: 5 to 30
Time of day: Post-lunch
Pace: Medium
Trainer Preparation Time: 1 to 5 minutes
Activity Duration: 15 minutes

Steps to Create
Prepare a slide or wall chart with the catch phrase: "I remember from the morning something beginning with . . ." If using a version with categories (see Tips section) then these will have to be prepared as well.

Steps to Run
Explain to the participants as follows:
1. "Remember when we were younger and played "I spy with my little eye"? Well this is a grown-up version of the same game with this (show them) catch phrase. Also we have added interest and stretched it a bit by asking you to use the last letter of the word stated before your turn as the start letter of the next item remembered"
2. The trainer captures the words on a flipchart

Suggested Debrief Strategy / Sample Questions
Split the group into appropriate teams with the following instructions:
1. Be specific and tell each other what happened during the activity
2. What word did each individual contribute?
3. What lies behind each word?

Working Example
There are times when new vocabulary is really important and of a foreign nature to participants. When this is the case and new concepts need the words to be anchored then go for this activity.

Tips, Tricks & Traps
If it stalls restart with the phrase "I remember from the morning something beginning with . . ." and use a random letter instead of the last latter of the previous word. Do not let the process stand in the way of the flow of learning!

To further stretch participants ask them to allocate the words choosing between several different categories of the material from the morning sessions.

Adult Learning Base Process: I Spy
Refer to **Adult Learning Base Process Reference Guide** for more information about this learning process.

Adult Learning Dashboard

This activity links participant's preferred style of learning. The following dashboard provides a quick reference to adult learning theorists and principles as part of the ID9® methodology.

This activity achieves the following level of Bloom's Taxonomy of the Cognitive Domain (Bloom et al 1956), shown with "X" in the following table.

Bloom's Taxonomy of the Cognitive Domain Level					
Knowledge	Comprehension	Application	Analysis	Synthesis	Evaluation
X					

This activity also achieves a link, shown with "X" in the following table, to participant's naturally occurring learning preferences. Global/Specific, Learning Modalities, Hemispheric Preference (Sperry, 1981), and Multiple Intelligences (Gardner, 1983) are referenced in ID9® methodology and process. This is not a complete list of links that are covered within the ID9® process however this dashboard aims to provide a quick reference for trainers to use to balance instructional design to provide equality for participants' learning preferences.

Global/Specific Learners		Learning Modalities (Sensory Intake)			Hemispheric Preference	
Global	Specific	Visual	Auditory	Kinesthetic	Left Brain	Right Brain
X	X	X	X	X	X	X

Multiple Intelligences								
Visual	Intrapersonal	Interpersonal	Musical	Mathematical / Logical	Linguistic	Kinesthetic	Naturalist	Existential
X	X	X		X	X			

43. Make the Right Connections

Learning outcome
Participants practice their ability to make the appropriate associations.

Overview
During this post-lunch review the trainer says a significant word (category) and participants call out all the various associated words (components) from the morning sessions that they recall.

In My Experience
A review activity that can turn into a mnemonic is just the thing to challenge and encourage participants.

The Hidden Twist
Later, when the significant word is mentioned, participants will readily recall the items associated with this key word.

Essential Data
Course type: Any
Group size: 5 to 30
Time of day: Post-lunch
Pace: Medium
Trainer Preparation Time: 5 minutes
Activity Duration: 15 minutes

Steps to Create
Determine a list of trigger words and write each one at the top of a flipchart page.

Steps to Run
1. Provide participants with self-adhesive cards
2. When the trainer calls out a word they write one word per card that they associate with the trigger word and post it on the relevant flipchart
3. Take a photo of each completed flipchart for the learning take home pack

Suggested Debrief Strategy/Sample Questions
Using the words associated with the trigger words devise a mnemonic to facilitate memorizing these items.

Working Example
When the big ticket items in the training intervention have lots of detail this activity works a treat.

Tips, Tricks & Traps
Afterwards participants' brains react a bit like computers and access the words the way they have "saved" them.

Adult Learning Base Process: Mnemonic
Refer to **Adult Learning Base Process Reference Guide** for more information about this learning process.

Adult Learning Dashboard

This activity links participant's preferred style of learning. The following dashboard provides a quick reference to adult learning theorists and principles as part of the ID9® methodology.

This activity achieves the following level of Bloom's Taxonomy of the Cognitive Domain (Bloom et al 1956), shown with "X" in the following table.

Bloom's Taxonomy of the Cognitive Domain Level					
Knowledge	Comprehension	Application	Analysis	Synthesis	Evaluation
X					

This activity also achieves a link, shown with "X" in the following table, to participant's naturally occurring learning preferences. Global/Specific, Learning Modalities, Hemispheric Preference (Sperry, 1981), and Multiple Intelligences (Gardner, 1983) are referenced in ID9® methodology and process. This is not a complete list of links that are covered within the ID9® process however this dashboard aims to provide a quick reference for trainers to use to balance instructional design to provide equality for participants' learning preferences.

Global/Specific Learners		Learning Modalities (Sensory Intake)			Hemispheric Preference	
Global	Specific	Visual	Auditory	Kinesthetic	Left Brain	Right Brain
X	X	X	X		X	X

Multiple Intelligences								
Visual	Intrapersonal	Interpersonal	Musical	Mathematical / Logical	Linguistic	Kinesthetic	Naturalist	Existential
X	X			X	X	X	X	

44. Mental Aerobics

Learning outcome
Equip participants with the big picture overview story that they need to bring back to the stakeholders in their business environment.

Overview
Animate participants after lunch during this post-lunch review by asking for a short statement about something learned that morning. Then another participant repeats the short statement and adds another appropriate piece, another participant then repeats these two items and adds a third and so on until a comprehensive list reviewing the morning's work is formed.

In My Experience
Being able to remember what has been explained empowers participants – memorizing is not always easy but memorizing by using the narrative tradition with repetition enlivens the process.

The Hidden Twist
Professional trainers are themselves taught the mantra: repeat, repeat, repeat without being boring!

Essential Data
Course type: Any
Group size: 5 to 30
Time of day: Post-lunch
Pace: Medium
Trainer Preparation Time: 5 minutes
Activity Duration: 15 minutes

Steps to Create
List the steps to run on a slide (see next point).

Steps to Run
1. The trainer starts with a short statement containing a key learning point from the sessions in the morning
2. A participant repeats this key learning point and adds another (different) one
3. The next participant repeats what has already been said and adds another one until a list of ten key learning points has been captured. In a group of thirty participants this would mean three lists of ten points giving a grand total of thirty key learning points
4. The elements are captured on a flipchart

Suggested Debrief Strategy/Sample Questions
The lists are displayed and each participant is asked to take three of the most meaningful key learning points for them, relate this to a real life work situation and explain to their neighbor how ONE will really make a difference back home.

Working Example
When there has been a great deal of information delivered to participants it is useful for them to recap in a way that encourages them to use the narrative tradition. Followed by leading them to choose what is highlighted for them means that they evaluate all items for significance and then have to choose one and elaborate.

Tips, Tricks & Traps
By focusing on what is remembered rather than on what has not yet been retained and then by focusing on what is important to each individual the atmosphere remains very positive.

Adult Learning Base Process: Memory Chain
Refer to **Adult Learning Base Process Reference Guide** for more information about this learning process.

Adult Learning Dashboard

This activity links participant's preferred style of learning. The following dashboard provides a quick reference to adult learning theorists and principles as part of the ID9® methodology.

This activity achieves the following level of Bloom's Taxonomy of the Cognitive Domain (Bloom et al 1956), shown with "X" in the following table.

Bloom's Taxonomy of the Cognitive Domain Level					
Knowledge	Comprehension	Application	Analysis	Synthesis	Evaluation
	X				

This activity also achieves a link, shown with "X" in the following table, to participant's naturally occurring learning preferences. Global/Specific, Learning Modalities, Hemispheric Preference (Sperry, 1981), and Multiple Intelligences (Gardner, 1983) are referenced in ID9® methodology and process. This is not a complete list of links that are covered within the ID9® process however this dashboard aims to provide a quick reference for trainers to use to balance instructional design to provide equality for participants' learning preferences.

Global/Specific Learners		Learning Modalities (Sensory Intake)			Hemispheric Preference	
Global	Specific	Visual	Auditory	Kinesthetic	Left Brain	Right Brain
X	X	X	X		X	X

Multiple Intelligences								
Visual	Intrapersonal	Interpersonal	Musical	Mathematical / Logical	Linguistic	Kinesthetic	Naturalist	Existential
X	X	X		X	X			

45. In my Survival Kit . . .

Learning outcome
During this post-lunch review prepare participants for when they leave the training room and get back into the real world of implementation.

Overview
In order to make this happen when they get back to their workplace participants may have to have a "survival kit" – the first participant identifies what they would have in their survival kit, the next participant adds something and so on until the survival kit is full.

In My Experience
At the start of every journey a bag must be packed with the correct items. Life after the training room intervention is another important professional journey and what could be better than a checklist to make that kit bag the best equipped bag possible?

The Hidden Twist
By placing what the participants identify into a kit bag drawn on a flipchart and keeping it highly visible on the wall participants view it for the rest of the course and may even feel drawn to add to it. Encourage them!

Essential Data
Course type: Any
Group size: 5 to 30
Time of day: Post-lunch
Pace: Medium
Trainer Preparation Time: 5 minutes
Activity Duration: 15 minutes

Steps to Create
Prepare a flipchart with an empty representation of a snazzy kit bag.

Steps to Run
Make sure that all participants have access to self-adhesive cards. Ask for contributions to the survival kit and ask that either the word or a drawing be committed to the self-adhesive card, placed in the kit bag on the flipchart.

Suggested Debrief Strategy/Sample Questions
The significance or use of the addition must be explained by the participant at the time it is posted.

Working Example
If this is a training intervention that includes new recruits to the subject matter, e.g., health care professionals who are destined to journey on into a world with many demands and responsibilities, a survival kit is just what they need. I did this once with a group embarking on the journey to becoming professional trainers and it proved to be a success when an item from the survival kit saved the day during the debut session of one of the participant's months later.

Tips, Tricks & Traps
If it is appropriate this could be a very physical activity and there could be an actual bag and items that can be placed in the bag by the participants. It could be a cumulative kit, or else an individual one, depending on the different needs. Could be that it might even be appropriate to make up such a survival kit and give one to each participant as they leave the training room.

Adult Learning Base Process: Learning Transfer Preparation
Refer to **Adult Learning Base Process Reference Guide** for more information about this learning process.

Adult Learning Dashboard

This activity links participant's preferred style of learning. The following dashboard provides a quick reference to adult learning theorists and principles as part of the ID9® methodology.

This activity achieves the following level of Bloom's Taxonomy of the Cognitive Domain (Bloom et al 1956), shown with "X" in the following table.

Bloom's Taxonomy of the Cognitive Domain Level					
Knowledge	Comprehension	Application	Analysis	Synthesis	Evaluation
	X				

This activity also achieves a link, shown with "X" in the following table, to participant's naturally occurring learning preferences. Global/Specific, Learning Modalities, Hemispheric Preference (Sperry, 1981), and Multiple Intelligences (Gardner, 1983) are referenced in ID9® methodology and process. This is not a complete list of links that are covered within the ID9® process however this dashboard aims to provide a quick reference for trainers to use to balance instructional design to provide equality for participants' learning preferences.

Global/Specific Learners		Learning Modalities (Sensory Intake)			Hemispheric Preference	
Global	Specific	Visual	Auditory	Kinesthetic	Left Brain	Right Brain
X	X	X		X	X	X

Multiple Intelligences								
Visual	Intrapersonal	Interpersonal	Musical	Mathematical / Logical	Linguistic	Kinesthetic	Naturalist	Existential
X	X	X			X	X	X	X

46. Action Implementation Plans

Learning outcome
Prepare the ground for participants to complete their Skill Development Action Plan (SDAP).

Overview
Inspire participants during this post-lunch review to implement what they have learned when they are back in the workplace by this review activity which enables them to make plans. Define categories of the material that has been delivered during the morning session and prompt participant input with the starting phrase: "When I am back at work I am going to . . ."

In My Experience
Commitment starts when we verbalize and by verbalizing publically others are inspired and so the SDAP grows along-side commitment.

The Hidden Twist
The items can be taken and typed up by the trainer in time to be incorporated into a "certificate" for signature at the end of the intervention to advance commitment and so the probability of implementation success.

Essential Data
Course type: Any
Group size: 5 to 30
Time of day: Post-lunch
Pace: Medium
Trainer Preparation Time: 5 minutes
Activity Duration: 15 minutes

Steps to Create
1. Set up the appropriate number of flipcharts
2. Head each flipchart with the relevant topic category and the catch phrase "When I am back at work I am going to . . ."
3. While participants are writing up their ideas play suitable background music quietly
4. The trainer should capture ideas on a slide for the debriefing activity

Steps to Run
1. Divide the participants into appropriate groups
2. Ask them to spend time at each flipchart and to write a maximum of two ways in which they foresee implementing what they have learned during the morning session when they return to their work place
3. Ensure your summary slide is ready to go and send it to the participants

Suggested Debrief Strategy/Sample Questions
Ask participants to rate themselves on a confidence scale between zero and ten (0 = zero confidence, 10 = total confidence) regarding their ability to implement the ideas that you show on the prepared summary slide.

Working Example
Getting participants to engage with the Learning Journal and subsequent Skill Development Action Plan can be a bit of a big ask of the uninitiated participant – this activity can be the spark that lights the journaling and action planning flames.

Tips, Tricks & Traps
This positive reinforcement of what participants remember rather than on honing in on what they may not yet have retained optimizes the atmosphere in the training room. A positive atmosphere supports participant learning and retention.

Adult Learning Base Process: Action Plan
Refer to **Adult Learning Base Process Reference Guide** for more information about this learning process.

Adult Learning Dashboard

This activity links participant's preferred style of learning. The following dashboard provides a quick reference to adult learning theorists and principles as part of the ID9® methodology.

This activity achieves the following level of Bloom's Taxonomy of the Cognitive Domain (Bloom et al 1956), shown with "X" in the following table.

Bloom's Taxonomy of the Cognitive Domain Level					
Knowledge	Comprehension	Application	Analysis	Synthesis	Evaluation
		X			

This activity also achieves a link, shown with "X" in the following table, to participant's naturally occurring learning preferences. Global/Specific, Learning Modalities, Hemispheric Preference (Sperry, 1981), and Multiple Intelligences (Gardner, 1983) are referenced in ID9® methodology and process. This is not a complete list of links that are covered within the ID9® process however this dashboard aims to provide a quick reference for trainers to use to balance instructional design to provide equality for participants' learning preferences.

Global/Specific Learners		Learning Modalities (Sensory Intake)			Hemispheric Preference	
Global	Specific	Visual	Auditory	Kinesthetic	Left Brain	Right Brain
X	X	X	X	X	X	X

Multiple Intelligences								
Visual	Intrapersonal	Interpersonal	Musical	Mathematical / Logical	Linguistic	Kinesthetic	Naturalist	Existential
X	X	X	X	X	X	X		

47. Make Choices to Walk the Talk

Learning outcome
Urge participants to make informed decisions.

Overview
Based on the work achieved during the morning session ask participants during this post-lunch review to devise a list of choices that will have to be faced if they are going to be able to implement what they have learned when they return to work. Their lists will be swapped with their neighbor and they will all have to work on the list they receive and make justified choices.

In My Experience
Making decisions can be quite a scary experience – it is great to achieve this in the safe environment of the training room before venturing out into the turbulent seas of the real world.

The Hidden Twist
By ensuring that the participants have to make choices working with the choices devised by another participant means that the choices available may be unfamiliar and uncomfortable and therefore more valuable!

Essential Data
Course type: Any
Group size: 5 to 10
Time of day: Post-lunch
Pace: Medium
Trainer Preparation Time: 5 minutes
Activity Duration: 15 minutes

Steps to Create
Prepare some back-up choices.

Steps to Run
1. Provide a suitable lined (three columns: one entitled Choice 1, the next entitled Choice 2 and the third entitled Why?) piece of paper for each participant
2. Ask them to devise lists of two choices: either the one in column 1 or the one in column 2 and so on
3. While participants are completing Step 2 play suitable background music quietly
4. Pass the list of choices to their neighbor who then has to make the choices

Suggested Debrief Strategy/Sample Questions
1. What was the reason behind each choice – write in the third column
2. Form groups to share how this activity contributes to determining decision points when working towards a goal

Working Example
There are topics where decision points and opportunity costs are more prevalent, for example in Project Management activities. This dry run at the process strengthens decision making and so enhances the possibility of implementation back at the office.

Tips, Tricks & Traps
This activity is beloved by trainers because it is all about application!

Adult Learning Base Process: Cooperative Learning
Refer to **Adult Learning Base Process Reference Guide** for more information about this learning process.

Adult Learning Dashboard
This activity links participant's preferred style of learning. The following dashboard provides a quick reference to adult learning theorists and principles as part of the ID9® methodology.

This activity achieves the following level of Bloom's Taxonomy of the Cognitive Domain (Bloom et al 1956), shown with "X" in the following table.

Bloom's Taxonomy of the Cognitive Domain Level					
Knowledge	Comprehension	Application	Analysis	Synthesis	Evaluation
				X	

This activity also achieves a link, shown with "X" in the following table, to participant's naturally occurring learning preferences. Global/Specific, Learning Modalities, Hemispheric Preference (Sperry, 1981), and Multiple Intelligences (Gardner, 1983) are referenced in ID9® methodology and process. This is not a complete list of links that are covered within the ID9® process however this dashboard aims to provide a quick reference for trainers to use to balance instructional design to provide equality for participants' learning preferences.

Global/Specific Learners		Learning Modalities (Sensory Intake)			Hemispheric Preference	
Global	Specific	Visual	Auditory	Kinesthetic	Left Brain	Right Brain
X	X	X	X	X	X	X

Multiple Intelligences								
Visual	Intrapersonal	Interpersonal	Musical	Mathematical / Logical	Linguistic	Kinesthetic	Naturalist	Existential
X	X	X	X	X	X	X	X	

48. Detect the Crime

Learning outcome
Encourage participants to identify when something is missing that they will really need if they are to make what they have learned come to life.

Overview
Hone participant observation skills using this detective game. During this post-lunch review a participant is chosen to be the suspect. Other participants avert their eyes. The suspect rearranges / removes one small segment of the material from the morning sessions. The rest of the participants are then challenged to detect the change.

In My Experience
There is a reason why we love detective stories. Awaken the hidden sleuths and they reap the benefit.

The Hidden Twist
By examining the scene of the "crime" the participants study the work that they did during the morning and by either detecting the change / theft or having it revealed to them this vital element will be remembered.

Essential Data
Course type: Any
Group size: 5 to 30
Time of day: Post-lunch
Pace: Medium
Trainer Preparation Time: 10 minutes
Activity Duration: 15 minutes

Steps to Create
Set up the appropriate number of scenarios using words and phrases on cards or using actual objects. It is essential that each of the scenarios have elements that can be re-arranged or removed.

Steps to Run
1. Ask for a volunteer or invite participants to catch a crumpled paper ball
2. Request that all, except the "criminal", avert their eyes
3. The "criminal" executes the "crime"
4. Participants are invited to detect the "crime"
5. Keep a list of "crimes"

Suggested Debrief Strategy/Sample Questions
Participants working in pairs or groups are asked:
1. The possible outcome given the "crime"
2. A method of remembering how to include all elements in the right order

Working Example
When training participants in a subject where it is critical that all elements are present (such as a manufacturing process) this is an entertaining and successful way of ensuring retention of material learned.

Tips, Tricks & Traps
The atmosphere must remain positive – with the use of the words associated with crime make sure to keep the tone on the side of the drama and intrigue not the possible tragedy.

Adult Learning Base Process: Spot the Problem
Refer to **Adult Learning Base Process Reference Guide** for more information about this learning process.

Adult Learning Dashboard

This activity links participant's preferred style of learning. The following dashboard provides a quick reference to adult learning theorists and principles as part of the ID9® methodology.

This activity achieves the following level of Bloom's Taxonomy of the Cognitive Domain (Bloom et al 1956), shown with "X" in the following table.

Bloom's Taxonomy of the Cognitive Domain Level					
Knowledge	Comprehension	Application	Analysis	Synthesis	Evaluation
X					

This activity also achieves a link, shown with "X" in the following table, to participant's naturally occurring learning preferences. Global/Specific, Learning Modalities, Hemispheric Preference (Sperry, 1981), and Multiple Intelligences (Gardner, 1983) are referenced in ID9® methodology and process. This is not a complete list of links that are covered within the ID9® process however this dashboard aims to provide a quick reference for trainers to use to balance instructional design to provide equality for participants' learning preferences.

Global/Specific Learners		Learning Modalities (Sensory Intake)			Hemispheric Preference	
Global	Specific	Visual	Auditory	Kinesthetic	Left Brain	Right Brain
X	X	X	X	X	X	X

Multiple Intelligences								
Visual	Intrapersonal	Interpersonal	Musical	Mathematical / Logical	Linguistic	Kinesthetic	Naturalist	Existential
X		X		X	X	X		

49. Bingo

Learning outcome
Participants examine their checklists for completeness.

Overview
Support participants' confidence by giving them the opportunity to play bingo during this post-lunch review. Participants are asked to write a checklist of all the elements that they remember from the morning sessions. Then the bingo master (the trainer) reads from a prepared valid master list the various elements and participants check off the items on their lists.

In My Experience
Bingo is familiar territory yet for participants creating their own bingo card this may be a new experience. It has to be based on what they have learned and then the tension to see if they have included all the right items comes to the fore.

The Hidden Twist
Checklists are created and this technique of developing checklists is reinforced.

Essential Data
Course type: Any
Group size: Any
Time of day: Post-lunch
Pace: Medium
Trainer Preparation Time: 10 minutes
Activity Duration: 10 minutes

Steps to Create
1. Design a valid master check list
2. Prepare a BINGO card for each participant

Steps to Run
1. Distribute the BINGO cards to all
2. Allow participants time to create their own list
3. While participants are completing Step 2 play suitable background music quietly
4. Start reading from the master list pausing long enough to allow participants to check off the items on their own list

Suggested Debrief Strategy/Sample Questions
Form pairs and then participants are asked to describe to their neighbor how they would change their checklist if they were going to write it again and encourage them to make the changes to their lists as they discuss.

Working Example
Some work situations can be daunting. If they are, this rubric of creating a bingo list as a fore runner to an actual checklist can take the pressure off in the stressful situation. It hands control to those who may feel disempowered.

Tips, Tricks & Traps
1. Good for novice participants
2. Giving a handout of the prepared master list at the end of the review activity consolidates the activity
3. A prize is not necessary – the thrill of shouting bingo is usually enough!

Adult Learning Base Process: Bingo
Refer to **Adult Learning Base Process Reference Guide** for more information about this learning process.

Adult Learning Dashboard

This activity links participant's preferred style of learning. The following dashboard provides a quick reference to adult learning theorists and principles as part of the ID9® methodology.

This activity achieves the following level of Bloom's Taxonomy of the Cognitive Domain (Bloom et al 1956), shown with "X" in the following table.

Bloom's Taxonomy of the Cognitive Domain Level					
Knowledge	Comprehension	Application	Analysis	Synthesis	Evaluation
X					

This activity also achieves a link, shown with "X" in the following table, to participant's naturally occurring learning preferences. Global/Specific, Learning Modalities, Hemispheric Preference (Sperry, 1981), and Multiple Intelligences (Gardner, 1983) are referenced in ID9® methodology and process. This is not a complete list of links that are covered within the ID9® process however this dashboard aims to provide a quick reference for trainers to use to balance instructional design to provide equality for participants' learning preferences.

Global/Specific Learners		Learning Modalities (Sensory Intake)			Hemispheric Preference	
Global	Specific	Visual	Auditory	Kinesthetic	Left Brain	Right Brain
	X		X	X	X	

Multiple Intelligences								
Visual	Intrapersonal	Interpersonal	Musical	Mathematical / Logical	Linguistic	Kinesthetic	Naturalist	Existential
	X		X		X		X	

50. Roles and Responsibilities

Learning outcome
Stimulate participants to enact the roles and responsibilities pertaining to what they have learned in the morning sessions.

Overview
During this post-lunch review roles are written on pieces of self-adhesive paper, turned over and mixed up. Participants select a piece of self-adhesive paper and, without looking, stick it on their forehead. Now everyone knows who everyone else is but no one knows who they themselves are – through careful questioning of others in the group they may discover their identity.

In My Experience
Asking the right questions, analyzing the answers, working out the roles and responsibilities and the place within the greater scheme of things by using what has been learned is an outstanding method of reviewing what has been learned and realizing how it can be utilized.

The Hidden Twist
False perceptions come out into the open and can evaporate when the reality is experienced – more effective than a whole lot of talk.

Essential Data
Course type: Especially good when learning about hierarchies
Group size: 5 to 30
Time of day: Post-lunch
Pace: Medium
Trainer Preparation Time: 10 minutes
Activity Duration: 15 minutes

Steps to Create
1. Write all the roles that have been discussed during the morning session on pieces of self-adhesive paper
2. Prepare the schematic of the correct roles, responsibilities and relationships

Steps to Run
1. The trainer facilitates the keeping of the identity of self a secret
2. When the labels are in place participants are encouraged to circulate and ask questions and to determine who they are by analyzing the answers and the reactions of those with whom they converse
3. After 5 minutes the participants are asked to stand in a formation with respect to other participants that depicts their role

Suggested Debrief Strategy/Sample Questions
1. The roles are revealed by taking off their label and reading it
2. How does this revelation help them to recognize the responsibilities of this role in their organization?
3. What were their thoughts during the activity and what are their thoughts now that they know who they represent?

Working Example
This is an excellent idea when participants are known to be challenged by rank and hierarchies.

Tips, Tricks & Traps
A good ending to the activity could be to ask all of the participants to stand in a position with respect to each other given who they think they are (labels still in place) and take a photo and then, if rearrangement is required to do so and, take another photo (also with labels in place) for a compare and contrast session.

Adult Learning Base Process: Match
Refer to **Adult Learning Base Process Reference Guide** for more information about this learning process.

Adult Learning Dashboard

This activity links participant's preferred style of learning. The following dashboard provides a quick reference to adult learning theorists and principles as part of the ID9® methodology.

This activity achieves the following level of Bloom's Taxonomy of the Cognitive Domain (Bloom et al 1956), shown with "X" in the following table.

Bloom's Taxonomy of the Cognitive Domain Level					
Knowledge	Comprehension	Application	Analysis	Synthesis	Evaluation
			X		

This activity also achieves a link, shown with "X" in the following table, to participant's naturally occurring learning preferences. Global/Specific, Learning Modalities, Hemispheric Preference (Sperry, 1981), and Multiple Intelligences (Gardner, 1983) are referenced in ID9® methodology and process. This is not a complete list of links that are covered within the ID9® process however this dashboard aims to provide a quick reference for trainers to use to balance instructional design to provide equality for participants' learning preferences.

Global/Specific Learners		Learning Modalities (Sensory Intake)			Hemispheric Preference	
Global	Specific	Visual	Auditory	Kinesthetic	Left Brain	Right Brain
X	X	X	X	X	X	X

Multiple Intelligences								
Visual	Intrapersonal	Interpersonal	Musical	Mathematical / Logical	Linguistic	Kinesthetic	Naturalist	Existential
X	X	X			X	X		X

51. Taking Stock

Learning outcome
During this post-lunch review boost participant's confidence by enabling them to list all the details of the subject they have learned.

Overview
On prepared sheets participants will build a body of information from the material delivered in the morning. Each sheet will contain columns headed with a title e.g. Country; Customer; Shelf Life; Method of Distribution etc. The trainer silently recites elements from a prepared list, is asked to stop and then when the element is said out loud (in this example "Product") participants complete the various columns as appropriate.

In My Experience
It is great to be able to tell the story of the big picture . . . and then to be able to complete that big picture overview with the details of the story. This review activity encourages participants to be able to fill in the details.

The Hidden Twist
This table can be used as a reference for the participants when they leave the course. It is self-made so of much more use than one that has been typed and just handed out without any participant effort having gone into its build.

Essential Data
Course type: It is particularly useful for technical training interventions when there are lots of precise details to retain.
Group size: Any
Time of day: Post-lunch
Pace: Medium
Trainer Preparation Time: 10 minutes
Activity Duration: 10 minutes

Steps to Create
1. Create the tables that have to be completed and ensure that there are enough copies to have one per participant
2. Determine the list of words to be recited silently to ensure that the activity will make perfect sense – use the example given above as a guide
3. Prepare a flipchart page for debriefing stage

Steps to Run
1. The trainer explains that the game is like the game played by children "Town, Country, River"
2. The trainer recites the list silently while music is playing
3. A participant stops the music, the trainer stops reciting and reveals the element
4. The clock starts ticking
5. All the participants complete a line in each column on their sheet
6. A sample is read out and everyone awards their neighbor the correct number of marks – a point for every new one and zero if it is repeat

Suggested Debrief Strategy/Sample Questions
Each participant reviews their marks, determines what else they need to know before they can apply what they have learned in the morning and shares this with the group by writing it on a prepared flipchart page.

Working Example
When participants are new to the corporate game and still finding their feet this activity can engender confidence. A checklist of their own making without too much stress!

Tips, Tricks & Traps
This activity is useful for a less enthusiastic group, because the concepts and materials are all given and they just need to be ordered.

Adult Learning Base Process: Table
Refer to **Adult Learning Base Process Reference Guide** for more information about this learning process.

Adult Learning Dashboard

This activity links participant's preferred style of learning. The following dashboard provides a quick reference to adult learning theorists and principles as part of the ID9® methodology.

This activity achieves the following level of Bloom's Taxonomy of the Cognitive Domain (Bloom et al 1956), shown with "X" in the following table.

Bloom's Taxonomy of the Cognitive Domain Level					
Knowledge	Comprehension	Application	Analysis	Synthesis	Evaluation
			X		

This activity also achieves a link, shown with "X" in the following table, to participant's naturally occurring learning preferences. Global/Specific, Learning Modalities, Hemispheric Preference (Sperry, 1981), and Multiple Intelligences (Gardner, 1983) are referenced in ID9® methodology and process. This is not a complete list of links that are covered within the ID9® process however this dashboard aims to provide a quick reference for trainers to use to balance instructional design to provide equality for participants' learning preferences.

Global/Specific Learners		Learning Modalities (Sensory Intake)			Hemispheric Preference	
Global	Specific	Visual	Auditory	Kinesthetic	Left Brain	Right Brain
X	X	X			X	

Multiple Intelligences								
Visual	Intrapersonal	Interpersonal	Musical	Mathematical / Logical	Linguistic	Kinesthetic	Naturalist	Existential
X	X		X	X	X		X	

52. Toast Master Sound Bites

Learning outcome
Inspire participants to be able to defend their implementation plans for their learning points.

Overview
During this post-lunch review all the topics from the morning sessions are printed or written on cards in a fishbowl. Participants, in turn, pick from the fish bowl and critique their topic for 30 seconds.

In My Experience
Speaking in public about the new learning points gathered during the training intervention is something that is often asked of participants when they return to the work place and using the Toast Master rubric prepares them well.

The Hidden Twist
The cards as well as containing a statement from the morning session may contain a problem related to the statement and the Toast Master needs to be nimble and appraise a solution to the problem which had also been given in the morning session.

Essential Data
Course type: Any
Group size: 5 to 15
Time of day: Post-lunch
Pace: Medium
Trainer Preparation Time: 10 minutes
Activity Duration: 15 minutes

Steps to Create
Write each possible topic from the morning sessions on cards and drop them into a fish bowl.

Steps to Run
1. The trainer directs participants to pick a card from the fish bowl. They should keep it blank side up until their turn to speak arrives
2. While participants are completing Step 1 play suitable background music quietly
3. With a crumpled paper toss determine the first speaker who then turns over the card, speaks for 30 seconds on the topic and throws the crumpled paper to the next participant to speak to their topic and so on until all have spoken

Suggested Debrief Strategy/Sample Questions
Turn to their neighbor and detail what they felt when they saw the topic, where they rate themselves out of ten (0 is zero and 10 is terrific) in terms of their confidence about this topic and what they think about this topic now that they have spoken about it spontaneously.

Working Example
When participants are at the leadership level and expected to run with what they have learned when they return to the workplace they need to be eloquent and verbally nimble. This is an excellent tried and trusted way to prepare them to welcome this otherwise potential ordeal.

Tips, Tricks & Traps
If participants run into a blank then they should know that they can ask others to help them remember solutions. To do this elegantly they need to know this upfront. Life will mirror art later on!

Adult Learning Base Process: Fish Bowl
Refer to **Adult Learning Base Process Reference Guide** for more information about this learning process.

Adult Learning Dashboard

This activity links participant's preferred style of learning. The following dashboard provides a quick reference to adult learning theorists and principles as part of the ID9® methodology.

This activity achieves the following level of Bloom's Taxonomy of the Cognitive Domain (Bloom et al 1956), shown with "X" in the following table.

Bloom's Taxonomy of the Cognitive Domain Level					
Knowledge	Comprehension	Application	Analysis	Synthesis	Evaluation
					X

This activity also achieves a link, shown with "X" in the following table, to participant's naturally occurring learning preferences. Global/Specific, Learning Modalities, Hemispheric Preference (Sperry, 1981), and Multiple Intelligences (Gardner, 1983) are referenced in ID9® methodology and process. This is not a complete list of links that are covered within the ID9® process however this dashboard aims to provide a quick reference for trainers to use to balance instructional design to provide equality for participants' learning preferences.

Global/Specific Learners		Learning Modalities (Sensory Intake)			Hemispheric Preference	
Global	Specific	Visual	Auditory	Kinesthetic	Left Brain	Right Brain
X	X	X	X	X	X	X

Multiple Intelligences								
Visual	Intrapersonal	Interpersonal	Musical	Mathematical / Logical	Linguistic	Kinesthetic	Naturalist	Existential
X	X	X	X		X	X		X

53. Quick Sand

Learning outcome
Participants think about an imaginary peer being stuck (i.e., the barriers they face) when applying their learning on-the-job and then they brainstorm solutions. Participants are taught to use Rico Clusters as a brainstorming technique.

Overview
This post-lunch review activity will give participants options to identify information, resources, support or help.

In My Experience
Participants help each other with ideas for additional resources. I used this activity when training a group of new hires. The activity benefited the participants by empowering them to review the available resources revealing the necessary information to get started when they get back to their desk.

The Hidden Twist
Participants focus on helping their imaginary peer when they are really helping themselves and other participants. The advantage of this activity of being this focused means that it frees up thinking and participants are not self-conscious.

Essential Data
Course type: Any.
Group size: 2 to 16 (optimal pairs or small groups), could work for 1:1.
Time of day: Post-lunch
Pace: Medium
Trainer Preparation Time: 15 minutes
Activity Duration: 15 minutes

Steps to Create
1. Create a handout that looks like quick sand, sand or rope
2. Create sample ideas for participants to fish out of a bag if they get stuck during the individual activity

Steps to Run
1. Group participants into small groups (3 to 5 participants). May also be conducted in pairs
2. Provide each participant with a hand-out (see above) and colored markers
3. Explain brainstorming technique called "Rico Clusters" and show a completed example
4. Begin activity individually and play suitable background music quietly until the group work begins
5. Choose ONE concept or process where an imaginary peer might get stuck – write it in the middle of the page
6. Then imagine you are your imaginary peer's manager, mentor or coach. Create a Rico Cluster using the resources discussed in the morning on how to get the imaginary peer unstuck
7. Add any additional resources to get the imaginary peer unstuck
8. Continue activity in groups
9. Each group works to find additional ideas to get the imaginary peer unstuck
10. Start clustering ideas together
11. Groups either select one Rico Cluster to present or the group presents the patterns as a result of their clustering.

Suggested Debrief Strategy/Sample Questions
1. What connections do you see as a result of clustering?
2. What additional resources did you find?
3. How does this relate to your role?
4. Summarize your key learning in one sentence

Working Example
Onboarding
New hires typically want to know where to find information. This is a great way to generate ideas on where to find information but also how to find information if you get stuck. Works equally well for process, conceptual and systems training interventions. This is a favorite activity with trainers! It is good for problem solving skills and helps participants to prepare for real life issues, and, if they are very imaginative even for worst case scenarios! It is an activity that is most helpful for participants to have experienced before they encounter immediate situations back at work.

Tips, Tricks & Traps

1. The trainer should watch time. The individual activity should take about 3 minutes. The group work should take about 7 minutes. Debrief and feedback should take the remaining 5 minutes.
2. If a participant is stuck, have some sample ideas ready that they could fish out of a bag
3. If a group is stuck, give hints as needed … such as "Remember the Manager's Resource Page we discussed?" That might help with ideas for Rico Cluster
4. Remind the group about Rico Clusters: Write down every idea. Now is not the time to criticize or evaluate the idea. Non-linear, no structure, quick release of expression, ideas or concepts will bubble up when clustered together

Adult Learning Base Process: Rico Clusters
Refer to **Adult Learning Base Process Reference Guide** for more information about this learning process.

Adult Learning Dashboard
This activity links participant's preferred style of learning. The following dashboard provides a quick reference to adult learning theorists and principles as part of the ID9® methodology.

This activity achieves the following level of Bloom's Taxonomy of the Cognitive Domain (Bloom et al 1956), shown with "X" in the following table.

Bloom's Taxonomy of the Cognitive Domain Level					
Knowledge	Comprehension	Application	Analysis	Synthesis	Evaluation
X					

This activity also achieves a link, shown with "X" in the following table, to participant's naturally occurring learning preferences. Global/Specific, Learning Modalities, Hemispheric Preference (Sperry, 1981), and Multiple Intelligences (Gardner, 1983) are referenced in ID9® methodology and process. This is not a complete list of links that are covered within the ID9® process however this dashboard aims to provide a quick reference for trainers to use to balance instructional design to provide equality for participants' learning preferences.

Global/Specific Learners		Learning Modalities (Sensory Intake)			Hemispheric Preference	
Global	Specific	Visual	Auditory	Kinesthetic	Left Brain	Right Brain
X	X	X	X	X	X	X

Multiple Intelligences								
Visual	Intrapersonal	Interpersonal	Musical	Mathematical / Logical	Linguistic	Kinesthetic	Naturalist	Existential
X	X	X	X		X	X	X	X

54. Oh no! But . . .

Learning outcome
Stir participants into action by exposing them to their own worst fears and having them solved by their peers using what they have garnered during the previous sessions.

Overview
A volunteer starts the post-lunch review activity by making a short statement using the material from the morning finishing with "Oh no, there's . . . " some barrier to its implementation. The next participant takes up the story by using a statement that removes the barrier only to say "Oh no, there's . . ." another barrier to implementation and the next participant explains why this barrier will be no problem and then introduces another barrier to be removed by the next participant and so on until all have engaged in removing barriers by using material learned in the morning sessions.

In My Experience
Everyone has fears when it comes to implementing what they have learned, they have answers and so do their colleagues. This review activity is a great opportunity to gain barrier busting tips for participants' own greatest fears from other participants using the learning points from the morning sessions.

The Hidden Twist
Participants gain insight into potential supporters within the network for contact after the training intervention. Trainer should take notes as the activity takes place to include in post course follow up.

Essential Data
Course type: Any
Group size: 5 to 10
Time of day: Post-lunch
Pace: Medium
Trainer Preparation Time: 15 minutes
Activity Duration: 15 minutes

Steps to Create
Prepare back up stories and barriers.

Steps to Run
1. The trainer asks the participants to stand in two lines slightly out of alignment
2. While participants are completing Step 1 play suitable background music quietly
3. The trainer explains the activity by telling the participants that they are going to recall items that they learned during the morning session, explain that item and then finish with a barrier to implementing that item with a view to having this barrier removed by the next participant diagonally opposite (hence the lack of alignment) when they take up the story

Suggested Debrief Strategy/Sample Questions
Test the confidence temperature: ask participants to state the number from zero (poor) to ten (super) and so to rank their ability to tackle issues head on when they return to the work place.

Working Example
In a situation fraught with problems participants need to know how to tackle them and whom they can contact for ideas. This activity builds competence and relationships. It is a lively activity that connects the training room to the real world.

Tips, Tricks & Traps
If the line-up does not work a ball throw to select the "volunteer" and to determine who will continue and address the barrier to implementation may help especially if participants are slow to come forward.

Adult Learning Base Process: Learning Transfer Preparation
Refer to **Adult Learning Base Process Reference Guide** for more information about this learning process.

Adult Learning Dashboard

This activity links participant's preferred style of learning. The following dashboard provides a quick reference to adult learning theorists and principles as part of the ID9® methodology.

This activity achieves the following level of Bloom's Taxonomy of the Cognitive Domain (Bloom et al 1956), shown with "X" in the following table.

Bloom's Taxonomy of the Cognitive Domain Level					
Knowledge	Comprehension	Application	Analysis	Synthesis	Evaluation
		X			

This activity also achieves a link, shown with "X" in the following table, to participant's naturally occurring learning preferences. Global/Specific, Learning Modalities, Hemispheric Preference (Sperry, 1981), and Multiple Intelligences (Gardner, 1983) are referenced in ID9® methodology and process. This is not a complete list of links that are covered within the ID9® process however this dashboard aims to provide a quick reference for trainers to use to balance instructional design to provide equality for participants' learning preferences.

Global/Specific Learners		Learning Modalities (Sensory Intake)			Hemispheric Preference	
Global	Specific	Visual	Auditory	Kinesthetic	Left Brain	Right Brain
	X		X	X	X	

Multiple Intelligences								
Visual	Intrapersonal	Interpersonal	Musical	Mathematical / Logical	Linguistic	Kinesthetic	Naturalist	Existential
	X	X	X		X	X		X

55. Anchors Away!

Learning outcome
Participants examine what they absorbed during the morning session. They practice using the Neuro Linguistic Programming technique of Chaining Anchors to establish where they are and where they want to go.

Overview
During this post-lunch review participants determine their present position regarding a particular topic and establish the goal they want to achieve.

In My Experience
After lunch I like to work with participants in a way that both settles and energizes – it sounds contradictory. With this activity a calm atmosphere is established and participants become revitalized ready to engage in the afternoon sessions.

The Hidden Twist
The big picture overview has prepared them for the fact that they are going to learn techniques to achieve their goal in the afternoon and that there is room for "process improvement" – not all the answers are there, some will come from the participants themselves during the afternoon sessions.

Essential Data
Course type: Any. There needs to be a significant difference between their present state and the desired state.
Group size: 4 to 20
Time of day: Post-lunch
Pace: Medium
Trainer Preparation Time: 15 minutes and the long strips of wall charts can be laminated and reused
Activity Duration: 15 minutes

Steps to Create
1. Ensure that the content delivered during the morning sessions gives the material needed for participants to determine present position (review) and to outline the future desired position (motivate)
2. Prepare long strips of wall charts with a clear start point and a clear end point on each – there should be a box at each point where details can be written
3. There should be no more than five steps from start to finish with blank boxes beside each point – these will be used in subsequent sessions during the afternoon

Steps to Run
1. Establish groups of four
2. Each group works to fill in the details for the start (innocence) and end point boxes (excellence) only
3. While participants are completing Step 2 play suitable background music quietly

Suggested Debrief Strategy/Sample Questions
A spokesperson from each group describes in THREE words the state of innocence and in a further THREE words the state of excellence while underlining / high lighting them in their group's long wall chart.

Working Example
This is a good activity in a situation where participants have to follow a procedure and are finding it difficult even though it is written, read and understood. If they deduce where they are in terms of their adoption of the procedure, what excellence looks like and then are encouraged to contribute to the uptake of the procedure they come to own the solution to the issue of getting to the desired state. If people do not have a goal how will they know when they have arrived? Participants are forced to look at the big picture and it might give them some breathing space and a chance to look outside the box. They get the chance to think about the outcome they want and what they would like their future to hold.

Tips, Tricks & Traps
The major problem here is to keep things moving and to make sure that only SIX words are underlined during the debriefing process.

Adult Learning Base Process: NLP Chaining Anchors
Refer to **Adult Learning Base Process Reference Guide** for more information about this learning process.

Adult Learning Dashboard

This activity links participant's preferred style of learning. The following dashboard provides a quick reference to adult learning theorists and principles as part of the ID9® methodology.

This activity achieves the following level of Bloom's Taxonomy of the Cognitive Domain (Bloom et al 1956), shown with "X" in the following table.

Bloom's Taxonomy of the Cognitive Domain Level					
Knowledge	Comprehension	Application	Analysis	Synthesis	Evaluation
					X

This activity also achieves a link, shown with "X" in the following table, to participant's naturally occurring learning preferences. Global/Specific, Learning Modalities, Hemispheric Preference (Sperry, 1981), and Multiple Intelligences (Gardner, 1983) are referenced in ID9® methodology and process. This is not a complete list of links that are covered within the ID9® process however this dashboard aims to provide a quick reference for trainers to use to balance instructional design to provide equality for participants' learning preferences.

Global/Specific Learners		Learning Modalities (Sensory Intake)			Hemispheric Preference	
Global	Specific	Visual	Auditory	Kinesthetic	Left Brain	Right Brain
X	X	X	X	X	X	X

Multiple Intelligences								
Visual	Intrapersonal	Interpersonal	Musical	Mathematical / Logical	Linguistic	Kinesthetic	Naturalist	Existential
X		X	X	X	X	X		X

56. Jog your Memory

Learning outcome
Assure participants that they can recall all the items (without exception) that they require to implement their key learning points.

Overview
During this post-lunch review promote participants' ability to recall by presenting them with a "picture" (either words and phrases or actual visual images) of what they have learned so far. They review the "picture" silently for a set time, the picture is then taken away and participants list all the important items in the "picture".

In My Experience
Checklists reassure participants and a self-made checklist ensures buy-in.

The Hidden Twist
By having to look at the "picture" participants are compelled to revisit the work of the morning and study. By having to recall, without the aid of the "picture", their actual learning level is tested without the participants being exposed to a counter-productive examination.

Essential Data
Course type: Any
Group size: 5 to 30
Time of day: Post-lunch
Pace: Medium
Trainer Preparation Time: 20 minutes
Activity Duration: 15 minutes

Steps to Create
Create either a verbal or pictorial list (or mixture of both) of the proceedings from the morning sessions.

Steps to Run
1. Allow participants a limited time to silently observe the creation
2. While participants are completing Step 1 play suitable background music quietly
3. Cover it
4. Participants must now recall all the elements and, if appropriate, in the right order

Suggested Debrief Strategy/Sample Questions
Ask each participant to write a list of the items. When the list is written pass the list to the person on their right who will correct it against the prepared solution on a slide. Each participant receives their list back marked appropriately. Each person is asked to critique their results with the person on their left and conclude with their strategy for ensuring that they remember all the elements in the correct order going forward.

Working Example
This is a variation on a game show that was popular in the 1970s. It is also a play on the ever popular Memory game. Familiarity with this technique means that it is quickly engaging and has the power to really stimulate recall. Participants who need to remember the items without searching too long when they are back in the real world will appreciate having undertaken this review activity.

Tips, Tricks & Traps
A variation would be to have participants create their own verbal and / or pictorial list – decide this according to the subject matter, the group size and the preparation time that the trainer has available.

Adult Learning Base Process: Metaphor
Refer to **Adult Learning Base Process Reference Guide** for more information about this learning process.

Adult Learning Dashboard

This activity links participant's preferred style of learning. The following dashboard provides a quick reference to adult learning theorists and principles as part of the ID9® methodology.

This activity achieves the following level of Bloom's Taxonomy of the Cognitive Domain (Bloom et al 1956), shown with "X" in the following table.

Bloom's Taxonomy of the Cognitive Domain Level					
Knowledge	Comprehension	Application	Analysis	Synthesis	Evaluation
X					

This activity also achieves a link, shown with "X" in the following table, to participant's naturally occurring learning preferences. Global/Specific, Learning Modalities, Hemispheric Preference (Sperry, 1981), and Multiple Intelligences (Gardner, 1983) are referenced in ID9® methodology and process. This is not a complete list of links that are covered within the ID9® process however this dashboard aims to provide a quick reference for trainers to use to balance instructional design to provide equality for participants' learning preferences.

Global/Specific Learners		Learning Modalities (Sensory Intake)			Hemispheric Preference	
Global	Specific	Visual	Auditory	Kinesthetic	Left Brain	Right Brain
X	X	X	X	X	X	X

Multiple Intelligences								
Visual	Intrapersonal	Interpersonal	Musical	Mathematical / Logical	Linguistic	Kinesthetic	Naturalist	Existential
X		X	X	X	X			

57. Standardize Before You Improvise

Learning outcome
Participants evaluate what they have learned during the last session or even during all the previous sessions by being exposed to a Mini Scenario during a post-lunch review which demands reflection on learning to date and supports them to start examining open ended problems in the afternoon sessions.

Overview
Participants listen to an exciting and yet familiar story which will be the catalyst for them to spring into action during the afternoon sessions.

In My Experience
When I tell a story that is well known and then reframe it, this has the right mix of being calming in that it is familiar and yet exciting because it has new meaning – that dangerous Post-lunch period where unease is coupled with slumber potential is thus seamlessly overcome.

The Hidden Twist
Participants reflect on what was gathered during the morning and are challenged with a new and exciting concept upon which they can build for the rest of the afternoon.

Essential Data
Course type: Any
Group size: 5 to 30
Time of day: Post-lunch
Pace: Medium
Trainer Preparation Time: 30 minutes
Activity Duration: 15 minutes

Steps to Create
1. Script the story, making sure that it links with the material in the morning
2. Provide self-adhesive cards and a prepared flipchart with a checklist template

Steps to Run
1. Tell the story
2. Ask participants to list items, on individual self-adhesive cards, which would be in the standard checklist up to the point where improvisation must occur based on what they have learned so far
3. While participants are completing Step 1 play suitable background music quietly
4. Ask the participants to converse with each other and to determine the order of the checklist items
5. Ask each participant to approach the flipchart template in logical turn and fix the checklist item in the right position

Suggested Debrief Strategy/Sample Questions
Tick the boxes on the participant constructed checklist up to the point of improvisation with the ok of the participants every step of the way. Emphasize that it is the standard checklist for the topic under discussion and that it is a candidate for lamination and work station display!

Working Example
For example, tell the story of the airplane landing in the Hudson River. Its pilot attributed the success of this landing to his following standard procedures as long as he could and then, and only then, improvising. The new standard checklist for aviation includes the manoeuvers of that day and so the frontiers of the standard checklist are pushed further out by improvisation finally making all of us safer. This equips the participants with a good and safe cushion to which they can always come back. Making it visual is a good idea. It gives a sense of security and the message that practice makes perfect. It is valuable to show that if there is a system that works and it is followed chances are things will work out especially if minds are open to improvization.

Tips, Tricks & Traps
The story must be familiar, the script dramatized and the delivery engaging / exciting. It has to be short and get to the point pronto.

Adult Learning Base Process: Case Study / Scenario
Refer to **Adult Learning Base Process Reference Guide** for more information about this learning process.

Adult Learning Dashboard

This activity links participant's preferred style of learning. The following dashboard provides a quick reference to adult learning theorists and principles as part of the ID9® methodology.

This activity achieves the following level of Bloom's Taxonomy of the Cognitive Domain (Bloom et al 1956), shown with "X" in the following table.

Bloom's Taxonomy of the Cognitive Domain Level					
Knowledge	Comprehension	Application	Analysis	Synthesis	Evaluation
		X			

This activity also achieves a link, shown with "X" in the following table, to participant's naturally occurring learning preferences. Global/Specific, Learning Modalities, Hemispheric Preference (Sperry, 1981), and Multiple Intelligences (Gardner, 1983) are referenced in ID9® methodology and process. This is not a complete list of links that are covered within the ID9® process however this dashboard aims to provide a quick reference for trainers to use to balance instructional design to provide equality for participants' learning preferences.

Global/Specific Learners		Learning Modalities (Sensory Intake)			Hemispheric Preference	
Global	Specific	Visual	Auditory	Kinesthetic	Left Brain	Right Brain
X	X	X	X	X	X	X

Multiple Intelligences								
Visual	Intrapersonal	Interpersonal	Musical	Mathematical / Logical	Linguistic	Kinesthetic	Naturalist	Existential
X	X	X	X	X	X	X		

58. Pinocchio Factor

Learning outcome
Challenge participants to find problems up front and so remove barriers to implementation. It is a tool to remind people of that corporate act of turning problems into opportunities.

Overview
During this post-lunch review boost critical thinking by exposing participants to prepared scenarios and challenging them to spot the problem by using what they have learned during the morning sessions.

In My Experience
By asking participants to find the problem they notice, acknowledge and retain what is there and also how the problem can be turned into an opportunity.

The Hidden Twist
The deliberate problems are subtle and really oblige participants to engage their critical sense and this will open the window for a debate activity in the afternoon.

Essential Data
Course type: Any
Group size: 5 to 30
Time of day: Post-lunch
Pace: Medium
Trainer Preparation Time: 30 minutes
Activity Duration: 15 minutes

Steps to Create
Prepare scenarios either verbal or pictorial to deliver to the participants. These scenarios must each contain subtle but real problems.

Steps to Run
1. Deliver the scenarios either to pairs or to small groups and ask them to spot the problem
2. While participants are completing Step 1 play suitable background music quietly

Suggested Debrief Strategy/Sample Questions
With the problem spotted each pair or small group is asked to:
1. Classify the problem
2. Outline the issues
3. Propose the opportunity
4. Evaluate the outcome

Working Example
In real life work situations where it is a foregone conclusion that it is going to be a tough sell to get the key learning points implemented it is a good idea to use this activity to prepare participants for the struggle. Participants leave the training room forewarned and forearmed.

Tips, Tricks & Traps
By asking participants to study what has already been delivered so as to identify a problem they subliminally revise all that they have already experienced painlessly! Trainers say that this is a very clever trick!

Adult Learning Base Process: Case Study / Scenario
Refer to **Adult Learning Base Process Reference Guide** for more information about this learning process.

Adult Learning Dashboard

This activity links participant's preferred style of learning. The following dashboard provides a quick reference to adult learning theorists and principles as part of the ID9® methodology.

This activity achieves the following level of Bloom's Taxonomy of the Cognitive Domain (Bloom et al 1956), shown with "X" in the following table.

Bloom's Taxonomy of the Cognitive Domain Level					
Knowledge	Comprehension	Application	Analysis	Synthesis	Evaluation
		X			

This activity also achieves a link, shown with "X" in the following table, to participant's naturally occurring learning preferences. Global/Specific, Learning Modalities, Hemispheric Preference (Sperry, 1981), and Multiple Intelligences (Gardner, 1983) are referenced in ID9® methodology and process. This is not a complete list of links that are covered within the ID9® process however this dashboard aims to provide a quick reference for trainers to use to balance instructional design to provide equality for participants' learning preferences.

Global/Specific Learners		Learning Modalities (Sensory Intake)			Hemispheric Preference	
Global	Specific	Visual	Auditory	Kinesthetic	Left Brain	Right Brain
X	X	X	X	X	X	X

Multiple Intelligences								
Visual	Intrapersonal	Interpersonal	Musical	Mathematical / Logical	Linguistic	Kinesthetic	Naturalist	Existential
X		X	X	X	X			

59. Find 10 and Fill the Gap

 Learning outcome
During this post-lunch review challenge participants to recall, discover and use what they have learned.

 Overview
Prepare a word search board where ten items from the morning session are hidden. Give participants time to search, find, mark and use these words to complete a gap filling hand-out.

 In My Experience
By making material hard to find and by making it important to find it so that it can be used further participants are really challenged and enjoy putting their brains in gear.

 The Hidden Twist
This activity combining seek and use events marries together two powerful motivators to drive implementation when participants are back in the workplace.

 Essential Data
Course type: Any
Group size: 5 to 30
Time of day: Post-lunch
Pace: Medium
Trainer Preparation Time: 30 minutes
Activity Duration: 15 minutes

 Steps to Create
1. Prepare the word search board
2. Prepare the text with the gaps

 Steps to Run
1. Give each participant the two pieces of paper
2. Ask that they search for and find the word and then use the word to fill the gap
3. While participants are completing Step 2 play suitable background music quietly
4. Watch the clock

 Suggested Debrief Strategy/Sample Questions
Now participants have a good vocabulary and recall of the important items from the morning sessions – what else do they want to know about the various items, what questions are raised by this activity?

 Working Example
A topic that has many words that are familiar and routines that are undertaken frequently lends itself to this activity – for example a retraining intervention because of non-compliance. Participants have to become very precise when finding the right word and using it in the appropriate place. It is a technique that can correct wrong perceptions and put participants back on the straight and narrow path.

 Tips, Tricks & Traps
When preparing the word search board it is important to use other real words not related to the subject matter and not just random letters, because mixing the morning's words with words that are not relevant will result in the most value to participants when they engage in the activity: they will have to use their critical thinking abilities.

 Adult Learning Base Process: Word Search
Refer to **Adult Learning Base Process Reference Guide** for more information about this learning process.

Adult Learning Dashboard

This activity links participant's preferred style of learning. The following dashboard provides a quick reference to adult learning theorists and principles as part of the ID9® methodology.

This activity achieves the following level of Bloom's Taxonomy of the Cognitive Domain (Bloom et al 1956), shown with "X" in the following table.

Bloom's Taxonomy of the Cognitive Domain Level					
Knowledge	Comprehension	Application	Analysis	Synthesis	Evaluation
		X			

This activity also achieves a link, shown with "X" in the following table, to participant's naturally occurring learning preferences. Global/Specific, Learning Modalities, Hemispheric Preference (Sperry, 1981), and Multiple Intelligences (Gardner, 1983) are referenced in ID9® methodology and process. This is not a complete list of links that are covered within the ID9® process however this dashboard aims to provide a quick reference for trainers to use to balance instructional design to provide equality for participants' learning preferences.

Global/Specific Learners		Learning Modalities (Sensory Intake)			Hemispheric Preference	
Global	Specific	Visual	Auditory	Kinesthetic	Left Brain	Right Brain
X	X	X			X	X

Multiple Intelligences								
Visual	Intrapersonal	Interpersonal	Musical	Mathematical / Logical	Linguistic	Kinesthetic	Naturalist	Existential
X	X		X	X	X		X	

60. Budget Magic

Learning outcome
Participants devise how to resource the business practices that their key learning points are encouraging them to implement during this post-lunch review.

Overview
Each participant comes back from lunch to find a budget sheet on their desk plus a bag of money (pretend money). They then complete the budget sheet and physically allocate the funds (piles of money) to their list of items remembered from the morning sessions to make the material come to life using limited resources.

In My Experience
We all know that money talks. When participants are given the chance to review what they have learned in terms of what happens to funds, this review brings their ability to implement into the realm of reality.

The Hidden Twist
By using the representational piles of pretend money participants are able to see the relative cost of items within their frame and across the frames of other participants.

Essential Data
Course type: Any
Group size: 5 to 30
Time of day: Post-lunch
Pace: Medium
Trainer Preparation Time: 30 minutes
Activity Duration: 15 minutes

Steps to Create
1. Prepare a budget sheet
2. Procure good quality fake money – make it more interesting by placing it in a mediaeval pouch

Steps to Run
1. Place the budget sheet and the pouch of money at each team place
2. Explain that each team now has the chance to determine the finances of the topics mentioned during the morning sessions
3. Ask them to place the money on the budget sheet in the relative proportions
4. While participants are completing Step 3 play suitable background music quietly

Suggested Debrief Strategy/Sample Questions
1. Each team observes the relative proportions of the other teams budgeting, returns to their own budget sheet and justifies any difference or similarity
2. How did this activity help?
3. What did you think initially, what do you think now?

Working Example
Implementing that which has been learned can be a heady thought which needs to be grounded if it has any chance at all. This activity prepares participants for the real world where business ideas meet budget constraints. It is ideal in situations where implementation is possible but may be quite challenging financially.

Tips, Tricks & Traps
To stretch this activity it would be interesting to have a Financial Controller holding the money filled mediaeval pouch and get participants to compete for funds based on the knowledge that they have gleaned from the sessions in the morning. This level of complexity would require fewer participants and tight scripting.

Adult Learning Base Process: Match
Refer to **Adult Learning Base Process Reference Guide** for more information about this learning process.

Adult Learning Dashboard

This activity links participant's preferred style of learning. The following dashboard provides a quick reference to adult learning theorists and principles as part of the ID9® methodology.

This activity achieves the following level of Bloom's Taxonomy of the Cognitive Domain (Bloom et al 1956), shown with "X" in the following table.

Bloom's Taxonomy of the Cognitive Domain Level					
Knowledge	Comprehension	Application	Analysis	Synthesis	Evaluation
			X		

This activity also achieves a link, shown with "X" in the following table, to participant's naturally occurring learning preferences. Global/Specific, Learning Modalities, Hemispheric Preference (Sperry, 1981), and Multiple Intelligences (Gardner, 1983) are referenced in ID9® methodology and process. This is not a complete list of links that are covered within the ID9® process however this dashboard aims to provide a quick reference for trainers to use to balance instructional design to provide equality for participants' learning preferences.

Global/Specific Learners		Learning Modalities (Sensory Intake)			Hemispheric Preference	
Global	Specific	Visual	Auditory	Kinesthetic	Left Brain	Right Brain
X	X	X	X	X	X	X

Multiple Intelligences								
Visual	Intrapersonal	Interpersonal	Musical	Mathematical / Logical	Linguistic	Kinesthetic	Naturalist	Existential
X		X	X	X		X	X	X

61. Limericks

Learning outcome
A self-designed mnemonic by participants engenders lasting buy-in.

Overview
A good way to check for learning is to allow participants to create a rhyme or another mnemonic about what they have learned – boost retention of the subject matter by giving time to participants to write a rhyme or chant (see TIPS, TRICKS AND TRAPS section) and share it during a post-lunch review.

In My Experience
This review activity nourishes our musical intelligence and stretches participants to find a new way to communicate what they have retained.

The Hidden Twist
Being required to condense key learning points into a short verse gives a stock cube effect. The learning points are condensed and can be carried around until needed and then expanded again (hydrated) to yield their full flavor.

Essential Data
Course type: Any
Group size: 5 to 30
Time of day: Post-lunch
Pace: Medium
Trainer Preparation Time: 30 minutes
Activity Duration: 15 minutes

Steps to Create
Create three examples: a Limerick, a visual and a short verse to illustrate what is expected of the participants.

Steps to Run
1. Divide the group into teams
2. Each team decides the precise form of their mnemonic (if they come up with something different from the examples so much the better!)
3. While participants are completing Step 2 play suitable background music quietly
4. Start the clock

Suggested Debrief Strategy/Sample Questions
Each team presents their mnemonic. Each team picks a different mnemonic to critique: in one sentence. The trainer collects the mnemonics and includes them all in the take home learning pack.

Working Example
This is an interesting activity to use when there are different roles and responsibilities that have to be known and respected (or any things that have to be associated with each other). Using a rhyme to create the link between the role and its corresponding responsibility is fun, memorable and effective in the long term. It is something that those who create it are proud to share.

Tips, Tricks & Traps
Some participants might be stressed by this activity if they are not good at creating so pairing up or building groups is essential and having one person choose the topic and the other creating the verse will help.

Some trainers are not convinced about the chanting idea – it can get a bit over the top. Use with care!

Adult Learning Base Process: Rhythmic Learning
Refer to **Adult Learning Base Process Reference Guide** for more information about this learning process.

Adult Learning Dashboard

This activity links participant's preferred style of learning. The following dashboard provides a quick reference to adult learning theorists and principles as part of the ID9® methodology.

This activity achieves the following level of Bloom's Taxonomy of the Cognitive Domain (Bloom et al 1956), shown with "X" in the following table.

Bloom's Taxonomy of the Cognitive Domain Level					
Knowledge	Comprehension	Application	Analysis	Synthesis	Evaluation
				X	

This activity also achieves a link, shown with "X" in the following table, to participant's naturally occurring learning preferences. Global/Specific, Learning Modalities, Hemispheric Preference (Sperry, 1981), and Multiple Intelligences (Gardner, 1983) are referenced in ID9® methodology and process. This is not a complete list of links that are covered within the ID9® process however this dashboard aims to provide a quick reference for trainers to use to balance instructional design to provide equality for participants' learning preferences.

Global/Specific Learners		Learning Modalities (Sensory Intake)			Hemispheric Preference	
Global	Specific	Visual	Auditory	Kinesthetic	Left Brain	Right Brain
X			X		X	X

Multiple Intelligences								
Visual	Intrapersonal	Interpersonal	Musical	Mathematical / Logical	Linguistic	Kinesthetic	Naturalist	Existential
		X	X		X			

62. Build Focus

Learning outcome
If participants can categorize what they have learned it potentiates focused implementation.

Overview
Participants are reassured during this post-lunch review that they have retained what they have learned by being challenged to assign different items from the morning sessions to the right categories.

In My Experience
An organized mind leads to smooth implementation – clutter does the opposite. By enabling participants to organize what they have learned the ability to implement expands exponentially.

The Hidden Twist
Being organized leads to self-control and self-control leads to increased performance at work. This review activity has many benefits.

Essential Data
Course type: Any
Group size: 5 to 30
Time of day: Post-lunch
Pace: Medium
Trainer Preparation Time: 30 minutes
Activity Duration: 15 minutes

Steps to Create
1. Present all the categories of material that have been delivered during the morning sessions on flipcharts
2. Prepare self-adhesive cards with all kinds of items belonging (and not belonging) to the stated categories

Steps to Run
1. Give each pair of participants a set of unique self-adhesive cards and ask them, in an orderly way, to allocate the items to the categories
2. While participants are completing Step 1 play suitable background music quietly

Suggested Debrief Strategy/Sample Questions
Ask participants to photograph each orderly flipchart result and to arrange the results in a slide so as to make a suitable group work hand-out.

Working Example
When you find that there is material in a training intervention contained in a table or matrix it is time to consider using this activity. Allow participants to create the table themselves! This way they will actually know and love this information!

Tips, Tricks & Traps
If this activity results in participants having to unpack and repack the information differently it will hinder retention of learning. Structure the props tightly to prevent this disaster!

Adult Learning Base Process: Match
Refer to **Adult Learning Base Process Reference Guide** for more information about this learning process.

Adult Learning Dashboard

This activity links participant's preferred style of learning. The following dashboard provides a quick reference to adult learning theorists and principles as part of the ID9® methodology.

This activity achieves the following level of Bloom's Taxonomy of the Cognitive Domain (Bloom et al 1956), shown with "X" in the following table.

Bloom's Taxonomy of the Cognitive Domain Level					
Knowledge	Comprehension	Application	Analysis	Synthesis	Evaluation
				X	

This activity also achieves a link, shown with "X" in the following table, to participant's naturally occurring learning preferences. Global/Specific, Learning Modalities, Hemispheric Preference (Sperry, 1981), and Multiple Intelligences (Gardner, 1983) are referenced in ID9® methodology and process. This is not a complete list of links that are covered within the ID9® process however this dashboard aims to provide a quick reference for trainers to use to balance instructional design to provide equality for participants' learning preferences.

Global/Specific Learners		Learning Modalities (Sensory Intake)			Hemispheric Preference	
Global	Specific	Visual	Auditory	Kinesthetic	Left Brain	Right Brain
X	X	X	X	X	X	X

Multiple Intelligences								
Visual	Intrapersonal	Interpersonal	Musical	Mathematical / Logical	Linguistic	Kinesthetic	Naturalist	Existential
X		X	X	X	X	X	X	

63. Business Consequences

Learning outcome
Boost participant's grasp of the complete array of details within the big picture.

Overview
A series of questions prompts participants to recall material from the morning session during a post-lunch review. Participants use either with words or pictures to write or draw on the top of a page their answer, folds it over (to cover their work) and passes it on. When the last prompt is reached the paper is passed on to be unfolded and read in its entirety by the relevant participant – the stories and artwork created should portray the work of the morning.

In My Experience
This review activity means that participants can verify that by learning the same things together they are building a community network capable of mutual support during the implementation phase.

The Hidden Twist
There will be a flow and continuity in the stories that will surprise and reassure participants that they are all on the same page going in the same direction.

Essential Data
Course type: Any
Group size: 5 to 10
Time of day: Post-lunch
Pace: Medium
Trainer Preparation Time: 30 minutes
Activity Duration: 15 minutes

Steps to Create
Design questions with a view to the answers flowing one after the other to tell the story recounted by the sessions in the morning.

Steps to Run
1. Provide each participant with an appropriate piece of lined paper
2. Read each question three times pausing and checking for comprehension and participant writing responses as appropriate
3. Ensure that the paper is folded before being passed on

Suggested Debrief Strategy/Sample Questions
When the last question is asked and answered the paper is passed to the next participant and each participant has a paper story to unfold. If the group is small enough everyone gets to read their story, if too large ask for five stories to be read and then check for lines in other stories that differ and give another perspective.

Working Example
A training intervention is often the scene of great networking. Where the group is spread apart geographically and needs a strong network to make things happen this activity illustrates very vividly that they have one story and is very powerful.

Tips, Tricks & Traps
Learning does not have to be fun but humor can be appropriate. This activity does lend itself to some funny things happening – if they do, make the most of them, or let the participants do so while at the same time holding firm to the idea of building a consolidated aligned story for the network.

Adult Learning Base Process: Brainstorming
Refer to **Adult Learning Base Process Reference Guide** for more information about this learning process.

Adult Learning Dashboard

This activity links participant's preferred style of learning. The following dashboard provides a quick reference to adult learning theorists and principles as part of the ID9® methodology.

This activity achieves the following level of Bloom's Taxonomy of the Cognitive Domain (Bloom et al 1956), shown with "X" in the following table.

Bloom's Taxonomy of the Cognitive Domain Level					
Knowledge	Comprehension	Application	Analysis	Synthesis	Evaluation
				X	

This activity also achieves a link, shown with "X" in the following table, to participant's naturally occurring learning preferences. Global/Specific, Learning Modalities, Hemispheric Preference (Sperry, 1981), and Multiple Intelligences (Gardner, 1983) are referenced in ID9® methodology and process. This is not a complete list of links that are covered within the ID9® process however this dashboard aims to provide a quick reference for trainers to use to balance instructional design to provide equality for participants' learning preferences.

Global/Specific Learners		Learning Modalities (Sensory Intake)			Hemispheric Preference	
Global	Specific	Visual	Auditory	Kinesthetic	Left Brain	Right Brain
X	X	X	X	X	X	X

Multiple Intelligences								
Visual	Intrapersonal	Interpersonal	Musical	Mathematical / Logical	Linguistic	Kinesthetic	Naturalist	Existential
X	X	X		X	X	X	X	

64. Get the Story Straight

Learning outcome
Embolden participants to take on the questions that will be raised by stakeholders in business life.

Overview
During this post-lunch review participants tell the story by reading a statement from a card delivered to them by the trainer which ends with a question and then they answer that question. Another card with the next aspect of the story is delivered to another participant by the trainer and so on until the conclusion and the story is told and the questions are answered.

In My Experience
In the real world there need to be detractors . . . by replying to their points clarity is reached. Practicing this before it happens by using what has been learned builds skills and therefore confidence.

The Hidden Twist
The trainer has the sequence of the story in their hands and selects the participants to tell the story in the correct order. It is tightly choreographed to ensure the right sequence and to engage the right participants at the right point in the sequence.

Essential Data
Course type: Any
Group size: 5 to 10
Time of day: Post-lunch
Pace: Medium
Trainer Preparation Time: 30 minutes
Activity Duration: 15 minutes

Steps to Create
Prepare the story cards with the question at the end.

Steps to Run
1. Hand out the cards: one to each participant or group depending on the number of participants
2. Each participant or group reads the card out loud in turn ending with the question and its answer
3. Every participant has a copy of the card and the question and is encouraged to take notes of the answers

Suggested Debrief Strategy/Sample Questions
1. What questions do these answers raise?
2. What are the possible answers to these new questions?
3. Do they have a possible Q and A now to use when they get back to work?

Working Example
Conceptual material needs to be exposed to the light of day and this approach means that the concepts must stand up to scrutiny through the rigors of this multiple perspective approach of asking and answering questions.

Tips, Tricks & Traps
A modification would be if the participants know the stakeholders well - then instead of the trainer preparing the questions the participants could think up the questions that stakeholders might ask.

Adult Learning Base Process: Questions and Answers
Refer to **Adult Learning Base Process Reference Guide** for more information about this learning process.

Adult Learning Dashboard
This activity links participant's preferred style of learning. The following dashboard provides a quick reference to adult learning theorists and principles as part of the ID9® methodology.

This activity achieves the following level of Bloom's Taxonomy of the Cognitive Domain (Bloom et al 1956), shown with "X" in the following table.

Bloom's Taxonomy of the Cognitive Domain Level					
Knowledge	Comprehension	Application	Analysis	Synthesis	Evaluation
				X	

This activity also achieves a link, shown with "X" in the following table, to participant's naturally occurring learning preferences. Global/Specific, Learning Modalities, Hemispheric Preference (Sperry, 1981), and Multiple Intelligences (Gardner, 1983) are referenced in ID9® methodology and process. This is not a complete list of links that are covered within the ID9® process however this dashboard aims to provide a quick reference for trainers to use to balance instructional design to provide equality for participants' learning preferences.

Global/Specific Learners		Learning Modalities (Sensory Intake)			Hemispheric Preference	
Global	Specific	Visual	Auditory	Kinesthetic	Left Brain	Right Brain
X	X		X		X	X

Multiple Intelligences								
Visual	Intrapersonal	Interpersonal	Musical	Mathematical / Logical	Linguistic	Kinesthetic	Naturalist	Existential
	X	X			X			

Chapter 5:
During Course:
Review Activities -
End of Day / Start of Day

Multi-day or Multi-session courses

Melanie Barn

About the Co-Author:

Melanie Barn

Melanie Barn (Mel) is an International Training Professional with many years of training and instructional design experience.

From an early age Mel was fascinated by training. Whether helping school mates with spelling, teaching juniors to play music, teaching horse-riding skills or coaching on the school sports field. She grew up in a sales and training environment and was inspired by her parents. Her mother was a highly-regarded business leader with an amazing sense of style and incredible ability to inspire people. It was her father who, as a training director, introduced the thrill of training techniques. He shared intriguing ideas such as adult learning styles, NLP and with funky acronyms like "KISS" and "SPIN". Mel wanted to know more!

After achieving a First Class Honors degree in Applied Biology, Mel could finally pursue her dream of a training career. Working in the Pharma-Biotech Industry, she built expertise in clinical research, website management and internal communications. Mel quickly found her niche as a Training Manager and earned her corporate reputation as a highly regarded International Trainer. She has been an invited speaker at a recognized UK pharmaceutical Trainer's Forum on two separate occasions.

Mel has developed and delivered an extensive portfolio of training programs. She is a specialist in designing interactive, outcome-driven training programs and has lead global training projects and training teams. Her instructional design experience spans a wide range of topics. Mel has used Mattiske's ID9® process since 2005. ID9® has revolutionized her training design beyond what she ever dreamed was possible!

Mel gets a big thrill from coaching other trainers to successfully design and deliver training. Her training mantra is "involve and inspire".

In 2010, Mel was able to realize another long-term dream, and relocated from the UK to the Mediterranean island of Cyprus. She lives by the sea with partner Keith, her spaniel Merlin and many cats! Her mum and dad are close by.

Thanks to the wonders of modern technology, Mel works for The Performance Company, as a Senior Instructional Designer and Trainer. Spare time is occupied by a passion for cooking, listening to music and learning Greek. As a semi-retired horse woman, Mel continues an obsession with animals and particularly enjoys taking Merlin to obedience classes – she's always training!

Chapter Introduction

This chapter provides start or end of day review activities for multi-day or multi-session courses. Give these start and end of day review activities a try and enjoy the results of more confident and motivated participants, who feel involved and inspired.

Multi-day courses are courses defined in this chapter as being split by an overnight break. For example a multi-day course might be a 2-day course which runs on 2 consecutive days. Multi-session courses are courses split by a longer period of time. For example, a 2-day course which is conducted with a week between each day (called a 1 + 1 course) or a virtual course of 5 x 2 hour sessions, run over 5 weeks.

So what are these activities for?

These start or end of day review activities take less than 30 minutes to run. They are used to review and summarize learning progress and provide opportunities to practice and "try out" new skills or techniques. They also help to boost participant confidence and motivation at a critical point in the course. The trainer has a final chance to observe and fill any significant learning gaps before taking participants forward.

Start of day reviews tend to be lower energy, that is, of slower to moderate pace. They are particularly useful for multi-session courses when memories need refreshing from the previous session. They are also a good way to 'break the ice', set the scene and connect participants to the topics at the beginning of each day of their course.

End of day activities tend to be higher energy, that is, faster-paced and highly kinesthetic. There is often nothing better than a highly kinesthetic or competitive end of day review to build some energy and finish with impact!

What makes these different to other reviews?

Start and end of day reviews tend to be of longer duration and can review a greater amount of course content than Mini- or Post-lunch Reviews (See previous Chapters).

They differ from a Major Review (see next Chapter) in several ways:
- Firstly, they are used at the start as well as the end of a day.
- Secondly, they can go beyond "must know" course content and review the finer details.
- Thirdly, they are often much more practical and provide opportunities for participants to practice and fine-tune their skills.

The activities suggested in this chapter have worked especially well for me. They are straightforward and generally easy to prepare and run. They are designed to engage as many different learning styles and preferences at once. Using these start and end of day review activities provides a great opportunity to give your training a boost. They may even help to revolutionize your training, as they did for mine. Give these start and end of day review activities a try and enjoy the results of more confident and motivated participants, who feel involved and inspired.

65. Wordstorm

Learning outcome
To recall key learning and content from topics covered.

Overview
During this end of day review activity small groups compete against each other. They fill a flipchart page with as many ideas, words, phrases, or symbols that they can recall from the topics specified.

Start of Day Review Activity	End of Day Review Activity
X	X

In my Experience
This is simple to prepare and easy to run. It is particularly good for reviewing factual or procedural content, such as regulations, procedures or Health and Safety training. The open nature of filling the page readily engages several learning preferences at once. The time allowed for the actual 'wordstorm' is enough to motivate participants to quickly write ideas. It is not so long that they run out of steam. 60 seconds to 3 minutes is recommended.

Anything goes with this activity as long as it helps participants remember key points. They may recall fun and meaningful moments from the course, such as donuts at break. All recall is great!

The Hidden Twist
This is a disguised way of getting participants to review and summarize their own knowledge. Additionally, if teams are creative they can unknowingly score bonus points. Based on the phrase "a picture paints a thousand words," teams score a bonus of 1,000 points for every picture/symbol drawn.

Essential Data
Course Type: Any, works best with factual or procedural content
Group size: 6–30 (Optimal. 1-5: Work in pairs or individually)
Time of day: End of Day. To use as a start of day review, remove the competition.
Pace: Fast and competitive
Trainer Preparation Time: 5 minutes
Activity Duration: 10-20 minutes

Steps to Create
1. Obtain blank flipchart paper and colored markers
2. Clearly identify topics for review
   - Refer to learning objectives and ensure alignment
3. Determine time allowed for the wordstorm (60 seconds to 3 minutes)
4. Optional: Prizes for winning team

Steps to Run
1. Regroup into groups of 3-5
2. Hand out a blank flipchart page and pens to each group
3. Explain instructions
   - Fill the flipchart with words, phrases, pictures, acronyms – anything you remember from [specify topics]/ the topics covered today
   - Set time allowed, e.g. 90 seconds
   - Say it's competitive – team with the most words wins
4. Start activity – shout 'go!'
   - Call out when half the allotted time has passed
   - Call out again with 10 seconds left and countdown to zero
5. Stop when time is up
6. Regroup to whole group: Each team reads out their words* to the whole group
   - * As one team reads, remaining teams cross out matching words on their page
   - Then another team read out – read only uncrossed* words
   - Go around teams until all uncrossed words are shared
7. Teams count up their total score
   - The scores 'TWIST':
     - Trainer asks – did anyone draw a picture or icon?
     - If yes, say "a picture paints a thousand words" – add 1,000 points to your total for every picture/symbol drawn (If no, mention bonus points missed)
     - Groups adjust score totals
8. Teams shout out final scores
9. Winners declared. Optional: Award prize

Suggested Debrief strategy
- **At the end**, trainer points out that the group has created their own summary
  - Trainer summarizes key points and patterns; or asks any of the following questions:
    - What do you notice about the ideas shared?
    - What patterns or repeating themes are there?
    - What unique items did you have that the other teams didn't?
- **During activity**, trainer notes important topics missed
  - Ask questions to recall missed topics
- Optional for debrief:
  - Ask each group: What are 2 acronyms you've used and what do they stand for?
  - Individuals select their #1 key word

Working Example
Regulations Training
Groups fill the flipchart with ideas about the regulations or 'procedures' covered. This might be names of regulations, regulating bodies, acronyms, examples, historical events that led to regulations, tips, do's and don'ts, etc. There is a lot of information to recall.

Tips, Tricks and Traps
- Remind group about the rules of brainstorming
- Be clear with instructions and scoring:
  ○ Clearly state that anything goes – fill the page with ideas!
  ○ 1 point for a word/acronym
  ○ 1 point for a phrase; not 1 point for each word in the phrase
- Play moderate-paced music during brainstorming. Not so loud that it distracts

Variation:
- Use Wordstorm as a learning activity. For example, used to explore what participants already know at the start of a course/topic
- **Virtual** session, use breakout groups or run as a whole group activity. Participants type into the Chat feature or use Annotation tools to write on a Whiteboard/slide

Adult Learning Base Process: Brainstorm
Refer to **Adult Learning Base Process Reference Guide** for more information about this learning process.

Adult Learning Dashboard
This activity links participant's preferred style of learning. The following dashboard provides a quick reference to adult learning theorists and principles as part of the ID9® methodology.

This activity achieves the following level of Bloom's Taxonomy of the Cognitive Domain (Bloom et al 1956), shown with "X" in the following table.

Bloom's Taxonomy of the Cognitive Domain Level					
Knowledge	Comprehension	Application	Analysis	Synthesis	Evaluation
X					

This activity also achieves a link, shown with "X" in the following table, to participant's naturally occurring learning preferences. Global/Specific, Learning Modalities, Hemispheric Preference (Sperry, 1981), and Multiple Intelligences (Gardner, 1983) are referenced in ID9® methodology and process. This is not a complete list of links that are covered within the ID9® process however this dashboard aims to provide a quick reference for trainers to use to balance instructional design to provide equality for participants' learning preferences.

Global/Specific Learners		Learning Modalities (Sensory Intake)			Hemispheric Preference	
Global	Specific	Visual	Auditory	Kinesthetic	Left Brain	Right Brain
X	X	X	X	X	X	X

Multiple Intelligences								
Visual	Intrapersonal	Interpersonal	Musical	Mathematical / Logical	Linguistic	Kinesthetic	Naturalist	Existential
X		X	X		X	X		

66. Rico Reflection

Learning outcome
To identify key learnings and commit to one action from topics covered.

Overview
Individuals use a "clustering" technique to write their thoughts about the course topics covered. Then they identify their key learnings and actions as they reflect on the written clusters. Finally, key learnings and actions are shared with a partner.

Start of Day Review Activity	End of Day Review Activity
X	X

In My Experience
Using Rico Clusters (developed by Gabriele Rico) encourages participants to indulge in a moment of personal reflection. Their minds wander and explore the course topics in an open and creative way. Rico Reflection is simple and takes only a few minutes. This makes it a great activity for larger participant groups. Participants only need a pen and paper. The technique appeals to creative, right-brained participants, while those with a left-brained preference will focus and analyze their thoughts.

The Hidden Twist
Participants are so absorbed by creating clusters that they engage in powerful reflection without realizing it. They are often surprised by what they identify. They also commit to an action, which is reinforced by sharing with a colleague.

Essential Data
Course Type – Any
Group Size – Any
Time of day – End of Day or Start of Day
Pace – Slow and focused
Trainer Preparation Time – 10 minutes
Activity Duration – 10-15 minutes

Steps to Create
- Obtain blank paper and pens (different colors if possible)
- Optional: Write an instructions summary for participant reference

Steps to Run
- Hand out to each participant a blank sheet of paper and pen(s)
- Explain the activity (Optional: Provide written instructions summary)
  - Write the name of the course/topic in a circle in the top third of the piece of paper
  - Let your mind wander from the name and think of other words
  - Write down each word that you think of. Put each one into a circle
  - Join the circles to each other with lines – there is no order
  - Let the words flow. If you sense a direction, follow it
  - Keep filling the page with words and circles
    - If you get stuck, move your pen. Trace over circles you've already created until another idea occurs
- Once the page is full, review your ideas and answer two questions –
  - 1) What is my key learning?
    - Highlight key words on the page and/or list key learnings
  - 2) What will I do with that learning?
    - Identify at least one action you can take
- Turn to the person next to you. Share key learning and one action

Suggested Debrief Strategy
Bring the whole group back together. Debrief using the following:
- What key learnings/action did you identify?
- How did the clusters help you? (What surprised you?)
- What else do you need to know before you can apply your learning?
- What is your first/next step to implement your action?

Working Example
Leadership Program
Useful for complex programs, such as a multi-day Leadership courses that involve lots of group work and group-based feedback. As an end of day activity it provides the opportunity to freely reflect and concentrate on personal thoughts, identifying key learnings and associated actions.

Computer Systems Training
Use Rico Reflection as an end of day activity following highly-interactive software or system training. It provides individuals with the opportunity to reflect and deeply consider their own key learnings and actions.

Tips, Tricks and Traps
- Keep the room quiet to aid a reflective mood
- Make sure participants stay focused – soft, slow music can help
- Check that actions are appropriate to the course objectives
- Be prepared for the speedy finisher! Ask questions on how they used the process (see debrief questions). Can they identify additional key learning/actions?

Variation:
Virtual session, participants complete this activity in their participant guide. They share with a partner using the Chat feature.

 Adult Learning Base Process: Rico Clusters and Metacognitive Reflection
Refer to **Adult Learning Base Process Reference Guide** for more information about this learning process.

 Adult Learning Dashboard
This activity links participant's preferred style of learning. The following dashboard provides a quick reference to adult learning theorists and principles as part of the ID9® methodology.

This activity achieves the following level of Bloom's Taxonomy of the Cognitive Domain (Bloom et al 1956), shown with "X" in the following table.

Bloom's Taxonomy of the Cognitive Domain Level					
Knowledge	Comprehension	Application	Analysis	Synthesis	Evaluation
	X				

This activity also achieves a link, shown with "X" in the following table, to participant's naturally occurring learning preferences. Global/Specific, Learning Modalities, Hemispheric Preference (Sperry, 1981), and Multiple Intelligences (Gardner, 1983) are referenced in ID9® methodology and process. This is not a complete list of links that are covered within the ID9® process however this dashboard aims to provide a quick reference for trainers to use to balance instructional design to provide equality for participants' learning preferences.

Global/Specific Learners		Learning Modalities (Sensory Intake)			Hemispheric Preference	
Global	Specific	Visual	Auditory	Kinesthetic	Left Brain	Right Brain
X	X	X	X	X	X	X

Multiple Intelligences								
Visual	Intrapersonal	Interpersonal	Musical	Mathematical / Logical	Linguistic	Kinesthetic	Naturalist	Existential
X	X	X	X	X	X	X		

. Mind Movie

Learning outcome
Participants use the 'Future Pace' NLP technique to mentally practice new skills or behaviors in a future, real-life scenario

Overview
Individuals visualize a future, real-life scenario in their mind – as a 'mind movie'. They imagine themselves conducting the perfect scenario. In the perfect scenario they should implement the desired new skills or behaviors exceptionally. They vividly imagine and rehearse their own actions, words and behaviors from start to finish. If they find themselves adopting any old habits or wrong behaviors these are instantly blocked and replaced with desired ones. After completing the visualization, individuals reflect on their 'mind movie' by answering questions. To debrief, they pair and share, or discuss experiences as a whole group.

Start of Day Review Activity	End of Day Review Activity
X	X

In my Experience
Most trainers feel at some stage as if they have to be a mindreader, or wish that we could telepathically project thoughts to our participants! As if by magic, here is an activity to help with that! This powerful visualization technique really helps participants to subconsciously embed new skills or behaviors into their minds. It is useful for any course involving a significant change. Do you want your participants to change their behavior? Or do you want them to follow a completely new process than before? Use this activity to help them take subconscious control of their learning and behavior.

The Hidden Twist
By mentally rehearsing the real-life situation in such a powerful and realistic way, the brain is subconsciously programmed with the new approach. If the visualization is delivered well, new behaviors can become almost automatic. Participants are often surprised by how easily they recall what to do when faced with the situation in real-life.

Essential Data
Course Type: Any course requiring a significant change outcome
Group size: 1 to 30 (Optimal)
Time of day: Start of day or end of day review
Pace: Slow and reflective
Trainer Preparation Time: 10-15 minutes
Activity Duration: 15-30 minutes

Steps to Create
1. Prepare for running the visualization (see Steps to Run)
   - Refer to learning objectives and ensure alignment
2. Create a debrief worksheet/page in participant guide (see Debrief Strategy)

Steps to Run
1. Participants identify a future situation where they will apply the new process/skills
   - Choose a scenario where an old habit/attitude would have been displayed
2. Conduct the visualization activity. Say:
   - Close your eyes and imagine you are there right now
   - You are carrying out the process/ You are applying the new skill
   - Step right into the scenario, imagine vividly what takes place and listen in to the soundtrack
     - See what you will see, hear what you will hear, feel what you will feel
   - Imagine the scenario from beginning to end – What are you saying? What are you doing? What are you thinking?
   - **If you have an old thought/use an old habit, immediately remove it – block it with a huge red no entry sign. Immediately switch to what you should be doing/saying
   - Visualize success! – Things are going perfectly for you, exactly as they should. See what you will see, hear what you will hear, feel what you will feel
3. Individuals reflect and answer questions in their worksheet/guide
4. Optional: Pair and share their scenarios and answers

Suggested Debrief Strategy
- Debrief whole group
- Questions for individual reflection:
  - Summarize your situation - What did you see, hear and feel?
  - What are you doing differently or what is new for you?
  - What did you do well in the rehearsal?
  - What must you avoid doing in the future?
  - What are 2 key things to remember when you do this for real?
- Whole group debrief – Choose from the following, based on the personal nature of the scenarios:
  - If sensitive, use pair and share as debrief. Then debrief #1 tip/action from individuals

○ Possible debrief questions for whole group:
- Being as specific as possible, what happened during the visualization?
- How did the visualization help you?
- On a scale from 1-10 (1 low, 10 high), what is your confidence level?
- What are 2 key things to remember when you do this for real?

Working Example
Evidence-based Interview Training

After training participants on the new interview process and arming them with some powerful questioning techniques, they visualize and rehearse their next interview. They systematically follow the new interview structure and mentally use some of the new interview questions. They block old habits and adjust questions to create stronger, more focused questions. The debrief reviews their experience and highlights benefits of the new process and questions.

Upgraded Data Entry System Training: Change Control is used after training participants on the new data entry process and data entry requirements. Participants rehearse making a system entry from start to finish. They follow all of the essential steps and ensure key elements are correctly entered. They work through the process and make mental corrections. The debrief reviews their experience and extracts the do's and don'ts of data entry.

Tips, Tricks and Traps
- Use a slow, soft and clear voice tone for the visualization
- If participants struggle to close their eyes, suggest that they fix on a single point in the room
- If participants find it difficult to visualize success, it may help to repeat the visualization
- Keep the mood in the room quiet during the reflection; slow, soft music can help

Variation:
Virtual session, this activity runs identically. Ensure good audio quality. Mute all participant lines during the visualization.

Adult Learning Base Processes: NLP – Future Pace, using sensory predicate phrases, and metacognitive reflection
Refer to **Adult Learning Base Process Reference Guide** for more information about this learning process.

Adult Learning Dashboard
This activity links participant's preferred style of learning. The following dashboard provides a quick reference to adult learning theorists and principles as part of the ID9® methodology.

This activity achieves the following level of Bloom's Taxonomy of the Cognitive Domain (Bloom et al 1956), shown with "X" in the following table.

Bloom's Taxonomy of the Cognitive Domain Level					
Knowledge	Comprehension	Application	Analysis	Synthesis	Evaluation
		X			

This activity also achieves a link, shown with "X" in the following table, to participant's naturally occurring learning preferences. Global/Specific, Learning Modalities, Hemispheric Preference (Sperry, 1981), and Multiple Intelligences (Gardner, 1983) are referenced in ID9® methodology and process. This is not a complete list of links that are covered within the ID9® process however this dashboard aims to provide a quick reference for trainers to use to balance instructional design to provide equality for participants' learning preferences.

Global/Specific Learners		Learning Modalities (Sensory Intake)			Hemispheric Preference	
Global	Specific	Visual	Auditory	Kinesthetic	Left Brain	Right Brain
X	X	X	X	X	X	X

Multiple Intelligences								
Visual	Intrapersonal	Interpersonal	Musical	Mathematical / Logical	Linguistic	Kinesthetic	Naturalist	Existential
X	X	X	X	X		X		

Start, Stop, Continue

Learning outcome
Participants classify activities and tasks from the course. They consider what they should and should not put into action.

Overview
Small groups review the topics covered during the course. They identify activities and tasks and then classify each one according to whether they are: 1) Something to start doing, 2) Something they should stop doing, or 3) Something they should continue to do. By the end participants create a summary of things to do (start or continue) and things to avoid (stop). Participants create their own personalized checklist to use as an action plan, which aids recall and supports implementation.

Start of Day Review Activity	End of Day Review Activity
X	X

In my Experience
This is a versatile activity which requires minimal trainer preparation. It works equally well as an individual activity. It provides an excellent review for procedural and role-specific training. Start, Stop, Continue is particularly useful when identification of roles and responsibilities is a key learning outcome. The activity works best if it can be repeated at least once per day through a multi-day course. This means the lists evolve across the entire course.

The Hidden Twist
The act of classification encourages participants to consider the impact/outcome of tasks. They translate an otherwise simple task list into something more instructive. They identify new activities, continuing activities and obsolete or unnecessary activities.

Essential Data
Course Type: Any, good for procedural or role-specific content
Group size: 4-30 (Optimal. 1-3: change to individual/ paired activity)
Time of day: Start of day or End of day
Pace: Moderate
Trainer Preparation Time: 5 minutes
Activity Duration: 10-30 minutes

Steps to Create
1. Obtain flipchart paper and pens
2. Clearly identify topics and roles
   - Is it only the participants' role, or multiple roles?
   - Refer to learning objectives and ensure alignment
3. Optional:
   - Prepare Start, Stop, and Continue flipcharts per group – see Steps to Run 3.
   - For individuals: Create a 3-column worksheet. Column headers: Start, Stop, Continue

Steps to Run
1. Regroup into groups of 3-5 (group same roles together)
2. Hand out 3 sheets of flipchart paper and pens to each group
3. Each group writes the following headings on their flipchart paper:
   - Start (Things to start doing)
   - Stop (Things to stop doing/ avoid)
   - Continue (Things to continue doing)
4. Specify/ allocate a role to each group
5. Explain instructions
   - Review the topics/ processes to this point
     - Identify tasks for your (allocated) role
     - Classify each task according to whether it should start, stop or continue
       - Record on the appropriate flipchart

Suggested Debrief Strategy
- Regroup to whole group: Each group presents their flipcharts
  - For one role: Ask groups to share what they should start, then stop, then continue
  - For different roles: Each group to present their start, stop, continue as a whole
- Possible debrief questions:
  - What tasks should you start?
  - What should you continue?
    - Are you doing more or less of that?
  - What must you stop/avoid?
  - What did you learn from this activity?
    - What's different/the same?
    - What surprised you?
    - How will it help you?
  - What are your expectations of others?
- If running as a small group activity, ensure debrief allows individuals to personalize the content

Working Example
Standard operating procedure (SOP) training
Having reviewed several topics or procedures, participants complete this review. For their own role, they identify potential tasks and classify these into Start, Stop or Continue. They could also identify the tasks and expectations of other roles in the same way.

Tips, Tricks and Traps
- Trainer or participants draw images/icons to symbolize Start, Stop and Continue. This further engages visual and creative (right-brained) learners.
- Prepare model answers for each role, as a post-activity job aid

- This activity provides an alternative to the Learning Journal
- Play soft music in the background during group work/ reflection

Variation:
- Start, Stop, Continue can be adapted for numerous course types and different reviews. It can be conducted in small groups, pairs or individually.
- **Virtual** session, use breakout groups or run as a whole group. Participants type ideas into the Chat feature or use Annotation tools to write on a Whiteboard/slide.

Adult Learning Base Process: Metacognitive Reflection and Naturalist
Refer to **Adult Learning Base Process Reference Guide** for more information about this learning process.

Adult Learning Dashboard
This activity links participant's preferred style of learning. The following dashboard provides a quick reference to adult learning theorists and principles as part of the ID9® methodology.

This activity achieves the following level of Bloom's Taxonomy of the Cognitive Domain (Bloom et al 1956), shown with "X" in the following table.

Bloom's Taxonomy of the Cognitive Domain Level					
Knowledge	Comprehension	Application	Analysis	Synthesis	Evaluation
	X				

This activity also achieves a link, shown with "X" in the following table, to participant's naturally occurring learning preferences. Global/Specific, Learning Modalities, Hemispheric Preference (Sperry, 1981), and Multiple Intelligences (Gardner, 1983) are referenced in ID9® methodology and process. This is not a complete list of links that are covered within the ID9® process however this dashboard aims to provide a quick reference for trainers to use to balance instructional design to provide equality for participants' learning preferences.

Global/Specific Learners		Learning Modalities (Sensory Intake)			Hemispheric Preference	
Global	Specific	Visual	Auditory	Kinesthetic	Left Brain	Right Brain
X	X	X	X	X	X	X

Multiple Intelligences								
Visual	Intrapersonal	Interpersonal	Musical	Mathematical / Logical	Linguistic	Kinesthetic	Naturalist	Existential
X		X	X	X	X	X	X	

69. What's the Story?

Learning outcome
Participants analyze a fictitious story or scenario in relation to key learning.

Overview
Pairs or individuals analyze a fictional story that provides examples of the course content in action. After reading the story, participants answer analysis questions designed to identify character's behaviors that relate to the course content.

Start of Day Review Activity	End of Day Review Activity
X	X

In my Experience
This activity is particularly useful for conceptual training content involving new skills, models, or principles. The story provides examples of how course content can be applied in a neutral setting. Alternatively, the message of the story can be indirectly related, by linking the moral or meaning of the story to the course objectives. Existing stories, such as an Aesop's fables, can be used, or the trainer can create a story.

The Hidden Twist
By reading a fictitious story and answering a few simple questions, participants are actually uncovering examples of applied learning. This analysis creates powerful memory links between the story and the course content.

Essential Data
Course Type: Conceptual or procedural training content
Group size: 1-50 (unlimited)
Time of day: Start or End of day review
Pace: Moderate
Trainer Preparation Time: 60 minutes
Activity Duration: 15-30 minutes

Steps to Create
1. Clearly identify topics for review
   - Refer to learning objectives and ensure alignment
2. Identify an existing story, or write a story which illustrates key concepts in action
3. Clearly identify links between the story and course content/ objectives
4. Write the analysis questions – these should help participants identify key points
5. Write model answers for trainer
6. Create a participant worksheet. Add images for visual appeal

Steps to Run
1. Hand out the worksheet
2. Pairs or individuals read the story
3. Then discuss and answer the questions

Suggested Debrief Strategy
- Debrief answers with the whole group
- Enrich the debrief with further questions:
  - What did you notice about the story as you were reading?
  - What was your first thought as you started reading? What are your thoughts now?
  - What do the characters in the story teach you?
  - In one sentence, what does this story mean for us/ teach us?

Working Example
Communication Skills
Using a fictitious conversation between two colleagues which illustrates the communication skills covered in the course. Participants read or "act out" the conversation. While analyzing the conversation, the participants identify the conversation structure, examples of high-impact questions, and good communication practices. Participants also identify areas for improvement and suggest things each character can do differently.

Tips, Tricks and Traps
- Stories are most effective if they illustrate both good and bad examples
- Use a font that is easy to read, such as Arial; Avoid Times New Roman!
- Play soft music in the background during group work (read and answer questions)
- Provide the trainer with model answers and highlighted examples for conducting the debrief
- This activity also works well as an overnight/Bridging task

Variation:
- Twist the activity. Have participants create a story or mock conversation to illustrate the main concepts from the course
- **Virtual** session, individuals complete the activity in their participant guide. Discuss and debrief answers with the whole group.

Adult Learning Base Process: Story or Case Study analysis
Refer to **Adult Learning Base Process Reference Guide** for more information about this learning process.

Adult Learning Dashboard

This activity links participant's preferred style of learning. The following dashboard provides a quick reference to adult learning theorists and principles as part of the ID9® methodology.

This activity achieves the following level of Bloom's Taxonomy of the Cognitive Domain (Bloom et al 1956), shown with "X" in the following table.

Bloom's Taxonomy of the Cognitive Domain Level					
Knowledge	Comprehension	Application	Analysis	Synthesis	Evaluation
			X		

This activity also achieves a link, shown with "X" in the following table, to participant's naturally occurring learning preferences. Global/Specific, Learning Modalities, Hemispheric Preference (Sperry, 1981), and Multiple Intelligences (Gardner, 1983) are referenced in ID9® methodology and process. This is not a complete list of links that are covered within the ID9® process however this dashboard aims to provide a quick reference for trainers to use to balance instructional design to provide equality for participants' learning preferences.

Global/Specific Learners		Learning Modalities (Sensory Intake)			Hemispheric Preference	
Global	Specific	Visual	Auditory	Kinesthetic	Left Brain	Right Brain
X	X	X	X	X	X	X

Multiple Intelligences								
Visual	Intrapersonal	Interpersonal	Musical	Mathematical / Logical	Linguistic	Kinesthetic	Naturalist	Existential
X	X	X	X	X	X	X	X	X

70. Set the Case

Learning outcome
Participants create a case study scenario for another group; then solve a case study set by others.

Overview
In pairs or small groups, participants set case studies for each other. Then they solve a case study that has been set by another group. Learning and idea-sharing is reinforced through a simple yet powerful debrief.

Start of Day Review Activity	End of Day Review Activity
X	X

In my Experience
This is straightforward and easy to prepare. Participants create their own highly relevant and practical scenarios. They analyze the case study. If appropriate, they can also practice through mini role play. Set the Case works well with a diverse group of participants who have varied experiences. It is really useful for problem solving.

The Hidden Twist
Application of learning happens when setting and when solving the cases. By setting a case, participants must consider different practical situations that others can use. By solving each other's cases participants are not only reviewing and practicing application. They also add perspectives, solve problems and provide ideas for solving real-life cases.

Essential Data
Course Type: Conceptual or procedural training content
Group size: 4-30 (Optimal. 1-4 work individually)
Time of day: Start or End of day review
Pace: Moderate
Trainer Preparation Time: 15-30 minutes
Activity Duration: 30 minutes

Steps to Create
1. Prepare the "set the case cards" template. Include section headings, or prompting questions – see following example
2. Define the case setting rules (see below)
3. Optional: Prepare an example or back-up case

Steps to Run
A: Set the Case (5 minutes)
- Regroup into pairs or small groups (no more than 5)
- Each group creates a brief case. It must be:
  - Relevant to their role/work and the course content
  - Written onto a Set the Case card
- Once completed, trainer collects the cards

B: Solve the Case (10-15 minutes)
- Distribute a case card to each group
- Explain the activity:
  - Read and discuss the case
  - Choose issues and areas to apply course content to
  - Examine and list potential solutions and actions
- Optional: Answer 3 debrief questions (See Debrief Strategy)

Sample set the case card:

Set the Case

Summary title:

Clearly describe the coaching scenario: Who is involved, what is the outline situation and why is coaching required?

Provide any further relevant background info:

Suggested Debrief Strategy
- Regroup to whole group
  - Each group summarizes their scenario and shares high level solutions
- Debrief questions for the case:
  - What are the main issues/ focus areas of this case?
  - How could the [course content] be applied to these issues/ focus areas?
  - What solutions/actions do you suggest?
    - [If role play: Run the role play and list top tips]
- To extend whole group debrief, select from the following questions:
  - How did you go about solving the case?
  - What did you do to apply [the model/ skills]?
  - What is your confidence level on a scale of 1-10? (1 low, 10 high)
  - What advice can you offer the case setters to deal with this situation?
  - How does the case you solved apply to you?
  - What did you learn from setting the case?
    - Which of the solutions proposed should help?

Working Example
Effective Coaching Course

Participants set a coaching case for each other – see following example. Participants review a coaching case. They practice applying the relevant coaching model and techniques learned. Case debrief questions:

- What are the main issues/ focus areas within this case? – They identify the issues
- How could the [course content] be applied to these? – They propose a summary of how the person should be coached (techniques and questions to use)
- What solutions do you suggest? – They suggest solutions to issues identified
- [If role play appropriate: practice this now and list top tips for application] – Optional: They can role play and try out their suggestions.

In this example debrief questions are tailored to cover use of the coaching model, conversation shape and use of questions to coach the person in the scenario.

Tips, Tricks and Traps

- Provide a template to make case setting consistent – see following example
- As pre-work ask participants to identify 1-2 real-life scenarios. This speeds up case setting
- Case setting could be completed as an overnight task. The analysis becomes start of day review
- Provide groups with a copy of solutions to the case they set
- Play soft music in the background during group work (set and solve the case)

Variation:

- Participants solve their own cases set
- **Virtual** session, use breakout groups, or whole group discussion. Discuss possible cases then work on 1-2 cases as a whole group. Participants could set and swap cases individually. Participants type their ideas into the Chat feature or use Annotation tools to write solutions on a Whiteboard/slide.

Adult Learning Base Process: Case Study

Refer to **Adult Learning Base Process Reference Guide** for more information about this learning process.

Adult Learning Dashboard

This activity links participant's preferred style of learning. The following dashboard provides a quick reference to adult learning theorists and principles as part of the ID9® methodology.

This activity achieves the following level of Bloom's Taxonomy of the Cognitive Domain (Bloom et al 1956), shown with "X" in the following table.

Bloom's Taxonomy of the Cognitive Domain Level					
Knowledge	Comprehension	Application	Analysis	Synthesis	Evaluation
			X	X	

This activity also achieves a link, shown with "X" in the following table, to participant's naturally occurring learning preferences. Global/Specific, Learning Modalities, Hemispheric Preference (Sperry, 1981), and Multiple Intelligences (Gardner, 1983) are referenced in ID9® methodology and process. This is not a complete list of links that are covered within the ID9® process however this dashboard aims to provide a quick reference for trainers to use to balance instructional design to provide equality for participants' learning preferences.

Global/Specific Learners		Learning Modalities (Sensory Intake)			Hemispheric Preference	
Global	Specific	Visual	Auditory	Kinesthetic	Left Brain	Right Brain
X	X	X	X	X	X	X

Multiple Intelligences								
Visual	Intrapersonal	Interpersonal	Musical	Mathematical / Logical	Linguistic	Kinesthetic	Naturalist	Existential
X		X	X	X	X	X		

71. Rapid Role Rounds

Learning Outcomes
Participants practice new skills/ techniques

Overview
A highly practical review. Provides "live" role play experience in a safe environment. Pairs practice a mini "live" role play. Then regroup to new pairs and practice a new scenario. The trainer can choose how many rounds are completed - at least two are recommended.

Start of Day Review Activity	End of Day Review Activity
X	X

In my Experience
Participants work in pairs to practice the skills or techniques learnt so far. This is particularly good as an end or start of day review for conceptual training content. For example leadership, communication, giving and receiving feedback, interviewing, handling conflict or stress management.

The Hidden Twist
Participants are so highly engaged in practicing quick and easy scenarios, they rapidly move from a state of uncertainly, to confidence in a short amount of time.

Essential Data
- Course Type: Conceptual training content
- Group size: 4-20 (Optimal. Less than 4: Work in pairs, trios or practice with the trainer. 20+ suggests that an additional trainer helps with facilitation and debrief)
- Time of day: Start or End of day review
- Pace: Moderate to fast, depending on the time limit set for each round
- Trainer Preparation Time: 60 minutes
- Activity Duration: 30 minutes

Steps to Create
1. Create the role play cards:
   - On each card provide a short scenario that participants will practice – see example below
   - Prepare a slide containing activity instructions. Include the main steps and time limits

Steps to Run
1. Regroup participants into pairs
2. Case 1: 5 minutes allowed
   - Hand out one role play card to each pair
   - Explain one person is practicing the case and the other is responding
   - Pairs read the role play card together
   - Each person prepares for their role (1-2 minutes)
   - 2-3 minutes to role play the scenario
3. Regroup for a whole group debrief, ask:
   - What went well?
   - What could you do better next time?
4. Case 2: 5 minutes allowed
   - With the same partner, switch roles
   - Hand out a new case card and repeat the activity
5. Cases 3 & 4: Switch Partners
   - Repeat 1-2 more rounds with a new case card
6. De-brief Whole Group

Example Case Card

Technique	Situation
	They made a personal remark towards you during a meeting you were chairing (because they didn't agree with what you were saying)

Suggested Debrief Strategy
- Debrief is conducted at two points:
- Debrief 1 (after first role play)
   - What went well?
   - What could you do better next time?
- Debrief 2 (at end of all rounds)
   - What happened during the practice rounds?
   - What is your confidence level on a scale from 1-10? (1 low, 10 high)
   - What were 1-2 key learnings for you?
   - Additional debrief questions:
     - How did you use the method(s) learned so far in the course?
     - Did anything change with more practice?
     - How well was your practice received?
     - What were your interactions like?
     - What went well/ what could improve?

Working Example
Giving and Receiving Feedback
Participants are provided with short feedback scenarios. They practice giving and receiving feedback. They must use the feedback method(s) provided during the course. Example scenarios:

A. You have been trying to teach a new co-worker basic principles of the main process in your Department. The new co-worker is joining your team from another Department and he or she has been introduced to you as a great worker who is very competent. However, he or she has been very slow to learn what you are trying to teach. Have a conversation, giving and receiving feedback to try to understand why your new co-worker is not learning as fast as you have expected.

B. A co-worker makes a personal remark* towards you during a team meeting (because he or she didn't agree with what you were saying). You need to give some feedback to address the situation and prevent it from reoccurring.

Tips, Tricks and Traps

- Make scenarios short and clear so participants can read them quickly. They should not distract from the overall goal to practice applying a skill or technique
- Provide an easy reference the skill/technique that participants should practice. This can be a visual, a job aid or checklist – See example below

- Play soft music in the background during group work/ reflection
- Provide the trainer with debrief notes, containing model answers and examples

Variation:

- On blank cards, ask participants to identify their own role play scenario. See "Set the Case"
- Virtual session, individuals or whole group analyze a scenario and plan what they would say. Willing volunteers demonstrate scenarios with the trainer or in pairs. The whole group observes and gives feedback.

Adult Learning Base Process: Live role play
Refer to **Adult Learning Base Process Reference Guide** for more information about this learning process.

Adult Learning Dashboard

This activity links participant's preferred style of learning. The following dashboard provides a quick reference to adult learning theorists and principles as part of the ID9® methodology.

This activity achieves the following level of Bloom's Taxonomy of the Cognitive Domain (Bloom et al 1956), shown with "X" in the following table.

Bloom's Taxonomy of the Cognitive Domain Level					
Knowledge	Comprehension	Application	Analysis	Synthesis	Evaluation
		X			

This activity also achieves a link, shown with "X" in the following table, to participant's naturally occurring learning preferences. Global/Specific, Learning Modalities, Hemispheric Preference (Sperry, 1981), and Multiple Intelligences (Gardner, 1983) are referenced in ID9® methodology and process. This is not a complete list of links that are covered within the ID9® process however this dashboard aims to provide a quick reference for trainers to use to balance instructional design to provide equality for participants' learning preferences.

Global/Specific Learners		Learning Modalities (Sensory Intake)			Hemispheric Preference	
Global	Specific	Visual	Auditory	Kinesthetic	Left Brain	Right Brain
X	X	X	X	X	X	X

Multiple Intelligences								
Visual	Intrapersonal	Interpersonal	Musical	Mathematical / Logical	Linguistic	Kinesthetic	Naturalist	Existential
X	X	X	X	X	X	X		

72. Close Encounters of the Fast Kind

Learning Outcomes
Participants apply new skills/ techniques

Overview
Based around the concept of "speed-dating". Participants sit in two rows, facing each other (see picture below). They have 90 seconds to share and practice a brief scenario with the person opposite. Then, participants rotate to the next partner, as directed. The trainer can choose how many rotations are completed. At least 4 rotations are recommended. All participants should be given the opportunity to practice their skills, as well as be practiced on.

Start of Day Review Activity	End of Day Review Activity
	X

In my Experience
This activity is good as a high-energy end of day review. It works well for conceptual training involving behaviors, such as communication skills, giving and receiving feedback, or handling conflict. The fast pace encourages participants to keep moving forward. Short bursts of practice time relieve the perceived pressure of "oh no, it's role play".

The Hidden Twist
The format enables participants to practice with different partners and gain a variety of experience in a short amount of time. Repetition reinforces learning. Practice makes perfect!

Essential Data
- Course Type: Conceptual training content
- Group size: 4-20 (Optimal. Less than 4: Work in pairs, or practice with the trainer. 20+ suggests that an additional trainer helps with facilitation and debrief)
- Time of day: End of day review
- Pace: Fast, due to the time limit on rotations
- Trainer Preparation Time: 60 minutes
- Activity Duration: 30 minutes

Steps to Create
1. Obtain a bell or another noisemaker to signal the rotations
2. Create the Mini case cards – see example below
   - These are short work-based cases. They briefly explain the scenario and provide an objective for something that participants need to get from the exchange
3. Prepare instructions/diagram for the rotation and movement during the activity – see example below

Steps to Run
1. Trainer arranges chairs. Participants seated in two equal rows, opposite each other (see picture below)
   - One row is Team A – they will practice the scenario. They stay in their seat for round 1
   - One row is Team B – they will be the recipients. They carry a case card
2. Hand out the case cards to Team B – one per person
3. Start the activity
   - Round 1: 7-8 minutes allowed
     - Team B shares the scenario on their case card with the opposite person in Team A
     - Then, they have 60 seconds to act out the scenario
     - When the bell sounds **Team B** rotates one place to the right
     - Repeat exchange of scenario followed by acting out the situation
     - Rotations take place until Team A have practiced at least 4 scenarios (or time is up)
   - Round 2: 7-8 minutes allowed.
     - Switch roles so that team B gets to practice scenarios. Team A carries the case cards
4. Debrief whole group

Sample Room Layout

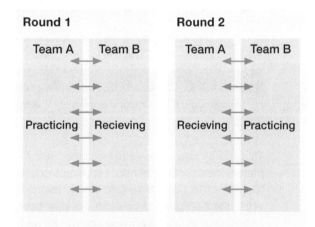

Suggested Debrief Strategy
- Use the following questions to debrief the whole group:
  - What happened during the rotations?
  - What is your confidence level on a scale from 1-10? (1 low, 10 high)
  - What were 1-2 key learnings for you?
  - Additional debrief questions:
    - How did you use the method(s) learned so far in the course?
    - What changed with more practice?

- How was your practice received?
- What were your interactions like?
- What went well/ what could improve?

Working Example
Influencing and Negotiation Skills
Participants use mini scenarios to practice the influencing and negotiation techniques they have learnt during the day. Example Case:
- You are implementing a new process and need to meet with the person opposite you next week in order to discuss the kick off meeting. You know they have a very busy schedule.
  Your objective: Get agreement to meet next week.

Tips, Tricks and Traps
- Provide a short break before the activity. This enables participants to relax and reflect on key learning so far. The trainer has time to rearrange the room.
- Prepare a slide containing high level activity instructions, to keep momentum going

- Make sure the cards are short and clear so that participants can read them easily
- Provide the trainer with debrief notes, containing model answers and examples
- Add a "musical chairs" theme: Use a track of music to guide the rotation. When the music stops it's time to rotate!

Variation:
- Virtual session, individuals or the whole group analyze some mini scenarios. They discuss what they would say. Willing volunteers demonstrate scenarios with the trainer or in pairs. The whole group observes and gives feedback.

Adult Learning Base Process
Role Play Technique and Speed Dating!
Refer to **Adult Learning Base Process Reference Guide** for more information about this learning process.

Adult Learning Dashboard
This activity links participant's preferred style of learning. The following dashboard provides a quick reference to adult learning theorists and principles as part of the ID9® methodology.

This activity achieves the following level of Bloom's Taxonomy of the Cognitive Domain (Bloom et al 1956), shown with "X" in the following table.

Bloom's Taxonomy of the Cognitive Domain Level					
Knowledge	Comprehension	Application	Analysis	Synthesis	Evaluation
		X			

This activity also achieves a link, shown with "X" in the following table, to participant's naturally occurring learning preferences. Global/Specific, Learning Modalities, Hemispheric Preference (Sperry, 1981), and Multiple Intelligences (Gardner, 1983) are referenced in ID9® methodology and process. This is not a complete list of links that are covered within the ID9® process however this dashboard aims to provide a quick reference for trainers to use to balance instructional design to provide equality for participants' learning preferences.

Global/Specific Learners		Learning Modalities (Sensory Intake)			Hemispheric Preference	
Global	Specific	Visual	Auditory	Kinesthetic	Left Brain	Right Brain
X	X	X	X	X	X	X

Multiple Intelligences								
Visual	Intrapersonal	Interpersonal	Musical	Mathematical/ Logical	Linguistic	Kinesthetic	Naturalist	Existential
X		X	X	X	X	X		

73. All a 'Board

Learning Outcomes
Participants use a commercial board game format to review key points from the course.

Overview
In this example, participants use the "Trivial Pursuit" board game format to review key learning. They use the game board and follow the general games rules. The main difference is the questions have been substituted to review the course.

Start of Day Review Activity	End of Day Review Activity
X	X

In my Experience
This activity uses an existing board game to add visual impact, creativity and variety to a simple set of quiz questions. All the trainer has to do is prepare the questions. The board, the game pieces and the rules (often most difficult and time-consuming to create) are on the shelf and ready to go! To stretch the learning, add a participant-generated category. Participants then write questions that are given to another group.

There are numerous board games that can be converted. These include "Scrabble", "Connect 4", "Snakes and Ladders/ Chutes and Ladders" and "Cluedo". Race games or strategic games tend to work best.

The Hidden Twist
Participants enjoy completing a familiar board game but the questions review course content and key learning.

Essential Data
- Course Type: Any
- Group size: 2-36 (Recommend groups of 4-6, one game board per group)
- Time of day: Start or End of day review
- Pace: Moderate. Speed up by adding a time limit.
- Trainer Preparation Time: 30 minutes
- Activity Duration: 20-30 minutes

Steps to Create
1. Buy "Trivial Pursuit" game boards and pieces – 1 for each group of 4-6 (check online auction sites)
2. Create questions based on content to be reviewed
   a. Ensure questions are in categories – at least 3 categories recommended
3. Assign each color of the board to a question category (double up the colors if only 3 categories)
4. Create a color key for the participants

Steps to Run
1. Provide game board and pieces to each group
2. Hand out new color key
3. Explain the "Trivial Pursuit" Rules – answer questions to "fill the pie"
4. Explain how to win: The person/ pair who complete their pie first. Or whoever has most of their pie filled after the time is up
5. Debrief whole group at the end

Suggested debrief strategy:
- How did the game unfold? (Who won?)
- Were there any difficult/ easy questions? (Which ones?)
- What's your #1 key takeaway?

Working Example
Company Induction
Use the "Trivial Pursuit" board and pieces, along with the following categories:
- Pink & Blue: Company Structure, Vision and Mission
- Brown & Green: Jargon and Acronyms
- Orange: Health and Safety Tips
- Yellow: Company History

Tips, Tricks and Traps
- Board games take a long time! Set a time limit and moderate the level of questions
- Write enough questions to keep everyone going to the end
- Add variety with a General Knowledge or "Joker" section about a completely different topic
- Remember to look for copyright restrictions on board games. For example, using "Trivial Pursuit", call the activity "Fill the Pie"
- Provide a list of questions and answers for the trainer
- Use themed music to start and finish the activity

Variation:
- **Virtual** session, complete one game as a whole group, with virtual teams of participants. The trainer uses one game board which is shown to participants using a webcam. The trainer asks the questions and participants shout out the answers. The trainer moves the pieces for the virtual teams. Consider using an online "roll the dice" app.

Adult Learning Base Process
Quiz/ Board game
Refer to **Adult Learning Base Process Reference**

Guide for more information about this learning process.

Adult Learning Dashboard

This activity links participant's preferred style of learning. The following dashboard provides a quick reference to adult learning theorists and principles as part of the ID9® methodology.

This activity achieves the following level of Bloom's Taxonomy of the Cognitive Domain (Bloom et al 1956), shown with "X" in the following table.

Bloom's Taxonomy of the Cognitive Domain Level					
Knowledge	Comprehension	Application	Analysis	Synthesis	Evaluation
	X				

This activity also achieves a link, shown with "X" in the following table, to participant's naturally occurring learning preferences. Global/Specific, Learning Modalities, Hemispheric Preference (Sperry, 1981), and Multiple Intelligences (Gardner, 1983) are referenced in ID9® methodology and process. This is not a complete list of links that are covered within the ID9® process however this dashboard aims to provide a quick reference for trainers to use to balance instructional design to provide equality for participants' learning preferences.

Global/Specific Learners		Learning Modalities (Sensory Intake)			Hemispheric Preference	
Global	Specific	Visual	Auditory	Kinesthetic	Left Brain	Right Brain
X	X	X	X	X	X	X

Multiple Intelligences								
Visual	Intrapersonal	Interpersonal	Musical	Mathematical/ Logical	Linguistic	Kinesthetic	Naturalist	Existential
X		X	X	X	X	X	X	

74. Find and Seek

Learning Outcomes
Participants solve clues/questions to physically locate information in relation to the course content

Overview
Pairs or small teams are provided with a series of questions or clues. In a treasure/scavenger hunt style, they solve a series of clues or answer questions to locate items or pieces of information. The activity ends once all clues are solved. The correct answers are discussed as a whole group.

Start of Day Review Activity	End of Day Review Activity
X	X

In my Experience
This is a highly kinesthetic and practical activity. It works well for procedural or technical/ systems training, when participants need to navigate around something or locate an item/information. They could be asked to locate information within a report, or a database. They could be identifying different areas or screens within systems or software. Or they could be locating specific tools or information within a document/template, or on a website.

The Hidden Twist
While simply answering review questions or solving clues, participants unconsciously learn to navigate around the item in question. They find paths to locate important information and tools that they will need to use back in the workplace.

Essential Data
- Course Type: Any, particularly good for procedural or technical training
- Group size: 1-40 (Optimal)
- Time of day: Start or End of day review
- Pace: Moderate (Fast if competition is created)
- Trainer Preparation Time: 30 minutes
- Activity Duration: 20-30 minutes

Steps to Create
1. Identify the key information/ actions that participants need to locate/ complete
2. Prepare a clue or question for each point
3. Write each one onto a clue card
4. Prepare an answer sheet for the trainer/ facilitator
5. If using treasure hunt style: on day of course place each clue into an envelope and hide appropriately

Steps to Run
1. Regroup into pairs, trios or small groups
2. Provide each group with a clue sheet, or the first clue
3. Begin the hunt
   a. Participants find the answer to each clue/ question
   b. Return to the room and indicate completion once finished
4. Debrief the answers with the whole group

Suggested Debrief Strategy
Use the following questions:
- How did the hunt go for your group?
- Were there any difficult/ easy clues? (Which ones?)
- How does this activity help you to locate/use this [tool] in the workplace?
- What's one new thing that you've learned from this activity?

Working Example
Budgeting and finance training
After completing training on how to use a new financial report and being shown where to locate relevant supporting documents participants complete the information seeker activity. The clues and questions get them to:

A. Identify different areas of the financial report that need to be completed with specific information
B. Locate supporting tools on the company intranet

Tips, Tricks and Traps:
- To write clues, focus on essential or mandatory information first. Once this is done, if further questions are required, use optional or less critical information.
- To inject some energy at the beginning or end of day, make the hunt competitive – Winners are first team to solve all clues; or those with the highest score
- Think about physical location of the information they need to find. If participants are using computers, where will these be located?
- Play low-volume energetic music in the background during group work (the information hunt)
- Prepare a stretch activity for early finishers
- Provide a list of questions and answers for the trainer to use in the debrief

Variation:
- Clues can be given all at once or sequentially in a treasure hunt format. If there are different levels of importance, clues can be assigned points. Then the objective is to score as many points as possible.

- **Virtual** session, participants solve the clues individually. Or the trainer gives clues one-by-one for the whole group to solve.

Adult Learning Base Process Scavenger Hunt/ Guided research
Refer to **Adult Learning Base Process Reference Guide** for more information about this learning process.

Adult Learning Dashboard

This activity links participant's preferred style of learning. The following dashboard provides a quick reference to adult learning theorists and principles as part of the ID9® methodology.

This activity achieves the following level of Bloom's Taxonomy of the Cognitive Domain (Bloom et al 1956), shown with "X" in the following table.

Bloom's Taxonomy of the Cognitive Domain Level					
Knowledge	Comprehension	Application	Analysis	Synthesis	Evaluation
	X	X			

This activity also achieves a link, shown with "X" in the following table, to participant's naturally occurring learning preferences. Global/Specific, Learning Modalities, Hemispheric Preference (Sperry, 1981), and Multiple Intelligences (Gardner, 1983) are referenced in ID9® methodology and process. This is not a complete list of links that are covered within the ID9® process however this dashboard aims to provide a quick reference for trainers to use to balance instructional design to provide equality for participants' learning preferences.

Global/Specific Learners		Learning Modalities (Sensory Intake)			Hemispheric Preference	
Global	Specific	Visual	Auditory	Kinesthetic	Left Brain	Right Brain
X	X	X	X	X	X	X

Multiple Intelligences								
Visual	Intrapersonal	Interpersonal	Musical	Mathematical/ Logical	Linguistic	Kinesthetic	Naturalist	Existential
X		X	X	X	X	X		

75. Arty-Facts Review

Learning Outcomes
Relate an abstract image to a fact, concept or key learning

Overview
Individuals select a picture card containing an abstract image. They reflect on the course and relate the image to a fact or concept learned. They then present their image, along with the related course fact – thus creating their "Arty-Fact"

Start of Day Review Activity	End of Day Review Activity
X	X

In my Experience
This activity works for many course types. It is particularly good for conceptual training content, such as leadership. The highly visual and creative approach opens up right-brain thinking and creativity for the entire group. The relationship identified between picture and content also gives the trainer insight into the participants' current perception of course topics.

The Hidden Twist
Creating a link from content learnt to a seemingly abstract image significantly deepens the thinking and heightens the learning process.

Essential Data
- Course Type: Any, best for conceptual training content
- Group size: 1-40
- Time of day: Start or End of day review
- Pace: Slow to moderate and reflective
- Trainer Preparation Time: 10-20 minutes
- Activity Duration: 10-20 minutes

Steps to Create
1. Create picture cards containing a selection of different abstract images – see following examples
2. Print each card to minimum A4/US Letter size
3. * Prior to the activity, lay the cards out in the room, ready for participants to select from

Steps to Run
1. Distribute picture cards (either laid out in the room for participants to choose a picture, or randomly distribute one card to each individual)
2. Participants consider their abstract image and relate it to a course fact, concept or key learning.
3. Individuals share their art and fact with the whole group
4. Then stick the picture onto the wall

Suggested Debrief Strategy
- Trainer to summarize at the end, or select from the following questions:
  - What do you notice about the ideas shared?
  - What patterns or repeating themes are there?
  - If you could select another picture, which one would you choose and why?
  - Which idea will you remember most?
  - What questions are raised by this activity?

Working Examples
Leadership training
A participant selects a picture of a pair of spectacles. The relationship is: Leadership is like a pair of glasses because you need clear vision. You sometimes need to switch lenses to see others' perspectives

Communication Skills: A participant selects a picture of a pair of spectacles. The link is: These spectacles represent communication because you need to observe body language during conversations. Also focus on providing clear communication.

Tips, Tricks and Traps
- Obscure or abstract images work better than obvious images
- Use photographs rather than cartoons for a more professional touch
- Once you have a set of picture cards, you can then use them for any course
- Play soft music in the background during the individual work (create arty-fact)

Variation:
- **Virtual session,** images can be provided on slide/whiteboard or in the participant guide

Adult Learning Base Process
Metaphors, Metacognitive Reflection, PLUS Right brain
Refer to **Adult Learning Base Process Reference Guide** for more information about this learning process.

With thanks to Aly Rumbelow

Example Picture Cards:

Adult Learning Dashboard

This activity links participant's preferred style of learning. The following dashboard provides a quick reference to adult learning theorists and principles as part of the ID9® methodology.

This activity achieves the following level of Bloom's Taxonomy of the Cognitive Domain (Bloom et al 1956), shown with "X" in the following table.

Bloom's Taxonomy of the Cognitive Domain Level					
Knowledge	Comprehension	Application	Analysis	Synthesis	Evaluation
			X		

This activity also achieves a link, shown with "X" in the following table, to participant's naturally occurring learning preferences. Global/Specific, Learning Modalities, Hemispheric Preference (Sperry, 1981), and Multiple Intelligences (Gardner, 1983) are referenced in ID9® methodology and process. This is not a complete list of links that are covered within the ID9® process however this dashboard aims to provide a quick reference for trainers to use to balance instructional design to provide equality for participants' learning preferences.

Global/Specific Learners		Learning Modalities (Sensory Intake)			Hemispheric Preference	
Global	Specific	Visual	Auditory	Kinesthetic	Left Brain	Right Brain
X	X	X	X	X	X	X

Multiple Intelligences								
Visual	Intrapersonal	Interpersonal	Musical	Mathematical/ Logical	Linguistic	Kinesthetic	Naturalist	Existential
X	X	X	X	X	X	X	X	

76. Big Deal Story

Learning Outcomes

Participants create a story about course content using abstract picture cards

Overview

Individuals are provided with a set of 3-5 picture cards. Each contains an abstract image. They use the images to create a story which incorporates the key points learned, to this point. They then present their cards and story to the whole group.

Start of Day Review Activity	End of Day Review Activity
X	X

In My Experience

This activity is relatively quick and easy to run. Participants are often surprised by how easily they use the images to generate a story. The varying stories and creative repetition of key messages aids learning and recall.

The Hidden Twist

Using abstract images to create a story about course content unconsciously elevates participants to a higher level of thinking. It adds immense power to the learning process. Sharing different stories about the same content in such a creative way provides reinforcement of memory and recall.

Essential Data

- Course Type: Any
- Group size: 1-40
- Time of day: Start or End of day review
- Pace: Moderate
- Trainer Preparation Time: 10-20 minutes
- Activity Duration: 20-30 minutes

Steps to Create

1. Create/obtain picture cards containing a selection of different abstract images. At least 3 cards per participant.
2. Print each card at similar size to a playing card

Steps to Run

1. Participants are 'dealt' a set of 3-5 picture cards
2. They use the cards to create a story about the course, to this point.
3. Individuals share their story with the whole group. They show corresponding image cards as they go along

Suggested Debrief Strategy

- Trainer to summarize at the end, or select from the following questions:
  - What do you notice about the stories shared?
  - What patterns or repeating themes are there?
  - Which ideas/ story will you remember most?

Working Example
Creative Business Thinking

Using a set of 3-5 picture cards, participants create a story about to the creative business thinking course content. They simultaneously use an additional creative thinking method!

Tips, Tricks and Traps

- Obscure or abstract images work better than obvious images
- Use photographs rather than cartoons for a more professional touch
- Play soft music in the background during individual reflection (create story)
- Commercial cards decks containing abstract images are available for purchase
- Creating your own cards: set up a Word/PowerPoint template which contains 6-8 images to a page
- Once you have a set of picture cards, you can then use them for any course

Variation:
- **Virtual session**, images can be provided on slide/whiteboard, in the participant guide, or sent to individuals as a personalized email attachment

Adult Learning Base Process
Storytelling, Metacognitive Reflection, PLUS Right brain processes
Refer to **Adult Learning Base Process Reference Guide** for more information about this learning process.

Adult Learning Dashboard

This activity links participant's preferred style of learning. The following dashboard provides a quick reference to adult learning theorists and principles as part of the ID9® methodology.

This activity achieves the following level of Bloom's Taxonomy of the Cognitive Domain (Bloom et al 1956), shown with "X" in the following table.

Bloom's Taxonomy of the Cognitive Domain Level					
Knowledge	Comprehension	Application	Analysis	Synthesis	Evaluation
				X	

This activity also achieves a link, shown with "X" in the following table, to participant's naturally occurring learning preferences. Global/Specific, Learning Modalities, Hemispheric Preference (Sperry, 1981), and Multiple Intelligences (Gardner, 1983) are referenced in ID9® methodology and process. This is not a complete list of links that are covered within the ID9® process however this dashboard aims to provide a quick reference for trainers to use to balance instructional design to provide equality for participants' learning preferences.

Global/Specific Learners		Learning Modalities (Sensory Intake)			Hemispheric Preference	
Global	Specific	Visual	Auditory	Kinesthetic	Left Brain	Right Brain
X	X	X	X	X	X	X

Multiple Intelligences								
Visual	Intrapersonal	Interpersonal	Musical	Mathematical/ Logical	Linguistic	Kinesthetic	Naturalist	Existential
X	X	X	X	X	X	X		

77. Top 10

Learning Outcomes
Participants prioritize their top key learning points from the session

Overview
In small groups, participants identify their top priority key learning points, or top tips for success.

Start of Day Review Activity	End of Day Review Activity
X	X

In My Experience
This is an extremely versatile reflection activity which can be used for all course types. It requires minimal trainer preparation. It can be run in under 10 minutes, and unlocks key learning from the session so far. This may include facts, actions, activities, Do's and Don'ts, instructions or skills. This is an interactive way of encouraging participants to reflect and prioritize their learning so far. The top 10 lists can be converted to a useful job aid.

The Hidden Twist
This is a disguised way to review key learning points at the end of a day. The act of prioritizing encourages participants to evaluate all key learning and identify the most valuable/important tips so far.

Essential Data
- Course Type: Any
- Group size: 4-40 (Optimal, for 1-4 participants convert to individual or paired activity)
- Time of day: Start or End of day review
- Pace: Moderate
- Trainer Preparation Time: 5 -20 minutes
- Activity Duration: 10-20 minutes

Steps to Create
1. Obtain blank flipchart paper and pens

Steps to Run
1. Regroup to small groups (3-5 participants)
2. Hand out to each group a blank flipchart and pens
3. Groups brainstorm their key learnings onto flipchart
4. Then prioritize their Top 10
5. Each group presents their top 10 to the whole group

Suggested Debrief Strategy
- Debrief the Top 10 lists
- Then ask questions to compare the priorities
  - Possible debrief questions:
    - How easy was it to prioritize? (If you could add another tip what would it be?)
    - How do your top 10 lists compare to each other?
    - What patterns or repeating themes are there?
    - What items would you "steal" from another group?
- Additional: Individuals to highlight their #1 key learning

Working Examples
New Appraisal Process Training:
- In groups participants list their top 10 key learnings, things to remember or actions about the new appraisal process.

Giving and receiving effective feedback
- Participants are given a "giving and receiving feedback Do's and Don'ts list" as a handout. In groups they review the list and prioritize their top 10. They create their own personalized guidance for giving and receiving feedback.

Tips, Tricks and Traps
- The Top 10 can be reduced to "Super Seven" or "Fantastic Five", even "Top Three"
- Provide stickers to aid prioritization through voting
- To incorporate Musical Intelligence add a music chart countdown theme and matching sounds, E.g. "Top of the Pops". Then conduct the debrief using this countdown style.
- Use as an end of day review. Convert the top 10 lists to a job aid. Provide the job aid as the next start of day activity. Ask participants, on further reflection, what would they add or change on the list?

Variations:
- The trainer provides a list of key learning points/ do's and don'ts as a handout (one per participant) or on giant flipchart (one per group). Participants prioritize their top 10 from this list.
- Virtual session, the top 10 lists can be created individually in the participant guide, or as a whole group on a slide/whiteboard

Adult Learning Base Process
Metacognitive
Refer to **Adult Learning Base Process Reference Guide** for more information about this learning process.

Adult Learning Dashboard

This activity links participant's preferred style of learning. The following dashboard provides a quick reference to adult learning theorists and principles as part of the ID9® methodology.

This activity achieves the following level of Bloom's Taxonomy of the Cognitive Domain (Bloom et al 1956), shown with "X" in the following table.

Bloom's Taxonomy of the Cognitive Domain Level					
Knowledge	Comprehension	Application	Analysis	Synthesis	Evaluation
	X				

This activity also achieves a link, shown with "X" in the following table, to participant's naturally occurring learning preferences. Global/Specific, Learning Modalities, Hemispheric Preference (Sperry, 1981), and Multiple Intelligences (Gardner, 1983) are referenced in ID9® methodology and process. This is not a complete list of links that are covered within the ID9® process however this dashboard aims to provide a quick reference for trainers to use to balance instructional design to provide equality for participants' learning preferences.

Global/Specific Learners		Learning Modalities (Sensory Intake)			Hemispheric Preference	
Global	Specific	Visual	Auditory	Kinesthetic	Left Brain	Right Brain
X	X	X	X	X	X	(X)

Multiple Intelligences								
Visual	Intrapersonal	Interpersonal	Musical	Mathematical/ Logical	Linguistic	Kinesthetic	Naturalist	Existential
X	X	X	X	X	X	X		

78. Match-Maker

Learning Outcomes
Participants define key terms or steps/stages from the course content

Overview
Each participant is given a card containing either a definition or a term from the course. As a whole group, participants interact to find the card that matches theirs. In doing so, they define key terms from the course.

Start of Day Review Activity	End of Day Review Activity
X	

In My Experience
This is simple and easy-to-run. It is based on the versatile "definition match" format. It ensures that participants know the definitions of important terms used during course. Or they can define steps of a process or model. It works well as a start of day review activity for many course types. It also doubles up as an icebreaker and connects participants to the course content. If terminology, definitions, processes or steps are involved in your training topic, this is the kind of easy yet powerful activity to keep in mind.

The Hidden Twist
Although they are completing one single step of a humble definition match, participants have to interact with many others to find their match. Thus, they review many terms and definitions along the way.

Essential Data
- Course Type: Any
- Group size: 6-20 (Optimal. For 1-6 participants give each participant more than one card, or switch to written format)
- Time of day: Start of Day Review (for multi-day or multi-session course)
- Pace: Moderate
- Trainer Preparation Time: 10-20 minutes
- Activity Duration: 5-15 minutes

Steps to Create
1. Choose up to 10 key terms. Write definitions for each one.
2. Create cards in 2 colors – one color for terms and one for definitions
3. Create an answer sheet for the trainer

Steps to Run
1. Hand out Terms and Definitions cards randomly to participants until all are distributed
2. Each participant should have at least one card
3. Participants find the person who has the term or definition which matches theirs
4. Once they have found their match, they stay together
5. Optional: If participants with >1 card to match: write their names on matching cards. They stick them onto the wall, and then continue with their next match.
6. Once everyone has made their match, each pair reads out their term and definition and responds to one debrief question (see debrief strategy)
7. If the match is correct, then further questioning and discussion can take place with the whole group. This adds depth to the learning.

Suggested Debrief Strategy
- Debrief each pair with the whole group
- Select from the following questions:
  - 'Where might you see this term?'
  - 'Who is likely to use this term?'
  - 'When might you use this term?'
  - 'Why is it important to know this definition?'
  - Ask further 'why' and 'what if' type questions to add depth to the learning

Working Example
Basic PowerPoint Training
- Term cards contain PowerPoint features with an associated icon, such as "Styles" and "View". Definitions cards describe what each feature is used for.

Communication skills - communication roadblocks
- Term cards contain different communication roadblocks. Definitions cards define each roadblock and give a practical example

Tips, Tricks and Traps
- This activity can be used for terms and definitions, defining acronyms, parts and descriptions, steps and associated actions, coaching models and example questions, etc.
- Play soft music in the background during the pairing up activity
- Provide a list of answers for the trainer to use in the debrief
- To quickly create the cards: Use glossaries found in reference manuals, participant workbooks, books and other course development aids

Variation:
- Once matched, pairs can add some further information to the definition card. E.g. Communication roadblocks – identify a strategy for overcoming this / PowerPoint Training – identify a tip or trap
- Virtual session, convert to on-screen with whole group. Or complete individually in the participant guide.

Adult Learning Base Process
Definition match – strongly kinesthetic
Refer to **Adult Learning Base Process Reference Guide** for more information about this learning process.

Adult Learning Dashboard

This activity links participant's preferred style of learning. The following dashboard provides a quick reference to adult learning theorists and principles as part of the ID9® methodology.

This activity achieves the following level of Bloom's Taxonomy of the Cognitive Domain (Bloom et al 1956), shown with "X" in the following table.

Bloom's Taxonomy of the Cognitive Domain Level					
Knowledge	Comprehension	Application	Analysis	Synthesis	Evaluation
X					

This activity also achieves a link, shown with "X" in the following table, to participant's naturally occurring learning preferences. Global/Specific, Learning Modalities, Hemispheric Preference (Sperry, 1981), and Multiple Intelligences (Gardner, 1983) are referenced in ID9® methodology and process. This is not a complete list of links that are covered within the ID9® process however this dashboard aims to provide a quick reference for trainers to use to balance instructional design to provide equality for participants' learning preferences.

Global/Specific Learners		Learning Modalities (Sensory Intake)			Hemispheric Preference	
Global	Specific	Visual	Auditory	Kinesthetic	Left Brain	Right Brain
X	X	X	X	X	X	X

Multiple Intelligences								
Visual	Intrapersonal	Interpersonal	Musical	Mathematical/ Logical	Linguistic	Kinesthetic	Naturalist	Existential
X		X	X	X	X	X		

79. Fast Five with Bonus Bank

Learning Outcomes
Participants answer questions to review key points from the course

Overview
A review quiz with a difference! Small groups (or individuals) "buzz in" and answer questions to score points. After answering a question correctly, they then gain control of a 'bonus' question. The bonus is a more detailed follow up question.

Start of Day Review Activity	End of Day Review Activity
X	X

In My Experience
This is a short duration start or end of day review. It can be a whole group shout out, with individuals keeping their own scores, or a competitive paired or small group activity.

The Hidden Twist
Not only is this a fast and creative way to ask review questions. The bonus questions add depth and detail. They heighten the learning experience.

Essential Data
- Course Type: Any
- Group size: 1-40
- Time of day: Start or End of day review
- Pace: Moderate to fast
- Trainer Preparation Time: 30 minutes
- Activity Duration: 10-15 minutes

Steps to Create
1. Create 5 questions to review key learning from the course, to this point
2. For each question, write a more in-depth bonus question. This is a direct follow-on question or could introduce a practical scenario for participants to consider.
3. Optional: Write each question and bonus onto PowerPoint slide/ flipchart
4. Optional: Obtain buzzers/ noisemakers

Steps to Run
1. Regroup to teams of 2-4 (or run as a whole group shout out)
2. Explain the rules and scoring
   a. Shout out/buzz in to answer the question
   b. First with correct answer gets control of the bonus
   c. 1 point for a correct answer
   d. Minus 1 point for an incorrect answer
3. Display each question in turn
4. Participants shout out/buzz in to answer
5. Debrief the answer and award/deduct 1 point
6. Then ask bonus question to the person/ team who gained control
7. Award/ deduct a bonus point according to their answer

Suggested Debrief Strategy
- Debrief answers at the time they are given
- Note specific gaps in learning and ensure gaps are filled before moving on
- Ask: What quiz question do you remember most and why?

Working Example
Coaching skills training
Questions review stages of the coaching conversation model used. For example "Expand and Focus" or "GROW". The bonuses are true/false questions about different example questions that can be used at each stage of the model.

Tips, Tricks and Traps
- To be quick, make bonus questions true or false or multiple choice
- To run a longer, deeper review, make bonus questions open-ended
- Use quiz-themed music to start and finish the activity; sound effects for right and wrong answers may also be appropriate
- Provide a list of answers for the trainer to debrief (include an image of any relevant model for easy reference)
- Tricks to ensure all participants remain engaged during bonus questions:
  o Involve all participants in confirming whether the bonus answers given are correct or not
  o Set a time limit for answering bonus questions
  o Announce that bonus questions can be "stolen" by others when an incorrect answer is given

- If available, an interactive response system can be used in place of the buzzers or shout out

Variation:
Virtual session, run in exactly the same way

Adult Learning Base Process
Quiz/ Review Questions
Refer to **Adult Learning Base Process Reference Guide** for more information about this learning process.

Adult Learning Dashboard

This activity links participant's preferred style of learning. The following dashboard provides a quick reference to adult learning theorists and principles as part of the ID9® methodology.

This activity achieves the following level of Bloom's Taxonomy of the Cognitive Domain (Bloom et al 1956), shown with "X" in the following table.

Bloom's Taxonomy of the Cognitive Domain Level					
Knowledge	Comprehension	Application	Analysis	Synthesis	Evaluation
X					

This activity also achieves a link, shown with "X" in the following table, to participant's naturally occurring learning preferences. Global/Specific, Learning Modalities, Hemispheric Preference (Sperry, 1981), and Multiple Intelligences (Gardner, 1983) are referenced in ID9® methodology and process. This is not a complete list of links that are covered within the ID9® process however this dashboard aims to provide a quick reference for trainers to use to balance instructional design to provide equality for participants' learning preferences.

Global/Specific Learners		Learning Modalities (Sensory Intake)			Hemispheric Preference	
Global	Specific	Visual	Auditory	Kinesthetic	Left Brain	Right Brain
X	X	X	X	X	X	X

Multiple Intelligences								
Visual	Intrapersonal	Interpersonal	Musical	Mathematical/ Logical	Linguistic	Kinesthetic	Naturalist	Existential
X	X	X	X	X	X	X		

80. Quick Fire Finale

Learning Outcomes

Participants answer questions to review key points from the course, to this point

Overview

In competition with each other, individuals or teams "buzz in" to answer questions and score points. Another twist on a competitive quiz review!

Start of Day Review Activity	End of Day Review Activity
	X

In My Experience

This activity is easy to prepare and run. It can be useful for any course type. It injects pace, to finish the day with a flourish! Run this as a whole group shout out, with participants keeping their own scores. Or run as an individual, paired or small group activity.

The Hidden Twist

Participants answer simple review questions but in a fast-paced, interactive and competitive way.

Essential Data

- Course Type: Any
- Group size: 6-40 (Optimal. For 1-6 participants adjust to pairs or individual activity)
- Time of day: End of day review (Remove competition for start of day activity)
- Pace: Fast and competitive
- Trainer Preparation Time: 15-30 minutes
- Activity Duration: 5-15 minutes

Steps to Create

1. Create 5-10 quiz questions (Refer to learning objectives)
2. Write 1 question onto each slide/ flipchart
3. Optional: Obtain noisemakers or buzzers
4. Optional: Obtain a suitable prize

Steps to Run

1. Regroup into small groups (of 3-4 per group)
2. Each group creates a team name. They also identify a word they can shout, or noise they will use to "buzz in"
3. While teams decide, the trainer prepares a Scorecard flipchart – see following example
   a. Write each team name in a grid format
4. Quiz begins!
5. Trainer asks each question in turn
6. The first team to buzz in (shout team word or make team noise) and give the correct answer scores 1 point
   a. Giving an incorrect answer loses 1 point
7. Trainer keeps scores on the scorecard
8. At the end, the team with the highest score wins
9. Optional: Award a prize to the winners

Example Scorecard:

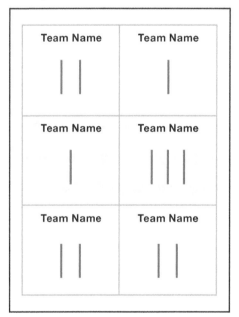

Suggested Debrief Strategy

- Debrief answers at the time they are given
- Note specific gaps in learning and ensure gaps are filled before moving on
- Ask: What's your #1 key learning?

Working Example
Sales Training 101

Uses 5-10 questions which review the core concepts of the sales training that day.

Advanced Microsoft Word

Uses 5-10 questions which review the main advanced features and actions for using MS Word

Tips, Tricks and Traps
- Use a combination of multiple choice, true/ false, fill the gap and/ or open-ended questions
- Provide a list of answers for the trainer to debrief
- Use quiz-themed music to start and finish the activity; sound effects for right and wrong answers may also be appropriate
- If available, an interactive response system can be used in place of the buzzers or shout out

Variation:
- Virtual session, run as whole group shout out or individual activity. Individuals can type answers into the chat feature. Alternatively individuals can be assigned to virtual teams and shout out answers to score points for their team.

Adult Learning Base Process
Quiz/ Review Questions
Refer to **Adult Learning Base Process Reference Guide** for more information about this learning process.

Adult Learning Dashboard

This activity links participant's preferred style of learning. The following dashboard provides a quick reference to adult learning theorists and principles as part of the ID9® methodology.

This activity achieves the following level of Bloom's Taxonomy of the Cognitive Domain (Bloom et al 1956), shown with "X" in the following table.

Bloom's Taxonomy of the Cognitive Domain Level					
Knowledge	Comprehension	Application	Analysis	Synthesis	Evaluation
X					

This activity also achieves a link, shown with "X" in the following table, to participant's naturally occurring learning preferences. Global/Specific, Learning Modalities, Hemispheric Preference (Sperry, 1981), and Multiple Intelligences (Gardner, 1983) are referenced in ID9® methodology and process. This is not a complete list of links that are covered within the ID9® process however this dashboard aims to provide a quick reference for trainers to use to balance instructional design to provide equality for participants' learning preferences.

Global/Specific Learners		Learning Modalities (Sensory Intake)			Hemispheric Preference	
Global	Specific	Visual	Auditory	Kinesthetic	Left Brain	Right Brain
X	X	X	X	X	X	X

Multiple Intelligences								
Visual	Intrapersonal	Interpersonal	Musical	Mathematical/ Logical	Linguistic	Kinesthetic	Naturalist	Existential
X		X	X	X	X	X		

Chapter 6:
During Course: Review Activities - End of Course

(Major Reviews)

Aly Rumbelow

About the Co-Author:

Aly Rumbelow

Aly is currently a Senior Learning & Development Manager at Amgen Ltd, a Global Biotechnology Company, where she forms part of the leadership of a global team of training professionals. She provides technical expertise and mentoring across the team and business. She is passionate about instructional design, interactive virtual training, new training technology and adult learning methodology.

In the 15 years that she has worked in the training environment, Aly has become an expert in the field of internal performance consulting and instructional design. She has designed and delivered high impact training programs to hundreds of corporate professionals and is known for her motivation and energy!

Chapter Introduction

Hello!

I am delighted to see you turn to Chapter 6 – the chapter that provides you with details of a number of tried and tested examples of end of course review activities.

One of the most essential activities within a training course is the end of course review. The end of course review activity is in place to assess whether your participants have met the learning objectives set out at the beginning of the course. It helps the trainer to "know that they know". The end of course review activity, also known as the Major Review, is your last chance to get your participants to a level where they can apply their learning back in the workplace, and help them do this in a safe environment. As soon as they walk out of your door, they will be expected to apply what they have learned.

End of course review activities are conducted just before the course summary, evaluation and close. If the training course is conducted over a number of days, then an end of day review should take place at the end of each day (see previous chapter). However, many of these end of course review activities presented in this chapter may also be used as end of day reviews. The longer the course duration,

the longer the review activity should take. Typically, in a one-day training program the end of course review activity takes approximately 30 minutes, however depending on the complexity of the program the end of course review activity could take longer.

In my experience, and according to the ID9® process, trainers should never leave an end of course review activity out of your course – if you are short for time, and then cut the course content NOT the end of course review!

In this chapter, I have ordered the activities by pace, starting with the slow and focused end of course activities, moving through to moderate, fast and ending in highly competitive activities.

Enjoy!

Aly Rumbelow

81. Checklist Charlie

Learning Outcomes
Participants are able to review the content of the topics covered and create a checklist of activities that need to be considered before using these topics back in the workplace.

Overview
This end of course review activity takes individual topics from the course content and helps participants to summarize the content. These items are then written up as a checklist which can be taken away and made use of in the future.

In My Experience
This is an extremely successful way of summarizing all the content covered within the training course. Participants work together in teams to create a separate checklist for each of the topics covered during the course.

The Hidden Twist
Not only do the participants review the course content within their groups but they also create a handy checklist that can be used in the future.

Essential Data
Course Type: Any courses covering up to 3 main topics that can be summarized as a checklist, e.g. how to prepare, deliver and evaluate a training session.
Group Size: 6-18
Time of Day: End of course review
Pace: Slow & focused
Time to Create: 5 mins
Activity Duration: 30 mins

Steps to Create
1. Design a blank A4 checklist template and add the topic title at the top of the table. Insert the following question to the top of the checklist "What is it that I need to do in order to achieve the topic", e.g. Prepare for a training session (see figure 1. below)
2. Repeat this for all topics covered during the course.
3. Print out all topic checklists, one per participant.

Sample Checklist

Checklist

Preparation	Complete

Steps to Run
1. Hand out each checklist to all participants.
2. Explain the rules:
   a. On the appropriate checklist, you will need to summarize the main course topic by listing the main ideas.
   b. You can use the course materials to help you and you can work in your group.
   c. You have 15 minutes to complete all of the checklists.
   d. After 15 minutes, I will ask for a volunteer from each table to present back on one of the topics. (5 minutes per topic).
3. Recommendation: While the participants are completing their checklists, play music softly in the background to aid concentration.

Debrief
1. While each group presents back on their topic, encourage the other groups to compare with their own checklist and add any additional items that are identified.
2. Once the topic has been presented back, ask the participants if they have any other items that were not mentioned so that the rest of the group can update their checklists further.
3. The trainer can encourage the participants to think more deeply by asking questions such as: If you didn't do X, what would happen?

Working Example
Conceptual - Train the Trainer
In this example, this one day training course covers preparation, delivery and evaluation of training. The participants are split into the three separate groups and look through all the content covered during the course in order to create 3 separate checklists; one checklist for things to do when preparing training, one checklist for things to do when delivering training, and one checklist for things to do when evaluating training. Each group presents back on one of the topics while the other teams review their checklist and add to it as appropriate.

Tips, Tricks & Traps
- Make sure that there is enough content in each topic to make up a checklist
- Keep to time! Do not go over the 15 mins to prepare the checklists and keep the debriefs brief! (max 5 minutes)
- Make the items on the checklist concise (no more than 6 words)
- While creating the checklists, the trainer should circulate each group to ensure that they are on the right track.
- Ask each of the participants to complete the checklists. If they don't – they won't have anything to take away with them!

Adult Learning Base Process – Metacognitive Reflection
Refer to **Adult Learning Base Process Reference Guide** for more information about this learning process.

Adult Learning Dashboard

This activity links participant's preferred style of learning. The following dashboard provides a quick reference to adult learning theorists and principles as part of the ID9® methodology.

This activity achieves the following level of Bloom's Taxonomy of the Cognitive Domain (Bloom et al 1956), shown with "X" in the following table.

Bloom's Taxonomy of the Cognitive Domain Level					
Knowledge	Comprehension	Application	Analysis	Synthesis	Evaluation
		X			

This activity also achieves a link, shown with "X" in the following table, to participant's naturally occurring learning preferences. Global/Specific, Learning Modalities, Hemispheric Preference (Sperry, 1981), and Multiple Intelligences (Gardner, 1983) are referenced in ID9® methodology and process. This is not a complete list of links that are covered within the ID9® process however this dashboard aims to provide a quick reference for trainers to use to balance instructional design to provide equality for participants' learning preferences.

Global/Specific Learners		Learning Modalities (Sensory Intake)			Hemispheric Preference	
Global	Specific	Visual	Auditory	Kinesthetic	Left Brain	Right Brain
X	X	X	X	X	X	

Multiple Intelligences								
Visual	Intrapersonal	Interpersonal	Musical	Mathematical/ Logical	Linguistic	Kinesthetic	Naturalist	Existential
X		X	X	X	X	X		

82. Steps to Success

Learning Outcomes
Participants are able to communicate the steps necessary to move from the present state to the desired state.

Overview
This end of course review activity encourages participants to pick out the main areas of focus from the course content which will help them to achieve the "desired" state. Each area of focus needs to build on the next.

During the activity, participants are asked to consider their emotions and feelings when they are in the present, "undesired" state and then how it feels when they imagine themselves in the "desired" state. These "emotionally charged" feelings help participants to realize success.

In My Experience
Due to the nature of this Adult Learning Base Process, a number of adult learning principles are incorporated within this activity which leads to a more in-depth review. The activity works best when participants have a significant difference between their present state and the desired state.

The Hidden Twist
Participants will be summarizing the course content as well as creating a step-by-step process of how to get to the desired state.

Essential Data
Course Type: Conceptual courses, e.g. Change Management and courses that follow a specific process where each new step builds upon the last.
Group Size: Any group size
Time of Day: End of course review
Pace: Slow & focused
Time to Create: 5 mins
Activity Duration: 20 mins

Steps to Create
1. Create the activity instructions and add to the Participant guide and/or a slide
2. Provide Post-it® notes

Steps to Run
1. The trainer asks the participants to remember a time when they were in the "undesired" state and ask them to reflect on how it felt to them.
2. The trainer then "breaks the state" an NLP term for cutting those thoughts. The trainer could ask the group to clear their minds and imagine a room of pure white, for example.
3. Now the trainer asks the participants to imagine themselves in the "desired" state. After 20 seconds or so, the trainer asks the participants to consider, introspectively "What are you feelings right now?"
4. Working individually, the participants review the course material covered and consider what will need to be implemented, the steps that will need to be take place in order to get to that "desired" state.
5. Now the participants must capture these steps on individual Post-it® notes and place the steps into the correct order.
6. Participants have 10 minutes to complete the process steps.

Debrief
1. After 10 minutes, the trainer asks participants to share their own steps with a partner
2. The pairs should then discuss the similarities and differences between their own steps and process. (5 mins)
3. The trainer should then ask for a volunteer from the group to share their "Steps to Success". (5 mins)

Working Example
Conceptual - Effective Communication
In this program participants who are struggling to communicate effectively to customers, teams or individuals have to introspectively consider what it looks like from the outside and how it feels to struggle to communicate. The trainer then breaks the state – asks participants to clear their minds of those thoughts, and now asks the group to introspectively consider and visualize themselves as being a great communicator. What does it look like and what does it feel like? Again, the trainer breaks the state and then asks the group to think about the logical steps that will need to be put in place in order to get to that desired place – being that great communicator. Each step will have been covered within the course content, and therefore, a review of the course content will be necessary to identify these steps.

Tips, Tricks & Traps
- Make sure that the course content follows a natural process for getting to the desired state
- The maximum number of steps should be 5.
- Circulate around the group to ensure that the participants are on the right track.

Adult Learning Base Process – NLP Future State
Refer to **Adult Learning Base Process Reference Guide** for more information about this learning process.

Adult Learning Dashboard

This activity links participant's preferred style of learning. The following dashboard provides a quick reference to adult learning theorists and principles as part of the ID9® methodology.

This activity achieves the following level of Bloom's Taxonomy of the Cognitive Domain (Bloom et al 1956), shown with "X" in the following table.

Bloom's Taxonomy of the Cognitive Domain Level					
Knowledge	Comprehension	Application	Analysis	Synthesis	Evaluation
			X		

This activity also achieves a link, shown with "X" in the following table, to participant's naturally occurring learning preferences. Global/Specific, Learning Modalities, Hemispheric Preference (Sperry, 1981), and Multiple Intelligences (Gardner, 1983) are referenced in ID9® methodology and process. This is not a complete list of links that are covered within the ID9® process however this dashboard aims to provide a quick reference for trainers to use to balance instructional design to provide equality for participants' learning preferences.

Global/Specific Learners		Learning Modalities (Sensory Intake)			Hemispheric Preference	
Global	Specific	Visual	Auditory	Kinesthetic	Left Brain	Right Brain
X		X	X	X	X	X

Multiple Intelligences								
Visual	Intrapersonal	Interpersonal	Musical	Mathematical/ Logical	Linguistic	Kinesthetic	Naturalist	Existential
X	X	X		X	X	X		

83. SWOB Analysis

Learning Outcomes

Participants review the course topics and are able to identify their own strengths and weaknesses with respect to the course content, analyze the opportunities and barriers to applying the learning back in the workplace and create a prioritized action plan.

Overview

During this end of course review activity, participants are able to classify, for each course topic the following:

Their personal strengths and weaknesses with the subject matter, any opportunities that can be gained from applying their newly acquired knowledge, skills and attitudes as well as determining an action plan to overcome any external barriers.

Using the SWOB Analysis Tool, (see fig. 2), participants populate the quadrants. Once done, they formulate a prioritized action plan by completing the Opportunities & Barriers Action Plan below.
(See fig. 3).

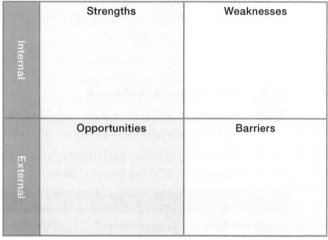

	Strengths	Weaknesses
Internal		
External	Opportunities	Barriers

Fig 2

What are my Opportunities for applying this learning at work?	What Actions do I need to take forward?	By When? (date for prioritizing)

What are my Barriers to applying this learning at work?	What Actions do I need to take forward?	By When? (date for prioritizing)

Fig 3

In My Experience

This is a focused and deep thinking end of course review. It uses higher-order reflection and helps participants to clearly see what to apply, when to apply it and how it should be applied back in the workplace.

The Hidden Twist

Participants not only review the course topics, but are able to personalize what their newly acquired knowledge, skills & attitudes mean for them. They also leave the course with a prioritized Personal Action Plan.

Essential Data

Course Type: Any
Group Size: Any
Time of Day: End of course Review
Pace: Slow & focused
Time to Create: 20-30 minutes
Activity Duration: 30-45 minutes

Steps to Create

1. Create a "SWOB Analysis" hand-out. Position the SWOB Analysis Tool (See Fig. 1) on the front of the document and then place the Opportunities & Barriers Action Plan Tool (see Fig. 2) on the reverse side of the document.
2. Make sure that both tools are large enough so that participants have enough space to complete them.
3. Multiply the number of topics by the number of participants and print. Each participant will need one hand-out per course topic.

Steps to Run

1. The Trainer hands out the SWOB Analysis and Opportunities & Barriers Action Plan Tool – one copy per topic covered in the course.
2. Next they explain the tool and how it is used:
   a. On the front side of the document you will see a SWOB Analysis tool. This is like a SWOT analysis, but instead of the T – Threats, we are using the word Barriers, thus SWOB and not SWOT.
   b. Complete the SWOB Analysis Tool.
   c. For the first course topic, write your personal strengths and weaknesses in the top two quadrants. What you do well and what you may need to practice, review or research further.
   d. Now move down to complete the opportunities quadrant. Here you need to consider what this new learning provides you as far as opportunities within your role, team, company etc.
   e. Now consider any Barriers that you may come across for applying this new learning within the said topic, for example, what is it that prevents you from implementing these new learnings? Now add these to the barriers quadrant.
   f. Once you have completed the SWOB analysis tool, turn the page over and complete the Opportunities & Barriers Action Plan Tool.
   g. Here you will transpose the opportunities & barriers from your SWOB tool, and consider what actions you will need to implement in order to take those opportunities forward and what you will need to do to overcome the identified barriers.
   h. You must also provide a date for implementation so that you can prioritize your actions.

3. Participants are then given 30 minutes to complete as many of the course topics / forms as they can.
4. Recommendation: As the participants are completing the activity, play music softly in the background to enhance the concentration.
5. As the review activity is taking place, the trainer must be available to answer any queries the participants may have.

Debrief

1. After 30 minutes, the trainer then asks the group "What have you learnt by developing this SWOB Analysis and Opportunities & Barriers Action Plan Tool?
2. Next, the trainer asks for a volunteer to share one of their SWOB Analyses with the rest of the group.
3. The trainer asks: Now thinking about those barriers that you have identified, what is your next step? What will you propose to overcome these barriers?
4. Now the trainer asks for another volunteer to share one of their SWOB Analyses and asks them to share what they have outlined in their Action Plan for one of their opportunities.

Working Example
Conceptual – Time Management
The topics for this one day instructor-led course could be:

- Prioritization
- Goal Setting
- Keeping Focus
- Self-Motivation

The review activity for this course would be to populate a SWOB Analysis and create a prioritized Opportunities & Barriers Action Plan for each topic.

Below is an example for the 2nd Topic above: Goal Setting.

	Strengths	Weaknesses
Internal	• I can use the SMART process for goal creation, (learnt today in the course) • I am able to turn my goals into specific tasks • I discuss my goals with other members of the team	• I tend to lose attention on long term goals. • I get easily distracted due to "fighting fires" • I miss the detail on some tasks resulting sometimes in a missed goal
	Opportunities	**Barriers**
External	• Our team now has a common language for creating SMART goals - making communication easier • We will be able to prioritize our goals more effectivelly • Team can be rewarded for a goal achievement	• Some team members may not be committed to the goals • Other departments are not on board with the goals

What are my Opportunities for applying this learning at work?	What Actions do I need to take forward?	By When? (date for prioritizing)
Our team now has a common language for creating SMART goals making communication easier	Ensure SMART Goal creation takes place in the goal setting process for next yeaer	1st November
Team can be rewarded for goal achievement	Set up a meeting with HR to discuss reward options	1st October

What are my Barriers to applying this learning at work?	What Actions do I need to take forward?	By When? (date for prioritizing)
Some team members may not be committed to the goals	Set up a separate team meeting to discuss the benefits of goal setting and involve the whole team in the goal setting process	10th October
Other departments are not on board with using SMART to create goals	Communicate the benefits & opportunities of creating SMART goals to the other department heads. Try to encourage bring this into company culture	1st October

Tips, Tricks & Traps

Consider using an example of a completed SWOB Analysis and Opportunities & Barriers Action Plan to show how to best complete the activity. Make sure that your instructions are clear when explaining how to use the tools.

Adult Learning Base Process – SWOT Analysis

Refer to **Adult Learning Base Process Reference Guide** for more information about this learning process.

Adult Learning Dashboard

This activity links participant's preferred style of learning. The following dashboard provides a quick reference to adult learning theorists and principles as part of the ID9® methodology.

This activity achieves the following level of Bloom's Taxonomy of the Cognitive Domain (Bloom et al 1956), shown with "X" in the following table.

Bloom's Taxonomy of the Cognitive Domain Level					
Knowledge	Comprehension	Application	Analysis	Synthesis	Evaluation
				X	

This activity also achieves a link, shown with "X" in the following table, to participant's naturally occurring learning preferences. Global/Specific, Learning Modalities, Hemispheric Preference (Sperry, 1981), and Multiple Intelligences (Gardner, 1983) are referenced in ID9® methodology and process. This is not a complete list of links that are covered within the ID9® process however this dashboard aims to provide a quick reference for trainers to use to balance instructional design to provide equality for participants' learning preferences.

Global/Specific Learners		Learning Modalities (Sensory Intake)			Hemispheric Preference	
Global	Specific	Visual	Auditory	Kinesthetic	Left Brain	Right Brain
X	X	X	X	X	X	X

Multiple Intelligences								
Visual	Intrapersonal	Interpersonal	Musical	Mathematical/ Logical	Linguistic	Kinesthetic	Naturalist	Existential
X	X	X	X	X	X	X	X	

84. Analyze & Optimize

Learning Outcomes
The participants complete an Analysis Table that they use to analyze whether their learning can be immediately applied back in the workplace. If their answer is YES, they construct a list of opportunities that this may have; if NO, they complete an Action Plan to help overcome these challenges.

Overview
During this end of course review activity, participants review the content covered in each course topic. They create a list of items they have learnt during the training course and then categorize them as to whether they can immediately implement this learning back in the workplace. If they can, they consider what opportunities and challenges may come up during the implementation stage.

In My Experience
This is a higher-order review activity, challenging the participants to evaluate their learning from the course in a structured and focused manner.

The Hidden Twist
Participants leave the course with a list of activities that they have learnt within the training course as well as a strategy for how to implement these learnings back in the workplace.

Essential Data
Course Type: Any
Group Size: Any
Time of Day: End of Course Review
Pace: Slow & Focused
Time to Create: 20 minutes
Activity Duration: 30-45 minutes

Steps to Create
1. Design an Analysis Table and an Action Plan. (see figs. 4 & 5)
2. Create a hand-out with the Analysis table at the top and the Action plan underneath.
3. Multiply the number of topics by the number of participants and print off that number. Each participant will need one hand-out per course topic.

Steps to Run
1. Distribute the hand-outs to all participants (one per topic)
2. Explain the rules:
   a. Using one Analysis Table per topic, list the learnings that you have taken from the course.
   b. Analyze whether you will be able to immediately implement this learning back in the workplace.
   c. If you can, then put a YES in column 2.
   d. Now move to the Opportunities column and write up what opportunities might arise further to this implementation.
   e. If you are unable to immediately implement this learning back in the workplace, put a NO in column 2.
   f. Now move to column 4 and list the challenges that you face that are preventing you from implementing this learning.
   g. Next, produce an action plan that will articulate how to overcome these challenges.
   h. You have 30 minutes to complete your first topic hand-out.
3. As the participants are completing the activity, play music softly in the background to enhance the concentration.

Topic Name			
What have I learnt	Am I able to apply this back in the Workplace Y / N	If YES: What Opportunities may arise	If NO: What Challenges will I need to overcome

Fig. 4

Topic Name	Action Plan	
What is my challenge?	What do I need to Implement in order to overcome this challenge?	When will I do this by?

Fig. 5

Debrief

1. The trainer asks for a volunteer to share one of their Learnings that gave rise to an opportunity.
2. The trainer asks why and what if questions to deepen the learning and provide clarity.
3. The trainer now asks for a volunteer to share one of their learnings that they will not be able to immediately implement back in the workplace.
4. The trainer says "Now thinking about that challenge that you have identified, what is your next step? What do you propose to overcome this challenge?"

Working Example
Conceptual – Communicating Effectively

For this Communicating Effectively training course, the topics covered are: Listening Skills, Presentation Skills, Using Positive Body Language and the Do's and Don'ts of email.

For each of those topics, participants look through their course materials and note down all the things that they have learnt, e.g., for listening skills the participant has learnt that in order to listen actively, they need to look at the person speaking, use affirmative body language and then paraphrase what they have just heard. Now the participant puts a YES in the column to state that they can immediately put this into practice back in the workplace.

For the next topic, presenting clearly, the participant has put a NO in the column to identify that they will not be able to use the newly acquired knowledge and skills for presenting immediately back in the workplace. The challenge is that currently in their role, they do not have the opportunity to deliver presentations.

Here, the participant now moves to the Action Plan, enters presentation Skills as the Topic Name, and lists the challenge as "No opportunity to present". In the next column, the participant writes, speak to my manager and ask if I can present my current project at the next team meeting, and follows this with a date of next week in the right hand column.

Tips, Tricks & Traps

Keep to time. The participants will need to complete the hand-outs for all topics. The trainer must therefore ask them to complete the remaining topics as a post-course review activity. (See chapter 8 for additional post-course review activities).

Adult Learning Base Process – Action Plan

Refer to **Adult Learning Base Process Reference Guide** for more information about this learning process.

Adult Learning Dashboard

This activity links participant's preferred style of learning. The following dashboard provides a quick reference to adult learning theorists and principles as part of the ID9® methodology.

This activity achieves the following level of Bloom's Taxonomy of the Cognitive Domain (Bloom et al 1956), shown with "X" in the following table.

Bloom's Taxonomy of the Cognitive Domain Level					
Knowledge	Comprehension	Application	Analysis	Synthesis	Evaluation
				X	

This activity also achieves a link, shown with "X" in the following table, to participant's naturally occurring learning preferences. Global/Specific, Learning Modalities, Hemispheric Preference (Sperry, 1981), and Multiple Intelligences (Gardner, 1983) are referenced in ID9® methodology and process. This is not a complete list of links that are covered within the ID9® process however this dashboard aims to provide a quick reference for trainers to use to balance instructional design to provide equality for participants' learning preferences.

Global/Specific Learners		Learning Modalities (Sensory Intake)			Hemispheric Preference	
Global	Specific	Visual	Auditory	Kinesthetic	Left Brain	Right Brain
X	X	X	X	X	X	X

Multiple Intelligences								
Visual	Intrapersonal	Interpersonal	Musical	Mathematical/ Logical	Linguistic	Kinesthetic	Naturalist	Existential
X	X	X	X	X	X	X	X	

85. "Deep-Pan" Action Plan!

Learning Outcomes
Participants create a well thought out action plan or set of goals to take forward with them when they return to the workplace.

Overview
This end of course review activity uses the PACER technique, a Neuro-Linguistic Programming (NLP) technique designed to help participants to individually think about what they want to achieve by using positive language to reinforce a results oriented approach. By using this technique, participants are able to produce well-formed outcomes that go above and beyond the normal SMART goal setting process.

In My Experience
This activity is highly effective due to the positive language that the participants use when writing their goals / actions / targets.

The Hidden Twist
Although on the surface this is an action plan or goal/target setting activity, the course content is reviewed before narrowing it down to the chosen actions/targets or goals.

Essential Data
Course Type: Conceptual
Group Size: Any group size
Time of Day: End of course review
Pace: Moderate
Time to Create: 5 mins
Activity Duration: 30-45 mins

Steps to Create
1. Create a document that shows the PACER table, (see Fig. 6) with the questions that the participants will need to ask themselves. As this is an in-depth action plan, each goal / target /action will be written on a separate table.
2. Leave enough space within the table in which the participants will write.

Steps to Run
1. Hand out one PACER table document to each participant
2. State what the PACER technique is, as described above.
3. Summarize and provide examples of each of the letters, P, A, C etc.

   P = Positive: Use positive language to describe the goal / target / action you want to achieve, e.g. "I want to be the best communicator in my team" as opposed to "I want to communicate better."

   A = Achievement: When thinking about achievement, think about the sensory evidence that will tell you when you have succeeded, e.g. how will it feel and what will it look like?

   C = Context: Under context, you should put with whom, where and when you want to achieve this and with who, where and when do you NOT want to achieve this!

   E = Ecology: In this section, think about how this goal / target / action is positioned. What is around it and what is going to get in the way of it? For example, if I lose 10% of my body weight, is my "better half" going to feel threatened by this?

   R = Resources: Here, you need to ask yourself "what is it that I need to achieve this"? How much time will it take? Will it cost anything? Who is going to support me? Do I have a role-model to aspire to?
4. Ask each participant to review the course materials and identify THREE goals / targets / actions that they want to achieve after the course.
5. Now the participants complete the PACER table for GOAL ONE.(See fig. 8)
6. The participants have 20 minutes to complete the table.
7. Recommendation: As the participants are completing their PACER table, play music softly in the background to aid concentration.

Debrief

1. As a debrief to this end of course review activity, ask the participants higher-order questions based on Blooms Taxonomy of the Cognitive Domain. If you want your participants to be able to apply their learning, use the appropriate language for application, e.g. How will you apply that, What would you predict and What evidence will you gather?

2. As a post-course activity, (see chapter 8 for alternative post-course activities), participants are asked to complete the PACER table for the other 2 goals /targets / actions they identified in step 4 above.

Working Example
Conceptual - Negotiation Skills

In this example, participants identify 3 goals / targets / actions to implement. These could be:

    a. Actively listening
    b. Identifying common ground
    c. Assertive communication

Participants are then asked to choose ONE of these three topics, and complete the PACER table within the next 20 minutes.

Sample PACER Table

You can see an example of the PACER table below, which gives the types of questions participants will need to ask themselves as they go through the document.

Step	Goal / Target / Action ONE
P ositive What do you want? What will this bring you?	
A chievement How will you know you are succeeding? How will you know when you have got it? What will you see, hear and feel? How will someone else know when you have got it? What is the first step? What is the last step?	
C ontext When, where and with who do you want it? When, where and with who do you NOT want it? How long for?	
E cology What time will this outcome need? Who else is affected and how will they feel? How does it fit in with your other outcomes? How does it increase your choices? What will happen if you get it? What will happen if you don't get it? What won't happen if you don't get it?	
R esources Can you start and maintain it? What resources have you already got? (skills, people, money, objects etc.) What resources do you need? Who has already succeeded in achieving this outcome?	

Fig 6

Tips, Tricks & Traps

While the participants complete this activity, the trainer should walk around each group to make sure that participants are on the right track, answer questions and provide examples if necessary.

As this activity encourages self-reflection it is not advised to ask for a volunteer to share their plan.

Do not underestimate the time that this activity can take. Remember, if you are short on time – cut the training course content and NOT the end of course review!

Adult Learning Base Process – NLP - Pacer

Refer to **Adult Learning Base Process Reference Guide** for more information about this learning process.

Adult Learning Dashboard

This activity links participant's preferred style of learning. The following dashboard provides a quick reference to adult learning theorists and principles as part of the ID9® methodology.

This activity achieves the following level of Bloom's Taxonomy of the Cognitive Domain (Bloom et al 1956), shown with "X" in the following table.

Bloom's Taxonomy of the Cognitive Domain Level					
Knowledge	Comprehension	Application	Analysis	Synthesis	Evaluation
			X		

This activity also achieves a link, shown with "X" in the following table, to participant's naturally occurring learning preferences. Global/Specific, Learning Modalities, Hemispheric Preference (Sperry, 1981), and Multiple Intelligences (Gardner, 1983) are referenced in ID9® methodology and process. This is not a complete list of links that are covered within the ID9® process however this dashboard aims to provide a quick reference for trainers to use to balance instructional design to provide equality for participants' learning preferences.

Global/Specific Learners		Learning Modalities (Sensory Intake)			Hemispheric Preference	
Global	Specific	Visual	Auditory	Kinesthetic	Left Brain	Right Brain
	X	X	X	X	X	

Multiple Intelligences								
Visual	Intrapersonal	Interpersonal	Musical	Mathematical/ Logical	Linguistic	Kinesthetic	Naturalist	Existential
X	X		X	X		X		

86. What Do You Think?

Learning Outcomes
Participants Are Able To Identify What They Now Know, Having Completed The Course, As Well As Why They Now Know It!

Overview
This End Of Course Review Activity Uses Metacognitive Reflection, The Process Of Thinking About Thinking, In Order To Recall The Course Content.

Participants Are Asked To Work With A Partner To Share 5 Things That They Have Learnt From The Course.

Once They Have Identified Those 5 Items, They Must Explain Why It Is That They Now Know Those Things And What It Was That Enhanced Their Knowledge, Skills Or Attitude.

In My Experience
This Activity Is Highly Effective Due To The Reflection Time That Each Individual Participant Takes. The Introspective Reflection Is A Key To The Success Of This Activity.

The Hidden Twist
As Participants Are Sharing What They Know With Each Other, They Are Able To Identify Additional Areas That They Now Know, Or Areas That They Still Need To Focus On.

Essential Data
Course Type: Any
Group Size: Any
Time Of Day: End Of Course Review
Pace: Slow & Focused
Time To Create: 5 Mins
Activity Duration: 30 Mins

Steps To Create
1. Create A 3-Column Table For The Participant Guide (Or As A Hand-Out) That Allows Participants To Enter The 5 Things That They Have Learnt From The Training Session/Course.
2. Suggested Column Titles Are: "Number" "What Have I Learnt?" And "What Was It That Enabled Me To Learn That?"

Steps To Run
1. Ask The Participants To Turn To The Appropriate Page In The Participant Guide (Or Distribute The Hand-Out)
2. The Trainer Asks Them To Take A Look Through The Course Content And Identify 5 Things That They Have Learnt During The Course. Each Of The 5 Items Are Entered Into The "What Have I Learnt?" Column.
3. Now The Participants Consider Why It Is They Now Know That And Summarize What It Was That Facilitated That Learning In The Second Column.
4. Once The Entries Are Complete They Must Turn To A Partner And In Turn, Say What It Is They Have Learnt And Why They Have Learnt It.
5. As The Participants Are Doing This, The Partner Is Encouraged To Ask Questions To Clarify Why That Learning Has Taken Place.
6. The Participants Have 20 Minutes To Complete This Task.

Debrief
1. After 20 Minutes, The Trainer Asks For 2 Or 3 Volunteers To Share One Item Each With The Group.
2. While The Debrief Is Taking Place, The Trainer Should Ask Open Questions To Bring Out More Information On The "Why" And "What Ifs" For Example, The Trainer Could Ask, "How Could You Apply That To X, Y Or Z?" Or "If You Were To Split That Down Into Component Parts, What Would Those Parts Be?"

Working Example
Conceptual - Communication Skills
Participants Could Consider The Following 5 Things That They Have Learnt During The Course: Listening Techniques, Presenting Clearly, Body Language, The Do's And Don'ts Of Email And Negotiating A Deal. For Each Of Those Topics, They Would Need To State What Helped Them To Learn It. For Example, For Listening Technique They Could State They Learnt How To Listen By Understanding The Concept Around Looking At The Person That Is Talking, Using Affirmative Body Language And Then Paraphrasing What You Have Just Heard And Then By Putting That Into Practice When They Partnered In The Mini Review Activity. (For Examples Of Mini Review Activities. (See Chapter 3).

Tips, Tricks & Traps
Don't Get Confused Between
  a) The Reason Why Someone Has Learnt It, E.g. It
     Is Part Of Their Individual Development Plan And
  b) Why Someone Has Learnt It, E.g. What Is It That
     Has Helped The Participant To Learn It?

Adult Learning Base Process – Metacognitive Reflection
Refer To **Adult Learning Base Process Reference Guide** For More Information About This Learning Process.

Adult Learning Dashboard

This activity links participant's preferred style of learning. The following dashboard provides a quick reference to adult learning theorists and principles as part of the ID9® methodology.

This activity achieves the following level of Bloom's Taxonomy of the Cognitive Domain (Bloom et al 1956), shown with "X" in the following table.

Bloom's Taxonomy of the Cognitive Domain Level					
Knowledge	Comprehension	Application	Analysis	Synthesis	Evaluation
			X		

This activity also achieves a link, shown with "X" in the following table, to participant's naturally occurring learning preferences. Global/Specific, Learning Modalities, Hemispheric Preference (Sperry, 1981), and Multiple Intelligences (Gardner, 1983) are referenced in ID9® methodology and process. This is not a complete list of links that are covered within the ID9® process however this dashboard aims to provide a quick reference for trainers to use to balance instructional design to provide equality for participants' learning preferences.

Global/Specific Learners		Learning Modalities (Sensory Intake)			Hemispheric Preference	
Global	Specific	Visual	Auditory	Kinesthetic	Left Brain	Right Brain
X	X	X	X	X	X	

Multiple Intelligences								
Visual	Intrapersonal	Interpersonal	Musical	Mathematical/ Logical	Linguistic	Kinesthetic	Naturalist	Existential
X	X	X		X	X	X		

87. Gallery Walk-About

Learning Outcomes
Participants review and discuss the content of all the flipcharts that have been created during the training course.

Overview
This end of course review activity uses visual, kinesthetic and auditory skills and helps embed the learning from the course by discussion with a partner.

During the course, each flipchart is stuck up around the room.

For this activity, participants take a partner with them and walk around the room stopping at each flipchart. They take it in turns to describe what is on the flipchart, the meaning and the learning relating to the topic. They discuss together the main points to that topic and any items that are pertinent, e.g. any top tips or "light bulb" moments they may have experienced while learning that topic.

In My Experience
This end of course activity is best used at the end of a two to three day course. The course must be a very interactive one where many of the activities or learnings are flipcharted. It is also a great activity to use when participants are tired! It gets them up to walk around the room but does not involve competitive group work.

The Hidden Twist
This activity involves metacognitive reflection. It allows participants to talk freely about their learnings from the course.

Essential Data
Course Type: Conceptual or Procedural
Group Size: Any group size
Time of Day: End of course review
Pace: Slow
Time to Create: Less than 5 mins
Activity Duration: 30 mins

Steps to Create
1. All that is needed to create this activity is the re-cycling of your flipcharts! How Eco-friendly is that?!

Steps to Run
1. Ask the participants to visualize that they are in an Art Gallery. Along the walls they can see priceless "pieces of art" (indicating the flipcharts)
2. Ask them to take a partner and their course notes, and along with their partner, walk around the gallery, taking in the priceless art.
3. They must discuss with each other the "art" – the content on the flipcharts, the meaning, the learning, and any other information that they can recall. They can turn to their course notes for additional information.
4. Ask the participants to take it in turn to lead the discussion as they come to a new "painting" (flipchart).
5. Recommendation: As the participants are walking around the "gallery" play music softly in the background to enhance the concentration.

Debrief
1. Once all "paintings" have been discussed, bring the group back together by asking the participants to return to their places.
2. The Trainer now asks for 2-3 volunteers to share with the rest of the group their favorite "piece of art" and explain:
   a. Which painting is their favorite
   b. What it the main idea / theme of the painting
   c. What is the relevance of this painting to the rest of the paintings in the gallery (e.g. to the rest of the course content or topic)

Working Example
Conceptual – Presentation Skills
During the Presentation Skills training, topics could include items such as.
- Delivery styles
- Using your Voice
- Creating a positive learning environment
- Using a flip chart
- Answering questions
- Asking questions
- Calming your nerves

All these topics will either have a pre-prepared flipchart, a flipchart review activity or a flipchart that is created during the course that the trainer has used to explain a topic further.

Every time a flipchart is used and finished with, hang it onto the classroom walls.

Participants grab a partner and walk about the room ("Gallery") to discuss the content of the flipcharts "Paintings".

Tips, Tricks & Traps

Check the layout of the classroom in advance to ensure that there is space around the room to hang your flipcharts.

Make sure that every flipchart that contains "must know" information is kept and stuck up on the walls of the classroom. It is recommended to pre-prepare your flipcharts (for those that you can) to ensure that they are easy to review and follow the ABC rule – Attractive, Big and Bold and key words CAPITALIZED.

If budget allows, use the flipcharts that have a sticky top edge to them which will save having to hang the flipcharts with Bluetac® or sticky tape.

Adult Learning Base Process – Metacognitive Reflection

Refer to **Adult Learning Base Process Reference Guide** for more information about this learning process.

Adult Learning Dashboard

This activity links participant's preferred style of learning. The following dashboard provides a quick reference to adult learning theorists and principles as part of the ID9® methodology.

This activity achieves the following level of Bloom's Taxonomy of the Cognitive Domain (Bloom et al 1956), shown with "X" in the following table.

Bloom's Taxonomy of the Cognitive Domain Level					
Knowledge	Comprehension	Application	Analysis	Synthesis	Evaluation
			X		

This activity also achieves a link, shown with "X" in the following table, to participant's naturally occurring learning preferences. Global/Specific, Learning Modalities, Hemispheric Preference (Sperry, 1981), and Multiple Intelligences (Gardner, 1983) are referenced in ID9® methodology and process. This is not a complete list of links that are covered within the ID9® process however this dashboard aims to provide a quick reference for trainers to use to balance instructional design to provide equality for participants' learning preferences.

Global/Specific Learners		Learning Modalities (Sensory Intake)			Hemispheric Preference	
Global	Specific	Visual	Auditory	Kinesthetic	Left Brain	Right Brain
X		X	X	X		X

Multiple Intelligences								
Visual	Intrapersonal	Interpersonal	Musical	Mathematical/ Logical	Linguistic	Kinesthetic	Naturalist	Existential
X		X	X	X		X		

88. 3 Minutes of Fame

Learning Outcomes

Participants deliver and listen to a 3-minute summary presentation on each of the topics covered during the training course.

Overview

This end of course review activity necessitates the participants to work in teams, blindly choose an instruction card, based on one of the topics covered during the training course from the trainer and deliver a 3-minute presentation following the instructions written on the card.

In My Experience

This end of course review activity is very effective and simple to run. It enhances team work and helps to précis the information in a clear and structured way. The instructions provide focus to the short presentation, and help to summarize the "must knows" from the course content.

The Hidden Twist

Each card covers a different "must know" topic from the course, therefore at the end of this activity, participants will have reviewed all the topics from the course.

Essential Data

Course Type: Any
Group Size: 8-20
Time of Day: End of course review
Pace: Moderate
Time to Create: 10 mins
Activity Duration: max 30 mins

Steps to Create

1. Looking at the course learning objectives, consider what it is that the participants need to show the trainer that they now know.
2. Create an instruction card for each of these "must know" topics, telling the participants what and how they need to present the topic.

Steps to Run

1. Keeping the card content hidden from the participants, the trainer asks each group to randomly pick an instruction card.
2. Each group has 5 minutes to prepare a 3-minute presentation, following the instructions on the card.
3. Recommendation: While the participants are preparing their presentation, play music softly in the background to aid concentration.

4. The groups are encouraged to use the course materials and information to hand and flipchart the information that they will present.
5. The groups choose a volunteer to present their task.
6. Each group takes it in turn to deliver the 3-minute presentation on their chosen topic.

Debrief

1. The debrief takes place during the end of course review itself. After each of the 3-minutes of fame has been delivered.
2. To add depth to the learning the trainer should ask "why" "how" and "what if" questions to the participants. Using the working example below, the following higher-order questions could be asked:
   a. Which painting is their favorite
   b. What it the main idea / theme of the painting
   c. What is the relevance of this painting to the rest of the paintings in the gallery (e.g. to the rest of the course content or topic)

Working Example
Procedural - Clinical Trial Regulations

Each group / team is given a number of cards to randomly pick one from. These cards contain the following information:
1. Explain to the group the differences between a guideline, a directive and a regulation
2. Name the 2 Types of review in the proposed Clinical trial Regulations and highlight 3 characteristics of each of them.
3. The Medicines for Human Use (Clinical Trial) Regulations of 2004 are arranged into 9 parts. List the main sections included in Parts 1, 4 and 5.
4. Name three documents that have changed under the new Pharmacovigilance legislation (2012) and highlight 2 characteristics of each of these versions.

Once each team has a card, they must turn it over and prepare a 3-minute presentation on their topic.

They will have 5 minutes to prepare the short presentation.

Once the preparation time is up, each group takes it in turn to present back to the rest of the group the information requested on their card.

After 3 minutes the trainer stops the group and the second group delivers their presentation.

Once all the groups have finished, the activity moves to the debrief.

Tips, Tricks & Traps
Make sure that you select the topics and instructions wisely to meet the Learning objectives of the course.

It is also very important to keep to time here. The groups have 3 minutes to complete their task. After 3 minutes, the trainer should ask the group to stop, whether they have finished or not.

Adult Learning Base Process – Teach Back
Refer to **Adult Learning Base Process Reference Guide** for more information about this learning process.

Adult Learning Dashboard

This activity links participant's preferred style of learning. The following dashboard provides a quick reference to adult learning theorists and principles as part of the ID9® methodology.

This activity achieves the following level of Bloom's Taxonomy of the Cognitive Domain (Bloom et al 1956), shown with "X" in the following table.

Bloom's Taxonomy of the Cognitive Domain Level					
Knowledge	Comprehension	Application	Analysis	Synthesis	Evaluation
		X			

This activity also achieves a link, shown with "X" in the following table, to participant's naturally occurring learning preferences. Global/Specific, Learning Modalities, Hemispheric Preference (Sperry, 1981), and Multiple Intelligences (Gardner, 1983) are referenced in ID9® methodology and process. This is not a complete list of links that are covered within the ID9® process however this dashboard aims to provide a quick reference for trainers to use to balance instructional design to provide equality for participants' learning preferences.

Global/Specific Learners		Learning Modalities (Sensory Intake)			Hemispheric Preference	
Global	Specific	Visual	Auditory	Kinesthetic	Left Brain	Right Brain
X		X	X	X	X	X

Multiple Intelligences								
Visual	Intrapersonal	Interpersonal	Musical	Mathematical/ Logical	Linguistic	Kinesthetic	Naturalist	Existential
X		X	X	X	X	X		

89. Quick Quiz

Learning Outcomes

Participants illustrate their newly acquired knowledge by completing an end of course quick quiz.

Overview

An informal activity where a number of questions are asked (in written form) based on the content of the course. Participants write on the answer sheets and once complete, the answers are then provided and verified/discussed.

In My Experience

This activity is a quick way to find out, whether your participants have understood the topic/s and are able to recall the data. Use this quiz to prompt further learning by asking some higher-order questions.

The Hidden Twist

As the answers are discussed during this activity, participants get a chance to identify topics that they need to review once again, during or after the training course.

Essential Data

Course Type: Procedural or Technical
Group Size: Any group size
Time of Day: End of course review (up to a half day course)
Pace: Moderate
Time to Create: 1 hour
Activity Duration: 10-15 mins

Steps to Create

1. Create 10 questions based on the "must know" topics covered during the course
2. Now enter these questions onto a word document providing sufficient space for the participants to write their answers.
3. Print off 1 question sheet per participant.
4. Create a "trainer's copy" that includes the answers and any pertinent information or examples that the trainer can refer to when running the activity.

Steps to Run

1. Hand out the question sheet to each participant.
2. Tell them that they have 10 minutes to answer the 10 questions on the question sheet.
3. Tell the participants when to start and then when to stop.
4. Review the questions, asking for volunteers to shout out the answers.

Debrief

As the trainer walks through the questions and answers, they clarify any items that were not answered correctly by briefly reviewing the necessary content. Use the "trainer's copy" mentioned above if necessary.

Working Example
Technical - International Conference on Harmonization (ICH)

This consists of a number of questions on the "must know" content of the training session.
The questions are set out on a word document similar to this:

<u>ICH Quick Quiz</u>

1. In which year did ICH discussions first begin?

    1988   1989   1990   1991

2. Which 3 regions did this involve?

3. The ICH guidelines are divided into 4 main areas:

    What is the fourth Category? _____

→ Safety	S
→ Quality	Q
→ Multidisciplinary	M
→ ??????	E

4. What does the "E6" guideline describe?

5. When did the "E6" guideline become effective?

    1995   1996   1997   1998

Fig 7

Tips, Tricks & Traps

This is a short end of course review activity and is better used at the end of a shorter course. It is important not to create anxiety for adult learners, therefore, at the beginning of the activity, you can say it's ok to get the questions wrong! Be careful not to criticize the participant if they have not answered the question correctly, rather say something like "In certain circumstances, your answer would have been right, can you describe when that would be?"

Adult Learning Base Process - Assessment
Refer to **Adult Learning Base Process Reference Guide** for more information about this learning process.

Adult Learning Dashboard

This activity links participant's preferred style of learning. The following dashboard provides a quick reference to adult learning theorists and principles as part of the ID9® methodology.

This activity achieves the following level of Bloom's Taxonomy of the Cognitive Domain (Bloom et al 1956), shown with "X" in the following table.

Bloom's Taxonomy of the Cognitive Domain Level					
Knowledge	Comprehension	Application	Analysis	Synthesis	Evaluation
	X				

This activity also achieves a link, shown with "X" in the following table, to participant's naturally occurring learning preferences. Global/Specific, Learning Modalities, Hemispheric Preference (Sperry, 1981), and Multiple Intelligences (Gardner, 1983) are referenced in ID9® methodology and process. This is not a complete list of links that are covered within the ID9® process however this dashboard aims to provide a quick reference for trainers to use to balance instructional design to provide equality for participants' learning preferences.

Global/Specific Learners		Learning Modalities (Sensory Intake)			Hemispheric Preference	
Global	Specific	Visual	Auditory	Kinesthetic	Left Brain	Right Brain
	X	X	X	X	X	

Multiple Intelligences								
Visual	Intrapersonal	Interpersonal	Musical	Mathematical/ Logical	Linguistic	Kinesthetic	Naturalist	Existential
X	X			X	X	X		

90. Simultaneous RP3

Learning Outcomes
Participants are able to try out newly acquired skills and see how it feels and looks from three different perspectives. (Triad Role Play)

Overview
This role play involves three roles, Role 1, Role 2 & an Observer. The whole group is split into teams of 3 with Role 1 practicing the new skills / knowledge acquired on Role 2. The Observer watches how Role 1 implements the newly acquired skills and the reaction to them of Role 2. Once the first role play has taken place, Role 1 moves to Role 2, Role 2 moves to the role of Observer and the Observer moves to take the place of role 1. This is repeated once more so that all 3 roles have been practiced by all 3 members of the group.

These role plays take place simultaneously. In doing this, each role-play takes place privately and no-one is forced onto "center stage".

In My Experience
Due to the nature of these simultaneous, private activities, this is a very low-threat activity. As each one of the participants experiences all three roles, they gain a more holistic understanding of the subject matter.

The Hidden Twist
This is a fantastic opportunity to put the newly acquired skills into practice. After all, it is known that "people learn best by doing".

Essential Data
Course Type: Conceptual
Group Size: 6 - 36
Time of Day: End of Course
Pace: Moderate
Time to Create: 2-3 hours
Activity Duration: 45 minutes

Steps to Create
1. Create 3 briefs for each group, one brief for Role 1, one brief for role 2 and a combination of both Role 1 & 2 for the Observer.
2. Print a set of all 3 briefs for each group.
3. Create an observation checklist for the observer role. Ensure that all skills or "must knows" are listed on the checklist in order to check that Role 1 is adhering to the new way of working.

Steps to Run
1. Split the participants into groups of 3.
2. Explain the rules:
   a. Each group will receive 3 briefs, one for each group member.
   b. There are 3 roles; Role 1, Role 2 & an Observer role.
   c. Role 1 will practice the newly acquired skills, Role 2 will be the role in receipt of the newly acquired skills, and Role 3 will observe the discussion.
   d. The Observer will receive both Role 1 and Role 2's briefs as well as an observation checklist in which to check that the newly acquired skills have been used in the role-play.
   e. Roles 1 & 2 conduct the role-play (in 5 minutes) and Role 3 observes Role 1 to check for adherence to the checklist.
   f. There now follows an in-group debrief (see below for details).
   g. Each group member will take the part of each role in rotation until he/she has completed all three roles.
   h. Once all the in-group debriefs have taken place, the trainer conducts an end of activity debrief. (see below for details).

In-Group Debrief
Each in-group debriefs (3 in all) will last 5 minutes.

The following questions should be asked.

- Role 1 – How do you think that went? Were you able to demonstrate the newly acquired skills? If not, what prevented you from doing so? Is there anything you would have done differently if you were to repeat the role-play?
- Role 2 – How did you feel as the "receiver" of Role 1's newly acquired skills? What techniques did you recognize?
- Observer – Did you see/hear the newly acquired skills in practice? How did you perceive Role 2 received them? Is there anything that Role 1 did not practice or could have done better?

End of Review Activity Trainer's debrief

The trainer thanks the participants for their interaction and asks the participants to re-group and sit back in their places.

For the last 15 minutes of this activity, the trainer uses higher-order questions to deepen the experiential learning. The trainer asks questions like:

- Would anyone like to share their experiences of this activity?
- Which do you conclude was the most useful role to play?
- What went well with that role?
- If you could repeat that activity, what would you do differently next time?
- How does that equate to the role you have at work?

Working Example
Basic Customer Service Training Course

This course could cover the basics of collecting information from a customer about a complaint and routing the call on to the appropriate resolver.

- Role 1 would be the customer service representative. They would need to ask the customer for their name, telephone number in case the call was inadvertently cut off, nature of the complaint and tell the customer what the next steps are in complaints process.
- Role 2 would be the customer. They would inform the customer service representative about the complaint, and provide all the details that they had been asked.
- Role 3 would be the Observer. The Observer would observe the customer service representative and use the observation checklist to ensure that all the new knowledge, skills and attitude had been implemented. The Observer would also watch the customer to see how they react to the customer service representative, for example, was it clear to Role 2 what information had been asked for by Role 1.

Tips, Tricks & Traps

The role of the observer is crucial to this activity; they are able to see the role play from an objective point of view as they are focused on viewing both Roles 1 & 2 in practice from an "outsider's" point of view.

By giving each participant the opportunity to play all three roles, participants are given a holistic picture and are able to empathize with their own customers after the training is implemented back in the workplace.

Make sure that your training room is big enough to accommodate all the role-plays.

Adult Learning Base Process – Triad Role Play

Refer to **Adult Learning Base Process Reference Guide** for more information about this learning process.

Adult Learning Dashboard

This activity links participant's preferred style of learning. The following dashboard provides a quick reference to adult learning theorists and principles as part of the ID9® methodology.

This activity achieves the following level of Bloom's Taxonomy of the Cognitive Domain (Bloom et al 1956), shown with "X" in the following table.

Bloom's Taxonomy of the Cognitive Domain Level					
Knowledge	Comprehension	Application	Analysis	Synthesis	Evaluation
					X

This activity also achieves a link, shown with "X" in the following table, to participant's naturally occurring learning preferences. Global/Specific, Learning Modalities, Hemispheric Preference (Sperry, 1981), and Multiple Intelligences (Gardner, 1983) are referenced in ID9® methodology and process. This is not a complete list of links that are covered within the ID9® process however this dashboard aims to provide a quick reference for trainers to use to balance instructional design to provide equality for participants' learning preferences.

Global/Specific Learners		Learning Modalities (Sensory Intake)			Hemispheric Preference	
Global	Specific	Visual	Auditory	Kinesthetic	Left Brain	Right Brain
X	X	X	X	X	X	X

Multiple Intelligences								
Visual	Intrapersonal	Interpersonal	Musical	Mathematical/ Logical	Linguistic	Kinesthetic	Naturalist	Existential
X	X	X		X	X	X		X

91. Words of Wisdom

Learning Outcomes
Participants are able to demonstrate that they can recall the "must knows" from the training course content.

Overview
This is a crossword activity. All the questions are based on content learnt throughout the training course. Participants complete the crossword individually or as a group activity.

In My Experience
This end of course activity is best used in a shorter training course – (up to 4 hours).

The Hidden Twist
This activity is a quiz in disguise! It helps the trainer to assess the learning within the group and re-view any areas that need more attention.

Essential Data
Course Type: Technical or Procedural
Group Size: 6 - 24
Time of Day: End of Course review
Pace: Moderate
Time to Create: 1-2 hours
Activity Duration: 20-30 minutes

Steps to Create
1. Look through the course content and select the areas that are the "must know" areas.
2. Create 20 questions around these "must know" areas.
3. Google search for a Free Online Crossword Maker or purchase one (these often have more options available).
4. Follow the instructions on the crossword maker, entering both questions and answers as appropriate.
5. Select the "Go" button and see the crossword taking shape.
6. Review the crossword and change if necessary.
7. Save as a .pdf file and cut & paste the crossword puzzle into your participant guide or onto a separate document to hand out to participants.

Steps to Run
1. Hand out the crossword puzzle to the participants or ask them to turn to the appropriate page within their participant guide.
2. Ask them to complete the crossword within the allotted time either individually, with a partner or as a group.
3. Once the time is up, move to the debrief.

Debrief
1. The trainer should now ask the questions in order and ask for the participants to share their answers.
2. While the debrief is taking place, the trainer should answer any questions that arise and try to provide examples to add depth to the learning.

Working Example
Technical – New Hire Orientation
Review the "must know" areas within the training course and make sure that you ask at least one question per "must know" area.

Questions could be like this:
1. The number of staff employed by the company in 2005.
2. The surname of the company's first CEO.
3. The name of the first product to come to market.
4. The number of company values that we work to.
5. The 7th word of the company Vision Statement.

Tips, Tricks & Traps
Make sure that your questions use appropriate language for crosswords, e.g. "Method by which the sales executive should confirm the order".

Ensure each question follows with the number of letters in the word/s in parenthesis, e.g. (7) or if the question has two words in the answer, like "in writing" show as (2, 7)

Adult Learning Base Process – Crossword
Refer to **Adult Learning Base Process Reference Guide** for more information about this learning process.

Adult Learning Dashboard

This activity links participant's preferred style of learning. The following dashboard provides a quick reference to adult learning theorists and principles as part of the ID9® methodology.

This activity achieves the following level of Bloom's Taxonomy of the Cognitive Domain (Bloom et al 1956), shown with "X" in the following table.

Bloom's Taxonomy of the Cognitive Domain Level					
Knowledge	Comprehension	Application	Analysis	Synthesis	Evaluation
X					

This activity also achieves a link, shown with "X" in the following table, to participant's naturally occurring learning preferences. Global/Specific, Learning Modalities, Hemispheric Preference (Sperry, 1981), and Multiple Intelligences (Gardner, 1983) are referenced in ID9® methodology and process. This is not a complete list of links that are covered within the ID9® process however this dashboard aims to provide a quick reference for trainers to use to balance instructional design to provide equality for participants' learning preferences.

Global/Specific Learners		Learning Modalities (Sensory Intake)			Hemispheric Preference	
Global	Specific	Visual	Auditory	Kinesthetic	Left Brain	Right Brain
X	X	X	X	X	X	

Multiple Intelligences								
Visual	Intrapersonal	Interpersonal	Musical	Mathematical/ Logical	Linguistic	Kinesthetic	Naturalist	Existential
X	X			X	X	X		

92. Process Challenge

Learning Outcomes
Participants correctly arrange the process from start to finish.

Overview
During this end of course activity, the participants are split into teams of 4-6 and are given a number of cards that once sorted, set out a process from start to finish.

In My Experience
This fast paced activity is perfect for staff who work on a process together, and who are dependent on each other to achieve the process.

The Hidden Twist
At the end of the activity, participants have reviewed the steps within the process but also, due to the nature the team activity, they used teamwork to complete the task. Teamwork is often important when working on a process in the workplace.

Essential Data
Course Type: Procedural
Group Size: maximum 30 (split into a maximum of 5 teams of 6)
Time of Day: End of course review
Pace: Moderate
Time to Create: 1-2 hours
Activity Duration: 20-30 mins

Steps to Create
1. Create a graphical representation of the process in the form of a process flow, including tasks, responsible persons and any decisions that need to be made.
2. Print on A4 or A3 (dependent on how complex the process is), one per participant.
3. Next print, laminate and cut up each part of the process (1 set of cards per group/team)
4. Put the cards into an envelope and seal it.

Steps to Run
1. Pass out the sealed envelopes - one to each group/team
2. The trainer asks the participants to close their course materials and make space on their tables to arrange the cards.
3. Next, the participants are asked to open the envelope and take out all the cards.
4. Now they attempt to put all the cards into the correct order.
5. They have 15 minutes to complete the task.
6. After 5 minutes, the teams move to the next table (clockwise direction) and have to check the accuracy of their neighbors' process flow.
7. The trainer passes out a copy of the correct process to each participant to use when the checking takes place.

Debrief
1. While the teams check each other's process flows for accuracy, if there are any questions or challenges around the process, the trainer must answer them as they come up.
2. To add greater depth to the learning, the trainer could also ask questions such as: "What would happen if you moved step 7 to step 9?", "How could you demonstrate that step x had taken place?" etc.

Working Example
Procedural – Company Appraisal Process
During the training, the company appraisal process is explained from start to finish. Once the process has been covered in whole, the participants have to replay this process in their mind and replicate it by sorting and placing the cards into the correct order.

Tips, Tricks & Traps

Some processes tend to be complicated! If this is the case, and your process is not linear, you could have a "skeleton process template" (see Fig. 8) on which the participants can place the correct cards. In this case, be careful to make all the steps the same size or the participants will look for the box size in which to fit the card, rather than consider the card content! Here is an example of a skeleton process template.

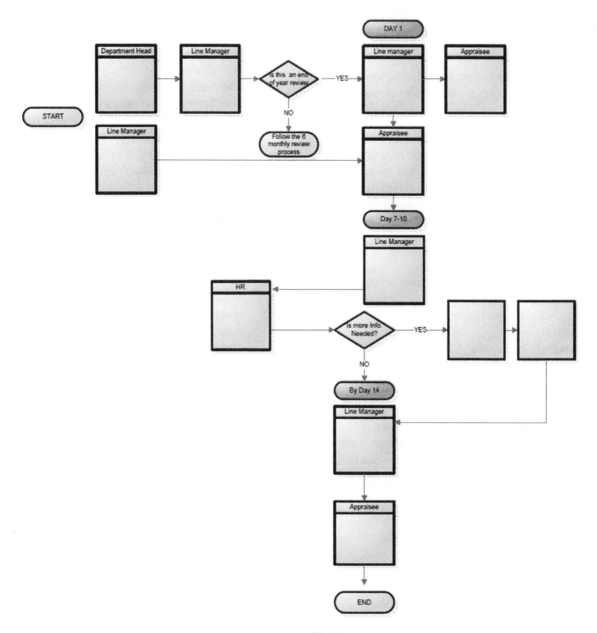

Fig 8

Adult Learning Base Process – Flow Chart

Refer to **Adult Learning Base Process Reference Guide** for more information about this learning process.

Adult Learning Dashboard

This activity links participant's preferred style of learning. The following dashboard provides a quick reference to adult learning theorists and principles as part of the ID9® methodology.

This activity achieves the following level of Bloom's Taxonomy of the Cognitive Domain (Bloom et al 1956), shown with "X" in the following table.

Bloom's Taxonomy of the Cognitive Domain Level					
Knowledge	Comprehension	Application	Analysis	Synthesis	Evaluation
		X			

This activity also achieves a link, shown with "X" in the following table, to participant's naturally occurring learning preferences. Global/Specific, Learning Modalities, Hemispheric Preference (Sperry, 1981), and Multiple Intelligences (Gardner, 1983) are referenced in ID9® methodology and process. This is not a complete list of links that are covered within the ID9® process however this dashboard aims to provide a quick reference for trainers to use to balance instructional design to provide equality for participants' learning preferences.

Global/Specific Learners		Learning Modalities (Sensory Intake)			Hemispheric Preference	
Global	Specific	Visual	Auditory	Kinesthetic	Left Brain	Right Brain
X	X	X	X	X	X	X

Multiple Intelligences								
Visual	Intrapersonal	Interpersonal	Musical	Mathematical/ Logical	Linguistic	Kinesthetic	Naturalist	Existential
X		X		X	X	X		

93. Agree or Disagree?

Learning Outcomes
Participants illustrate their newly acquired knowledge by completing an end of course INTERACTIVE quiz.

Overview
Similar to a True / False activity, this informal end of course review activity consists of a number of statements, read by the trainer on the content of the course. Participants hold up their answer cards (green Agree card on one side, red Disagree card on the other) in response to the statement.

In My Experience
This activity is a quick and engaging way to find out whether your participants have understood the course topic/s.

The Hidden Twist
Unlike a True / False activity that is very much, black & white; either right or wrong, the Agree / Disagree activity is much more "grey" and can be open to interpretation. In technical or procedural training, the answers are likely to be clear cut – either Agree (true) or Disagree (False), however when conducting a conceptual course, by its nature, it is much more open to discussion. Given this difference, the participants are able to have a more impactful discussion which will lead to higher-order questions and reflection.

Fig 9

Essential Data
Course Type: Any
Group Size: Any group size
Time of Day: End of course review (up to half day course)
Pace: Fast
Time to Create: 1 hour
Activity Duration: 15-20 mins

Steps to Create
1. Create 10 questions or statements based on the "must know" topics covered.
2. On the same document, give examples of when it is appropriate to agree, and when appropriate to disagree, to help with the debrief.
3. Create the answer cards. You will need a green box with the word AGREE in the middle and a red box with DISAGREE in the middle. (See Fig. 9)
4. Print off as many copies of each answer type as there are participants.
5. Laminate the two sides together and cut around the edges to form a single AGREE/DISAGREE card.

Steps to Run
1. Hand out one AGREE/DISAGREE card to each participant.
2. Trainer explains the rules:
   a. I will ask you 10 questions or statements, based on the subject matter that we have covered in the course.
   b. Your answer to each question or statement is either AGREE or DISAGREE.
   c. You must hold up your cards, revealing your answer.

Debrief
1. The debrief takes place as the activity progresses.
2. The trainer discusses the answers given by using examples if appropriate and probing with higher-order questions to deepen the learning.
3. Some of the questions in the working example below could be followed up, by the trainer with:
   a. Question 2: Can you show me how else you could copy & paste inside a document
   b. Question 6: When would you want to insert a macro into a word document?
   c. Question 8: There is another way to undo an action. Can anyone demonstrate that to me?
   d. What led you to disagree with statement x?
   e. Can you explain your reasoning behind your answer?
   f. Does anyone else use that process? Etc.

Working Example
Technical – Microsoft Word Short cut keys
The course covers short cut keys within Microsoft Word. It is an interactive course where participants practice the short cut keys within Microsoft Word itself.

For the end of course review activity, participants are asked to hold up their answer cards to the following AGREE or DISAGREE questions:

1. You can find anything in a document by selecting Ctrl + F
2. The short cut keys for Copy & Paste are Ctrl + C & Ctrl + P
3. If you want your lines to appear as double spacing, select Ctrl + 2
4. To go back to single line spacing, you press Ctrl + 2 once more
5. The short cut key for underlining words is Ctrl + U
6. To insert a macro in Microsoft Word, select Alt + F8
7. In order to display the Save As dialogue box, you must press F11
8. You can undo an action by pressing Ctrl + Z
9. To select all the content on the page, press Ctrl + J
10. F1 brings up Microsoft Help Online

Tips, Tricks & Traps
Make sure that you leave enough time to complete this end of course review activity. It will take longer than a standard True/False activity.

Adult Learning Base Process - Assessment
Refer to **Adult Learning Base Process Reference Guide** for more information about this learning process.

Adult Learning Dashboard

This activity links participant's preferred style of learning. The following dashboard provides a quick reference to adult learning theorists and principles as part of the ID9® methodology.

This activity achieves the following level of Bloom's Taxonomy of the Cognitive Domain (Bloom et al 1956), shown with "X" in the following table.

Bloom's Taxonomy of the Cognitive Domain Level					
Knowledge	Comprehension	Application	Analysis	Synthesis	Evaluation
		X			

This activity also achieves a link, shown with "X" in the following table, to participant's naturally occurring learning preferences. Global/Specific, Learning Modalities, Hemispheric Preference (Sperry, 1981), and Multiple Intelligences (Gardner, 1983) are referenced in ID9® methodology and process. This is not a complete list of links that are covered within the ID9® process however this dashboard aims to provide a quick reference for trainers to use to balance instructional design to provide equality for participants' learning preferences.

Global/Specific Learners		Learning Modalities (Sensory Intake)			Hemispheric Preference	
Global	Specific	Visual	Auditory	Kinesthetic	Left Brain	Right Brain
X	X	X	X	X	X	

Multiple Intelligences								
Visual	Intrapersonal	Interpersonal	Musical	Mathematical/ Logical	Linguistic	Kinesthetic	Naturalist	Existential
X	X			X	X	X		

94. Speed Review

Learning Outcomes
Each participant shares 3 things that they have learnt from the course and how they will use or implement those things back in the workplace.

Overview
Speed dating with a twist! This end of course review activity will be done in a "speed dating style" where participants will sit opposite each other where one half of the group, say the A's will stay in one place and their pairs, say the B's will move. During each cycle, each pair has to share their 3 key learnings from the course and how they will apply those learnings back in the workplace. (Each learning and application should take no more than 30 seconds – 3 minutes in total). There will then be a 2 minute silence so that each pair can summarize what they have just heard. All the B's then move to the next chair and sit opposite their next "date" to repeat the process. This continues until all the A's have dated all the B's. (See Fig. 10)

In My Experience
This is a great way to share learnings and application ideas in a very time efficient manner! It is time limited and therefore participants have to provide their information in a concise and succinct way.

The Hidden Twist
Participants will end up with a list of learnings and ideas for application that they can take away with them to implement back in the workplace. (The more participants, the longer the list!)

Essential Data
Course Type: Any
Group Size: 8 - 24
Time of Day: End of course
Pace: Fast
Time to Create: 20 minutes
Activity Duration: (dependent on number of participants – 8 = 20 minutes, 24 = 1 hour)

Steps to Create
1. Visualize your room set-up and identify how you will lay out the chairs for this activity. You will need the participants to be able to write on something (a desk, or if more practical, a clipboard)
2. If using clipboards, ensure you have one per participant and they are able to clip the learning / application sheets for each "partner" to it.
3. Create the learning / application sheet. Draw 3 columns. In the first column title, put Name. This will be the name of the "partner". In the second column title put "What 3 things have you learned? In the third column title put "How will you apply this back in the workplace?
4. Each row will have sufficient space to write all 3 learnings and how they will be applied.
5. Print out the learning / application sheets. Each participant will need the same number of sheets as 50% of the number of participants on the course.

Steps to Run
1. Set up the room to accommodate the activity. See above.
2. Split the group into two halves. You can do this by giving each participant a number one, or two; name them an apple or banana; or an A or B.
3. All the A's on one side and all the B's on the other. The A's will keep their seats during the activity. The B's will move to the next A after each 5 minutes.
4. Now hand out the Learning / Application sheets, as many as needed for the 50% of participants.
5. Ask the participants to take a pen and get ready for their "date"!
6. Each A shares their 3 learnings and applications for those learnings with the B opposite them. They have 1.5 minutes to do that.
7. The trainer says "change over" and each B shares their 3 learnings and applications for those learnings with the A opposite them. They also have 1.5 minutes.
8. Now the trainer says "stop" and both A & B summarize their "date's" learning and application onto the learning / application sheet.
9. After 2 minutes (now at 5 minutes), the Trainer says "B's now move on".
10. Each B takes their place opposite the next A in line and the process is repeated.
11. Once all the B's have exchanged with all the A's, the activity is complete.

Debrief

The trainer asks the participants how many learnings and ideas for application they have summarized on their Learning / Applications sheets. The participant with the most learnings / applications is asked to share them with the rest of the group.

During this time, any questions that come up are discussed and clarifications provided.

Working Example
Technical – Train the Trainer

Participants share with each of their "partners" three things that they learnt during the train-the-trainer course, and how they will implement or apply those learnings back in the workplace.
The first A participant shares with the first B participant their ideas and then this is repeated by the first B sharing their ideas with the first A.

These ideas could be something along these lines:

1. It is very important to listen actively during the training session and I can do this back in the workplace by making sure I look at my participants and use positive affirmation.
2. When using my voice, I must try to enhance the way I deliver my message. I can do this back in the workplace by using inflection in my voice.
3. I must make my flipcharts impactful. I can do this by following the ABC rule. I can make pre-prepare them and make them Attractive, Big & Bold and by Capitalizing key words.

Tips, Tricks & Traps

It is important to get the name of your "partner". When you get back to the workplace, you may want to ask a question about their learning and application.

This activity can be used for any type of instructor-led training course.

If you have an uneven number, have that person sit with one of the A's and be an observer.

Make sure that for the number of participants in the room you have enough space to set up the chairs/ tables or chairs and clipboards.

Adult Learning Base Process – Key Learning

Refer to **Adult Learning Base Process Reference Guide** for more information about this learning process.

Sample Room Layout:

Round 1

6 ⟷ 6
5 ⟷ 5
4 ⟷ 4
A's   B's
3 ⟷ 3
2 ⟷ 2
1 ⟷ 1

Round 2

6 ⟷ 5
5 ⟷ 4
4 ⟷ 3
A's   B's
3 ⟷ 2
2 ⟷ 1
1 ⟷ 6

Round 3

6 ⟷ 4
5 ⟷ 3
4 ⟷ 2
A's   B's
3 ⟷ 1
2 ⟷ 6
1 ⟷ 5

Adult Learning Dashboard

This activity links participant's preferred style of learning. The following dashboard provides a quick reference to adult learning theorists and principles as part of the ID9® methodology.

This activity achieves the following level of Bloom's Taxonomy of the Cognitive Domain (Bloom et al 1956), shown with "X" in the following table.

Bloom's Taxonomy of the Cognitive Domain Level					
Knowledge	Comprehension	Application	Analysis	Synthesis	Evaluation
		X			

This activity also achieves a link, shown with "X" in the following table, to participant's naturally occurring learning preferences. Global/Specific, Learning Modalities, Hemispheric Preference (Sperry, 1981), and Multiple Intelligences (Gardner, 1983) are referenced in ID9® methodology and process. This is not a complete list of links that are covered within the ID9® process however this dashboard aims to provide a quick reference for trainers to use to balance instructional design to provide equality for participants' learning preferences.

Global/Specific Learners		Learning Modalities (Sensory Intake)			Hemispheric Preference	
Global	Specific	Visual	Auditory	Kinesthetic	Left Brain	Right Brain
X	X	X	X	X	X	

Multiple Intelligences								
Visual	Intrapersonal	Interpersonal	Musical	Mathematical/ Logical	Linguistic	Kinesthetic	Naturalist	Existential
X	X	X		X	X	X		

95. Whose side are you on anyway?

Learning Outcomes
Participants review and embed the course content by answering a number of True/False questions.

Overview
In this end of course review activity, participants are asked a number of True/False questions, ideally 10, on the whole of the course content. They have to move to one side of the room if they believe the answer to be True and the other side of the room if they believe the answer to be False. Once participants have chosen "their side" the trainer gives them one opportunity to change their minds and move to the other side if wished. A debrief occurs after each question is answered.

In My Experience
This is a great kinesthetic activity that re-charges, and motivates the individual participants. As it is a short activity, it is best to use this for a shorter training course, (up to 4 hours).

The Hidden Twist
This highly charged activity covers all of the must knows in an engaging way.

Essential Data
Course Type: Procedural or Technical
Group Size: 10-24
Time of Day: End of course Review
Pace: Fast
Time to Create: 20-30 minutes
Activity Duration: 10 minutes

Steps to Create
1. Create 10 questions based on the "must know" topic content.
2. Create a document and insert a 2-column table.
3. Place the questions, row by row, into the left hand table column.
4. Enter the answers, providing any pertinent examples into the right hand column.
5. Print out one copy for the trainer and one copy for each participant.

Steps to Run
1. Arrange the furniture, should you need to, to provide space for the participants to move from one side of room to the other without colliding into chairs, tables etc.
2. Explain the rules:
   a. The participants will be asked to move into the center of the room, half way between one side of the room to the other.
   b. The trainer will ask a True / False question.
   c. If you think the answer to the question is True, you should move to this side of the room (trainer points to the side)
   d. If you think the answer to the question is False, you should move to the other side of the room (trainer points to that side).
   e. In total, 10 questions will be asked.
   f. Once you have moved to the side of the room you believe the answer to be, you will have ONE opportunity to change your mind and move to the opposite side of the room.

Debrief
1. The debrief takes place after each question has been asked. The trainer will confirm which answer was correct, True or False.
2. The trainer will ask "why" and "what if" questions and ask for examples of the participants to add further depth to the learning.

Working Example
Technical – Process Training
Any process can be reviewed by using this shorter end of course review activity. Example questions for this training are:

The Sales Manager is accountable for x, y & z

The Sales Director completes form A and passes onto the Sales Manager

If Step 3 was taken out of the process, x would happen

Customers have 14 days to raise a customer complaint

Tips, Tricks & Traps

Make sure that your room size is large enough to accommodate a row of participants on each side of the room.

Giving the participants one opportunity to change sides is a great idea and helps to deepen the learning in the debrief e.g. the trainer can ask questions like "What is it that made you change your mind and move to the other side?"

As the answers of the questions will be either True or False, the questions must be very clearly written.

Adult Learning Base Process - Assessment

Refer to **Adult Learning Base Process Reference Guide** for more information about this learning process.

Adult Learning Dashboard

This activity links participant's preferred style of learning. The following dashboard provides a quick reference to adult learning theorists and principles as part of the ID9® methodology.

This activity achieves the following level of Bloom's Taxonomy of the Cognitive Domain (Bloom et al 1956), shown with "X" in the following table.

Bloom's Taxonomy of the Cognitive Domain Level					
Knowledge	Comprehension	Application	Analysis	Synthesis	Evaluation
	X				

This activity also achieves a link, shown with "X" in the following table, to participant's naturally occurring learning preferences. Global/Specific, Learning Modalities, Hemispheric Preference (Sperry, 1981), and Multiple Intelligences (Gardner, 1983) are referenced in ID9® methodology and process. This is not a complete list of links that are covered within the ID9® process however this dashboard aims to provide a quick reference for trainers to use to balance instructional design to provide equality for participants' learning preferences.

Global/Specific Learners		Learning Modalities (Sensory Intake)			Hemispheric Preference	
Global	Specific	Visual	Auditory	Kinesthetic	Left Brain	Right Brain
X			X	X	X	

Multiple Intelligences								
Visual	Intrapersonal	Interpersonal	Musical	Mathematical/ Logical	Linguistic	Kinesthetic	Naturalist	Existential
	X			X	X	X		

96. Killer Questions

Learning Outcomes
Participants are able to ask and answer questions based on the materials covered during the course.

Overview
This end of course review activity splits the group up into two teams. Each team has to review the course content and create 5 "Killer Questions" for the alternate team. The harder the question the better! Both teams ask their questions in order, e.g. Team A asks their first question, and then Team B asks their first question. If the alternate team answers the question correctly, they score one point. If not, the questioning team scores the point. The team with the most points after all 5 questions have been asked is the winning team.

In My Experience
This activity is great fun! It's also a great end of course activity if you want to finish the course on a high. It promotes team building and can be quite competitive. (Great if you can relate that to one of your company values!)

The Hidden Twist
As participants are searching through the course notes for their killer questions, they are actually reviewing the materials in detail and discussing course content while they search.

Essential Data
Course Type: Any
Group Size: 8-16 (for more participants, see the Tips, Tricks & Traps section below)
Time of Day: End of course review
Pace: Fast & Highly Competitive
Time to Create: 2 mins
Activity Duration: 30-45 mins

Steps to Create
All you need is a pre-prepared flipchart with three columns, Column 1 lists the question numbers, column two is for Team A's point score and column 3 is for Team B's score.

Have a coin to toss to see which team starts their questions first.

Steps to Run
1. Split the group into two teams.
2. Ask the teams to look through their course materials and get them to come up with 5 "Killer Questions" for the alternate team.
3. The question detail MUST have been covered during the course.
4. They have 10 minutes to prepare their questions.
5. Recommendation: While the participants are preparing their questions, play faster music softly in the background to enhance the energy and competitiveness.
6. After 10 minutes, toss a coin to see which team starts first.
7. Team A asks Team B their first question. If Team B answers the question correctly, they receive one point, and Team A does not score – However, if Team B does not answer the question correctly, then Team A will score the point.
8. The trainer marks this up on the flipchart against Question Number 1.
9. Now it is the turn of Team B to ask Team A their first question and the same happen - If Team A answers the question correctly, Team A receives a point, if not, then Team B receives the point and the trainer marks this up against question number 1.
10. Continue until all questions have been asked and answered by each team.
11. The team with the most points is the winning team.

Debrief
1. The debrief for this course takes place during the activity. If any clarifications are needed regarding the course material, these are discussed during the activity at the point of asking. If Trainer suspects that depth of learning is missing or wants to point the teams to cover the "must know" topics in more detail, the can intersperse some What, How, and What if questions when appropriate.

Working Example
Technical – New Hire Orientation
The following killer questions could be created for the alternate team

1. How many staff were employed by the company in 2005?
2. What was the name of the company's first CEO?
3. What date, dd/mm/yy, did the company's first product come to market?
4. What is the company's Vision Statement (must be word-for-word)
5. We are appraised on our 6 company values. What is the fourth company value? (word-for-word)

In order to intersperse the questions with higher-order questions, the trainer could follow up with the following examples:

1. What happened in 2006 to that changed that figure?
2. What would you predict was the reason for his retirement?
3. What would have happened to the company had that product not come to market at that time?
4. When and how is our Vision Statement used within our daily work?
5. Why are our company values so important to us?

Tips, Tricks & Traps
The activity can become rather competitive! Make sure that your participants are aware that the trainer's decision is FINAL!!

If you have more than 16 participants in your group, you could still run this end of course review activity, but you could assign those additional participants the role of an adjudicator as part of an adjudicating panel (max 4).

If the course has been delivered by more than one trainer, each team can use one trainer as their "Mascot". The mascot could act as a Subject Matter Expert and assist their team with the answer to ONE of the questions, for a one point forfeit. The trainers could "play-up" their mascot roles and become competitive too!

Adult Learning Base Process – Competitive Metacognitive
Refer to **Adult Learning Base Process Reference Guide** for more information about this learning process.

Adult Learning Dashboard

This activity links participant's preferred style of learning. The following dashboard provides a quick reference to adult learning theorists and principles as part of the ID9® methodology.

This activity achieves the following level of Bloom's Taxonomy of the Cognitive Domain (Bloom et al 1956), shown with "X" in the following table.

Bloom's Taxonomy of the Cognitive Domain Level					
Knowledge	Comprehension	Application	Analysis	Synthesis	Evaluation
		X			

This activity also achieves a link, shown with "X" in the following table, to participant's naturally occurring learning preferences. Global/Specific, Learning Modalities, Hemispheric Preference (Sperry, 1981), and Multiple Intelligences (Gardner, 1983) are referenced in ID9® methodology and process. This is not a complete list of links that are covered within the ID9® process however this dashboard aims to provide a quick reference for trainers to use to balance instructional design to provide equality for participants' learning preferences.

Global/Specific Learners		Learning Modalities (Sensory Intake)			Hemispheric Preference	
Global	Specific	Visual	Auditory	Kinesthetic	Left Brain	Right Brain
X		X	X	X		X

Multiple Intelligences								
Visual	Intrapersonal	Interpersonal	Musical	Mathematical/ Logical	Linguistic	Kinesthetic	Naturalist	Existential
X		X	X	X		X		

97. Changing Tables

Learning Outcomes
Participants are able to complete a number of review activities that represent the "must know" content of the training course.

Overview
Nothing to do with babies! This competitive end of course review activity combines a number of short review activities on the main course topics that participants have to complete. It is like the learning stations learning activity but rather than learning they are reviewing! Each group of participants starts a few minutes apart at the same table. They then rotate around the tables in a fast a time as possible making sure that the activity is completed in the most accurate fashion.

Once they have completed all review activities, the end of course review activity is complete. The winning team is the team that completes the short review activities the most accurately and in the fastest time.

In My Experience
This activity is great for being able to apply those Adult Learning Principles! By ensuring that each review activity contains a selection of different learning styles, the whole spectrum of learning styles can be incorporated into one deliciously mixed and rich activity!

The Hidden Twist
As each table contains a review activity for each topic from the course, the whole of the course content is covered in an interactive and competitive way.

Essential Data
Course Type: Any
Group Size: 8-24
Time of Day: End of course review
Pace: Highly Competitive
Time to Create: 2-3 hours
Activity Duration: 30 minutes

Steps to Create
1. Create at least four simple review activities based on the course topics and prepare the materials necessary to run them. (See chapters 3, 4 & 5 for examples of review activities).
2. Print off all the materials needed for each activity.
3. Include the answer sheets or information capture tables in the participant guides or on one to two sheets of paper.

Steps to Run
1. Tell the participants that this activity will be timed and the group to correctly complete the whole activity in the shortest length of time will be the winners.
2. The trainer provides the activity instructions.
   a. All participants must close their books / course materials
   b. Each group/team is given one answer sheet
   c. Choose the running order of the groups (e.g. who will start, come second, third etc.)
   d. The first group start their stopwatch (most mobile phones have a stopwatch!) and they start at the first activity table.
   e. Once group1 has completed the first activity, they "change table" to the second activity table.
   f. Now group 2 can start their stopwatch and move to the first activity table.
   g. Continue this way until all groups have started.
   h. Once group 1 finishes the last activity on the last table, they stop their stopwatch and make a note of the time taken to complete all the tables.
   i. The trainer continues in this way until all groups have finished and all times have been noted.
   j. The winning team will have the quickest time with the most accurately completed activities.
3. As the end of course review activity is taking place, play some fast up-beat music to enhance the competitiveness.

Debrief
1. The trainer brings the group back together and asks them to sit back at their places.
2. Each of the short review activities are de-briefed and answers checked.
3. The groups take it in turns to feed-back on each of the review activities.
4. While the debrief is taking place, the trainer should ask "why" and "what if" questions to add depth to the learning and provide clarity when needed.

Working Example
Technical – New Hire Orientation

A one day new hire orientation course covers the following topics: Company strategy; Company History; Functions and locations; Our Products; Our Future.

Five tables are set up in the training room and a short review activity is placed at each table. The activities cover the must knows from each of the 5 topics, for example, for the functions and location review, a map could be placed at the table listing all the functions within the company. The groups would have to list on their answer sheet the cities in which there are company offices and which functions are located in each city.

Participants visit each table and complete the activities as fast as they can until all groups have completed all 5 of the review activities.

Tips, Tricks & Traps
It is important to make sure that all the activities take a similar time to complete. This way you will be able to stagger the teams more easily and avoid a bottleneck in the flow of the activity.

Adult Learning Base Process – Learning Stations
Refer to **Adult Learning Base Process Reference Guide** for more information about this learning process.

Adult Learning Dashboard

This activity links participant's preferred style of learning. The following dashboard provides a quick reference to adult learning theorists and principles as part of the ID9® methodology.

This activity achieves the following level of Bloom's Taxonomy of the Cognitive Domain (Bloom et al 1956), shown with "X" in the following table.

Bloom's Taxonomy of the Cognitive Domain Level					
Knowledge	Comprehension	Application	Analysis	Synthesis	Evaluation
	X				

This activity also achieves a link, shown with "X" in the following table, to participant's naturally occurring learning preferences. Global/Specific, Learning Modalities, Hemispheric Preference (Sperry, 1981), and Multiple Intelligences (Gardner, 1983) are referenced in ID9® methodology and process. This is not a complete list of links that are covered within the ID9® process however this dashboard aims to provide a quick reference for trainers to use to balance instructional design to provide equality for participants' learning preferences.

Global/Specific Learners		Learning Modalities (Sensory Intake)			Hemispheric Preference	
Global	Specific	Visual	Auditory	Kinesthetic	Left Brain	Right Brain
X	X	X	X	X	X	X

Multiple Intelligences								
Visual	Intrapersonal	Interpersonal	Musical	Mathematical/ Logical	Linguistic	Kinesthetic	Naturalist	Existential
X		X	X	X	X	X		

Chapter 7:
Bridging Tasks for Participants Learning and Review Activities

Alison Asbury

About the Co-Author:

Alison Asbury

Alison is a Training & Development Manager for a large biopharmaceutical company in California. For the past seven years, she has developed and delivered process and system training to lead Clinical Research and Data Management staff to higher levels of performance. She has delivered virtual training to learners around the globe and has travelled to India, Ireland and South Africa to deliver face-to-face training.

Alison specializes in process improvement implementations and change management, and is particularly adept at virtual training delivery to large, geographically-diverse audiences.

Alison plans to continue to learn and grow as a training professional and of course... travel!

Chapter Introduction

Bridging tasks can best be defined as any learning or review activity that occurs in between instructor-led classes. Bridging tasks can be completed individually, in pairs or in small groups without trainer or manager intervention.

Bridging tasks extend the classroom and the learning. It allows the learner to interact with the materials in new ways, in their own time, at their own pace. It allows them to explore new ideas they might not have had time to develop in class. Bridging tasks allow the learner to stretch and prepares them for their next in-class training. Bridging tasks are debriefed when the participants reconvene and steps are provided within the chapter to assist with the debrief process.

Bridging tasks that are considered 'learning activities' are when participants are completing the activity with the intent of learning new and not previously presented material. Learning activities are defined as 'first time learning' activities. Bridging tasks that are completed by participants as 'review activities' aim to review materials learned in previous training sessions. Review activities are defined as 'second or subsequent learning' activities.

This chapter provides ideas on different types of bridging tasks. Some are learning activities to extend the classroom and the learning. Some are review activities to increase retention and allow the participants to practice what they've learned. Some are simple and some are more complex and require more time for the learner to complete. As a trainer, take the challenge – some of these activities may seem too difficult or may appear complex for learners to complete. Bridging tasks extend the learning, advance skills and knowledge and embed retention. When completed bridging tasks are another step towards maximizing learning transfer and application. Let participants surprise you when they complete their bridging tasks … and themselves!

98. ABC Review (Article or Book Chapter Review)

Learning Outcomes
During this bridging task participants will review an article or book chapter in the time between classes. In doing this review as a bridging task, the learner has extra time to review material related to the class. This is a way of providing material without using precious class time.

Overview
This bridging task provides additional material or review material to reinforce learning.

Bridging Task – Learning Activity	Bridging Task – Review Activity
X	X

In My Experience
An article or book chapter review is a great way to provide additional perspectives. Learners can note their response to the materials. They can feel free to agree or disagree with the material provided. They are not agreeing or disagreeing with the instructor or one of their peers, they are simply agreeing or disagreeing with the point of view of the article or book chapter author.

The Hidden Twist
In reviewing the article or book chapter and formulating their response to it, the learner is solidifying their understanding of the material. This is a good learning or review activity when you are trying to reach higher level learning objectives like evaluating content.

Essential Data
COURSE TYPE: Any
GROUP SIZE: 1 – 20 (Optimal), 20+ (Debrief in small groups, not whole group together)
TIME OF DAY: Bridging Task
PACE: Slow
Trainer Preparation Time: 1 hour
Bridging Task Duration: 30 minutes - 1 hour

Steps to Create
1. Find one or more articles or book chapters related to the topic
2. Create a handout with the article or book chapter provided. The handout should include review questions so that article or book chapter can be discussed consistently when debriefed in the next session.

Steps to Run
1. Provide handout to participants
2. Ask participants to review the article or book chapter and answer the questions provided in the handout
3. Provide due date for bridging task*

Suggested Debrief Strategy / Sample Questions
In the next session, ask participants their reaction to the article or book chapter.
- What was their initial reaction?
- How did it make them feel?
- Did they support or reject the position stated in the article or book chapter immediately?
- Did their view change over time?

Working Example
Customer Service or Sales Training
This bridging task works best if the article or book chapter can be somewhat controversial. Try to pick an article or book chapter that may spark different emotional responses. Participants will engage more with content that makes them feel something – either positive or negative. This bridging task also lends itself to debate preparation.

This bridging task works well with customer service or sales training. The article or book chapter is about a customer call that goes horribly wrong. Learners will be able to reflect – have they ever encountered or witnessed something similar? Can they think of strategies to either avoid or repair if a similar situation happens to them?

Tips, Tricks & Traps
Ask participants open-ended questions. Let them reflect and formulate their own opinions to the material. Formulating their response and providing the rationale behind it are important to learning and aid retention.

Adult Learning Base Process – Research
Refer to **Adult Learning Base Process Reference Guide** for more information about this learning process.

Adult Learning Dashboard

This activity links participant's preferred style of learning. The following dashboard provides a quick reference to adult learning theorists and principles as part of the ID9® methodology.

This activity achieves the following level of Bloom's Taxonomy of the Cognitive Domain (Bloom et al 1956), shown with "X" in the following table.

Bloom's Taxonomy of the Cognitive Domain Level					
Knowledge	Comprehension	Application	Analysis	Synthesis	Evaluation
X	X		X		X

This activity also achieves a link, shown with "X" in the following table, to participant's naturally occurring learning preferences. Global/Specific, Learning Modalities, Hemispheric Preference (Sperry, 1981), and Multiple Intelligences (Gardner, 1983) are referenced in ID9® methodology and process. This is not a complete list of links that are covered within the ID9® process however this dashboard aims to provide a quick reference for trainers to use to balance instructional design to provide equality for participants' learning preferences.

Global/Specific Learners		Learning Modalities (Sensory Intake)			Hemispheric Preference	
Global	Specific	Visual	Auditory	Kinesthetic	Left Brain	Right Brain
X		X		X		X

Multiple Intelligences								
Visual	Intrapersonal	Interpersonal	Musical	Mathematical/ Logical	Linguistic	Kinesthetic	Naturalist	Existential
X	X			X	X	X		

99. Channel Your Inner Oprah (Conduct an Informational Interview)

Learning Outcomes
Learners conduct an interview to gather information, make connections, network and gain new insight.

Overview
In this bridging task, learners will conduct an interview with a peer, classmate, friend or family member on a topic related to the material.

Bridging Task – Learning Activity	Bridging Task – Review Activity
X	

In My Experience
Conducting an informational interview with another person passionate about the same topic is as enjoyable as it is enlightening. Conducting an informational interview provides insights and connections the learner would not have thought of on their own. It also provides a networking opportunity that will live beyond the course.

The Hidden Twist
In conducting the informational interview and putting the questions and responses to paper, the new information, connections and insights are solidified. Additional connections and insights might be gained while reflecting on the interview.

Essential Data
COURSE TYPE: Any
GROUP SIZE: 1 – 20 (Optimal), 20+ (Debrief in small groups, not whole group together)
TIME OF DAY: Bridging Task
PACE: Medium
Trainer Preparation Time: 30 minutes
Bridging Task Duration: 30 – 45 minutes (15 minutes for interview and 15 minutes to write up findings)

Steps to Create
1. Create a handout with interview topic and suggested questions

Steps to Run
1. Provide the handout to participants
2. Ask participants to conduct an informational interview with either a peer, co-worker, classmate, friend or family member
3. Provide due date for bridging task

Suggested Debrief Strategy/Sample Questions
In the next session, ask participants what new information they learned. What were you surprised to learn? What connections or new insights did you make as a result of the interview?

Working Example
Instructional Design
During the ID9® training we were exploring the topic of mobile learning. Our bridging task was to interview one of our classmates on mobile learning. The following interview questions were asked:
- Were they using mobile learning?
- How were they implementing mobile learning?
- What was their organization's mobile learning strategy?

I interviewed a classmate within my same company but in a different training organization in a different part of the world. I was fascinated to learn about what my classmate was working on. It sparked all sorts of new ideas that I wanted to explore and as well it created a new person in my professional network.

Tips, Tricks & Traps
- Let participants know that the handout questions can be used to guide the conversation but not all questions need to be asked or answered. The conversation should flow organically.
- For virtual sessions: If participants are to interview each other and are located in different locations, consider pairing up participants based on time zone. Or consider pairing up participants in different locations. It's engaging to interview someone from a different location than your own.

Adult Learning Base Process – Interview
Refer to **Adult Learning Base Process Reference Guide** for more information about this learning process.

Adult Learning Dashboard

This activity links participant's preferred style of learning. The following dashboard provides a quick reference to adult learning theorists and principles as part of the ID9® methodology.

This activity achieves the following level of Bloom's Taxonomy of the Cognitive Domain (Bloom et al 1956), shown with "X" in the following table.

Bloom's Taxonomy of the Cognitive Domain Level					
Knowledge	Comprehension	Application	Analysis	Synthesis	Evaluation
X	X		X	X	X

This activity also achieves a link, shown with "X" in the following table, to participant's naturally occurring learning preferences. Global/Specific, Learning Modalities, Hemispheric Preference (Sperry, 1981), and Multiple Intelligences (Gardner, 1983) are referenced in ID9® methodology and process. This is not a complete list of links that are covered within the ID9® process however this dashboard aims to provide a quick reference for trainers to use to balance instructional design to provide equality for participants' learning preferences.

Global/Specific Learners		Learning Modalities (Sensory Intake)			Hemispheric Preference	
Global	Specific	Visual	Auditory	Kinesthetic	Left Brain	Right Brain
X		X	X	X	X	X

Multiple Intelligences								
Visual	Intrapersonal	Interpersonal	Musical	Mathematical/ Logical	Linguistic	Kinesthetic	Naturalist	Existential
X	X	X			X	X		

100. I Spy

Learning Outcomes
Learners will visualize and walk through a past or upcoming interaction. Learners will think about the interaction from their perspective, the other person's perspective and a third observer perspective. If a past interaction is reviewed, this bridging task may provide the learner with insight on what went well, what did not go well and what they can do differently next time to improve the outcome. If an upcoming interaction is previewed, this bridging task will enable the learner to practice the interaction and see other perspectives. This will help the learner prepare for the interaction.

Overview
This bridging task uses the NLP technique of Perceptual Positions. Perceptual Positions allows the learner to review or preview an interaction as self, other and observer. It provides the learner an opportunity to consider these different perspectives and what they can do to help the interaction in a positive manner.

Bridging Task – Learning Activity	Bridging Task – Review Activity
X	X

In My Experience
This bridging task will help learners realize that preparation for an important interaction can only help the interaction go more smoothly. The learner will feel more relaxed having done the preparation and the other person will be impressed with the preparation done.

The Hidden Twist
This bridging task is about changing behavior. This bridging task allows learners to look at their role in an interaction from multiple perspectives. This bridging task may provide the learner the insight needed to change their behavior for a successful interaction.

Essential Data
COURSE TYPE: Any
GROUP SIZE: 1 – 20 (Optimal), 20+ (Debrief in small groups, not whole group together)
TIME OF DAY: Bridging Task
PACE: Slow
Trainer Preparation Time: 30 minutes
Bridging Task Duration: 30 minutes

Steps to Create
Create a handout with following:
a. Information on the NLP technique of Perceptual Positions
b. Instructions for the bridging task
c. Space for participants to write down their answers

Steps to Run
1. Provide the handout to participants
2. Ask each participant to think of a recent interaction or upcoming interaction that they would like to review
3. Ask participants to review or preview the interaction selected as self, other and observer
4. Ask participants to write a couple of sentences from each perspective
a. What did you see, hear and feel from each perspective?
5. Repeat each perspective to provide greater insight
6. Ask participants to write a couple of sentences about what they learned from the second round
7. Provide due date for bridging task

Suggested Debrief Strategy/Sample Questions
Manager / Trainer check-in:
• If possible, review and provide feedback prior to next session. If participant is struggling, request that they schedule a coaching session.

At the start of the next session:
• Depending on the size of the group, review the bridging task at the next session. What was their experience? Did the bridging task provide insight that changed the way they saw the interaction? What will they do same/differently in future interactions? Or if they previewed, did it change their strategy for the upcoming interaction?

Working Example
Negotiation Skills
This bridging task would work well for a course on negotiation skills. If the negotiation is reviewed, this bridging task will help the learner prepare for the next negotiation. If the negotiation is previewed, this will help the learner internalize that preparation prior to any negotiation is helpful.

Tips, Tricks & Traps
• Remind participants to "break state" before they move to the next perspective
• Remind participants if they get stuck to reach out for help. The instructor can help as well as a fellow participant.

Adult Learning Base Process
NLP - Perceptual Positions
Refer to **Adult Learning Base Process Reference**
Guide for more information about this learning process.

Adult Learning Dashboard

This activity links participant's preferred style of learning. The following dashboard provides a quick reference to adult learning theorists and principles as part of the ID9® methodology.

This activity achieves the following level of Bloom's Taxonomy of the Cognitive Domain (Bloom et al 1956), shown with "X" in the following table.

Bloom's Taxonomy of the Cognitive Domain Level					
Knowledge	Comprehension	Application	Analysis	Synthesis	Evaluation
	X	X			X

This activity also achieves a link, shown with "X" in the following table, to participant's naturally occurring learning preferences. Global/Specific, Learning Modalities, Hemispheric Preference (Sperry, 1981), and Multiple Intelligences (Gardner, 1983) are referenced in ID9® methodology and process. This is not a complete list of links that are covered within the ID9® process however this dashboard aims to provide a quick reference for trainers to use to balance instructional design to provide equality for participants' learning preferences.

Global/Specific Learners		Learning Modalities (Sensory Intake)			Hemispheric Preference	
Global	Specific	Visual	Auditory	Kinesthetic	Left Brain	Right Brain
X		X		X	X	

Multiple Intelligences								
Visual	Intrapersonal	Interpersonal	Musical	Mathematical/ Logical	Linguistic	Kinesthetic	Naturalist	Existential
X	X				X	X		

101. Hurdles

Learning Outcomes
Learners will reflect on what they've learned and will think about how to implement.

Overview
In this bridging task, learners will reflect on what they've learned and will think about the hurdles they might encounter when implementing.

Bridging Task – Learning Activity	Bridging Task – Review Activity
	X

In My Experience
This bridging task provides learners the opportunity to pause and think about what they've just learned. This pause and reflection helps to solidify learning. It might also bring new insights to light or bring up new questions for the learner to explore further.

The Hidden Twist
In thinking about the hurdles they might encounter, learners start to plan how to overcome the hurdles.

Essential Data
COURSE TYPE: Any
GROUP SIZE: 1 – 20 (Optimal), 20+ (Debrief in small groups, not whole group together)
TIME OF DAY: Bridging Task
PACE: Slow
Trainer Preparation Time: 30 minutes
Bridging Task Duration: 30 minutes

Steps to Create
1. Create a handout for participant's reflection – see Sample Handout

Sample Handout:

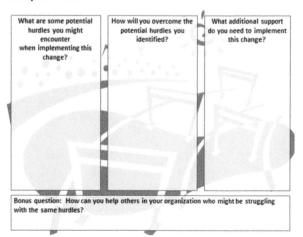

Steps to Run
1. Provide handout to participants
2. Ask participants to reflect on the change they have just learned about. This could be a change in behavior, organizational change or a change in process.
   a. What are some potential hurdles you might encounter when implementing this change?
   b. How will you overcome the potential hurdles you identified?
   c. What additional support do you need to implement this change?
   d. How can you help others in your organization who might be struggling with the same hurdles?
3. Provide due date for bridging task

Suggested Debrief Strategy/Sample Questions
In the next session, ask participants to list the potential hurdles they identified and potential solutions to overcome those hurdles. Can other participants expand on potential solutions? What additional support do they need? How can they help others who might struggle with the same hurdles?

Working Example
Process Training
This is a good bridging task for a class on a new or changing process. This bridging task provides the pause for reflection needed to implement a change. This bridging task provides the opportunity to discuss concerns and helps participants through the concern to possible solutions. This bridging task will help the participant realize most perceived hurdles have easy solutions. This bridging task will provide the opportunity for participants to identify the support they need to implement the change as well as how they can help others.

Tips, Tricks & Traps

As the instructor, you will want to review the results of this bridging task prior to the next session. That way you will know going into the next session if participants are struggling or resistant to change. If a participant has uncovered a hurdle they can't think of a potential solution for, you can brainstorm or research potential solutions prior to the next session so that the participant, other participants and next session are not derailed.

Adult Learning Base Process
Metacognitive Reflection
Refer to **Adult Learning Base Process Reference Guide** for more information about this learning process.

Adult Learning Dashboard

This activity links participant's preferred style of learning. The following dashboard provides a quick reference to adult learning theorists and principles as part of the ID9® methodology.

This activity achieves the following level of Bloom's Taxonomy of the Cognitive Domain (Bloom et al 1956), shown with "X" in the following table.

Bloom's Taxonomy of the Cognitive Domain Level					
Knowledge	Comprehension	Application	Analysis	Synthesis	Evaluation
	X	X	X		

This activity also achieves a link, shown with "X" in the following table, to participant's naturally occurring learning preferences. Global/Specific, Learning Modalities, Hemispheric Preference (Sperry, 1981), and Multiple Intelligences (Gardner, 1983) are referenced in ID9® methodology and process. This is not a complete list of links that are covered within the ID9® process however this dashboard aims to provide a quick reference for trainers to use to balance instructional design to provide equality for participants' learning preferences.

Global/Specific Learners		Learning Modalities (Sensory Intake)			Hemispheric Preference	
Global	Specific	Visual	Auditory	Kinesthetic	Left Brain	Right Brain
	X	X		X		X

Multiple Intelligences								
Visual	Intrapersonal	Interpersonal	Musical	Mathematical/ Logical	Linguistic	Kinesthetic	Naturalist	Existential
X	X			X	X	X	X	X

102. Name Calling

Learning Outcomes
Learners will reflect on what they've learned and will start to think about the topic more broadly. This expansion in thought lends itself to more creative thought patterns and additional connections made with the material which increases retention.

Overview
In this bridging task, learners will reflect on what they've learned and will think about whom else to go to for information or who else might like to gain knowledge of the topic discussed.

Bridging Task – Learning Activity	Bridging Task – Review Activity
	X

In My Experience
This bridging task provides learners the opportunity to pause and think about what they've just learned. People like to help others and share their knowledge. Learners feel good about sharing what they've just learned and they potentially help the person they share the information with.

The Hidden Twist
In thinking about who else might like to gain knowledge of the topic discussed, the learner may actually reach out to those individuals thus sharing knowledge organically throughout the organization.

Essential Data
COURSE TYPE: Any
GROUP SIZE: 1 – 20 (Optimal), 20+ (Debrief in small groups, not whole group together)
TIME OF DAY: Bridging Task
PACE: Slow
Trainer Preparation Time: 30 minutes
Bridging Task Duration: 30 minutes

Steps to Create
1. Create handout for participant's reflection – see Sample Handout

Sample Handout:

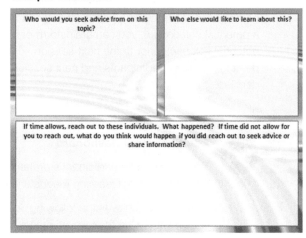

Steps to Run
Provide handout to participants
1. Ask participants to reflect on what they have learned
   a. Who would you seek advice from on this topic?
   b. Who else would like to learn about this?
   c. If time allows, reach out to these individuals. What happened? If time did not allow for you to reach out, what do you think would happen if you did reach out to seek advice or share information?
2. Provide due date for bridging task

Suggested Debrief Strategy/Sample Questions
In the next session, ask participants:
- Who did you think of to seek advice from? Why? Were you able to reach out to them? If yes, what happened? If no, what do you think would happen if you reached out to them?
- Who else would like to learn about this? Why? Were you able to reach out to them? If yes, what happened? If no, what do you think would happen if you reached out to them?

Working Example
Process Training
This is a good bridging task for a class on a new or changed process. Learners will think about whom to get advice from. If they are able to reach out to these individuals, it provides an opportunity to discuss the new or changed process and learn more about the benefits to the organization. (As a trainer, you will want to reach out to managers, stakeholders and the project team so they are aware staff may be reaching out to them. Work with the project team to provide management with a brief synopsis of the new or changed process.) Learners will think about whom to share this information with. If they are able to reach out to these individuals, it provides the opportunity for the knowledge to cascade through the organization organically. I once received a "Word of Mouth" Award. It was for process training where the organization was so excited about the new process that they told their friends to attend the training.

Tips, Tricks & Traps
In process training, if it is an organizational change that's already been agreed to by leadership, its best practice to add a disclaimer not to question the rationale behind the process. It's better to focus on the benefits of the process to the organization. It's best to give learners an outlet for questions and suggestions regarding the new or changed process (i.e. their manager, a leadership team member that is also a stakeholder in the new or changed process, an email inbox manned by the project team implementing the new or changed process, etc.)

Adult Learning Base Process
Metacognitive Reflection
Refer to **Adult Learning Base Process Reference Guide** for more information about this learning process.

Adult Learning Dashboard

This activity links participant's preferred style of learning. The following dashboard provides a quick reference to adult learning theorists and principles as part of the ID9® methodology.

This activity achieves the following level of Bloom's Taxonomy of the Cognitive Domain (Bloom et al 1956), shown with "X" in the following table.

Bloom's Taxonomy of the Cognitive Domain Level					
Knowledge	Comprehension	Application	Analysis	Synthesis	Evaluation
X	X	X			

This activity also achieves a link, shown with "X" in the following table, to participant's naturally occurring learning preferences. Global/Specific, Learning Modalities, Hemispheric Preference (Sperry, 1981), and Multiple Intelligences (Gardner, 1983) are referenced in ID9® methodology and process. This is not a complete list of links that are covered within the ID9® process however this dashboard aims to provide a quick reference for trainers to use to balance instructional design to provide equality for participants' learning preferences.

Global/Specific Learners		Learning Modalities (Sensory Intake)			Hemispheric Preference	
Global	Specific	Visual	Auditory	Kinesthetic	Left Brain	Right Brain
X	X	X	X	X		X

Multiple Intelligences								
Visual	Intrapersonal	Interpersonal	Musical	Mathematical/ Logical	Linguistic	Kinesthetic	Naturalist	Existential
X	X	X			X	X	X	X

103. Blog-O-Rama

Learning Outcomes
This bridging task is another way to solidify learning and increase retention.

Overview
In this bridging task, participants will write a blog. This could either be a private or public blog. If a private blog, the blog could serve as a Learning Journal. This is where the learner can reflect on their learning, highlight key points and document a Skill Development Action Plan. If a public blog, the blog could serve as an area where participants can submit their assignments, answer questions from the instructor or other participants or bounce ideas off each other.

Bridging Task – Learning Activity	Bridging Task – Review Activity
	X

In My Experience
Writing a blog is similar to keeping a journal and is a way to track progress. Learners can take notes, highlight key areas of interest and set goals. The blog is an engaging way to go back in time and look at all that has been learned and the progress made on goals.

The Hidden Twist
Do you want to set up a class blog or do you want learners to set up their own blog? Either way, learners are not only thinking and writing about what they've learned thereby increasing retention, they are learning about blogging too! That's pretty cool.

Essential Data
COURSE TYPE: Any

GROUP SIZE: Any, 5 – 20 (Optimal), 20+ (Consider debriefing within the blog as well)

TIME OF DAY: Bridging Task

PACE: Fast – Medium (Depends on amount of writing per blog. Short and quick blog posts could be fast paced. Lengthier blog posts would be at a more moderate pace)

Trainer Preparation Time: 1 - 5 hours (depending on experience)

Bridging Task Duration: 1 - 2 hours

Steps to Create
1. If creating a class blog, you will need to set up the blog. If participants are setting up individual blogs, you'll need to provide set up instructions to participants.
   You will find lots of information with a simple internet search.

Steps to Run
1. Decide: Class or individual blogs?
2. Decide: Public or private?
3. If a class blog, you'll provide participants with the blog address. Additionally, you'll provide the assignment. What are participants going to write about? Are they reviewing an article and providing comments? Are they expected to comment on each other's work? Are they answering questions you'll post to the blog? Are they keeping a public learning journal where they can highlight their key learning (and learn from each other)?
4. If individual blogs, you'll provide participants with instructions to set up. Again, you'll provide the assignment. What are participants going to write about? Are they keeping a learning journal and setting goals? This is a good place to track a Skills Development Action Plan that only you and the participant have access to.
5. Provide due date for bridging task.

Suggested Debrief Strategy/Sample Questions
In the next session, ask participants:
- What did you blog about? What did you learn about through blogging? What was your favorite key learning? Now that you've blogged, will you continue blogging?

Working Example
Writing Skills in Business Communication
Blogging might work well for a Writing Skills in Business Communication class. Participants can practice writing business communications and can post to the class for feedback.

Tips, Tricks & Traps
Make sure you are comfortable blogging prior to using this bridging task for a class. Test it out with friends or co-workers first. You'll need to help participants trouble shoot when they run into problems to have this bridging task run smoothly.

Adult Learning Base Process
Journaling
Refer to **Adult Learning Base Process Reference Guide** for more information about this learning process.

Adult Learning Dashboard
This activity links participant's preferred style of learning. The following dashboard provides a quick reference to adult learning theorists and principles as part of the ID9® methodology.

This activity achieves the following level of Bloom's Taxonomy of the Cognitive Domain (Bloom et al 1956), shown with "X" in the following table.

Bloom's Taxonomy of the Cognitive Domain Level					
Knowledge	Comprehension	Application	Analysis	Synthesis	Evaluation
X	X		X	X	X

This activity also achieves a link, shown with "X" in the following table, to participant's naturally occurring learning preferences. Global/Specific, Learning Modalities, Hemispheric Preference (Sperry, 1981), and Multiple Intelligences (Gardner, 1983) are referenced in ID9® methodology and process. This is not a complete list of links that are covered within the ID9® process however this dashboard aims to provide a quick reference for trainers to use to balance instructional design to provide equality for participants' learning preferences.

Global/Specific Learners		Learning Modalities (Sensory Intake)			Hemispheric Preference	
Global	Specific	Visual	Auditory	Kinesthetic	Left Brain	Right Brain
X	X	X		X		X

Multiple Intelligences								
Visual	Intrapersonal	Interpersonal	Musical	Mathematical / Logical	Linguistic	Kinesthetic	Naturalist	Existential
X	X	X			X	X		

104. Do Good

Learning Outcomes
In this bridging task, participants 'do good' while getting actual experience using what they are learning. By using what they are learning, participants get to practice and spend more time with the materials. They might encounter issues or raise questions they would not have otherwise. All this helps to increase retention. Additionally, by being able to practice what is being taught, learner confidence increases as well.

Overview
In this bridging task, participants should actually do whatever they are being trained on. The hidden twist is that in doing this bridging task, participants are also doing well for their community.

Bridging Task – Learning Activity	Bridging Task – Review Activity
	X

In My Experience
This bridging task is a great way to get learners to engage with the materials. They are really using the materials and tools they are learning about. Plus they are doing so in a way that helps others. It's a win-win.

The Hidden Twist
You can also add a little competition to the mix. If you set up the bridging task so that participants are completing a project to raise money, the participant who raises the most money can win a prize. The prize could be related to the class, like a book on project management or additional coaching time with the instructor.

Essential Data
COURSE TYPE: Any course where participants can volunteer their time to practice the skills learned in class.

GROUP SIZE: 1 - 20 (Optimal)

TIME OF DAY: Bridging Task

PACE: Medium

Trainer Preparation Time: 2 hours

Bridging Task Duration: 5 - 10 hours or more depending on project

Steps to Create
1. Create instructions on how to use Project Management class materials and Project Management tools to complete a project

Steps to Run
1. Instruct participants to:
   a. Select a project
   b. Select a stakeholder (for this bridging task, this is typically the instructor)
   c. Draft a plan that includes communication, budget, timeline and resources available. Get stakeholder approval.
   d. Once approved by the stakeholder, get started on the project and provide regular updates. Timing of regular updates should be suggested in the communication plan and approved by the stakeholder.
   e. Complete the project and donate the money raised to charity.

Suggested Debrief Strategy/Sample Questions
In the next session, ask participants:
- What hurdles are you running into in managing or completing your project? How can you overcome those hurdles? (These are typically the same type of obstacles they would run into for any project – issues with communication, budget, timeline, resources or quality.)
- If the bridging task includes competition, update participants on where they stand. This might spur some additionally fund raising efforts to increase standings. Nobody likes to finish last.

Working Example
Project Management
This bridging task would work well for a Project Management class. All class materials and tools can be utilized. Participants will get practice using the skills learned in class. For example, the bridging task could be to complete a project to raise money with all proceeds being donated to charity. Other examples might be classes on instructional design, developing and delivering training or building eLearning courses. Training associations offer links to volunteer opportunities. This is a great way to practice Project Management skills in a fun, competitive and safe way.

Tips, Tricks & Traps
This is not an easy bridging task to complete.
This requires a significant time commitment from
participants. Adding an element of highly engaging
participation and competition helps. Plus participants
know at the end, they will be donating money to a
charity the class selected. When they encounter
hurdles or frustration, this will keep them going.

Adult Learning Base Process
Application Project
Refer to **Adult Learning Base Process Reference**
Guide for more information about this learning process.

Adult Learning Dashboard
This activity links participant's preferred style of learning. The following dashboard provides a quick
reference to adult learning theorists and principles as part of the ID9® methodology.

This activity achieves the following level of Bloom's Taxonomy of the Cognitive Domain (Bloom et al 1956),
shown with "X" in the following table.

Bloom's Taxonomy of the Cognitive Domain Level					
Knowledge	Comprehension	Application	Analysis	Synthesis	Evaluation
X	X	X			

This activity also achieves a link, shown with "X" in the following table, to participant's naturally occurring learning
preferences. Global/Specific, Learning Modalities, Hemispheric Preference (Sperry, 1981), and Multiple Intelligences
(Gardner, 1983) are referenced in ID9® methodology and process. This is not a complete list of links that are covered
within the ID9® process however this dashboard aims to provide a quick reference for trainers to use to balance
instructional design to provide equality for participants' learning preferences.

Global/Specific Learners		Learning Modalities (Sensory Intake)			Hemispheric Preference	
Global	Specific	Visual	Auditory	Kinesthetic	Left Brain	Right Brain
X		X		X		X

Multiple Intelligences								
Visual	Intrapersonal	Interpersonal	Musical	Mathematical / Logical	Linguistic	Kinesthetic	Naturalist	Existential
X	X	X			X	X		X

105. Prepare for Success (for Negotiation Training)

Learning Outcomes

It helps to be prepared when going into any negotiation – from buying a new car or house to negotiation that next big deal. In this bridging task, participants will practice using a negotiation planning worksheet. In working through the negotiation planning worksheet, participants will also work on their questioning skills (i.e. making sure they are asking the right questions to get to a win-win negotiation).

Similar conversation guides and planning worksheets can be prepared for other topics of training. Use the following activity as the foundation to spark ideas for your subject matter.

Bridging Task – Learning Activity	Bridging Task – Review Activity
	X

Overview

In this bridging task, participants will review a recent negotiation or practice negotiating with a partner.

In My Experience

Everyone needs negotiation skills. This bridging task strengthens skills learned in negotiation training. It allows the learner to practice using the negotiation tools provided in class. Typically this includes a negotiation planning worksheet.

The Hidden Twist

In business, it helps to be prepared. That goes for any business interaction from job interview, to tough negotiation, to delivering a speech. In this bridging task, participants will learn the benefits of preparation. In learning the benefits of preparation, they may see how it can help in many other aspects of their business and personal lives.

Essential Data

COURSE TYPE: Negotiation Skills

GROUP SIZE: 2 – 20 (Optimal)

TIME OF DAY: Bridging Task

PACE: Medium

Trainer Preparation Time: 30 minutes - 2 hours

Bridging Task Duration: 30 minutes – 1 hour

Steps to Create

1. If participants are going to review a recent negotiation, create a handout with review questions.
   a. Did they prepare for this negotiation? If yes, what did they do to prepare for this negotiation? If no, go back and simulate preparing for the negotiation. Would this have helped in the negotiation? If so, how?
2. If participants are going to practice a negotiation, create scenarios for each partner pair. Each scenario for each partner pair will tell the story of the upcoming negotiation and provide each partner with information regarding their part of the negotiation. The scenario will include highest and lowest buy or sell amounts and if there is a best alternative to a negotiated agreement (BATNA) for either party.

Steps to Run

Provide the negotiation planning worksheet.

1. Provide instructions on how to use the negotiation planning worksheet
2. Provide handout with review questions or assign partners and provide scenarios
3. Provide due date for bridging task

Suggested Debrief Strategy/Sample Questions

Negotiation Review

In the next session, review the handout questions. Ask participants:

- Did they prepare for the negotiation?
  o If yes, what did they do to prepare for the negotiation? Did the preparation help the negotiation go more smoothly or have a successful outcome? If yes, how? If no, what would have helped the negotiation?
  o If no, were they able to go back and simulate prepare for the negotiation? Would this have helped in the negotiation? If so, how? What will they do differently in a future negation?

Negotiation Practice

In the next session, ask participants:

- How did the negotiation go? Did you have enough information? If no, what additional questions did you ask? What was the outcome of the negotiation?

Working Example
Negotiation Skills
This is a great bridging task for a Negotiation Skills class. If done in a classroom setting or online, consider recording participants performing the negotiation. Review the recording with participants so they can learn even more from the interaction.

Tips, Tricks & Traps
In creating the negotiation scenarios, provide enough information to get participants started but try to leave some information out so that participants have to think about what questions need to be asked. In negotiating, typically the buyer knows how much they

want to spend and the highest amount they are willing to spend. The seller doesn't know this information and typically has to ask questions to figure this information out. Likewise, the seller knows the absolute bottom they are willing to sell for and the buyer needs to ask questions. In any negotiation, there can be a win-win outcome. It takes questioning and listening to get there.

Adult Learning Base Process
Application Project
Refer to **Adult Learning Base Process Reference Guide** for more information about this learning process.

Adult Learning Dashboard
This activity links participant's preferred style of learning. The following dashboard provides a quick reference to adult learning theorists and principles as part of the ID9® methodology.

This activity achieves the following level of Bloom's Taxonomy of the Cognitive Domain (Bloom et al 1956), shown with "X" in the following table.

Bloom's Taxonomy of the Cognitive Domain Level					
Knowledge	Comprehension	Application	Analysis	Synthesis	Evaluation
X	X	X			

This activity also achieves a link, shown with "X" in the following table, to participant's naturally occurring learning preferences. Global/Specific, Learning Modalities, Hemispheric Preference (Sperry, 1981), and Multiple Intelligences (Gardner, 1983) are referenced in ID9® methodology and process. This is not a complete list of links that are covered within the ID9® process however this dashboard aims to provide a quick reference for trainers to use to balance instructional design to provide equality for participants' learning preferences.

Global/Specific Learners		Learning Modalities (Sensory Intake)			Hemispheric Preference	
Global	Specific	Visual	Auditory	Kinesthetic	Left Brain	Right Brain
	X	X	X	X		X

Multiple Intelligences								
Visual	Intrapersonal	Interpersonal	Musical	Mathematical / Logical	Linguistic	Kinesthetic	Naturalist	Existential
X	X	X		X	X	X		

106. Toastmasters (for Presentation Skills Training)

Learning Outcomes

Learners gain valuable experience in practicing presentation or public speaking skills.

Overview

In this bridging task, participants use the camera app on their smartphone to record a speech or presentation.

Bridging Task – Learning Activity	Bridging Task – Review Activity
	X

In My Experience

This bridging task helps learners practice what they've learned and lets them review their speech or presentation in action. The camera doesn't lie … they'll be able to see areas they are doing well and areas that need improvement. They can continue to practice by recording themselves until they feel confident delivering the material to a live audience.

The Hidden Twist

Learners will gain valuable insight that preparation and practice for an upcoming speech or presentation helps to ensure success.

Essential Data

COURSE TYPE: Communication Skills, Presentations Skills, Public Speaking

GROUP SIZE: 1 – 20 (Smaller class size is optimal so the instructor can review recordings and provide feedback to participants individually)

TIME OF DAY: Bridging Task

PACE: Medium

Trainer Preparation Time: 30 minutes

Bridging Task Duration: 30 minutes - 1 hour

Steps to Create

1. Create a handout with instructions to participants
   a. Provide instructions on how to record using camera app on iPhone or smartphone.
   b. Are you going to give them a topic to give a speech or presentation on or are they thinking of a topic themselves?
   c. Provide the duration of the speech or presentation.

Steps to Run

1. Provide handout to participants
2. Review bridging task with participants
   a. Are there any participants that do not have access to an iPhone or smartphone? You will need to have a plan to deal with this. Are there loaner recording devices available (cameras, camcorders, etc.)? Can time be scheduled with the instructor or other participant to use their recording device?
3. Are you going to review the recordings or are the recordings practice for a live speech to be delivered in the next class?
   a. If you are going to review the recordings, provide a due date to submit the recording(s) to the instructor.

Suggested Debrief Strategy/Sample Questions

If you are reviewing the recording(s) individually with the participant, ask what went well and what are the areas they would like to improve upon? You can provide additional feedback as well. Ask how the participant felt after practicing by recording? More confident? Aware of areas that needed practice or improvement? Did recording help them prepare the materials? Did it make them go back and re-write parts that didn't flow?

If the bridging task is practice for a live speech or presentation to be delivered in class, ask how the recording helped prepare for the live speech or presentation? How did they feel after they practiced? Did they record more than once? How did they feel after each additional recording?

Working Example
Public Speaking / Presentation skills

This bridging task works well for a class on public speaking or presentation skills. Delivering a speech takes practice. Practicing a speech by recording it forces the participant to say each word – not just practice it in their head. It will allow them to see what parts they might stumble on and might need to re-word for the appropriate flow. It will let them see areas that need improvement. Are they mumbling? Are they looking down? What are they doing with their hands? What is their body language?

Tips, Tricks & Traps
This bridging task does not take a lot of time to create but it may take significant time to provide individual feedback. Think about the class size and if you can effectively provide feedback individually. Consider keeping the course size small if providing feedback individually.

 Adult Learning Base Process
Application Project
Refer to **Adult Learning Base Process Reference Guide** for more information about this learning process.

 Adult Learning Dashboard
This activity links participant's preferred style of learning. The following dashboard provides a quick reference to adult learning theorists and principles as part of the ID9® methodology.

This activity achieves the following level of Bloom's Taxonomy of the Cognitive Domain (Bloom et al 1956), shown with "X" in the following table.

Bloom's Taxonomy of the Cognitive Domain Level					
Knowledge	Comprehension	Application	Analysis	Synthesis	Evaluation
X	X	X			

This activity also achieves a link, shown with "X" in the following table, to participant's naturally occurring learning preferences. Global/Specific, Learning Modalities, Hemispheric Preference (Sperry, 1981), and Multiple Intelligences (Gardner, 1983) are referenced in ID9® methodology and process. This is not a complete list of links that are covered within the ID9® process however this dashboard aims to provide a quick reference for trainers to use to balance instructional design to provide equality for participants' learning preferences.

Global/Specific Learners		Learning Modalities (Sensory Intake)			Hemispheric Preference	
Global	Specific	Visual	Auditory	Kinesthetic	Left Brain	Right Brain
	X	X	X	X	X	

Multiple Intelligences								
Visual	Intrapersonal	Interpersonal	Musical	Mathematical / Logical	Linguistic	Kinesthetic	Naturalist	Existential
X	X				X	X		

107. Reviewed and Improved

Learning Outcomes

Participants will solidify their learning by reviewing training material and make recommendations for improvement. The recommendations for improvement will be based on what the course has taught them about instructional design.

Overview

In this bridging task, participants will review existing training material and make recommendations for improvements.

Bridging Task – Learning Activity	Bridging Task – Review Activity
	X

In My Experience

This bridging task helps participants identify flaws in instructional design in existing training material. By reviewing the principles of instructional design, participants are increasing their retention. Additionally, by identifying flaws in existing training material, participants will be less likely to create training material that do not adhere to the principles of instructional design.

The Hidden Twist

Participants will be able to take those recommendations forward and actually improve the training material reviewed. This benefits the organization and future participants of the improved upon training material.

Essential Data

COURSE TYPE: Train the Trainer; Instructional Design

GROUP SIZE: 1 – 20+

TIME OF DAY: Bridging Task

PACE: Slow

Trainer Preparation Time: 15 - 30 minutes

Bridging Task Duration: 30 minutes - 1 hour

Steps to Create

1. Create a handout with instructions to participants

Steps to Run

1. Provide handout to participants
2. Ask participants to select existing training materials for review
3. Provide due date to submit recommendations for improvement

Suggested Debrief Strategy/Sample Questions

Ask participants to share their recommendations with the class. Ask each participant: If this recommendation was incorporated into the existing training materials, what would the learner of the new and improved training experience? How does the recommended improvement increase learning, review and/or retention?

Working Example
Instructional Design

This bridging task works well for a class on instructional design. Participants can select existing training materials and think of ways to improve upon those materials. They could focus on improving the overall design or they could focus on improving one aspect of the training, for example adding review questions.

Tips, Tricks & Traps

Ask participants to stretch and actually implement the improvements recommended.

Adult Learning Base Process
Metacognitive Reflection

Refer to **Adult Learning Base Process Reference Guide** for more information about this learning process.

Adult Learning Dashboard
This activity links participant's preferred style of learning. The following dashboard provides a quick reference to adult learning theorists and principles as part of the ID9® methodology.

This activity achieves the following level of Bloom's Taxonomy of the Cognitive Domain (Bloom et al 1956), shown with "X" in the following table.

Bloom's Taxonomy of the Cognitive Domain Level					
Knowledge	Comprehension	Application	Analysis	Synthesis	Evaluation
X	X	X	X	X	X

This activity also achieves a link, shown with "X" in the following table, to participant's naturally occurring learning preferences. Global/Specific, Learning Modalities, Hemispheric Preference (Sperry, 1981), and Multiple Intelligences (Gardner, 1983) are referenced in ID9® methodology and process. This is not a complete list of links that are covered within the ID9® process however this dashboard aims to provide a quick reference for trainers to use to balance instructional design to provide equality for participants' learning preferences.

Global/Specific Learners		Learning Modalities (Sensory Intake)			Hemispheric Preference	
Global	Specific	Visual	Auditory	Kinesthetic	Left Brain	Right Brain
	X	X		X		X

Multiple Intelligences								
Visual	Intrapersonal	Interpersonal	Musical	Mathematical / Logical	Linguistic	Kinesthetic	Naturalist	Existential
X	X				X	X		

Chapter 8:
Post-Course Tasks for Participants - Application of Learning Activities
Emma Lambert

About the Co-Author:

Emma Lambert

Emma Lambert discovered her love of teaching in 1995 when she qualified as a nurse and took a teaching qualification (C&G 7307 Further and Adult Education Teaching Certificate) to improve her chances of promotion in nursing. Little did she know then that she was opening a door to a whole new passion. Since then there have been a number other qualifications, including those in teaching and training which have taken her through a number of roles in the clinical setting and finally to the pharmaceutical industry where she has been in leadership and management roles all of which have involved teaching or training, including designing whole curricula, either formally or informally for her team. Currently Global Head Learning Operations and Quality at Novartis AG Switzerland Emma continues to build her knowledge of the science behind teaching and training and feed her passion for the speciality.

Chapter Introduction

Hello, so perhaps you have already read the other chapters in this book or perhaps this is just where it fell open as you dived in. Whatever the case, don't flip to another chapter yet!

As professional trainers we work hard to make sure that our learning objectives are action based and measurable, our content is correct and relevant and our delivery lights fires for our participants whatever their learning preference and motivation to learn. We give our hearts and souls in the delivery of the training and often we wave goodbye at the end of the training course and hope for the best. So doesn't it break your heart when you hear feedback along the lines of, "That training was no good, I sent Joe on it and he still does exactly the same as he did before?"

There is only so much we can do as trainers. When we realize that a training intervention is not just 'getting participants through the training', that is, moving a person from the beginning of the training course to the end we shift from 'professional presenter' to 'professional trainer'. To get participants to a behavior change means that something needs to be in place to encourage, support, motivate and drive participants to do what was originally designed in the training objectives (Mattiske: High Performance Learning Model).

In Chapter 1, I provided pre-course activities to engage, motivate and kick-start the learning process. This chapter wraps up the learning path by providing post-course activities to maximize the possibility that participants apply what they have learned. This book-end of pre- and post-learning activities extends the learning intervention and moves from an 'event' to a 'process'.

Engaging participants and keeping learning going after the 'event' can be challenging for trainers. Traditionally participants have thought of training as occasion, with a free lunch, and perhaps considered it a 'day off from real work'. The post-course tasks prolong your training influence and reinforce the message that training is a journey, not a day trip, and sends a strong message that participants need to do something more than just attend – they need to apply what they have learned.

Additionally, in Chapter 9, my friend and colleague Susan Giddens presents ways to engage participants' managers in the post-course process to drive learning application. When post-course activities are given to participants and Susan's activities given to managers learning application takes off with participants applying what they've learned with skyrocketed motivation.

108. I learned you learned

Learning Outcome
Accelerating the application of learning to the workplace

Overview
This activity encourages participants to think broadly around what they have learned in the classroom and examine how they can apply the learning in the workplace.

In My Experience
Participants typically leave the classroom with varying degrees of motivation to apply what they have learned. Approximately 15% of them will apply the learning spontaneously (Brinkerhoff 2006) but the other 85% will require some assistance in transferring learning to behavior. This activity allows participants to reflect on their learning individually then bring it back to the group setting to discuss and explore the practicalities of applying what they have learned back on the job. I used this simple activity to follow up initial training on a new system being introduced to an organization. Participants subsequently created their own forum for sharing tips and ideas for using the system.

The Hidden Twist
Over time participants will begin to develop their own self-evaluation processes allowing them to see ways of transferring learning to the workplace and so accelerating the pace of behavior change. They will also learn from each other about how to apply their learning.

Essential Data
Course Type: Any

Group Size: Pairs, small or whole group

Time of day: 30 days post-course

Pace: Intermediate as dictated by the group

Time to Create: 15 minutes

Time to run: 30-60 minutes depending upon group size

Steps to Create
- Create flip charts with the following statements, one per flip chart
  - I have applied xxxx from the course to my workplace
  - The result of doing this has been xxxx
  - Since the course I have learned
  - I would like to share this tip
  - The thing I found that did not really work well was xxxxx
  - I think this xxxx would have made it work better
- Create a hand out of these statements to give to participants at the end of the course with the explanation that you will meet to discuss the responses post-course

Steps to Run
- Arrange a meeting of the group a month after the class
- Have the statements on the flipcharts around the wall in order
- After greeting the participants and allowing them to settle in the room ask for a volunteer to start the session
- The trainer then facilitates the session recording answers and encouraging discussion and questioning of each other
- To close the session ask the participants if they would find it useful to share ideas again and if so ask somebody to facilitate an informal follow up
- Tell participants that they can contact you if they need any assistance in running the session

Suggested Debrief Strategy / Sample Questions
By priming the participants with the statements before the session you are reinforcing the expectation that they will apply the learning.

Ask participants what they think will be the next step in their learning process related to this

Working Example
This activity is particularly useful following a course where specific actions are required, for example the introduction of a new process or system with clearly defined steps or operating procedures.

Tips, Tricks and Traps
- Identify one or two high performance learners (Mattiske) and prime them before the session so that you have somebody to start the discussion
- Set the date for the follow up at the same time as the date for the training
- Ensure participants know that this session is part of the course follow up and that completion will not be recorded in LMS unless this step is taken
- Have one or two tips about the system or process to hand in case discussion is slow
- Make sure that any tips or tricks identified by participants do not invalidate the system or process or result in non-compliance

Adult Learning Base Process
Metacognitive Self Reflection
Refer to **Adult Learning Base Process Reference Guide** for more information about this learning process.

Adult Learning Dashboard
This activity links participant's preferred style of learning. The following dashboard provides a quick reference to adult learning theorists and principles as part of the ID9® methodology.

This activity achieves the following level of Bloom's Taxonomy of the Cognitive Domain (Bloom et al 1956), shown with "X" in the following table.

Bloom's Taxonomy of the Cognitive Domain Level					
Knowledge	Comprehension	Application	Analysis	Synthesis	Evaluation
		X			

This activity also achieves a link, shown with "X" in the following table, to participant's naturally occurring learning preferences. Global/Specific, Learning Modalities, Hemispheric Preference (Sperry, 1981), and Multiple Intelligences (Gardner, 1983) are referenced in ID9® methodology and process. This is not a complete list of links that are covered within the ID9® process however this dashboard aims to provide a quick reference for trainers to use to balance instructional design to provide equality for participants' learning preferences.

Global/Specific Learners		Learning Modalities (Sensory Intake)			Hemispheric Preference	
Global	Specific	Visual	Auditory	Kinesthetic	Left Brain	Right Brain
X	X	X	X	X	X	X

Multiple Intelligences								
Visual	Intrapersonal	Interpersonal	Musical	Mathematical / Logical	Linguistic	Kinesthetic	Naturalist	Existential
X	X	X	X	X	X	X		X

109. Dropping Anchor

Learning Outcome

Creating a strategy for applying the learning from the classroom to the workplace and optimizing the chance of embedding a behavior change

Overview

This activity is designed to assist the participant in identifying the key steps in implementing learning and encouraging them to follow the steps to apply the new learning in the workplace in a measured manner

In My Experience

A good training course will have participants motivated and excited at the end but that motivation can soon wane when the reality of being back at the workplace and good intentions can come to nothing. This activity encourages the participant to not only think about what they want to do but how they will do it and the potential barriers they face. By asking them to write all of this down you increase the chance of them taking action and by adding in a review meeting where you will discuss the progress you are optimizing the chance of the participant taking the learning back to apply on the job.

The Hidden Twist

Participants are given an opportunity to reflect upon what they have learned and to analyze what needs to be done and how in order to demonstrate the expected behavior from the course. In doing this they can identify potential barriers to implementation and think of ways to overcome these. Additionally, committing the actions to paper can improve the chances of making the changes required rather than just thinking about them. Moreover in revisiting the plan you really encourage the participant do take action and you as the trainer can collect data for the organization to identify barriers and issues that are preventing the change take place and feed it back to the business to encourage them to take action where needed. Finally, you are building networks and encouraging exchange of information so that participants can continue to learn from each other after the course.

Essential Data

Course Type: Any but particularly good for training on new systems or processes where an clear behavior is identified

Group Size: Any

Time of day: This is a post-course activity that should be carried out around six weeks after the course

Pace: moderate

Time to create: 15 minutes at the end of the course

Time to run: Allow approximately 10 minutes per participant per session

Steps to Create

- At the end of the course ask the participants to identify one thing they will definitely do to apply their learning in their work place. If they have been using a learning journal and are transferring items from this to an action plan ask them just to highlight the thing they feel is key
- Ask the participant to write down the steps they will need to take in order to reach the place they want to be an estimate how long they will need to achieve them
- Inform participants that you will meet six weeks after the course (virtually or in person) to discuss progress
- Set up the meeting and send out the invitation with the course invitation and make sure participants know that they are expected to attend this debrief

Steps to Run

- The trainer opens the meeting by welcoming participants back and then facilitates the meeting making sure that all participants contribute and encouraging the participants to offer advice and suggestions where needed

Suggested Debrief Strategy/Sample Questions

In this activity the trainer is the facilitator and should start proceedings by asking for a volunteer to revisit their agreed action and walk the group through what it was and how they have progressed and what barriers have they encountered or sources of support have they found.

If a participant reports a problem or barrier ask the group if they have met this issue and if so what have they done to alleviate it and if not what strategies could they suggest.

Make sure that all participants report back on progress and if they have not made any identify why they have been unable to.

Working Example
Process Training

I used this activity to follow up on training on a process which had not been followed correctly previously and had resulted in a situation that potentially could have been dangerous and would have had serious consequences had it been picked up in an audit rather than by an internal team member. Thus it was essential that particular steps were implemented and we wanted to really anchor them in the organization. We found that this process really encouraged people to think about what they had to do and how they would actually do it. We also discovered that an air of competition pushed people to do more than just the one thing. On the other side of the coin we discovered massive resistance from one particular group of people that was having a major impact on implementing the process. By engaging the managers we were able to identify that the resistance was caused by the genuine belief that this group of people were right and the new process was incorrect. By including this group in the training we were able to correct that belief and optimize the implementation of the process. A key learning here was not all resistance comes from reluctance to change and that we might never have known about this issue had we not run the post-course activity.

Tips, Tricks and Traps

- Identify your high performance learners and brief one of them beforehand to start the discussion
- Ensure the actions taken are compliant and in line with the objectives
- Ensure that participants know that you are going to report on any significant barriers to implementation in advance and assure them of anonymity of required, then make sure you keep to this
- Do not allow any one participant to answer all the questions
- Do not allow criticism of participants who have not made progress but make it clear that action is expected
- Remember that you are there as a facilitator, you want the participants to share their knowledge and feel good about what they have accomplished so don't offer all the advice and answers, encourage the group to do this and to challenge any dubious advice, only step in if really needed.

Adult Learning Base Process
NLP Chaining Anchors
Refer to **Adult Learning Base Process Reference Guide** for more information about this learning process.

Adult Learning Dashboard

This activity links participant's preferred style of learning. The following dashboard provides a quick reference to adult learning theorists and principles as part of the ID9® methodology.

This activity achieves the following level of Bloom's Taxonomy of the Cognitive Domain (Bloom et al 1956), shown with "X" in the following table.

Bloom's Taxonomy of the Cognitive Domain Level					
Knowledge	Comprehension	Application	Analysis	Synthesis	Evaluation
		X			

This activity also achieves a link, shown with "X" in the following table, to participant's naturally occurring learning preferences. Global/Specific, Learning Modalities, Hemispheric Preference (Sperry, 1981), and Multiple Intelligences (Gardner, 1983) are referenced in ID9® methodology and process. This is not a complete list of links that are covered within the ID9® process however this dashboard aims to provide a quick reference for trainers to use to balance instructional design to provide equality for participants' learning preferences.

Global/Specific Learners		Learning Modalities (Sensory Intake)			Hemispheric Preference	
Global	Specific	Visual	Auditory	Kinesthetic	Left Brain	Right Brain
X	X	X	X	X	X	X

Multiple Intelligences								
Visual	Intrapersonal	Interpersonal	Musical	Mathematical / Logical	Linguistic	Kinesthetic	Naturalist	Existential
X	X	X		X	X	X		X

110. Postcards from the Edge

Learning Outcome
Fostering commitment to applying one learning action as a result of attending the course

Overview
This activity is designed to channel the participant into making a commitment to applying at least one thing that they have learned during the course by writing it on a post card and giving it to a fellow participant who will send it to them at an agreed interval asking how they are getting on with this commitment.

In My Experience
Participants typically give their postcard to somebody with whom they have built a rapport and the postcard helps to facilitate the relationship continuing after the course so that networks build. As with other similar activities, committing in writing increases the chances of action being taken and the reminder of your promise and the prospect of having to admit to your peers that you have not followed up on your agreed action helps to promote application further.

The Hidden Twist
In order to identify a key action the participant has to review the participant guide and their notes. Thus you are encouraging reflection on and evaluation of the course content. The participant then has to consider what it is possible to adopt and how they would achieve this. This engages both right and left brain preferences as there is a requirement to analyze the learning, plan what needs to be done to achieve this and consider the potential outcomes of the scenario. By putting this in writing and giving it to a colleague we can improve the chances of the participant making the changes required rather than just thinking about them. Moreover receiving the card with a question that demands an answer really encourages the participant to take action. By making sure that the course is not recorded as complete until this activity has been completed you also optimize the chances of change Finally, you are building networks and encouraging exchange of information so that participants can continue to learn from each other after the course.

Essential Data
Course Type: Any but particularly good for management or leadership training where a key behavior or skill can be identified

Group Size: Any

Time of day: This is a post-course activity that should be carried out at the end of the course and around twelve weeks after the course

Pace: moderate

Time to create: 20 minutes at the end of the course

Time to run: Minimal as participants will do it themselves, all you have to do is check that it has been done.

Steps to Create
- Have postcards printed with the name of the course on the front and on half the back the statement I(their name) will take the action below as a result of attending the (name of course) course
- Create a template for the participant to send back on receiving their card

Steps to Run
- At the end of the course ask the participants to revisit the participant guide and their notes and to identify one thing they will definitely do to apply their learning in their work place. If they have been using a learning journal and are transferring items from this to an action plan ask them just to highlight the thing they feel is key
- Ask the participant to complete the postcard and write their work address on the right hand side.
- Ask the participant to hand the postcard to a fellow participant
- Ask the recipient of the card to keep it safe and to send it to the person three months after the end of the course with the question "How is it going?"
- Tell the participants that on receiving their own card back they should contact the sender to tell them how it has gone using the template provided and copying in the rest of the group and the trainer
- Send a reminder to the group to send the postcards at the agreed time

Suggested Debrief Strategy/Sample Questions

This activity hands the responsibility for the post-course implementation and follow up squarely to the participants but ensures that the trainer gets feedback on implementation which can be a valuable contribution to metrics, especially the level three (Kirkpatrick) behavior change and consequently also the return on expectation. When creating the template for the feedback consider using questions such as

- What steps did you take to implement your learning?
- What are the remaining actions you need to take?
- What were your first barriers and how did you overcome them
- What are the positive results you have seen from this action
- Can you identify any negative results and what are they
- If you have not been able to apply this learning what are the things that need to happen in order for you to do so?
- Can you summarize your feelings about what you have learned in one sentence?
- What will be your next action as a result of this course?

Working Example
Leadership training

This activity is used in one of our key leadership training programs and it has the effect of really focusing participants in on what they want to apply initially from a vast selection of new skills. Knowing that they will be asked how they have done with this is a powerful motivator to take action or at least look at why it cannot be taken and develop a strategy in order to feedback to their peers

Tips, Tricks and Traps

- Make sure everybody fills in a card
- Remember to send a reminder
- Provide the participants with a list of e-mail addresses so that they can respond with the feedback
- Let the participants know that their training record will not be marked as complete until this activity has been received

Adult Learning Base Process
Action Planning

Refer to **Adult Learning Base Process Reference Guide** for more information about this learning process.

Adult Learning Dashboard

This activity links participant's preferred style of learning. The following dashboard provides a quick reference to adult learning theorists and principles as part of the ID9® methodology.

This activity achieves the following level of Bloom's Taxonomy of the Cognitive Domain (Bloom et al 1956), shown with "X" in the following table.

Bloom's Taxonomy of the Cognitive Domain Level					
Knowledge	Comprehension	Application	Analysis	Synthesis	Evaluation
		X			

This activity also achieves a link, shown with "X" in the following table, to participant's naturally occurring learning preferences. Global/Specific, Learning Modalities, Hemispheric Preference (Sperry, 1981), and Multiple Intelligences (Gardner, 1983) are referenced in ID9® methodology and process. This is not a complete list of links that are covered within the ID9® process however this dashboard aims to provide a quick reference for trainers to use to balance instructional design to provide equality for participants' learning preferences.

Global/Specific Learners		Learning Modalities (Sensory Intake)			Hemispheric Preference	
Global	Specific	Visual	Auditory	Kinesthetic	Left Brain	Right Brain
X	X	X	X	X	X	X

Multiple Intelligences								
Visual	Intrapersonal	Interpersonal	Musical	Mathematical / Logical	Linguistic	Kinesthetic	Naturalist	Existential
X	X	X		X	X	X	X	X

111. Pass it forward

Learning Outcome

Reinforcement of learning by revisiting and teaching a colleague

Overview

In this activity the participant has to take all or part of the course and teach it to a colleague within an agreed timeframe. The recipient is then asked to feedback on the participant by way of an evaluation form sent out by the trainer.

In My Experience

Participants enjoy sharing their knowledge with somebody whether it is their closest colleague or a whole team of people. The trick is to make sure that people do not feel overwhelmed or daunted by the task by ensuring they finish the course confident in their knowledge.

The Hidden Twist

In order to teach the agreed material the participant has to study the participant guide, reference materials provided and their own notes and then reconstruct the key messages in a meaningful way. Thus we have the opportunity to take the participant right through Blooms Taxonomy of the Cognitive Domain (Bloom 1956) checking that the participant has learned the key points, can interpret them and explain them, break them down and put them back together again and appraise their learning. While all this is going on the participant is revisiting and reinforcing their knowledge and passing it on in a cascade.

If the participant is a trainer and this is part of a train the trainer course you also get to check their instructional design skills and topic balancing!

Essential Data

Course Type: This is particularly good for train the trainer courses where you want to make sure that the trainer has really picked up the key points and understands and can defend and appraise them.

Group Size: Any

Time of day: This is a post-course activity that should be carried out after the course within an agreed timeframe

Pace: moderate

Time to create: 1 hour

Time to run: Minimal as participants will do it themselves, all the trainer has to do is review the evaluation forms to make sure that the learning is correct

Steps to Create

* Create a briefing document that covers:
  o What the participant is to teach
  o The timeline for completion
  o Instructions on how to send the evaluation forms back
* Create an evaluation form with questions which will check that the participant has learned correctly and delivered the messages in a meaningful way.

Steps to Run

* At the end of the course distribute the briefing document
* Send an electronic copy of the evaluation form to participants
* Inform participants of the deadline for submission of the evaluations
* Inform participants that their training record will not be marked as complete until this activity has been completed

Suggested Debrief Strategy/Sample Questions

The key to this activity is in the evaluation form so you need to make sure you ask the right questions. These will need to be specific to the task but you can use some generics such as:

* Summarize what you have learned in one sentence
* What are the possibilities around applying this learning
* If you had to rate your knowledge of this subject on a scale of 0 to 10 what score would you give yourself and why
* What questions did you have after this session
* On a scale of 0 to 10 how well did xxxxx answer them

Working Example

This is one of my favorite post-course activities as it really focusses the participants on what they have done and makes them deconstruct their own learning and put it back together again in a way they can pass on. It works as a review and reinforcement while sharing the knowledge too. It works best when you have participants who have a knowledge of training but can also be used with people who have no training background as long as the briefing is thorough in what you want people to do. I have seen participants do all sorts of things from the PowerPoint of key messages from those who are not trainers to some really innovative and interactive sessions from those who are. One participant (a professional trainer) did such a good job of this task that the course was redesigned to include her activity as it was better than the existing one!

Tips, Tricks and Traps
- If the people on the course are not trainers make sure they are not overwhelmed by this task by making sure the briefing sets out what they need to do.
- If you really want to take this activity one step further you can arrange to debrief the participant in a short meeting once you have received their evaluations
- You can ask the participant to teach to one or many depending on your desired outcome
- Read the evaluations and make sure you address any incorrect learning
- Tailor your evaluation form to the course objectives to ensure they have been met. For example if an objective is " Explain process A" make sure you ask a question that ascertains if they have done this

Adult Learning Base Process
Teach Back
Refer to **Adult Learning Base Process Reference Guide** for more information about this learning process.

Adult Learning Dashboard
This activity links participant's preferred style of learning. The following dashboard provides a quick reference to adult learning theorists and principles as part of the ID9® methodology.

This activity achieves the following level of Bloom's Taxonomy of the Cognitive Domain (Bloom et al 1956), shown with "X" in the following table.

Bloom's Taxonomy of the Cognitive Domain Level					
Knowledge	Comprehension	Application	Analysis	Synthesis	Evaluation
					X

This activity also achieves a link, shown with "X" in the following table, to participant's naturally occurring learning preferences. Global/Specific, Learning Modalities, Hemispheric Preference (Sperry, 1981), and Multiple Intelligences (Gardner, 1983) are referenced in ID9® methodology and process. This is not a complete list of links that are covered within the ID9® process however this dashboard aims to provide a quick reference for trainers to use to balance instructional design to provide equality for participants' learning preferences.

Global/Specific Learners		Learning Modalities (Sensory Intake)			Hemispheric Preference	
Global	Specific	Visual	Auditory	Kinesthetic	Left Brain	Right Brain
X	X	X	X	X	X	X

Multiple Intelligences								
Visual	Intrapersonal	Interpersonal	Musical	Mathematical / Logical	Linguistic	Kinesthetic	Naturalist	Existential
X	X	X		X	X	X		X

112. Aren't I clever!

Learning Outcome
Positive reinforcement of the value of the training.

Overview
For this activity the participant is asked to identify and report back on one positive outcome of the training course. This can be done in a number of ways including a meeting, in person or virtual, to report back on what has worked well following training.

In My Experience
Most people enjoy talking about a success but do be aware that in some cultures this just won't work as it will be seen as impolite bragging.

Participants sometimes struggle to identify a success so make sure they can approach you for help if they are struggling with what to bring to the meeting and remember that a success is a success no matter how small it seems.

The Hidden Twist
The participant has to implement some aspect of the training in order to have something to report on at the post-course meeting. By focusing in on success the trainer reinforces the value of the training and can perhaps get some good metrics and marketing for the course! As different people will have different markers of success you can engage all types of learners and capture the key motivators personal to the participant.

Essential Data
Course Type: Any

Group Size: Any

Time of day: This is a post-course activity that should be carried out after the course within an agreed timeframe

Pace: Quick

Time to create: 1 hour

Time to run: Allow five minutes per participant for the presentation of their story and two minutes for questions

Steps to Create
- Create a briefing document that tells the participant
  o The venue, date and time of the follow up meeting
  o Joining instructions for the meeting if it is a virtual one
  o Your expectations, for example:
    - At the follow up meeting please be prepared to tell your colleagues
    - 1 thing you have successfully implemented from the course
    - Why you feel it has been a success
    - What the positive impact has been on you and your team/colleagues
    - How that has made you feel
    - You will have x minutes to present your success story

Steps to Run
- At the end of the course distribute the briefing document

Suggested Debrief Strategy/Sample Questions
The trainer should open this meeting with a quick review of what people were asked to do and ask for a volunteer to start the process. Example questions can be found in the section above. As a trainer listen to the predicate phrases the participant uses in their feedback and formulate any follow up questions around that to make sure you really hook them into their own success.

Working Example
This activity works well because you have asked the participants to find a success and so they are not exposing any failings and making themselves vulnerable in from of their peers. What often happens is that people bring one success but on hearing what others have done find that they have more than one success or get ideas as to what they can do next with their new knowledge or skill.

Tips, Tricks and Traps
- In advance of the meeting ask one participant if they would be happy to go first if nobody volunteers
- Make sure people know that they have a set time to present and enforce that
- The activity revolves around successes so if issues arise help to facilitate a positive outcome such as "so that was quite a mountain you had to climb but well done for getting around it"
- Encourage everybody to participate in the discussion by linking stories with synergies or similar outcomes
- Don't allow one person to dominate as it will shut down the meeting

Adult Learning Base Process
Metacognitive Reflection
Refer to **Adult Learning Base Process Reference**
Guide for more information about this learning process.

Adult Learning Dashboard
This activity links participant's preferred style of learning. The following dashboard provides a quick reference to adult learning theorists and principles as part of the ID9® methodology.

This activity achieves the following level of Bloom's Taxonomy of the Cognitive Domain (Bloom et al 1956), shown with "X" in the following table.

Bloom's Taxonomy of the Cognitive Domain Level					
Knowledge	Comprehension	Application	Analysis	Synthesis	Evaluation
			X		

This activity also achieves a link, shown with "X" in the following table, to participant's naturally occurring learning preferences. Global/Specific, Learning Modalities, Hemispheric Preference (Sperry, 1981), and Multiple Intelligences (Gardner, 1983) are referenced in ID9® methodology and process. This is not a complete list of links that are covered within the ID9® process however this dashboard aims to provide a quick reference for trainers to use to balance instructional design to provide equality for participants' learning preferences.

Global/Specific Learners		Learning Modalities (Sensory Intake)			Hemispheric Preference	
Global	Specific	Visual	Auditory	Kinesthetic	Left Brain	Right Brain
X	X	X	X	X	X	X

Multiple Intelligences								
Visual	Intrapersonal	Interpersonal	Musical	Mathematical / Logical	Linguistic	Kinesthetic	Naturalist	Existential
	X	X		X	X			X

113. Cartoon Time

Learning Outcome

Reinforcement of key learning from the training

Overview

Participants are asked to create a cartoon depicting the key thing they learned at the training and have since applied. These are returned to the trainer and compiled into a booklet which is sent out to the participants as a reminder of the key points of the course. The cartoon can be as funny as people like and you can even offer a prize for the best

In My Experience

Some participants can feel that this task is too difficult because they do not consider themselves to have the skills to complete it. Make sure you have some examples of very simple cartoons as well as more complex ones and give participants any tools you have such as web sites that may help.

The Hidden Twist

The participant has to revisit the participant guide and their notes to decide on a ley learning thus they are reviewing and reinforcing their learning. The trainer can ascertain that the correct things have been learned and may even get some useful material for marketing the course!

Essential Data

Course Type: Any

Group Size: Any

Time of day: This is a post-course activity that should be carried out after the course within an agreed timeframe

Pace: Quick

Time to create: Thirty Minutes

Time to run: Minimal

Steps to Create

- Create a briefing document that tells the participant what you want them to do
  - o Create a cartoon that illustrates the key thing you have learned from this course
  - o You can make it as humorous or as serious as you like
  - o You can draw it or use any other tool to create it but you may find a web based cartoon creator useful (search for free cartoon creation tool on the internet)
  - o Send your cartoon back to me at xxxxxx by xx xx xx
  - o I will compile a booklet of the cartoons so that we can share them
  - o Below is an example to guide you

Steps to Run

- Distribute the briefing document
- Explain the steps and answer any questions

Sample completed Cartoon Time Activity

Suggested Debrief Strategy/ Sample Questions

The debrief for this is really simple as all the trainer has to do is collate all the cartoons in a booklet and send them out with a message to the participants.

Working Example

This activity has brought some really great results as people can let go and present their findings in any way they like.

Tips, Tricks and Traps

- In this activity can be daunting for those who do not consider themselves creative or artistic so have some examples and tools such as the link to Chogger.com available
- Make sure people know you will share them in case they are tempted to show colleagues in an unflattering light
- You can use this activity in a number of ways for instance you could change the brief to make the cartoon about one thing they will start or stop doing as a result of the course
- You can use this activity for pre-course work by changing the scenario for example to cover what the participant would like to be saying when they finish the course and link it to an expectations and concerns activity
- If you prefer, send a cartoon strip that has already been created and participants simply fill in the conversation based on their key learnings from the course (see example).

Sample Handout/Poster for Cartoon Time Activity

Adult Learning Base Process
Metacognitive Reflection

Refer to Adult Learning Base Process Reference Guide for more information about this learning process.

Adult Learning Dashboard

This activity links participant's preferred style of learning. The following dashboard provides a quick reference to adult learning theorists and principles as part of the ID9® methodology.

This activity achieves the following level of Bloom's Taxonomy of the Cognitive Domain (Bloom et al 1956), shown with "X" in the following table.

Bloom's Taxonomy of the Cognitive Domain Level					
Knowledge	Comprehension	Application	Analysis	Synthesis	Evaluation
		X			

This activity also achieves a link, shown with "X" in the following table, to participant's naturally occurring learning preferences. Global/Specific, Learning Modalities, Hemispheric Preference (Sperry, 1981), and Multiple Intelligences (Gardner, 1983) are referenced in ID9® methodology and process. This is not a complete list of links that are covered within the ID9® process however this dashboard aims to provide a quick reference for trainers to use to balance instructional design to provide equality for participants' learning preferences.

Global/Specific Learners		Learning Modalities (Sensory Intake)			Hemispheric Preference	
Global	Specific	Visual	Auditory	Kinesthetic	Left Brain	Right Brain
X	X	X		X	X	X

Multiple Intelligences								
Visual	Intrapersonal	Interpersonal	Musical	Mathematical / Logical	Linguistic	Kinesthetic	Naturalist	Existential
X	X				X	X	X	X

114. It's a gift

Learning Outcome
The participant can revisit the key points from the course as they move forward to apply their learning

Overview
The trainer uses photographs of participants, flipcharts, tasks, events, quotes etc. throughout the course to create a booklet, photo montage or slide show of the course for the participant to keep and refer to.

In My Experience
Participants love to receive this kind of post-course gift and will review it if only at the very least to see if their picture is flattering! Therefore it is an excellent way of encouraging reflection on the course and the key points which you will have made sure are most prominent.

The Hidden Twist
In reviewing the "gift" the participant is revisiting the highlights of the course

Essential Data
Course Type: Any

Group Size: Any

Time of day: This is a post-course activity that should be carried out after the course within an agreed timeframe

Pace: Moderate

Time to create: 30 Minutes to 30 days depending on the complexity and graphic design quality that you create!

Time to run: Minimal

Steps to Create
- During the course the trainer takes photographs of tasks, flip charts, activities, events and participants
- Note down quotes, quips and stories
- After the course have these collated into a format of your choice according to your budget
- Send them to the participant after the course with a message thanking them for participating

Steps to Run
- After the course send out the gift

Suggested Debrief Strategy/Sample Questions
No real debrief is needed apart from a nicely worded message thanking the participant for taking part in the course and expressing your hope that they find the gift useful as an aid to remembering the course.

Working Example
These "gifts" are really well received and can be as elaborate as budget allows or as simple as it dictates. If a theme has been used during the training then the follow up gift can also use this theme. In one training course where the theme was journeys the gift was sent in a miniature suitcase to continue the theme.

Tips, Tricks and Traps
- Get permission from the participants to use their photographs in writing, if necessary
- If you are using quotes make sure you have permission for this too, preferably in writing
- A standard disclaimer and permission form covers the above points nicely
- Beware of any restrictions on the use of photography on some company sites
- Don't put anything unflattering or demotivating. Remember you want people's motivation to heighten, not drop!

Adult Learning Base Process
Collage
Refer to **Adult Learning Base Process Reference Guide** for more information about this learning process.

Adult Learning Dashboard

This activity links participant's preferred style of learning. The following dashboard provides a quick reference to adult learning theorists and principles as part of the ID9® methodology.

This activity achieves the following level of Bloom's Taxonomy of the Cognitive Domain (Bloom et al 1956), shown with "X" in the following table.

Bloom's Taxonomy of the Cognitive Domain Level					
Knowledge	Comprehension	Application	Analysis	Synthesis	Evaluation
		X			

This activity also achieves a link, shown with "X" in the following table, to participant's naturally occurring learning preferences. Global/Specific, Learning Modalities, Hemispheric Preference (Sperry, 1981), and Multiple Intelligences (Gardner, 1983) are referenced in ID9® methodology and process. This is not a complete list of links that are covered within the ID9® process however this dashboard aims to provide a quick reference for trainers to use to balance instructional design to provide equality for participants' learning preferences.

Global/Specific Learners		Learning Modalities (Sensory Intake)			Hemispheric Preference	
Global	Specific	Visual	Auditory	Kinesthetic	Left Brain	Right Brain
X	X	X		X	X	X

Multiple Intelligences								
Visual	Intrapersonal	Interpersonal	Musical	Mathematical / Logical	Linguistic	Kinesthetic	Naturalist	Existential
X	X	X	X	X	X		X	X

115. How's it going?

Learning Outcome

Participants discuss key learning points from the course and the application of them in the workplace. They also analyze any barriers they experienced in applying the learning and explain the strategies they employed to overcome them.

Overview

The trainer holds a post-course telephone conference/virtual meeting approximately three months after the course and uses targeted questions to facilitate the discussion and analysis of what they have learned and applied.

In My Experience

This is a simple activity that takes very little work yet has a big impact. Participants are usually very keen to tell their peers what they have applied and the challenges they have faced.

The Hidden Twist

In discussing what they have applied the participants are reviewing and reinforcing what they learned. They are also analyzing the barriers they encountered and sharing the solutions they came up with. In this way you are engaging whole brain learning by hooking in the analytical and the creative elements and, if you use a virtual meeting platform such as Live Meeting or WebEx you can capture your visual, auditory and kinesthetic learners. Finally you are setting the expectation that there will actually be post-course application of learning.

Essential Data

Course Type – Any

Group Size – Any

Time of day – This is a post-course activity that should be carried out after the course within an agreed timeframe

Pace – Moderate

Time to create- Around 1 hour

Time to run – Allow a maximum of 10 minutes per participant.

Steps to Create

- Write a maximum of five targeted questions, for example:
  o What were your first thoughts on your key learning from the course and what are they now?
  o What are the barriers you have encountered in implementing your learning?
  o What challenges have you faced in taking your new ideas back to the workplace?
  o Describe your key success and how it made you felt
  o What will be your next steps?
  o What else do you want to know about this topic and how will you meet this requirement
- Organize a post-course meeting and ensure that the date of it is included in the course joining instructions along with the information that it is a requirement of completing the course that they attend

Steps to Run

- Distribute the questions at the end of the course
- Explain that all participants are expected to contribute at the post-course meeting
- Facilitate the meeting using the tools available in your virtual meeting platform and allow the speaking participant to take control of the screen to engage the kinesthetic learner

Suggested Debrief Strategy/Sample Questions

Use questions that will encourage the participants to review what they have learned but remember to try to use higher order questions, how and what rather than can and are, to prompt deep reflection and analysis.

Working Example

People usually like to share successes, especially if they have been achieved in the face of some adversity such as resistance from colleagues or superiors. This activity pushes participants to look for successes they would not necessarily have classed as such. I have often been surprised by the ingenuity of people in applying their learning and overcoming barriers and this activity allows collaboration and sharing of ideas and can become ongoing peer coaching and a support network.

Tips, Tricks and Traps
- Encourage participants to prepare for the meeting by putting together something they can share such as a slide, drawing, journal entry
- Brief one of your high performance learners in advance so that they can begin the discussion as this is often the trickiest part of such a meeting
- Encourage participants to stay in touch and share ideas and support
- Do not be tempted to ask too many questions
- Keep people focused on success despite barriers
- Make sure every participant actually participates
- Send out a reminder with the questions about five days before the meeting
- Have some references and further reading available for those who want to know more

Adult Learning Base Process
Action Planning
Refer to **Adult Learning Base Process Reference Guide** for more information about this learning process.

Adult Learning Dashboard
This activity links participant's preferred style of learning. The following dashboard provides a quick reference to adult learning theorists and principles as part of the ID9® methodology.

This activity achieves the following level of Bloom's Taxonomy of the Cognitive Domain (Bloom et al 1956), shown with "X" in the following table.

Bloom's Taxonomy of the Cognitive Domain Level					
Knowledge	Comprehension	Application	Analysis	Synthesis	Evaluation
			X		

This activity also achieves a link, shown with "X" in the following table, to participant's naturally occurring learning preferences. Global/Specific, Learning Modalities, Hemispheric Preference (Sperry, 1981), and Multiple Intelligences (Gardner, 1983) are referenced in ID9® methodology and process. This is not a complete list of links that are covered within the ID9® process however this dashboard aims to provide a quick reference for trainers to use to balance instructional design to provide equality for participants' learning preferences.

Global/Specific Learners		Learning Modalities (Sensory Intake)			Hemispheric Preference	
Global	Specific	Visual	Auditory	Kinesthetic	Left Brain	Right Brain
X	X	X	X	X	X	X

Multiple Intelligences								
Visual	Intrapersonal	Interpersonal	Musical	Mathematical / Logical	Linguistic	Kinesthetic	Naturalist	Existential
X	X	X		X	X	X		X

116. Quizzical Questions

Learning Outcome
Participants use their course notes to answer questions thus reviewing the work and, with appropriately written questions, are encouraged to examine how they have applied their learning.

Overview
The trainer writes questions which direct participants back to the participant guide and notes they made. The questions refer to application of learning and can be multiple choice or free text answers.

In My Experience
This activity can be a simple one sheet multiple choice quiz or a longer activity with free text answers according to course length and content.

The Hidden Twist
You are directing people back to course materials and reminding them that there is an expectation that learning will be applied. You may also find that participant's answers provide you, the trainer, with some valuable metrics!

Essential Data
Course Type: Any

Group Size: Any

Time of day: This is a post-course activity that should be carried out after the course within an agreed timeframe

Pace: Moderate

Time to create: Around 1 hour

Time to run: Dependent on length of quiz

Steps to Create
- Refer to the course aim and objectives and write questions pertaining to what can and should be applied

Steps to Run
- Send the questions out post-course with details of the time for submission of answers and the address to send them to
- Inform participants that post-course work is part of the completion criteria for the course

Suggested Debrief Strategy/Sample Questions
Create these according to your aim and objectives

Working Example
Computer system training
Following system training I used this activity to assess learning application and was able to get some really good metrics for course evaluation as well as finding myself with an excellent source of tips, tricks and frequently asked questions which I was able to publish on the intranet for all to see.

Tips, Tricks and Traps
- Write questions that go beyond just testing retention of knowledge
- Ensure your questions are relevant to the course aim and objectives
- Consider sharing the answers but make sure you tell participants in advance that you will do this
- Compile a tips and tricks package from the answers
- Consider using some of the outputs to develop an FAQ page or hand out
- You may like to arrange a post quiz debrief call
- If there is evidence of misapplication or incorrect knowledge you must make sure you address it

Adult Learning Base Process
Question & Answer
Refer to **Adult Learning Base Process Reference Guide** for more information about this learning process.

Adult Learning Dashboard

This activity links participant's preferred style of learning. The following dashboard provides a quick reference to adult learning theorists and principles as part of the ID9® methodology.

This activity achieves the following level of Bloom's Taxonomy of the Cognitive Domain (Bloom et al 1956), shown with "X" in the following table.

Bloom's Taxonomy of the Cognitive Domain Level					
Knowledge	Comprehension	Application	Analysis	Synthesis	Evaluation
		X			

This activity also achieves a link, shown with "X" in the following table, to participant's naturally occurring learning preferences. Global/Specific, Learning Modalities, Hemispheric Preference (Sperry, 1981), and Multiple Intelligences (Gardner, 1983) are referenced in ID9® methodology and process. This is not a complete list of links that are covered within the ID9® process however this dashboard aims to provide a quick reference for trainers to use to balance instructional design to provide equality for participants' learning preferences.

Global/Specific Learners		Learning Modalities (Sensory Intake)			Hemispheric Preference	
Global	Specific	Visual	Auditory	Kinesthetic	Left Brain	Right Brain
X	X	X	X	X	X	X

Multiple Intelligences								
Visual	Intrapersonal	Interpersonal	Musical	Mathematical / Logical	Linguistic	Kinesthetic	Naturalist	Existential
X	X	X		X	X	X		X

Chapter 9:
Supporting the Learning Activities for Managers and Trainers
(pre- bridging & post-)

Susan Giddens

About the Co-Author:

Susan Giddens

In 2006, Susan Giddens received her Master's Degree in Education with a specialty in Instructional Technologies from San Francisco State University, USA. Upon graduation Susan embarked on her career in training and worked with an eLearning company in San Francisco. Today, Susan's role as Senior Training Manager for Genentech, Inc., a leading biotechnology company, challenges her to create interactive and engaging training with often highly scientific training content.

Susan has conducted training globally. In her current role, Susan has influenced learning and development to increase the quality of training delivery which focuses on having minimum training time with maximum learning transfer and application. Susan truly has a 'seat at the table' working with senior leaders and key stakeholders on organizational initiatives that impact people and processes. She successfully engages SMEs (Subject Matter Experts) from project kick-off to having them facilitate as expert trainers, delivering the programs that her department has written.

One of her great strengths is creating a support network that surrounds participants before, during, and after training by providing high quality learning materials, engaging the participant's manager from the announcement of the training throughout the entire journey, keeping key stakeholders informed about the progress of learning programs and providing ways for participants to access resource materials to assist them in their learning application.

Susan began her journey with ID9® already having a strong foundation knowledge of instructional design and after just a few hours in the ID9® Level 1 (Silver) class Susan was able to transfer her theoretical knowledge to practical application. Now, some years later, and with her completion of the Platinum course (hence this book!), Susan has applied ID9® across her work and continues to be passionate about training always seeking ways to improve the quality of learning and development.

Chapter Introduction

The Participant's Manager is critical to the success of training. By inviting the managers to engage with the learning process can sometimes be challenging for trainers, uncomfortable for managers or even undesired by the organization. Many organizations consider training is for the 'training department' and that participants attend the courses and somehow by magic are expected to put into practice what they have learned, that is learning application.

Managers play a critical part of whether participants apply their learning, or not. On one hand, if a manager is supportive of the learning process, checks in with participants before and after training and is there to support and guide them throughout their journey participants motivation and willingness to change their behavior is heightened. On the other, that is when managers are unsupportive, even an unintended quip after the training course like 'well, that's not the way we do it around here' can deflate the motivation of the participant and result in them not applying anything they have learned from the training course which in turn makes training a complete waste of time and resources.

On first glance, it is relatively easy to inform managers what their direct reports will be learning in the upcoming training course, and after the course what challenges direct reports experienced in training. However, when we as instructional designers, trainers and training managers leave out this part of the process we are leaving out a critical step. This step of engaging participant's managers can truly set up the learning through a pre-training activity, accelerate learning during training and embed learning and close the loop post-training.

However, at times it may be difficult to engage managers and get support from your organization to do so. You may feel like you're trying to climb a mountain, but like climbing a mountain the reward is great. Actively engaging managers enables managers to develop their staff to achieve workplace goals and shows the training department's value in a whole new and improved way.

Throughout this chapter you will see a diagram that details which roles can/should participate in each activity. The following roles are defined as:

- **Trainer** – the person who conducts the training program
- **The Support Network** (i.e. people involved in supporting the participant towards implementation of the program learning – i.e. application of learning)
  - o **Manager** – the manager of the participant
  - o **Coach** – someone who takes the role of coach who is not the participant's manager. This could also be a **SME,** a Subject Matter Expert in the content of the training course or an **External Partner,** a person or organization who has been contracted by the company to conduct the training
  - o **Key Stakeholder** – a key influencer in the learning process (perhaps a senior leader)
- **Participant** – the participant who attends the training program

In some cases, it's the trainer and manager only, in other cases the trainer will create something and pass it to the manager, the key stakeholder or another role for implementation. The goal of each activity is to ensure the managers have the knowledge and tools available to them to support their direct report's learning and strive for transfer and application of learning.

I hope the activities listed in this chapter will help you take your training programs to new heights and to engage and influence managers with the collective aim of increasing participant motivation towards learning application.

117. "Learning and the Manager's Role": A Mini-Course for Managers

Who's involved?

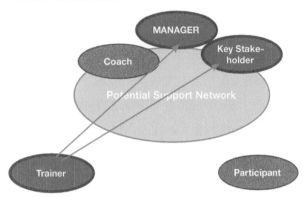

Learning Outcome

By the end of this activity, Managers should have a strong understanding of the different learning styles, their specific training department needs and their role in supporting their direct reports across the learning process. In addition, the one-on-one time with the Trainer develops a strong foundation for further collaboration and assessment of the organizational development requirements. The meeting is between the Trainer and the Manager, or the Trainer and Key Stakeholders

Pre-training	Bridging Task	Post-Training
X		

Overview

This activity is conducted prior to a major review of the organization's training strategy, before a major rollout of a new training initiative or periodically to refresh the minds of managers and the role they play in training success

In My Experience

This is a very quick activity that has maximum impact. After the session Managers have clarity on their role and their impact on the learning process. Many managers may not have ever thought about how they can positively or negatively influence learning application. Conducting this mini-course brings managers on board and creates a common language. It also strengthens a networking link between the training department and the functional business.

Essential Data

- Course Type: Any
- Group Size: Less than 5 managers schedule individual meetings; 5 or more use mini-course
- When: Periodically, as needed
- Time Required: 30 minutes

Steps to create

The Trainer develops and delivers a mini training module entitled "Learning and the Manager's Role" to Managers which includes the following key points:

1. The training department's philosophy
   - Present the training philosophy and include the focus on learning application (not just 'training for training sake')
   - Discuss the roles that impact training success (trainer, manager, key stakeholder, participant etc)
2. The goals around training
   - Provide the broader training strategy and plan
   - Provide specifics on upcoming training programs where their direct reports are involved
3. The scope and impact of training, including:
   - A single training program can teach Leaners new required ways of working, however it is after the participants leave the classroom that the behavior change or new skill must be implemented.
   - It is the manager's role to ensure their direct reports are behaving in the new way, using the new skills, applying the new process, using the new system as defined by process and training.

Tips, Tricks and Traps

- Choose the most appropriate time and place to conduct the training.
- Try not to include this training in an overcommitted management meeting schedule where this mini-course may risk being viewed as an add-on or after thought
- Leadership endorsement of Managers playing a hands-on role in the training process is critical. If you feel there is a lack of support from Managers towards the concept of supporting learning, consider conducting this "Mini-course" with the Leadership team first to build momentum and then present it to Managers.
- The content of this mini course can also be used as an agenda for individual meetings with managers. This is suggested where there are less than five managers.

Adult Learning Base Process:
Social Proof / Training Strategy
Refer to **Adult Learning Base Process Reference Guide** for more information about this learning process.

Adult Learning Datasheet:
This activity links participant's preferred style of learning. The following dashboard provides a quick reference to adult learning theorists and principles as part of the ID9® methodology.

This activity achieves the following level of Bloom's Taxonomy of the Cognitive Domain (Bloom et al 1956), shown with "X" in the following table.

Bloom's Taxonomy of the Cognitive Domain Level					
Knowledge	Comprehension	Application	Analysis	Synthesis	Evaluation
X					

This activity also achieves a link, shown with "X" in the following table, to participant's naturally occurring learning preferences. Global/Specific, Learning Modalities, Hemispheric Preference (Sperry, 1981), and Multiple Intelligences (Gardner, 1983) are referenced in ID9® methodology and process. This is not a complete list of links that are covered within the ID9® process however this dashboard aims to provide a quick reference for trainers to use to balance instructional design to provide equality for participants' learning preferences.

Global/Specific Learners		Learning Modalities (Sensory Intake)			Hemispheric Preference	
Global	Specific	Visual	Auditory	Kinesthetic	Left Brain	Right Brain
X	X	X			X	

Multiple Intelligences								
Visual	Intrapersonal	Interpersonal	Musical	Mathematical / Logical	Linguistic	Kinesthetic	Naturalist	Existential
X	X	X						X

118. See Learning, Hear Learning, and Do Learning: A Pre-Learning Discussion

Who's involved?

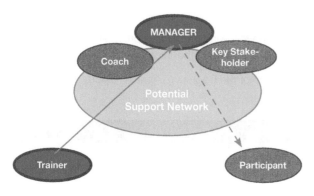

Learning Outcome

Using a questionnaire Manager's have participants answer questions about the upcoming course, focusing in on their expectations and concerns. Apart from creating a valuable process to prepare participants for the training by answering the questions, by the end of this activity, both Manager and Participant may have a perspective on how the Participant prefers to take in new information. The answers to the questionnaire can be provided to the trainer before the training.

Pre-training	Bridging Task	Post-Training
X		

Overview

1. Prior to starting a new training program, prepare the Managers to conduct a one-on-one discussion with their Participants to talk about the upcoming training and in doing so also identify their preferred learning style.

   The discussion between manager and participant should focus on activating the three different representational systems of visual, auditory and kinesthetic as they review the Pre-Course Discussion Questions (see below) together. Confirm the Manager understands how to interpret the questions to effectively map out their Participant's learning style.

2. The Manager distributes questions to the Participant together with the course outline (including the course aim and objectives) at least three days prior to the discussion and sets the expectation that both the manager and the participant should complete the questionnaire prior to meeting.

3. The Manager conducts the meeting with the Participant to discuss the following:
   • Responses to the Pre-Course questions

• Variances between the responses between what the manager has written when compared to the participant
• Expectations for attending training
• Any next steps to prepare for training.

In My Experience

This activity seeks to engage managers in the learning process by having them complete a similar questionnaire as the participant. By having both manager and participant answer the questions they will most likely read the course outline and think about the expectations of the upcoming course. This means that the manger can confidently discuss the training course and that the participant has begun the learning process prior to arriving at the training.

Essential Data

• Course Type: Any
• Group Size: 1:1 with Participant and Manager
• When: Three days prior to training
• Time Required: 10-15 minutes

Steps to create

1. Create two questionnaires, one for the Manager and the other for the Participant using the following questions as a guideline. ou may choose to include on the Manager's questionnaire the 'hidden learning style' column if you wish, or not.

Pre-Course Discussion Questions:

Participant to complete...	Manager to complete...	Hidden learning style
Describe how you are going to take the plunge into the course content.	Describe how your direct report might take the plunge into the course content.	Kinesthetic (take the plunge)
Discuss the skills/learning that that you want to keep an eye on that will enhance your abilities by attending this course.	Discuss the skills/learning that that you want your direct report to keep an eye on that will enhance your abilities by attending this course.	Visual (keep an eye on)
Explain how you are going to interact with course content. What do you think you'll see, hear and do during the course?	Explain how your direct report might interact with course content. What do you think he or she will see, hear and do during the course?	Auditory, Visual or Kinesthetic (see, hear, do)
Using your own words, reframe the course objectives that you feel will have the most impact on your development.	Using your own words, reframe the course objectives that you feel will have the most impact on your direct report's development.	Auditory (in your own words)

2. Optional – Prepare a handout explaining NLP Predicate Phrases to provide context around learning modalities, that is, visual, auditory and kinesthetic.

3. Provide Managers with a straight forward guidance document explaining the process.

   a. Meet with your direct report at least three days prior to the course start date

   b. Either before or at the meeting provide your direct report with the questionnaire. If the questionnaire is provided during the meeting questions may be discussed together, or allow them some time to write answers before discussing and comparing.

   c. On completion discuss:
      i. Responses to the Pre-Course questions
      ii. Variances between the responses between what the manager has written when compared to the participant
      iii. The Manager's and Organization's Expectations for attending training
      iv. Interesting points around visual, auditory and kinesthetic learning preferences
      v. Any next steps to prepare for training'

Tips, Tricks and Traps
- Encourage managers to really think through their answers
- Remind managers why the organization is investing in the specific training program and the program aim
- Ensure managers are very clear on why their direct report has been nominated or has self-nominated for training and how this training benefits their role, the effectiveness of their team and overall, for the organization
- If managers are hesitant or resistant offer to attend the meeting with the manager helping to guide the process.

Adult Learning Base Process:
NLP Sensory Predicate Words and Phrases
Refer to **Adult Learning Base Process Reference Guide** for more information about this learning process.

Adult Learning Datasheet:
This activity links participant's preferred style of learning. The following dashboard provides a quick reference to adult learning theorists and principles as part of the ID9® methodology.

This activity achieves the following level of Bloom's Taxonomy of the Cognitive Domain (Bloom et al 1956), shown with "X" in the following table.

Bloom's Taxonomy of the Cognitive Domain Level					
Knowledge	Comprehension	Application	Analysis	Synthesis	Evaluation
		X			

This activity also achieves a link, shown with "X" in the following table, to participant's naturally occurring learning preferences. Global/Specific, Learning Modalities, Hemispheric Preference (Sperry, 1981), and Multiple Intelligences (Gardner, 1983) are referenced in ID9® methodology and process. This is not a complete list of links that are covered within the ID9® process however this dashboard aims to provide a quick reference for trainers to use to balance instructional design to provide equality for participants' learning preferences.

Global/Specific Learners		Learning Modalities (Sensory Intake)			Hemispheric Preference	
Global	Specific	Visual	Auditory	Kinesthetic	Left Brain	Right Brain
	X		X			

Multiple Intelligences								
Visual	Intrapersonal	Interpersonal	Musical	Mathematical / Logical	Linguistic	Kinesthetic	Naturalist	Existential
		X			X	X		

119. Water Cooler Cards: Meaningful Conversations about Recent Training

Who's involved?

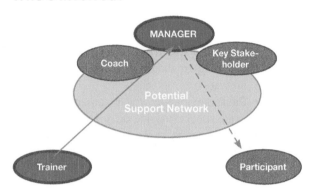

Learning Outcome

As part of the instructional design process create a quick-reference card (Water Cooler Card) that outlines key training points and questions to help participant's Managers gauge the effectiveness and impact of a recent training program. Once the trainer provides the Manager with the Water Cooler Cards, the Manager interacts with the Participant.

Pre-training	Bridging Task	Post-Training
	X	X

Overview

Managers don't always have to have formal meetings to follow-up after training. Casual encounters in the office, for example, around the water cooler, can often be as effective as a formal post-course meeting. However, managers need to know the questions to ask and this is where trainers and instructional designers can help managers to be prepared for these "Water Cooler" discussions. As part of the materials created for the program, create a "Water Cooler Card" for the Manager to reference when engaging with Participants in casual encounters. Water Cooler Cards are intended to gather general perceptions about the effectiveness of the training rather than specifics about the content of the program.

In My Experience

Water Cooler cards are quick and easy to create and the managers I work with appreciate that the training department is setting them up for success by providing targeted questions that they can ask when they see their direct report following training. In addition, the relationship between the trainer, the training department and the manager is strengthened as this activity builds an opportunity to show value to Managers. The end goal is that by managers engaging in follow-up conversations Participants feeling supported not only by their Manager but the organization as it sends a strong message that the training is important and that they are supported after the training course to apply what they have learned.

Essential Data

- Course Type: Any
- Group Size: Any
- When: After training session
- Time Required: 5-15 minutes

Steps to create

- Review course content and summarizes the key points
- Create open-ended questions around the key points and course content
- Creates a Water Cooler Card (postcard size) and populates questions.
  - o What did you do well during training?
  - o What were your initial thoughts around the new process/product? What are your thoughts now?
  - o What else do you need to know to be successful?
- Distribute the card just prior to the training course to participant's managers, or immediately following it with guidance on how and when to use the Water Cooler Card. This can be done in a meeting or individually with managers.

Tips, Tricks and Traps

- Use the Water Cooler Card immediately after training to reinforce with the Participant how important training is to the organization
- Consider creating a series of Water Cooler Cards that can be used over time. For example, create a set of cards with questions that address the Bloom's Taxonomy generally or specifically such as Analysis and Synthesis.
- Manager role may be replaced and/or enhanced by the use of a peer coach or non-aligned coach.

Adult Learning Base Process:
Action Planning
Refer to **Adult Learning Base Process Reference**
Guide for more information about this learning process.

Adult Learning Datasheet:
This activity links participant's preferred style of learning. The following dashboard provides a quick reference to adult learning theorists and principles as part of the ID9® methodology.

This activity achieves the following level of Bloom's Taxonomy of the Cognitive Domain (Bloom et al 1956), shown with "X" in the following table.

Bloom's Taxonomy of the Cognitive Domain Level					
Knowledge	Comprehension	Application	Analysis	Synthesis	Evaluation
		X	X	X	X

This activity also achieves a link, shown with "X" in the following table, to participant's naturally occurring learning preferences. Global/Specific, Learning Modalities, Hemispheric Preference (Sperry, 1981), and Multiple Intelligences (Gardner, 1983) are referenced in ID9® methodology and process. This is not a complete list of links that are covered within the ID9® process however this dashboard aims to provide a quick reference for trainers to use to balance instructional design to provide equality for participants' learning preferences.

Global/Specific Learners		Learning Modalities (Sensory Intake)			Hemispheric Preference	
Global	Specific	Visual	Auditory	Kinesthetic	Left Brain	Right Brain
X	X	X	X		X	

Multiple Intelligences								
Visual	Intrapersonal	Interpersonal	Musical	Mathematical / Logical	Linguistic	Kinesthetic	Naturalist	Existential
X					X			

120. Questioning Cards: Meaningful Conversations about Recent Training

Who's involved?

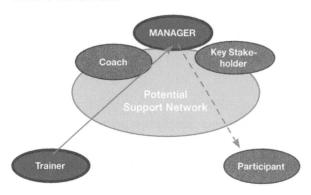

Learning Outcome

Pre-training	Bridging Task	Post-Training
	X	X

Overview

By the end of this activity, Managers should have a set of "Questioning Cards" based on the new process, product, technology or professional development skills in order to guide them through a meaningful conversation with their direct reports. Asking these questions draws out key information from the learning program.

Note: Questioning Cards address specific content from the learning program whereas Water Cooler Cards are intended to gather general perceptions about the effectiveness of the training.

Once the Questioning Cards are provided to the manager, the manager interacts with the participant.

In My Experience

Like Water Cooler cards (please see previous activity) Question Cards are quick and easy to create. Designed to focus in specifically on the content trained, questions will assist the manager in having meaningful conversations to support their direct reports either as a bridging task (in between training sessions) or as post-training support.

As mentioned in the previous activity, Water Cooler Cards, by providing Managers with questions supports the manager so that they can support their direct report who has attended the training program. When we've done this the managers I work with appreciate and value the training department more highly. Generally I've used these after a training course has finished, but if you were running a split program (for example several sessions over a period of time) Questioning Cards could be used successfully in-between sessions as a bridging task.

Essential Data

- **Course Type:** Any
- **Group Size:** 1-5
- **When:** After training
- **Time Required:** 5-30 minutes

Steps to create

1. Trainer or Instructional Designer creates cards based on the topics covered in training. The total number will vary but each card should deep-dive on one main idea / concept / process.
2. Trainer or Instructional Designer conducts informational session with Manager(s) to distribute cards and explain the content.
3. Managers use the Questioning Cards when meeting individually or to their team who have attended the training. During the meeting they assess what the Participant knows, where gaps might exist, specific areas where he / she is strong and to support the learner as they embark on their application of the learning.

Sample:

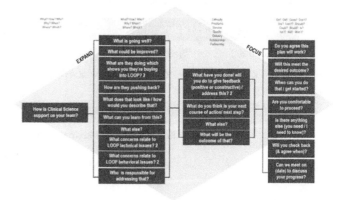

Tips, Tricks and Traps

- Conduct a mini-role play at the Manager's staff meeting to demonstrate how to use the questioning cards.
- When designing questions, start with open-ended questions to open up the conversation and get the participant/s talking. Then, change the questions to closed questions to focus in on specifics as the participants reveal what he/she knows, doesn't know, and requires more additional support. Finish off the questions with action based questions related to the participant moving forward to implement their action plan and apply their learning

Adult Learning Base Process:
Action Planning
Refer to **Adult Learning Base Process Reference**
Guide for more information about this learning process.

Adult Learning Datasheet:
This activity links participant's preferred style of learning. The following dashboard provides a quick reference to adult learning theorists and principles as part of the ID9® methodology.

This activity achieves the following level of Bloom's Taxonomy of the Cognitive Domain (Bloom et al 1956), shown with "X" in the following table.

Bloom's Taxonomy of the Cognitive Domain Level					
Knowledge	Comprehension	Application	Analysis	Synthesis	Evaluation
	X	X			

This activity also achieves a link, shown with "X" in the following table, to participant's naturally occurring learning preferences. Global/Specific, Learning Modalities, Hemispheric Preference (Sperry, 1981), and Multiple Intelligences (Gardner, 1983) are referenced in ID9® methodology and process. This is not a complete list of links that are covered within the ID9® process however this dashboard aims to provide a quick reference for trainers to use to balance instructional design to provide equality for participants' learning preferences.

Global/Specific Learners		Learning Modalities (Sensory Intake)			Hemispheric Preference	
Global	Specific	Visual	Auditory	Kinesthetic	Left Brain	Right Brain
	X		X		X	

Multiple Intelligences								
Visual	Intrapersonal	Interpersonal	Musical	Mathematical / Logical	Linguistic	Kinesthetic	Naturalist	Existential

121. Picture Replay: Summarizing Training Content for Managers

Who's involved?

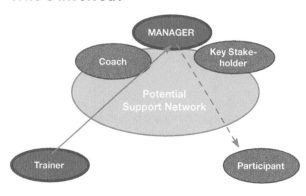

Learning Outcome
By the end of this activity, Managers will have a high level visual summary of the training content that can be used for various learning applications.

Pre-training	Bridging Task	Post-Training
		X

Overview
This activity provides a visual snapshot of key learning points from the course graphically summarized onto one page. Once the trainer has provided this to Managers, they then engage in a meeting with the participant/s

In My Experience
As a visual learner myself I learn best through pictures and color. In this activity the trainer needs to summarize the key points from the training program using pictures and only minimal words. This could be set out as a collage, photos in a tiled formation or if you or a graphic artist has the skills into a hand drawn illustration. For conceptual content (e.g. leadership, change, delegation, communication) choose photos that have been used from the course materials together with choosing key concepts taught from the program. For process type content, the process itself can be used in a very graphical way (see example below using the process from a customer service training program).

Essential Data
- Course Type: Any
- Group Size: 1-10
- When: After training
- Where/How: 1:1, Staff Meeting, Team Meeting
- Time Required: 10-30 minutes

Steps to create
As general guidance, the picture should be graphical, contain limited number of word and stay in the "big picture."
1. Trainer (or graphic designer with guidance from the Trainer / Instructional Designer) develops a one-page picture that summarizes the course.
2. Manager utilizes this image in one-on-one discussions or in team meetings.
3. Write guiding questions for the manager to ask or discussion points to use in conjunction with the picture.

Sample Questions (using Bloom's Taxonomy to guide the conversation)
- What parts of the course content can you see in this picture? (Knowledge)
- Describe what is in the picture and how it relates to the overall course or details within the course. (Comprehension)
- Rate your own ability to apply these concepts) and explain how they are applying each concept into their daily activities (Application)
  Explain what you are doing different now as a result of the course. What about in the future? (Application)
- Analyze one or more parts of the picture. How does each relate to your workplace? (Analysis)

- Articulate how they differentiate between these concepts or ideas presented in this learning program compared to previous trainings (Synthesis)
- Now that you are starting to apply this new process/content, how does this process compare to what we were using/doing before? (Evaluation)

Tips, Tricks and Traps
- Choosing the content is important. Use key concepts and processes from the training course using your learning objectives to guide you in choosing only the most important content from the program.

- Find a resource (e.g. graphic designer) that can design the picture as a cartoon, sketch or something of a creative nature. Make it interesting while keeping the theme relative to the content.
- Apply as many key points as possible distilling only to the 'must knows' from the course.
- Provide the Manager with a recommendation on how to use this picture with guiding questions.

Adult Learning Base Process:
Storytelling and Higher order questions.
Refer to **Adult Learning Base Process Reference Guide** for more information about this learning process.

Adult Learning Datasheet:
This activity links participant's preferred style of learning. The following dashboard provides a quick reference to adult learning theorists and principles as part of the ID9® methodology.

This activity achieves the following level of Bloom's Taxonomy of the Cognitive Domain (Bloom et al 1956), shown with "X" in the following table.

Bloom's Taxonomy of the Cognitive Domain Level					
Knowledge	Comprehension	Application	Analysis	Synthesis	Evaluation
X	X	X	X	X	X

This activity also achieves a link, shown with "X" in the following table, to participant's naturally occurring learning preferences. Global/Specific, Learning Modalities, Hemispheric Preference (Sperry, 1981), and Multiple Intelligences (Gardner, 1983) are referenced in ID9® methodology and process. This is not a complete list of links that are covered within the ID9® process however this dashboard aims to provide a quick reference for trainers to use to balance instructional design to provide equality for participants' learning preferences.

Global/Specific Learners		Learning Modalities (Sensory Intake)			Hemispheric Preference	
Global	Specific	Visual	Auditory	Kinesthetic	Left Brain	Right Brain
X	X	X	X		X	X

Multiple Intelligences								
Visual	Intrapersonal	Interpersonal	Musical	Mathematical / Logical	Linguistic	Kinesthetic	Naturalist	Existential
X	X				X			X

122. Play that Movie: Using Alternative Medias to Discuss Training Impact

Who's involved?

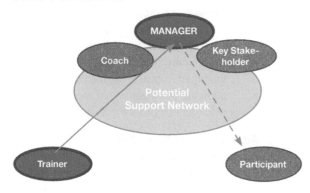

Learning Outcome
By the end of this activity, Managers will be able to creatively discuss the training impact to his / her direct reports.

Pre-training	Bridging Task	Post-Training
	X	X

Overview
The Trainer selects a movie or scene from a movie that clearly depicts one or more of the ideas/concepts presented in training. The Trainer then creates a briefing kit for the Manager with the movie and notes on the specific scene to play, how it relates to the training, and key questions / expected answers to ask the Participants.

In My Experience
Who doesn't love movies? Using movies as a training process has been successful probably since movies were invented and this activity extends that concept to an effective activity in between training sessions (bridging task) or post-training. Supporting the manager with a full briefing kit (i.e. a mini trainer's guide) boosts the manager's confidence and be creative, innovative and supportive with the trainer behind the scenes doing the work for them.

Essential Data
- Course Type: Any
- Group Size: 2-20
- When: After training session
- Where/How: 1:1, staff meeting, team meeting, offsite
- Time Required: 15-60 minutes

Steps to create
1. Choose a movie that relates to the content of the course. (There are excellent online resources with suggestions for all types of content, e.g. Leadership, Change, Motivation, Process etc.)
2. Either provide the managers with enough DVD copies of the movie for each team member, or provide 1 DVD for the manager to play a scene from a movie.
3. Create a Manager's Movie Briefing Kit
   a. Ask the following questions:
      - What does this film or clip illustrate? How does this apply to the training? (Comprehension)
      - Compare this movie clip to what you learned in the training session? How do the two relate? (Evaluation)
      - Differentiate between what you learned in training and how you are modifying it to use in your daily activities? (Analysis and Synthesis)

Tips, Tricks and Traps
- Be very careful about 'publicly' playing movies as you could inadvertently be breaking copyright. Even playing a movie in a meeting room in your office may be considered breaking copyright. To be certain that you are not giving a copy of the movie as a DVD to each participant to watch before the meeting means that copyright is covered and that you are not playing the movie in public.
- Make sure the movie is relevant to the age group of the participants. Playing an old fashioned movie may not resonate with younger employees

Adult Learning Base Process: Storytelling
Refer to **Adult Learning Base Process Reference Guide** for more information about this learning process.

Adult Learning Datasheet:
This activity links participant's preferred style of learning. The following dashboard provides a quick reference to adult learning theorists and principles as part of the ID9® methodology.

This activity achieves the following level of Bloom's Taxonomy of the Cognitive Domain (Bloom et al 1956), shown with "X" in the following table.

Bloom's Taxonomy of the Cognitive Domain Level					
Knowledge	Comprehension	Application	Analysis	Synthesis	Evaluation
	X	X	X	X	X

This activity also achieves a link, shown with "X" in the following table, to participant's naturally occurring learning preferences. Global/Specific, Learning Modalities, Hemispheric Preference (Sperry, 1981), and Multiple Intelligences (Gardner, 1983) are referenced in ID9® methodology and process. This is not a complete list of links that are covered within the ID9® process however this dashboard aims to provide a quick reference for trainers to use to balance instructional design to provide equality for participants' learning preferences.

Global/Specific Learners		Learning Modalities (Sensory Intake)			Hemispheric Preference	
Global	Specific	Visual	Auditory	Kinesthetic	Left Brain	Right Brain
	X	X	X			X

Multiple Intelligences								
Visual	Intrapersonal	Interpersonal	Musical	Mathematical / Logical	Linguistic	Kinesthetic	Naturalist	Existential

123. Mind Map Learning Application

Who's involved?

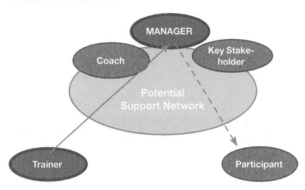

Learning Outcome
By the end of this activity, Managers and / or Coaches will be able to explore with the Participants ideas or concepts that were presented in training.

Pre-training	Bridging Task	Post-Training
	X	X

Overview
The trainer or instructional designer creates a worksheet to list the relevant topics from training. These topics should be presented to the manager a list of between 2-7 topics or key elements from the training program. These topics will form the branches of the mind map. Smaller and more minor concepts may create sub-branches on the mind map.

In My Experience
The idea is for the Participant to map what he/she has learned and who he/she will apply the learning. The worksheet gives the manager insight to what might come up in the mind mapping process and allows the manager to access what was learned in the training session, how the Participant is applying and synthesizing the learning as well as insights to potential gaps that the manager can then work with the Participant (or trainer/coach) to help fill. This results in a supported and engaged Participant.

Essential Data
- Course Type: Any
- Group Size: 1-20
- When: After training session
- Where/How: 1:1, staff meeting, team meeting
- Time Required: 2-15 minutes

Steps to create
1. Examples of key topics might include key learning, tools, impact, challenges, and processes and so on. Work from the course outline for the list of topics and from participant materials to spark ideas for other key elements from the course.
2. Provide an overview on 'how to mind map' with an example to show managers what their groups might create
3. Suggest a format for the meeting that the manager will hold with the team:
   a. Introduce mind mapping (show an example)
   b. List the key topics/concepts from the training program
   c. Participants in small groups or pairs create a mind map (using flipchart or poster paper)
   d. Participants present their mind map in a 1-2 minute summary to the whole group

Tips, Tricks and Traps
- If mind mapping is a new concept for managers and or participants, ensure that they are shown how to mind map
- This activity can be done a few times with the same content where the central theme of the mind map is examples of real life work situations. (For example: the customer service process in different types of customer interaction situations) This provides an exploration of how the learning is being applied to new situations, if applicable.

Adult Learning Base Process:
Mind Mapping
Refer to **Adult Learning Base Process Reference Guide** for more information about this learning process.

Adult Learning Datasheet:
This activity links participant's preferred style of learning. The following dashboard provides a quick reference to adult learning theorists and principles as part of the ID9® methodology.

This activity achieves the following level of Bloom's Taxonomy of the Cognitive Domain (Bloom et al 1956), shown with "X" in the following table.

Bloom's Taxonomy of the Cognitive Domain Level					
Knowledge	Comprehension	Application	Analysis	Synthesis	Evaluation
		X			X

This activity also achieves a link, shown with "X" in the following table, to participant's naturally occurring learning preferences. Global/Specific, Learning Modalities, Hemispheric Preference (Sperry, 1981), and Multiple Intelligences (Gardner, 1983) are referenced in ID9® methodology and process. This is not a complete list of links that are covered within the ID9® process however this dashboard aims to provide a quick reference for trainers to use to balance instructional design to provide equality for participants' learning preferences.

Global/Specific Learners		Learning Modalities (Sensory Intake)			Hemispheric Preference	
Global	Specific	Visual	Auditory	Kinesthetic	Left Brain	Right Brain
X	X	X		X		X

Multiple Intelligences								
Visual	Intrapersonal	Interpersonal	Musical	Mathematical / Logical	Linguistic	Kinesthetic	Naturalist	Existential
X						X		

124. Breaking News! Connecting Training to Real World Events

Who's involved?

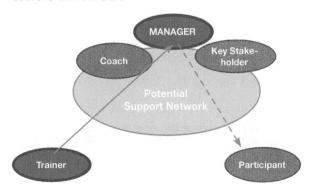

Learning Outcome
By the end of this activity, the Managers will be able to connect the training to the outside world, increasing the relevancy of the training session for Participants.

Pre-training	Bridging Task	Post-Training
X	X	X

Overview
Utilizing real world news articles to help set context for training helps motivate participants. As a pre-training activity managers can help participants to focus on the information that will be presented in the upcoming training program. As a bridging task the Managers can use the article to debrief the session if the activity is done post training.

In My Experience
Leadership

During a leadership program a bridging task was assigned to research Fortune 500 leaders and what set them apart followed by a series of reflective questions regarding the relevance of what their research linked to the content of the training program. Then, as a start of the next session review activity participants presented their research. The results were surprising, as not only did participants undertake the project and present back to the group, many had reached out to the leaders that they had researched and contacted them directly for further insights, therefore increasing their business network.

Essential Data
- Course Type: Any
- Group Size: 2-20
- When: Before and after training session
- Where/How: Email distribution, 1:1, staff meeting, team meeting
- Time Required: 2-15 minutes

Steps to create
- The Trainer / Instructional Designer identify a news article relevant to the training session. They create a package for the Manager that includes:
  - The article (or link)
  - Explanation on how it relates to the course content
  - Suggested debriefing questions
    - Being as specific as possible, tell me how the article relates to what you learned in training.
    - How does the article help you relate to the course content? How does the article help you imagine new possibilities?
  - The Manager distributes the information as it makes sense for his / her team (team meeting discussion, one-on-one discussion, and email with notes explaining the context).

Tips, Tricks and Traps
- Be sure to document the source and include in managers packet. Some good resources include Newsweek, Bloomberg Business Week, Times, US News and World Report, BBC News.
- Sometimes a direct link between the article and training course is suited to the course, however, for conceptual type courses (e.g. leadership, change, management etc.) sometimes focusing on what other companies are doing well or mistakes other companies have made provides for a rich conversation between the manager and their team.

Adult Learning Base Process: Storytelling
Refer to Adult Learning Base Process Reference Guide for more information about this learning process.

Adult Learning Datasheet:
This activity links participant's preferred style of learning. The following dashboard provides a quick reference to adult learning theorists and principles as part of the ID9® methodology.

This activity achieves the following level of Bloom's Taxonomy of the Cognitive Domain (Bloom et al 1956), shown with "X" in the following table.

Bloom's Taxonomy of the Cognitive Domain Level					
Knowledge	Comprehension	Application	Analysis	Synthesis	Evaluation
	X	X	X		

This activity also achieves a link, shown with "X" in the following table, to participant's naturally occurring learning preferences. Global/Specific, Learning Modalities, Hemispheric Preference (Sperry, 1981), and Multiple Intelligences (Gardner, 1983) are referenced in ID9® methodology and process. This is not a complete list of links that are covered within the ID9® process however this dashboard aims to provide a quick reference for trainers to use to balance instructional design to provide equality for participants' learning preferences.

Global/Specific Learners		Learning Modalities (Sensory Intake)			Hemispheric Preference	
Global	Specific	Visual	Auditory	Kinesthetic	Left Brain	Right Brain
X	X	X	X		X	

Multiple Intelligences								
Visual	Intrapersonal	Interpersonal	Musical	Mathematical / Logical	Linguistic	Kinesthetic	Naturalist	Existential
X	X	X			X			

125. Closing the Loop: Smart Conversations to Synchronize Managers, Trainers and Coaches

Who's involved?

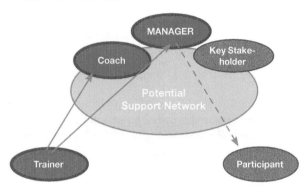

Learning Outcome
Aligning Managers, Trainers and Coaches on how to support the Participant in the application of a new process, system or product.

Pre-training	Bridging Task	Post-Training
X		X

Overview
Closing the Loop is a series of conversations between the Manager, Trainer and Coach before and after the training program. The conversations will focus on obtaining a holistic view of the Participant(s), including strengths, struggles and areas to focus coaching. Once briefed by the Trainer, the Manager then conducts the meeting with participant/s.

In My Experience
Gaining alignment from participant's managers and coaches (if they are assigned to the program) before the training begins means that support is high before the course has started! You might be reading this thinking…that could never happen in my organization but I challenge you to try it! I've found that by reaching out to managers and having a very brief conversation increases the motivation for the manager to take on an active supporting role throughout the learning process. If you have coaches assigned to participants as well as managers bring them into this conversation. The end result is that everyone is on the same page and focused on the learning outcomes, that is, to achieve learning application for each participant.

Essential Data
- Course Type: Any
- Group Size: Less than 20 managers the recommendation is Phone calls; more than 20, the recommendation is email
- When: Before and after training
- Where/How: Email, phone call, 1:1
- Time Required: 15 min before session; 15 minutes after session = 30 minutes total

Steps to create
1. Before the learning program
   - The Trainer initiates a quick conversation with the Manager / Coach to confirm expectations on what his / her direct reports will get out of the training.
   - This conversation can be a brief (10-15 minutes) phone call or email chain that addresses the Manager's / Coach's viewpoint on where the Participant's may struggle, skills to focus on during the training and the key competencies the trainer can help the Participant zero in on during training.
2. After the training session
   - The Trainer conducts a training debrief with the Manager and/or Coach informing on the Participant's progress.
   - This brief discussion or email updates on the learning session (e.g. success the Participant experienced, challenges the Participant experienced, and perspective on potential super users)
   - After the training debrief, the Manager and or Coach follows up with the Participant to confirm they felt about the training, what they think their successes and challenges were and how the Participant will be applying the learning and the action plan to overcoming the challenges.

Sample Questions:

Pre-training Session (Trainer and Manager):
- What challenges do you think your direct report will face during training?
- Does your direct report have any particular areas of development that I should be aware of that I (the trainer) could help them focus on during training?

Post-training Debrief (Trainer and Manager):
- Summary on what the Participant experienced from a success point of view; challenges point of view. Do you as the trainer think this person can support others during implementation or use?

Post-training Session (Manager to Participant):
- What were your successes during learning?
- What were your challenges? What are your next steps to overcoming the challenges? What time frame will you be implementing your next steps?

Adult Learning Base Process:
Action Planning
Refer to Adult Learning Base Process Reference Guide for more information about this learning process.

Tips, Tricks and Traps
1. Keep interactions short but meaningful. The idea is not to burden the Manager or Coach with extra work but really to empower the Manager by knowing what occurred during training specific to their direct report(s).
2. Trainers should provide detailed examples, reference specific concept / ideas and stay fact based when debriefing on the training session.

Adult Learning Datasheet:
This activity links participant's preferred style of learning. The following dashboard provides a quick reference to adult learning theorists and principles as part of the ID9® methodology.

This activity achieves the following level of Bloom's Taxonomy of the Cognitive Domain (Bloom et al 1956), shown with "X" in the following table.

Bloom's Taxonomy of the Cognitive Domain Level					
Knowledge	Comprehension	Application	Analysis	Synthesis	Evaluation
X					

This activity also achieves a link, shown with "X" in the following table, to participant's naturally occurring learning preferences. Global/Specific, Learning Modalities, Hemispheric Preference (Sperry, 1981), and Multiple Intelligences (Gardner, 1983) are referenced in ID9® methodology and process. This is not a complete list of links that are covered within the ID9® process however this dashboard aims to provide a quick reference for trainers to use to balance instructional design to provide equality for participants' learning preferences.

Global/Specific Learners		Learning Modalities (Sensory Intake)			Hemispheric Preference	
Global	Specific	Visual	Auditory	Kinesthetic	Left Brain	Right Brain
X	X	X	X			

Multiple Intelligences								
Visual	Intrapersonal	Interpersonal	Musical	Mathematical / Logical	Linguistic	Kinesthetic	Naturalist	Existential
X								

126. Rico Review: Identifying Challenges and Successes for Training

Who's involved?

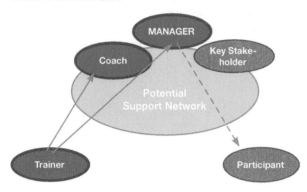

Learning Outcome

By the end of this activity, Managers and / or Coaches will have insight to the obstacles and successes the Participants are experiencing. These insights will allow Managers and Coaches to help clear the obstacles and help reward success.

Pre-training	Bridging Task	Post-Training
		X

Overview

Rico Clustering is a form of non-linear note taking which is especially effective to visually brainstorm what participants have applied from their training and what obstacles or barriers they are facing as they implement their learning.

In My Experience

When managers and or coaches are provided with a method to guide their conversations, be it questioning, 6 Thinking Hats, or in this case Rico Clusters the conversation between their direct reports and teams often results in the meeting becoming more in depth and valuable. This activity really gets people talking and celebrating what's already been done and talking without fear of what hasn't yet been implemented. It gives Managers and or Coaches an opportunity to reward success and also create some action planning around those areas of learning where participants are stuck, or haven't had an opportunity to apply.

Essential Data

- Course Type: Any
- Group Size: 5-20 people
- When: After training
- Where/How: Team Meeting, Staff meeting
- Time Required: 15-30 minutes

Steps to create

Using Rico Clusters, Participants work with their Manager and/or Coach to document the challenges / obstacles and benefits / success factors to implementing the learning.

1. Trainer provides the Manager with a course outline. Talking through the course outline the trainer discusses with the Manager and or Coach their thoughts on how their team is going so far with implementing their learning. Using the course outline to guide the conversation discuss the topics, ideas and concepts that are potentially facing obstacles and what is being successfully applied already.

2. The trainer suggests a meeting agenda:
   a. Gather the team together (participants from the course who report to the manager or are coachees of the coach)
   b. Review the course outline as a group
   c. Divide the team into two groups: Challenges & Successes
   d. Briefly overview Rico Clusters and how this process works
   e. Using Rico Clusters the 'Challenges' team and 'Successes' team create a flipchart/poster of their experience so far
      i. 'Challenges' Group expands on their work by creating suggestions to overcome the challenges with what they learned in the course
      ii. 'Successes' Group expands on how they can achieve further traction and learning application with what they learned in the course.
   f. Each group presents back to the whole group
   g. Manager/Coach summarizes, making suggestions for further success, removal of barriers and challenges, and encourages the group towards 100% learning application.

3. Managers organize a working session dividing the team into two groups (Challenges, Success) with to brainstorm, via Rico Clusters following the suggested agenda

4. Trainer checks in with Manager/Coach after the meeting for an update on what happened and next steps.

Tips, Tricks and Traps
- Managers and or coaches may not know all of the answers about the detail of what their team members are applying. It's important for the trainer to be very supportive of the manager/coach even if their knowledge of what's happening with their group is scant.
- The trainer might attend the meeting, but it's recommended that if this happens that the trainer leaves it to the manager/coach to facilitate the meeting. This way the responsibility for applying the learning transfers to the manager/coach and the participants.
- Use flip charts or scratch paper to document the Rico Clusters. Try to make the brainstorming a visible as possible.

- The 'Successes' group may directly counter the Challenges group's assumptions and ideas as a way to move the discussion forward.
- The Manager should serve as facilitator and help guide his/her group to better success and/or increased motivation.

Adult Learning Base Process:
Rico Clusters
Refer to Adult Learning Base Process Reference Guide for more information about this learning process.

Adult Learning Datasheet:
This activity links participant's preferred style of learning. The following dashboard provides a quick reference to adult learning theorists and principles as part of the ID9® methodology.

This activity achieves the following level of Bloom's Taxonomy of the Cognitive Domain (Bloom et al 1956), shown with "X" in the following table.

Bloom's Taxonomy of the Cognitive Domain Level					
Knowledge	Comprehension	Application	Analysis	Synthesis	Evaluation
	X				

This activity also achieves a link, shown with "X" in the following table, to participant's naturally occurring learning preferences. Global/Specific, Learning Modalities, Hemispheric Preference (Sperry, 1981), and Multiple Intelligences (Gardner, 1983) are referenced in ID9® methodology and process. This is not a complete list of links that are covered within the ID9® process however this dashboard aims to provide a quick reference for trainers to use to balance instructional design to provide equality for participants' learning preferences.

Global/Specific Learners		Learning Modalities (Sensory Intake)			Hemispheric Preference	
Global	Specific	Visual	Auditory	Kinesthetic	Left Brain	Right Brain
	X	X	X	X		X

Multiple Intelligences								
Visual	Intrapersonal	Interpersonal	Musical	Mathematical / Logical	Linguistic	Kinesthetic	Naturalist	Existential
X	X	X			X	X		

127. Learning Application by Bestseller

Who's involved?

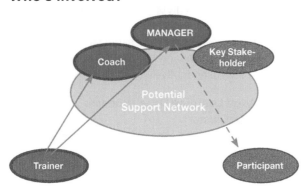

Learning Outcome

The manager reengages the Participants and learning from a specific training program by looking to bestselling books for inspiration and direction. This technique not only reinforces the learning it speaks to the relevancy of the content when a current bestselling book is introduced.

Pre-training	Bridging Task	Post-Training
	X	X

Overview

For this activity the trainer or instructional designer should research current best-selling books and authors relevant to the training content. After completing the research and select an appropriate book (or books, more than one can be selected), the trainer/ instructional designer writes up a summary on the book, highlighting key ideas that relate to the training content. Additional summary items should include page number and paragraphs with key quotes that the manager can use during a meeting.

In My Experience

This has been an activity that I've conducted with great success. The book, at the very least, updates participant's business book library, and brings to the forefront popular thinking creating a very valuable and rich discussion. Here are some books and ideas to start with:

- Blink: The Power of Thinking Without Thinking by Malcolm Gladwell: What was your blink response to the new system? After training or further investigation do you have a different response?

- Good to Great: Why Some Companies Make the Leap...And Others Don't by Jim Collins: How do we go from good to great now that we know more?

- The 4-Hour Workweek: Escape 9-5, Live Anywhere, and Join the New Rich by Timothy Ferriss – How can we as a team or department create efficiencies that will allow us to work smarter (and less hours) not harder and longer?

Essential Data

- Course Type: Any
- Group Size: 1-25
- When: After training session
- Where/How: 1:1, staff meeting, team meeting, off-site
- Time Required: 10-20 minutes

Steps to create

- The trainer should send one or more copies of the book along with the briefing kit (book summary, key quotes, and a description of how it relates to the content), to the manager within one week of the training program ending.

- The manager can then use the book and summary to have conversations with direct reports. If the trainer sends several copies the manager can distribute them as he/she sees fit.

Tips, Tricks and Traps

- Be careful of copyright. Using long excerpts from a book may inadvertently break copyright so to be 100% safe, it's suggested that a copy of the book be given to each participant.
- Check the online book stores bestseller lists in the 'business book' section. This will provide you with the most up-to-date bestsellers.
- Biographies of leading business people and influencers can also be chosen. Learning from how they created success, their setbacks throughout their careers, the businesses that they created can all link to some types of training content.
- I know it may sound obvious, but as a trainer and instructional designer make sure YOU have read the book! The last thing that you need is to have to 'wing it' through a conversation with a participant or their manager when you haven't read the book yourself!

Adult Learning Base Process:
Metacognitive Reflection

Refer to Adult Learning Base Process Reference Guide for more information about this learning process.

Adult Learning Datasheet:
This activity links participant's preferred style of learning. The following dashboard provides a quick reference to adult learning theorists and principles as part of the ID9® methodology.

This activity achieves the following level of Bloom's Taxonomy of the Cognitive Domain (Bloom et al 1956), shown with "X" in the following table.

Bloom's Taxonomy of the Cognitive Domain Level					
Knowledge	Comprehension	Application	Analysis	Synthesis	Evaluation
X	X	X			

This activity also achieves a link, shown with "X" in the following table, to participant's naturally occurring learning preferences. Global/Specific, Learning Modalities, Hemispheric Preference (Sperry, 1981), and Multiple Intelligences (Gardner, 1983) are referenced in ID9® methodology and process. This is not a complete list of links that are covered within the ID9® process however this dashboard aims to provide a quick reference for trainers to use to balance instructional design to provide equality for participants' learning preferences.

Global/Specific Learners		Learning Modalities (Sensory Intake)			Hemispheric Preference	
Global	Specific	Visual	Auditory	Kinesthetic	Left Brain	Right Brain
	X		X		X	

Multiple Intelligences								
Visual	Intrapersonal	Interpersonal	Musical	Mathematical / Logical	Linguistic	Kinesthetic	Naturalist	Existential
					X			

Chapter 10:
Adult Learning Base
Processes Reference Guide
Catherine Mattiske

Adult Learning Base Processes Reference Guide

The following training processes are used in **Training Activities That Work.** It is not intended to be an exhaustive list of all training methods but rather is provided as a quick reference glossary of training methods of delivery that are noted in Chapters 1-9.

Adult Learning Base Process	Definition
Action Plan	Action planning can be especially helpful in proving participants with an opportunity to set goals and actions in preparation for learning transfer and learning application. You can provide the framework for the action plan form and ask participants to fill in the questions, or you can ask them to create their own form. In ID9® Action Plans may be used as a review activity or form part of a continuous activity throughout the duration of the training program.
Assessment	A way of determining a participant's level of knowledge, skill, expertise or behavior in a given area. Typically assessments or tests before and after the training. Self-assessment may be conducted in many different ways. Assessment can be individual or a team activity answering questions regarding the content. Generally in ID9® Assessments are Formative Assessments rather than Summative Assessments however Summative Assessments often may need to follow Formative Assessments due to compliance requirements within a regulated workplace.
Bingo	A game in which players mark off numbers on cards as the numbers are drawn randomly by a caller, the winner being the first person to mark off all their numbers. In ID9® Bingo may be adapted as a learning or review activity or as an icebreaker.
Board Game	A game that involves the movement of counters or other objects round a board. In ID9® a board game (either commercially purchased or created from scratch) may be adapted as a learning or review activity and is particularly useful as a Major Review.
Brainstorming	A group method for collecting ideas and suggestions from the participants. This technique is used to problem solve and collect information by stimulating creative thinking through unrestrained and spontaneous participation in discussion. In ID9® learning and review activities can be based around the Brainstorming method and is especially useful as a learning activity for unchartered uses for new content.
Case Study	A technique where the participants are asked to investigate a situation or problem and report their findings, causes and/or solutions. Participants gather and organize relevant materials and report their findings. In ID9® learning and review activities can be based around the Case Study structures and are particularly useful for activating new skills and knowledge in a simulated learning environment.
Chaining Anchors (NLP)	Neuro Linguistic Programming teaches that we constantly make "anchors" (associations) between what we see, hear and feel and our emotional states. Chaining Anchors is a sequential process of moving to a significantly different state. In ID9® learning and review activities can be based around the Chaining Anchors technique and is especially useful when participants have a significant difference between their present state and the desired state. Each state builds on the one before until the desired state is reached.
Cooperative Learning	Cooperative learning is a method of instruction that has participants working together in groups, usually with the goal of completing a specific task. In ID9® Cooperative Learning can be created as a learning or review activity. Cooperative Learning can help participants develop leadership skills and the ability to work with others as a team.
Crossword	A puzzle consisting of a grid of squares and blanks into which words crossing vertically and horizontally are written according to clues. In ID9® crosswords can be created as a learning or review activity.

Adult Learning Base Process	Definition
Debrief	A debrief is conducted by the trainer as the final step to a learning or review activity. During the debrief the trainer checks the results of the activity, provides feedback, fills gaps in learning and ensures that participants are confident to move on to the next session of content.
Eureka Effect	The eureka effect, also known as the aha! effect, refers to the common human experience of suddenly understanding a previously incomprehensible problem or concept.
Fishbowl	In ID9® learning and review activities can be based on the 'fishbowl' approach whereby participants draw from a bowl, hat, or bag cards with questions, steps of a process, mini-case studies, etc.
Flow Chart	A diagram of the sequence of movements or actions of people or things involved in a complex system or activity. In ID9® learning and review activities can be based around working with flowcharts to map processes, create action plans, etc.
Future Pace (NLP)	This technique is used in NLP exercises in order to test the effectiveness of a change intervention. Mentally rehearsing a future result so that the desired outcome automatically occurs.
Guided Research	Also known as Inquiry-based learning or Enquiry-based learning, Guided Research describes approaches to learning that are based on the investigation of questions, scenarios or problems - often assisted by a trainer. Participants will identify and research issues and questions to develop their knowledge or solutions. Guided Research learning includes problem-based learning, and is generally used in small scale investigations and projects, as well as research.
Higher Order Questions	Higher order thinking, based on learning taxonomies such as Bloom's Taxonomy links to the process of asking questions thus elevating the basic question to 'Higher Order Questions'. The idea is that some types of learning require more cognitive processing than others, but also have more generalized benefits.
I Spy	A children's game in which one player specifies the first letter of an object they can see, the other players then having to guess the identity of this object. In ID9® learning and review activities can be based around I Spy for sophisticated research projects, scavenger hunts for content, usability possibilities for new content, etc.
In-Tray Diagnosis	A variant of Diagnosis Problem case is the In-Tray Diagnosis in which participants are presented a number of documents that might be found in their in-trays, or email inbox. In ID9® learning and review activities can be based around In-Tray Diagnosis for sophisticated case studies, role plays, time sensitive action taking, etc.
Key Learning	Notable information discovered while performing an activity, utilizing a tool, creating a deliverable, etc. When key learnings are shared, productivity can be gained by warning others of pitfalls or informing others of valuable short cuts, tips, etc.
Kinesthetic	Kinesthetic learning (also known as tactile learning) is a learning style in which learning takes place by the participant carrying out a physical activity, rather than listening to a lecture or watching a demonstration.
Learning Journal	The Learning Journal is a systematic way of documenting learning and collecting information for self-analysis and reflection. Participants can also be given specific questions that spark ideas for journal entries.

Adult Learning Base Process	Definition
Learning Stations	In the training room information on a variety of topics is set out in different places in the training room. Participants, individually, in pairs or small groups, visit each Learning Station to complete a learning or review activity, undertake a research project, etc.
Learning Transfer	Today, transfer of learning is usually described as the process and the effective extent to which past experiences (also referred to as the transfer source) affect learning and performance in a new situation (the transfer target).
Live Role Play	"Live" or "Hot" role-playing, deals with real people (the participants) and their actual problems with others-on the job, at home, in the community, elsewhere in the everyday world.
Match / Matching	Participants match items of content, for example, terms and definitions, dates to a timeline, etc.
Memory Chain	Participants create a chain of content based on repetition of all parts of the process/content heard from prior participants in the 'chain'.
Metacognitive Reflection	Reflecting on what we know. Participants have thoughts, notions, and intuitions about their own knowledge and thinking. Flavell (1979) describes three kinds of metacognitive knowledge: Awareness of knowledge—understanding what one knows, what one does not know, and what one wants to know, Awareness of thinking—understanding cognitive tasks and the nature of what is required to complete them, and Awareness of thinking strategies—understanding approaches to directing learning.
Metaphor	A figure of speech in which a word or phrase is applied to an object or action to which it is not literally applicable. In ID9® themes for a single piece of content within the training program or the entire training program can be based around a metaphor.
Mind Mapping	A mind map is a diagram used to visually outline information. A mind map is often created around a single word or text, placed in the center, to which associated ideas, words and concepts are added. Major categories radiate from a central node, and lesser categories are sub-branches of larger branches. Categories can represent words, ideas, tasks, or other items related to a central key word or idea. In ID9® learning and review activities can be based around Mind Mapping as individual, paired, small group or whole group activations.
Mnemonic	A system such as a pattern of letters, ideas, or associations which assists in remembering something. For example: the popular Mnemonic for star types is O Be A Fine Girl Kiss Me. In ID9® learning and review activities can be based around creating a Mnemonic to aid recall of complex content.
Naturalist Intelligence	Naturalist Intelligence is one of Howard Gardner's Nine Multiple Intelligences. It involves how sensitive an individual is towards nature and the world around them. In ID9® learning and review activities can be based around the Naturalist Intelligence to classify content based on a set of criteria.
Neuro-Linguistic Programming (NLP)	Neuro-Linguistic Programming (NLP) is an approach to communication, personal development, and psychotherapy created by Richard Bandler and John Grinder in California, USA in the 1970s.
Open-ended Problem	Most case assignments require participants to answer an open-ended question or develop a solution to an open-ended problem with multiple potential solutions.
Pacer (NLP)	A NLP process for goal setting: Positive, Achievement, Context, Ecology and Resources.

Adult Learning Base Process	Definition
Perceptual Positions (NLP)	Perceptual Positions is a NLP technique where participants mentally review (or preview) a situation from a number of different standpoints in order to enrich their appreciation of what is involved.
Questions and Answers	A classic learning or review activity where questions are posed to participants to answer.
Quiz / Review Questions	A classic learning or review activity where questions are posed to participants to answer.
Rhythmic Learning	Participants create a rhythm, rhyme or rap using a regular, repeated pattern of sounds and or movements to aid retention of complex step-by-step processes or other learning content.
Rico Clusters	Rico Clusters involve freely putting random ideas and connections down on a piece of paper or as a group on a flipchart/whiteboard and then analyzing the connections to create clusters which may spark new ideas and creativity.
Right Brain Processes	Learning and review activities that engage the Right Brain Processes which include participants who prefer to use feeling, are "big picture" oriented, where imagination rules, use symbols and images, present and future, philosophy & religion, can "get it" (i.e. meaning), believe, appreciate, have spatial perception, know object function, are fantasy based, present possibilities, are impetuous and risk taking.
Role Play	Acting out of specific situations with the group to demonstrate ways to handle specific situations or problems. In a Role Play the trainer sets the scene and tells the participants their roles, but doesn't tell the outcome - the participants have to create the 'action.' The outcome of a Role Play is less predictable than a demonstration. Role Plays are useful when participants need to discover something for themselves, or when they are ready to practice a skill.
Role Play Technique using Speed Dating	An acting out of specific situations with the group to demonstrate ways to handle specific situations or problems using the format of "Speed Dating" which is an organized social activity in which people seeking romantic relationships and have a series of short conversations with potential partners in order to determine whether there is mutual interest. Replacing the 'romantic relationship' notion with a series of mini case studies, conversations related to the content, or short scenarios provides an accelerated pace for learning key content.
Scavenger Hunt	A game, typically played in an extensive outdoor area, in which participants have to collect a number of miscellaneous objects. In ID9® learning and review activities can be based around the Scavenger Hunt activity format to find content based on a set of criteria.
Scenario	An abridged case study.
Sensory Predicate Words and Phrases (NLP)	A Predicate Phrase gives a clue to visual, auditory or kinesthetic learning preference where the main verb provides the clue and all the words related to that verb except the subject. For example, "That rings a bell", where 'ring' is auditory and the subject is recalling prior knowledge.
Socratic Method	A method of teaching by question and answer. In ID9® learning and review activities can be based around the Socratic Method format to explore content to an in-depth level. ID9® promotes the use of the Socratic Method as one of many pre-course learning activity structures but can be used for other higher-order learning or review activities.

Adult Learning Base Process	Definition
Spot the Problem/ Error	A training method where participants seek out the 'false' or 'incorrect' information within a case study, example or piece of content. In ID9® learning and review activities can be based around the Spot the Error format and is especially useful as a review activity structure.
Step Mix	A training method where participants un-jumble a process, example or piece of content. In ID9® learning and review activities can be based around the Step Mix format and is especially useful as a review activity structure.
Story or Case Study Analysis	A training method where participants analyze a Story or Case Study and relate it to content that they have already learned or are about to learn. In ID9® learning and review activities can be based around the Story or Case Study Analysis format and is especially useful as a pre-course activity, bridging task or review activity structure.
Storytelling	Storytelling is the conveying of events in words, and images, often by improvisation or embellishment. Crucial elements of stories and storytelling include plot, characters, and narrative point of view. In ID9® learning and review activities can be based around Storytelling and is especially useful for attaching meaning to content.
Supporting Data and Documents	Research Documents and papers can be provided to participants to use to answer a series of questions or case study scenarios. In ID9® learning and review activities can be based around providing Supporting Data and Documents and is especially useful for analyzing complex content and processes.
SWOT Analysis	A study undertaken by an organization to identify its internal strengths and weaknesses, as well as its external opportunities and threats. In ID9® learning and review activities can be based around providing SWOT analysis and is especially useful for analyzing future action planning thus establishing grounded and realistic learning transfer and application.
Table	Research documents and papers can be provided to participants in the form of data Tables which participants analyze. In ID9® learning and review activities can be based around providing Tables of data and information and is especially useful for analyzing complex content and processes to construct meaning from a number of disparate parts.
Teach-back	As a learning activity Teach-back is a training method where participants individually, in pairs or small groups research a particular piece of content and teach it to the whole group. As a review activity, participants review information that they have learned and then present key elements to the whole group.
Triad/ Trio Role Play	See Role Play. This form of role play is conducted with three participants in each group, one participant usually taking the role of 'observer' providing feedback to the other two participants.
True or False Questions	Preparing a series of statements each of which is to be judged as true or false; "a true-false test" enables participants to identify true content and analyze what would make false statements true.
Word Search	A puzzle consisting of letters arranged in a grid, containing several hidden words written in any direction. In ID9® learning and review activities can be based around creating a Word Search puzzle and is especially useful for teaching complex terminology where spelling of terms is important.

Appendix A:
Theoretical Research Reference

Overarching influence for ID9®

ID9® is a constructivist approach to learning design that encourages collaborative experiential learning. The ID9® framework and process was developed in 1997 by Catherine Mattiske (Born 1964).

ID9® is a process that builds on learning through the use of learning activities and confirms new knowledge through structured review activities

The influences from theory on the design and development of instructional systems design which create the foundation to ID9® can be drawn from several areas of research including learning and psychological theory.

To enable further understanding of the 'learning theory' that has led toward our current knowledge on the application of learning and the need for aligning learning interventions to individual and corporate objectives, the following summary of researched authors is provided.

Constructivism

One of the four major learning theory schools, constructivism is the belief that learners, having some prior knowledge and experience as a basis from which to test out their hypotheses, build their own set of content to solve a particular set of problems posed by the instructor. Constructivism is a *learner-centric* educational paradigm, in which content is constructed by the learners in a team based collaborative learning, a constructivist learning environment, as well as by the instructor. Learner-centric theories embodied in constructivism focus on the importance of the learners over the instructor to the instructional activity. In the active learning education paradigm of constructivism the instructor is no longer a primary intermediary and single conduit of knowledge between the learners and the learning experience. All knowledge need not past first through the instructor. The instructor instead becomes a catalyst, a coach, and a program manager directing projects that centre upon solving a particular problem, not an intermediary or a barrier between content and the students. With constructivism learner enquiry and discovery, learner autonomy, and self-motivation of the learner are critical elements to the success of the learning processes.

There are many learning theories that fall under the educational paradigm of constructivism, such as Len Vygotsky's *social development theory*, Jean Lave's *situated learning*. Two that are most often cited as preeminent examples of constructivism are Piaget's *developmental learning* theory and Bruner's *discovery learning* theory.

Major Influential ID9® Theorists:

The development of the ID9® framework and process (Mattiske 1997) was influenced by Benjamin Bloom (1913 – 1999), John Dewey (1859 – 1952), Jerome Seymore Bruner (Born 1915), Robert Mills Gagne (1916 – 2002), Howard Earl Gardner (Born 1943), Hermann Ebbinghaus (1850 – 1909) and Marton and Saljo (Published 1976). The theories and models presented by these authors are major influences that form foundation for the ID9® framework and process.

- Benjamin Bloom: Bloom's Taxonomy – the use of verbs to describe learning objectives, content and outcomes
- John Dewey: Experiential learning
- Jerome Seymore Bruner: Constructivism and the role of structure in learning
- Robert Mills Gagne: The building block for ID9®'s step 5 'Topic Rotation'
- Howard Earl Gardner: The use of Multiple Intelligences in course design
- Hermann Ebbinghaus: Primacy and Recency - overarching influence over ID9® process
- Marton and Saljo: Deep Learning principles for ID9®

Major Influential ID9® Theorists Reference Table

Author	Birth / Death	System / Model / Theory	Brief overview of contribution to theory	Theory linking to ID9®	Influence on ID9® concept and steps
Hermann Ebbinghaus	1850 - 1909	• Learning Curve / Memory – Retention Curve • The 'Serial Position Effect' called Primacy and Recency	Demonstrated the 'higher mental processes' of learning where the mastery of facts resulted from the number of times something was learnt and developed the 'rate of forgetting'. Concluded learning past mastery produced 'over learning' which increased the 'rate of forgetting'. Ebbinghaus's 'Serial Position Effect' or the Primacy and Recency of memory suggested that the first and last things learnt are the easily and most accurately recalled.	The work on learning and retention curves supports this theory that if meaningful learning is to occur attaching new learning to an individual's schema will encourage a 'deep learning' methodology. Primacy and Recency form the overarching structure for ID9®. Primacy and Recency influenced is felt from the Welcome through to the Close. Within ID9® course design, the first and last things learnt effects of Primacy and Recency are used in each of the topic reviews and activities. Primacy and Recency also provides influence over the running sheet structure and identifies the placement of training breaks.	Primacy and Recency form the overarching structure for ID9® Step 6: Major Review – Repetition, Reflection and Review linked to learning objectives demonstrates retention of new learning and mastery of new knowledge. The effects of Primacy and Recency highlight the importance of ID9®'s opening and closing phases, i.e. step's 1 to 4 and steps 7 to 9.
John Dewey	1859 – 1952	• Constructivist Learning Theory / Philosophy of Experiential Learning / Practical Problem-Based Learning	Learning comes from experience and believed in the unity of theory and practice. These thoughts formed the origins of experiential learning from Kolb and others. Dewey raised the important issue of vocational education and its role within traditional education.	Dewey believed traditional learning drew on cultural heritage for learning content as well as promoting a learners desire to learn new and current content. A sound educational experience involved the continuity and interaction between learner and what was learned. Dewey emphasized experience, experiment, purposeful learning and freedom to learn through 'progressive education'.	Step 3: Big Picture Overview – connect course objectives and outcomes with each participant. Step 4: Connect – activity designed to connect the learning to each participant. Step 5: Topic Rotation Tool – Drawing together adult learning engagement methods, styles and experiential learning to assist in the transfer and application process. Step 6: Major Review – Repetition, Reflection and Review linked to learning objectives demonstrates retention of new learning and mastery of new knowledge.
Benjamin Bloom	1913 - 1999	• Contributed to the classification of educational objectives and to the theory of mastery-learning	Bloom's Taxonomy was created in 1956 under the leadership of educational psychologist Dr. Benjamin Bloom in order to promote higher forms of thinking in education, such as analyzing and evaluating, rather than just remembering facts (rote learning). They are Cognitive, Affective and Psychomotor. Trainers often refer to these three categories as KSA (Knowledge, Skills, and Attitude). This taxonomy of learning behaviors can be thought of as "the goals of the learning process." That is, after a learning episode, the learner should have acquired new skills, knowledge, and/or attitudes	While Bloom's Taxonomy has been quite useful in that it has extended learning from simply remembering to more complex cognitive structures, such as analyzing and evaluating, newer models have come along. It has also become more useful with the revised taxonomy in the mid-nineties However, one useful model is the Structure of Observed Learning Outcome (SOLO) taxonomy. It is a model that describes levels of increasing complexity in a learner's understanding of subjects (Biggs, Collis, 1982). See Biggs below.	ID9® draws on Bloom's Taxonomy as an overall targeted approach when developing the course outline, the learning objectives and then integrating them into the learning design Step 5: Topic Rotation Tool – Drawing together adult learning engagement methods and styles to assist in the transfer and application process

Author	Birth / Death	System / Model / Theory	Brief overview of contribution to theory	Theory linking to ID9®	Influence on ID9® concept and steps
Jerome Seymore Bruner	Born 1915	• Social Constructivism / Cognitive Learning Theory	Educational Psychology / Genetic Epistemology / Assimilation and Accommodation / Different levels and types of learning requires a different type of instruction Bruner's `spiral curriculum' theory suggests that learners learn progressively by understand increasingly difficult concepts through a process of step by step discovery Bruner believes learning is a dynamic process and that learner's construct or build knowledge based upon their existing knowledge	Bruner suggested that the forming of concepts, categories and problem solving procedures are possible from both the external environment and an individual's own ability to conceptualize. Bruner's view is that the role of structure in learning, rather than simply the mastery of facts and techniques, was the center of the classic problem of the application of learning. Bruner put forward his evolving ideas about the building of learning structures, and the way in which they affect a learner's ability to construct, build on and transform learning introspectively Bruner builds on Socratic traditions and suggests learning design is essential to enable learners to actively construct and build on existing knowledge Bruner's four principles of his Theory of Instruction: Readiness: Learner's must have a predisposition to learn so their experiences and context must be considered Structure: The content must be structured so that it can be grasped by the learner Sequence: Material must be presented in the most effective sequence Generation: Good learning should encourage extrapolation, manipulation and filling in of the gaps, just beyond the learner's existing knowledge	ID9® is a constructivist approach to learning design that encourages collaborative experiential learning ID9® is a process that builds on learning through the use of learning activities and confirms new knowledge through structured review activities
Robert Mills Gagne	1916 – 2002	• Conditions of Learning	Gagne looked at the events of learning as a series of phases, using the cognitive steps of coding, storing, retrieving and transferring information. Gagne suggested that, since the purpose of instruction is learning, the central focus for rational derivation of instructional techniques is the human learner. Development of rationally sound instructional procedures must take into account learner characteristics such as initiate capacities, experimental maturity, and current knowledge states. Such factors become parameters of the design of any particular program of instruction	Gagne's Nine Steps of Designing Learning Instruction: 1. Gain attention: Present stimulus to ensure reception of instruction. 2. Tell the learners the learning objective: What will the pupil gain from the instruction? 3. Stimulate recall of prior learning: Ask for recall of existing relevant knowledge. 4. Present the stimulus: Display the content. 5. Provide learning guidance 6. Elicit performance: Learners respond to demonstrate knowledge. 7. Provide feedback: Give informative feedback on the learner's performance. 8. Assess performance: More performance and more feedback, to reinforce information. 9. Enhance retention and transfer to other contexts	The building block for ID9®'s step 5 'Topic Rotation'

Author	Birth / Death	System / Model / Theory	Brief overview of contribution to theory	Theory linking to ID9®	Influence on ID9® concept and steps
Howard Earl Gardner	Born 1943	• Theory of Multiple Intelligences	Gardner developed the theory of `Multiple Intelligences' in 1983 which suggest that there are many different types of intelligences that can be measured to determine the potential of learners. Gardner's Multiple Intelligences theory utilizes aspects of cognitive and developmental psychology, anthropology and sociology to explain human intellect	Gardner's Multiple Intelligence theory is ideally suited to a student-centered approach, and allows designers to structure aligned activities to include, enhance and cultivate an individual's strengths and weaknesses, encouraging learners to explore their intelligence	Gardiner's Multiple Intelligence theory is used as the guiding principle across the ID9® process to create a participant centered approach to learning. Multiple Intelligences is a formal checkpoint in the ID9® process to create balance across the entire program. Step 4: Connect – activity designed to connect the learning to each participant
Marton & Soljo	Published 1976	• Surface and Deep Learning	Deep and Surface are two approaches to learning. Surface learning is the simple memorization of facts, for example learning facts to pass an exam, whereas Deep learning is where learner's search for meaning. Deep learning engages in a more active dialogue with the content of the learning. It is as if the learner is constantly asking himself questions such as "How do the various parts of the learning relate to each other?"; "Is the meaning of the learning consistent or are there any logical gaps?"; "How does this relate to what I already know?" and so on. A surface approach to learning is the lack of such an active and reflective attitude toward acquiring new learning.	Participants can take different approaches to learning at different times. These approaches are not stable traits and depending upon individual motivation and interest in the content some participants will tend towards taking a deep approach while others will tend towards a surface approach. Effective facilitation can influence participants to take a deep approach, while poor facilitation can influence participants to take a surface approach. Biggs (1999) defines good facilitation as the encouragement of a deep approach to learning.	A Deep Learning approach is a guiding principle for all steps of the ID9® process

Supportive ID9® Theorists:

Further theories and models which are supportive influences to the ID9® framework and process are John Biggs (Born 1934), David Kolb (Born 1939), Jean Piaget (1896 – 1980), Burrhus Frederic Skinner (1904 – 1990), David A. (Anthony) Sousa, Roger Sperry (1913 – 1994), and Edward Thorndike (1874 – 1949).

- John Biggs: Constructive alignment of learning, surface and deep learning and the SOLO Taxonomy
- David Kolb: Experiential learning
- Jean Piaget: Constructivism, progressively building and constructing upon learning and the importance of learning activities
- Burrhus Frederic Skinner: Learning feedback, learning reinforcement and self-paced learning
- David A. (Anthony) Sousa: Importance of emotions, feedback, past experiences and meaning in adult learning.
- Roger Sperry: Left-Right brain and adult learning engagement methods and styles
- Edward Thorndike: Adult learning theory

Supportive ID9® Theorists Reference Table

Author	Birth / Death	System / Model / Theory	Brief overview of contribution to theory	Theory linking to ID9®	Influence on ID9® concept and steps
Edward Thorndike	1874 – 1949	• Adult Learning / Active Learning	Thorndike's research developed two significant theories of learning, concluding that children and adults learn in different ways and that learning is a series of neural connections. Thorndike is considered the father of `adult learning theory' and `connectionism'. Thorndike pioneered the concept of learning transfer, i.e. the degree to which learning transfers into the actual performance of skills and knowledge.	Thorndike contributed to the theory of adult education and his completion, arithmetic, vocabulary, and directions or CAVD test that form the basis for modern intelligence testing. Thorndike suggested that adults bring prior experience to training and therefore learn differently to children. These prior experiences need to be considered when designing adult learning.	ID9® maximizes learning transfer through the use of adult learning principles. Step 5: Topic Rotation Tool – Drawing together adult learning engagement methods and styles to assist in the transfer and application process.
Jean Piaget	1896 - 1980	• Theory of cognitive development and epistemological which when viewed together was called "genetic epistemology".	The theory of constructivism, like cognitivist, promotes a move from the `assimilation' of new knowledge, i.e. `surface learning', to a focus on knowledge `accommodation', or `deep learning' principles. With constructivism leaner enquiry and discovery, learner autonomy, and self-motivation of the learner are critical elements to the success of the learning processes.	Both theories suggest that learners scaffold new knowledge to existing schemas; however constructivists believe that this is achieved by individual interpretation accelerated by motivation and intention. The level of learner motivation is dependent upon the degree to which a learner moves, or is allowed to move, from passive learning to active and engaged learning, i.e. learner's actively `pull' knowledge instead of a passive `push'. Learner engagement is further enhanced through the use of intervention learning activities that are aligned to espoused learning outcomes.	ID9® includes training and review activities integrated within all steps of the ID9® Framework and Process. The ID9® Framework is built on providing learning support to participants and individual motivation and intention. Step 3: Big Picture Overview – connect course objectives and outcomes with each participant. Step 4: Connect – activity designed to connect the learning to each participant. Step 5: Topic Rotation Tool – Drawing together adult learning engagement methods and styles to assist in the transfer and application process. Step 6: Major Review – Repetition, Reflection and Review linked to learning objectives demonstrates retention of new learning and mastery of new knowledge.

Author	Birth / Death	System / Model / Theory	Brief overview of contribution to theory	Theory linking to ID9®	Influence on ID9® concept and steps
Burrhus Frederic Skinner	1904 - 1990	• Programmed Learning / Learning Behaviors / Experimental Analysis of Behavior.	Learning feedback and reinforcement. Skinner's view was that learning was best achieved when the desired behaviors from a learning program were created through repeated and reinforced approaches. Skinner believed that there was a distinct difference between effective learning and what was actually being delivered in a traditional learning environment. He believed that traditional delivery such as lecturing failed to confirm a learner's learning during the delivery, running the risk of learners being left behind.	Skinner linked behaviorist theory and his thoughts on effective learning to that of self-paced learning and proposed an alternative teaching technique in 1958 called 'programmed learning'. Skinner suggested delivering this 'programmed learning' via what he termed 'the learning machine', a learning technique that has four steps: • Within a lineal program learners progress from one frame of information to another in small steps. • Prior to moving to the next frame of information a learners correct and incorrect responses must be reinforced or corrected. • Immediate feedback acts as reinforcement to learned material. • Self-paced learning allows learning to proceed at the learners pace.	Step 4: Connect – activity designed to connect the learning to each participant. Step 5: Topic Rotation Tool – Drawing together adult learning engagement methods and styles to assist in the transfer and application process. Step 6: Major Review – Repetition, Reflection and Review linked to learning objectives demonstrates retention of new learning and mastery of new knowledge.
Roger Sperry	1913 - 1994	• Split-Brain (Left-Right Brain) research.	Sperry asked the simple question Nature or nurture? Sperry's work led to the understanding that the right and left brain hemispheres have a complimentary relationship and paved the way for new developments in cognitive neuroscience.	Sperry conducted "split-brain" studies on the connection between the brain's left and right hemispheres, proving that neural circuitry is specifically 'wired' for specific functions, and showing that the two sides of the brain can operate almost independently.	Step 5: Topic Rotation Tool – Drawing together adult learning engagement methods and styles to assist in the transfer and application process

Author	Birth / Death	System / Model / Theory	Brief overview of contribution to theory	Theory linking to ID9®	Influence on ID9® concept and steps
John Biggs	Born 1934	• Constructive Alignment of Learning / Deep and Surface Learning / SOLO Taxonomy for assessing learning outcomes / 3P's of Teaching and Learning.	Constructive alignment is a constructivist understanding of the nature of learning, and an aligned design for outcomes-based teaching education. The SOLO Taxonomy builds on Bloom's Taxonomy and aids both trainers and learners in understanding the learning process. The model consists of five levels in the order of understanding: • Pre-structural - The learner doesn't understand the lesson and uses a much too simple means of going about it—the learner is unsure about the lesson or subject. • Uni-structural - The learner's response only focuses on one relevant aspect—the learner has only a basic concept about the subject. • Multi-structural - The learner's response focuses on several relevant aspects but they are treated independently—the learner has several concepts about the subject but they are disconnected. Assessment of this level is primarily quantitative. • Relational - The different aspects have become integrated into a coherent whole—the learner has mastered the complexity of the subject by being able to join all the parts together. This level is what is normally meant by an adequate understanding of a subject. • Extended abstract - The previous integrated whole may be conceptualized at a higher level of abstraction and generalized to a new topic or area—the learner is now able to create new ideas based on her mastery of the subject.	There are two basic concepts behind constructive alignment: • Learners construct meaning from what they do to learn. This concept derives from cognitive psychology and constructivist theory, and recognizes the importance of linking new material to concepts and experiences in the learner's memory and the extrapolation to possible future scenarios via the abstraction of basic principles through reflection. • The facilitator makes a deliberate alignment between the planned learning activities and the learning outcomes. This is a conscious effort to provide the learner with a clearly specified goal, a well-designed learning activity or activities that are appropriate for the task, and well-designed assessment criteria for giving feedback to the learner.	Step 1: Aim – Early engagement, participant centered learning and a positive learning environment creates a platform for 'DEEP' learning. Step 3: Big Picture Overview – connect course objectives and outcomes with each participant. Step 4: Connect – activity designed to connect the learning to each participant. Step 5: Topic Rotation Tool – Drawing together adult learning engagement methods and styles to assist in the transfer and application process. Step 8: Evaluation – the importance of assessing learning.

Author	Birth / Death	System / Model / Theory	Brief overview of contribution to theory	Theory linking to ID9®	Influence on ID9® concept and steps
David Kolb	Born 1939	• Kolb developed (with Roger Fry) the Experiential Learning Model (ELM) • Kolb is also known for developing the Learning Style Inventory (LSI)	Influenced by Dewey and Piaget, Kolb developed the Experiential Learning Model (ELM) which is composed of four elements: • concrete experience • observation of and reflection on that experience • formation of abstract concepts based upon the reflection • testing the new concepts • (repeat). The influencing factors of ELM were experiential learning, the individual and social change, career development, and executive and professional education. Kolb is renowned in educational circles for his Learning Style Inventory (LSI). His model is built upon the idea that learning preferences can be described using two continuums: active experimentation-reflective observation and abstract conceptualization-concrete experience.	Knowing an individual's learning style enables learning to be designed and orientated according to the preferred method. That said, everyone responds to and needs the stimulus of all types of learning styles to one extent or another - it's a matter of using emphasis that fits best with the given situation and an individual's learning style preferences. Kolb's Learning Style Inventory (LSI) results in identifying four types of learners: converger (active experimentation-abstract conceptualization), accommodator (active experimentation-concrete experience), assimilator (reflective observation-abstract conceptualization), and diverger (reflective observation-concrete experience). The LSI is designed to determine an individual's learning preference.	Some elements of the experiential learning model and the learning style inventory, based on observation and reflection of the learning experience and an individual's learning styles, are included in the ID9® process, however neither Kolb's ELM or LSI are used in their entirety

Author	Birth / Death	System / Model / Theory	Brief overview of contribution to theory	Theory linking to ID9®	Influence on ID9® concept and steps
David Sousa		• Sousa is known for brain research, instructional skills, and education at the Pre-K to 12, university and adult levels.	Sousa is an international consultant in educational neuroscience and author of 15 books that suggest ways that educators and parents can translate current brain research into strategies for improving learning and is a member of the Cognitive Neuroscience Society Sousa suggested four key factors affect the intensity of a learner's intrinsic motivation in any given situation: emotions, feedback, past experiences, and meaning. These factors are all connected and influence one another to some degree: The brain pays more attention to stimuli and events that are accompanied by emotions. The brain regions associated with motivation are more active in subjects who are learning tasks and receiving feedback than in subjects doing the same tasks with no feedback. Past experiences always affect new learning. As we learn something new, our brain transfers into working memory any long-stored items it perceives as related to the new information. These items interact with new learning to help us interpret information and extract meaning, which is part of the principle called transfer. The search for meaning is innate. As a learning episode ends, the brain decides whether to encode the new learning into long-term memory or let it fade away. It's an important decision because people cannot recall—let alone implement—learning that their brains have not stored.	Adults attach meaning to new learning by drawing on a multitude of past experiences, but they may not find a match that makes it relevant. When a participant in a professional development activity asks, "Why do I need to know this?" that individual is neither readily connecting the day's menu of learning to past teaching experiences nor accepting it as meaningful. To create experiences that participants perceive as meaningful, professional development leaders should: • Directly connect the new initiative to job-related goals. For example, activities that show precisely how participants can use new strategies to help them learn new content are more valuable than general suggestions. • Present the topic over enough time and in enough depth so participants gain a thorough understanding of how it relates to their work. It is unwise, for instance, to expect participants to make in-depth connections in a one-hour workshop, especially if there are no follow-up activities. • Use instruction modalities other than "telling." Participants need to see the strategy modeled and then apply it themselves soon thereafter. When participants actively participate in a demonstration of the primacy-recency effect, for example, they more clearly recognize that the brain remembers best the first and last items presented in a learning episode—and they are more likely to sequence instruction with this phenomenon in mind. • Initiate action research. Conducting action research in the classroom enables facilitators to personally assess the effectiveness of a new strategy, obtain validation for incorporating new strategies into their repertoire, and investigate specific problems that affect their teaching. • Promote study groups around the topic. As group members exchange new research and share in-class experiences, they can analyze why—and under what conditions — a strategy is effective. Participating in study groups helps facilitators who are reluctant to try out new ideas gain confidence.	Step 1: Aim – Early engagement, participant centered learning and a positive learning environment creates a platform for 'DEEP' learning Step 3: Big Picture Overview – connect course objectives and outcomes with each participant Step 4: Connect – activity designed to connect the learning to each participant Step 5: Topic Rotation Tool – Drawing together adult learning engagement methods and styles to assist in the transfer and application process

Other ID9® Theoretical Influences:

The work of the following authors have also influenced or link to the ID9® framework and process (listed in order of approximate birth date): Socrates, Plato, Aristotle, Thomas Hobbs, Rene Descartes, John Locke, George Berkley, Thomas Reid, David Hume, Jean-Jacques Rousseau, Immanuel Kant, Franz-Joseph Gall, James Mill (father of John Stuart Mill), John Stuart Mill, Charles Robert Darwin, William James, Ivan Petrivich Pavlov, Mary Calkins, Edward Bradford Titchener, James Rowland Angell, Montessori, Carl Jung, John Broadus Watson, Kurt Lewin, Lev Vygotsky, Carl Rogers, Malcolm Shepherd Knowles, Donald Kirkpatrick, David Ausubel, George Miller, Albert Bandura, Allen Paivio, Eric Kandel, Edward de Bono, John Favell, Bernice McCarthy, Jay Cross, Robin Fogarty, Atkinson-Shiffrin Memory Model, Black & Wiliam, Honey & Mumford and Jean Lave.

Other ID9® Theoretical Influences Reference Table

Author	Birth / Death	System / Model / Theory	Brief overview of contribution to theory	Theory linking to ID9®	Influence on ID9® concept and steps
Socrates	469 - 399 BC	• Socratic Method / Socratic Irony / The Power of Questioning / Did not write one word – this task was left to his students Plato and Aristotle	Human morality and the definition of wisdom. The Socratic Method is no more than a teacher using the occasional open or inductive question (Clark, D. 2012) Sophisticated e-learning is allowing us to realize the potential of a scalable Socratic approach without the need for one-on-one teaching. Through the use of technology-based tools that allow search, questioning and now adaptive learning (through real-time chat boxes etc.) Socratic learning can be truly realized on scale (Clark, D. 2012).	Socrates believed that, for certain types of learning, questioning and dialogue allows the learner to generate their own ideas and conclusions.	Step 5: Topic Rotation Tool – Drawing together adult learning engagement methods, styles and the power of questioning to assist in the transfer and application process. The Socratic approach is taught as part of the Certified ID9® Professional program.
Plato	428 - 348 BC	• Nativism / Life-long Learning	Inherent or innate knowledge where new knowledge was gained by reflecting on the content of one's mind. This he termed the 'Mind's Eye' or turning our thoughts inward and that our senses mislead and alter new knowledge. Plato's Reminiscence Theory of Knowledge heavily influenced Christianity.	Plato believed an educational system should be designed to determine the abilities of individuals and that training should be provide to enhance and strengthen these abilities. Plato mapped out a developmental educational theory that rested on the Greek philosophy of 'Mind and Body' and saw education as a process of 'Life-long Learning'.	ID9® includes building reflective activities for participants to reflect on their existing and potential learning of new knowledge.
Aristotle	384 BC – 322 BC	• Empiricism / Laws of Attraction / Laws of Associationism / Theory of the Golden Mean (everything in moderation) and Theory of Learning	Knowledge is external to the mind / Sensory experience is the basis of all knowledge / The rise of mnemonics Aristotle believed 'learning by doing' was fundamental to learning.	Aristotle supported active participation in the learning process and understood education to be more than the mere transmission of knowledge, it was the preparation for participation in life and therefore a tool for life-long learning.	ID9® includes training and review activities and social learning techniques integrated within all steps of the process and discusses the importance of mnemonics.
Thomas Hobbs	1588 - 1679	• Social Contract Tradition	Supported Aristotle's and also believed sensory impressions were the source of all knowledge / Modern founder of Social Contract Tradition.	Hobbs studied the importance of an individual's sensors in relation to learning and believed that one's sensors drew knowledge from the external environment. Parallels can be drawn between the works of Aristotle and Hobbs. Both highlighted the role of an individual's sensors in acquiring new knowledge and links this to the more recent work on VAK (refer Neil Fleming below).	Step 5: Topic Rotation Tool – Drawing together adult learning engagement methods and learning styles to assist in the transfer and application process.
Rene Descartes	1596 – 1650	• Modern Philosophy (1640)	Supported Plato's Theory of 'Innate Ideas' / Coined the term Behaviorism / "I think therefore I Am".	Descartes concluded, if he doubted, then something or someone must be doing the doubting, therefore the very fact that he doubted proved his existence. The simple meaning of the phrase is that if one is skeptical of existence, which is in and of itself proof that he does exist.	Through the ID9® process of building learning and review activities participants are provided structure to 'think' and are provided with planned ways to extend their thinking, overcome doubt to establish confidence for learning application.

Author	Birth / Death	System / Model / Theory	Brief overview of contribution to theory	Theory linking to ID9®	Influence on ID9® concept and steps
John Locke	1632 - 1704	• Infant Mind / the Learning Environment	Supporter of Hobbs / The Mind is a 'blank state' for experience to write on. Locke was critical of traditional schooling of the day, describing them as poor influences both physically and mentally on positive learning.	Locke recommending building a learner's character, developing good habits of acquiring new knowledge, the inclusion of a positive learning environment and the addition of pleasure and play in learning.	ID9® is a constructivist approach to learning design that encourages collaborative experiential learning. ID9® includes learning and review activities and social learning techniques integrated within all steps of the process.
George Berkley	1685 - 1753	• Immaterialism / Subjective Idealism / The Master Argument	Berkeley's immaterialism is open to "gross misinterpretation" and was built on two entirely distinct and varied premises: (1) active mind or spirit, perceiving, thinking, and willing, and (2) passive objects of mind, namely sensible ideas (sense-data) or imaginable ideas. In his work The Master Argument he had to show that matter was an abstract concept with no real world existence that passed itself off as an object of immediate experience. But this is not an argument against abstract concepts as the Master Argument seems to suggest. Rather it is an argument against poor uses of abstraction and useless abstract concepts that cloak themselves as objects of immediate experience.	What Berkley is getting at in the Three Dialogues is that the concept of matter is a useless abstraction that is often confused for being an object of immediate experience and that we can get by without it. Conceptual topics in training often leave the learner thinking that theoretical approaches to concepts have little or no relevance in their day-to-day workplace. However abstract concepts should be transformed to the concrete where possible as part of the instructional design process.	ID9® is a constructivist approach to learning design that encourages collaborative experiential learning. Where topics trained are conceptual by nature (professional development type topics) conceptual concepts should be transitioned where possible to the concrete allowing for immediate real-world experience.
Thomas Reid	1710 – 1796	• 27 Faculties of the Mind	Reid believed that common sense should be at the foundation of all philosophical inquiry. He disagreed with Hume, who asserted that we can never know what an external world consists of as our knowledge is limited to the ideas in the mind, and George Berkeley, who asserted that the external world is merely ideas in the mind. By contrast, Reid claimed that the foundations upon which our sensus communis are built justify our belief that there is an external world.	Thomas Reid was one of the founders of the "common sense" school of philosophy. He is also well known for his criticisms of Locke's view of personal identity and Hume's view of causation. Much of the view developed in the Inquiry reappears in the Intellectual Powers, which expands his epistemological picture beyond the apprehension of the world through the senses to consideration of memory, imagination, knowledge concerning kinds of things, the nature of judgment, reasoning and taste.	Step 5: Topic Rotation Tool – Drawing together adult learning engagement methods and learning styles to assist in the transfer and application process. Building a common sense approach and perception equals reality into learning interventions and maintaining a positive learning climate are foundations to ID9®.
David Hume	1711 - 1776	• Problem of Causation / Induction / Is-ought Problem	Hume strove to create a total naturalistic "science of man" that examined the psychological basis of human nature. In stark opposition to the rationalists who preceded him, most notably Descartes, he concluded that desire rather than reason governed human behavior, saying: "Reason is, and ought only to be the slave of the passions." A prominent figure in the skeptical philosophical tradition and a strong empiricist, he argued against the existence of innate ideas, concluding instead that humans have knowledge only of things they directly experience.	According to Hume, we reason inductively by associating constantly conjoined events, and it is the mental act of association that is the basis of our concept of causation.	Step 5: Topic Rotation Tool – Drawing together adult learning engagement methods and learning styles to assist in the transfer and application process. The ID9® process begins each topic with associative reflection moving from the known to the unknown.

Author	Birth / Death	System / Model / Theory	Brief overview of contribution to theory	Theory linking to ID9®	Influence on ID9® concept and steps
Jean-Jacques Rousseau	1712 - 1778	• Child-Centric Education	Rousseau developed the concept of "child-centered" education. His essential idea is that education should be carried out, so far as possible, in harmony with the development of the child's natural capacities by a process of apparently autonomous discovery. This was in opposition to teachers providing learners with what they thought was important to learn.	Rousseau's work is the formation of what is more commonly known today as Learner-Centered educational principles. Today's self-paced modules of e-Learning emulate the principles of Rousseau's learner-centric ideals.	ID9® is a constructivist approach to learning design that encourages collaborative experiential learning.
Immanuel Kant	1724 – 1804	• Categorical Imperative / Critique of Pure Reason / Importance of Schemata	Transcendental Idealism / Synthetica Priori / Noumenon / Sapereaude / Nebular Hypothesis . Believed that much knowledge was inborn.	Kant argued that experience is purely subjective without first being processed by pure reason. He also said that using reason without applying it to experience only leads to theoretical illusions.	ID9® is a constructivist approach to learning design that encourages collaborative experiential learning. The ID9® process ensures participants build on experience, learn linear and conceptual content in a pragmatic and tangible form and apply it to real-world application during the training session.
Franz-Joseph Gall	1758 – 1828	• Phrenology / Phrenology Chart / Formal Discipline of Learning	The study of the sections or faculties of the brain.	Gall believed that with practice, strengthening faculties of the brain improved learning.	Step 5: Topic Rotation Tool – Drawing together adult learning engagement methods and styles to assist in the transfer and application process (i.e. Left / Right brain) Step 6: Major Review – Repetition, Reflection and Review linked to learning objectives demonstrates retention of new learning and mastery of new knowledge.
James Mill (father of John Stuart Mill)	1773 – 1829	• Associationism	Mill wrote the Analysis of the Phenomena of the Human Mind and believed that the analysis of complex emotional states included affections, aesthetic emotions and moral sentiments. Mill attempted to resolve emotional state into two categories; pleasurable and painful sensations.	James Mill also elaborated on Hume's associationism. The elder Mill saw the mind as passively functioning by the law of contiguity, with the law of frequency and a law of vividness "stamping in" the association. His emphasis on the law of frequency as the key to learning makes his approach very similar to the behaviorists in the twentieth century. But he is most famous for being the father of John Stuart Mill.	Step 4: Connect – activity designed to connect the learning to each participant. Step 5: Topic Rotation Tool – Drawing together adult learning engagement methods and styles to assist in the transfer and application process (i.e. Left / Right brain).
John Stuart Mill	1806 – 1873	• Associationism / Laws of Experience • The Whole is Different from the Sum of its Parts	Is the sum of sensations and ideas joined by the Laws of Contiguity or Similarity.	Mill revised his father's work and believed that complex ideas were created via association; the resulting whole was more than just the sum of its parts.	Step 4: Connect – activity designed to connect the learning to each participant. Step 5: Topic Rotation Tool – Drawing together adult learning engagement methods and styles to assist in the transfer and application process (i.e. Left / Right brain).

Author	Birth / Death	System / Model / Theory	Brief overview of contribution to theory	Theory linking to ID9®	Influence on ID9® concept and steps
Charles Robert Darwin	1809 – 1882	• Natural Selection • "ignorance more frequently begets confidence than does knowledge"(Darwin, C. 1871, p. 3)	Origin of the species / Voyage of the Beagle. Darwin suggested there was no difference between humans and 'lower animals'. Casting doubt on the works of Plato, Descartes and Kant and therefore Christianity. The skills that engender competence in a particular domain are often the very same skills necessary to evaluate competence in that domain–one's own or anyone else's. Because of this, incompetent individuals lack what cognitive psychologists variously term metacognition (Everson & Tobias, 1998), metamemory (Klin, Guizman, & Levine, 1997), metacomprehension (Maki, Jonas, & Kallod, 1994), or self-monitoring skills (Chi, Glaser, & Rees, 1982). These terms refer to the ability to know how well one is performing, when one is likely to be accurate in judgment, and when one is likely to be in error. (Unskilled and Unaware of It: How Difficulties in Recognizing One's Own Incompetence Lead to Inflated Self-Assessments, Kruger, J and Dunning, D, 1999).	When people are incompetent in the strategies they adopt to achieve success and satisfaction, they suffer a dual burden: Not only do they reach erroneous conclusions and make unfortunate choices, but their incompetence robs them of the ability to realize it. Incompetent individuals lack the metacognitive skills necessary for accurate self- assessment.	Step 3: Big Picture Overview – connect course objectives and outcomes with each participant. The ID9® Framework and Process creates behavioral learning objectives based on 'what equals good' and therefore sets a competency standard for participants to reach. Self-assessment is based on criteria as well as personal reflection creating a pragmatic measured approach to form competency accuracy. Metacognitive reflection is an ID9® program level balance check.
William James	1842 – 1910	• Functionalism / The Principles of Psychology/ Learning by Doing	James was heavily influenced by Dewey and Kolb and believed that the utility of consciousness and behavior in adjusting to one's environment was a product of mental events, both rational and irrational and therefore were emotional reactions. James's philosophy of 'learning by doing' included a learner's association to the learning, interest in and attention during learning and the will and motivation to learn.	The early work on the importance of attaching new knowledge to prior experiences suggests the significance of and connections to a learner's schema. Learner's learn through experiences that turn into useful and habitual behaviors through actions.	Step 2: Icebreaker – Creates a safe and positive learning environment. Step 3: Big Picture Overview – connect course objectives and outcomes with each participant. Step 4: Connect – activity designed to connect the learning to each participant.
Ivan Petrivich Pavlov	1849 – 1936	• The Behaviorist Theory of Classic and Operant Conditioning / Behavior Modification	Transmarginal inhibition. Pavlov concluded it was possible to learn how to artificially create human disorganization for the purpose of controlling and reorienting human behavior. He was the first to coin the phrase `attention deficit disorder' or ADD. Pavlov recognized that there are two distinct types of responses: unconditioned responses to stimuli, the innate response to stimuli that occurs naturally without any learning involved and conditioned responses to stimuli, the learned response or habitual response.	Pavlov's work suggested that a formal or controlled learning environment, isolated from external influences, provided learners with a controlled state for effective learning.	Step 2: Icebreaker – Creates a safe and positive learning environment.

Author	Birth / Death	System / Model / Theory	Brief overview of contribution to theory	Theory linking to ID9®	Influence on ID9® concept and steps
Mary Calkins	1863 - 1930	• Theory of Self / Paired Associate Technique • Self-psychology	Calkins created the paired-associate technique, a research method where colors are paired with numbers and the colors are presented again for recall. Two underlying forms of psychology in vogue at the time were "atomistic psychology" and the "science of selves." Calkins was the first to "discover" the psychology of selves. She called it reconciliation between structural and functional psychology. Her first basic definition of her psychology is as follows: "All sciences deal with facts, and there are two great classes of facts-Selves and Facts-for-the-Selves. But the second of these great groups, the Facts-for-the-Selves, is again capable of an important division into internal and external facts. To the first class belong precepts, images, memories, thoughts, emotions and volitions, inner events as we may call them; to the second class belong the things and the events of the outside world, the physical facts, as we may name them. The physical sciences study these common and apparently independent or external facts; psychology as distinguished from them is the science of consciousness, the study of selves and the inner facts-for-selves (cited in Strunk, 1972).	Methods of recall used within review techniques.	Step 5: Topic Rotation Tool – Drawing together adult learning engagement methods and styles to assist in the transfer and application process (i.e. Left / Right brain). Methods of recall used within review techniques.
Edward Bradford Titchener	1867 – 1927	• Structuralism / 'Raw' Thought	Student of Wundt / Own feelings and sensations relate to the behavior of others and that of the learning experience. Titchener created his version of psychology that described the structure of the mind; structuralism.	Titchener differentiated particular types of sensations: auditory sensation, for example, he divided into "tones" and "noises"; ideas and perceptions he considered to be formed from sensations; "ideational type" was related to the type of sensation on which an idea was based, e.g., sound or vision, a spoken conversation or words on a page. Titchener believed that if the basic components of the mind could be defined and categorized, the structure of mental processes and higher thinking could be determined. What each element of the mind is, how those elements interact with each other and why they interact in the ways that they do was the basis of reasoning that Titchener used in trying to find structure to the mind.	Step 5: Topic Rotation Tool – Drawing together adult learning engagement methods and styles to assist in the transfer and application process (i.e. including VAK as sensory influences within instructional design).
James Rowland Angell	1869 - 1949	• Constructivist Learning Theory	Believed that the goal of psychology should be to study the significance of learned behavior when adapting it to the environment.	Contemporary psychology theories have strongly influenced research and thinking around pedagogy, knowledge management, the application of learning and instructional design. 'Behaviorism', 'cognitivism' and 'cognitive theory', and 'cognitive constructivism' have dominated learning centered pedagogy, theories of psychology and learning design for the past century.	Step 1: Aim – Early engagement, participant centered learning and a positive learning environment. Step 5: Topic Rotation Tool – Drawing together adult learning engagement methods and styles to assist in the transfer and application process.

Author	Birth / Death	System / Model / Theory	Brief overview of contribution to theory	Theory linking to ID9®	Influence on ID9® concept and steps
Montessori	1870 - 1952	• The Philosophy of Montessori Education	Believed in Learner-Centered Learning through experiential learning and practical problem-based learning.	Montessori influenced Piaget with the concept of learner-centered learning for children. Montessori methods involve: • Movement enhances thinking and learning • An increased sense of control improves learning and well-being • Increased motivation improves learning • Extrinsic assessments reduces motivation • Collaboration is conducive to learning • Learning is deeper and richer when situated in meaningful contexts • Interactions assist with learning • The importance of a positive learning environment	ID9® is a constructivist approach to learning design that encourages collaborative experiential learning. ID9® includes training and review activities and social learning techniques integrated within all steps of the process.
Carl Jung	1875 - 1961	His theories include: The concept of introversion and extraversion , The concept of the complex, The concept of collective unconscious, which is shared by all people and includes the archetypes and Synchronicity as a mode of relationship that is not causal.	Jung proposed and developed the concepts of the extraverted and the introverted personality, archetypes, and the collective unconscious.	The Myers-Briggs Type Indicator (MBTI), a popular psychometric instrument, has been developed from Jung's theories.	Step 5: Topic Rotation Tool – Drawing together adult learning engagement methods and styles to assist in the transfer and application process.
John Broadus Watson	1878 – 1959	• Behavioral Science / Study of Consciousness	Founder of Behaviorism. He believed that the study of behavior was more relevant than the study of consciousness as it was observable behavior and therefore able to be studied scientifically. Watson stated that psychology should focus on the "behavior" of the individual, not their consciousness.	Watson discovered that the kinesthetic sense controlled behavior. Within his "behaviorism", Watson put the emphasis on external behavior of people and their reactions to given situations, rather than the internal, mental state of those people.	Step 5: Topic Rotation Tool – Drawing together adult learning engagement methods and styles to assist in the transfer and application process (i.e. including VAK as sensory influences within instructional design).
Kurt Lewin	1890 - 1947	• The "founder of social psychology" and was one of the first to study group dynamics and organizational development. Lewin was the first to coin the term 'Action Research'	Lewin described change as a three-stage process. The first stage he called "unfreezing". It involved overcoming inertia and dismantling the existing "mind set". It must be part of surviving. Defense mechanisms have to be bypassed. In the second stage the change occurs. This is typically a period of confusion and transition. We are aware that the old ways are being challenged but we do not have a clear picture as to what we are replacing them with yet. The third and final stage he called "freezing". The new mindset is crystallizing and one's comfort level is returning to previous levels.	This describes the process of intrinsic behavior change and the method used by individuals to transfer their new learning, however it fails to address extrinsic influences limiting and therefore inhibiting the behavior change process.	Step 5: Topic Rotation Tool – Drawing together adult learning engagement methods and styles to assist in the transfer and application process.
Lev Vygotsky	1896 - 1934	• Social Constructivism / social development theory • Founder of holistic theory of human cultural and biosocial development commonly referred to as cultural-historical psychology or Activity Theory	Vygotsky also posited a concept of the Zone of Proximal Development, often understood to refer to the way in which the acquisition of new knowledge is dependent on previous learning, as well as the availability of instruction.	Individuals learn through interactivity and play which formed the basis for the concept of social learning.	ID9® is a constructivist approach to learning design that encourages collaborative experiential learning. ID9® includes training and review activities and social learning techniques integrated within all steps of the process.

Author	Birth / Death	System / Model / Theory	Brief overview of contribution to theory	Theory linking to ID9®	Influence on ID9® concept and steps
Carl Rogers	1902 – 1987	• Coach, Mentoring and Student-Centric Techniques	Influence by Dewey, Rogers was the first to identify the relationship between teacher or trainer and learner as moving toward the facilitator of the learning and the learner. Roger's belief was that through Socratic questioning a more open dialogue between facilitator and learner occurs, which encourages a more positive learning environment.	Socratic questioning is a method for encouraging learners to contribute and participate in the learning and is therefore a learner-centric technique.	Aligns with the principles of ID9® and with TPC's Confident Facilitation Skills approach.
Malcolm Shepherd Knowles	1913 – 1997	• Theory of Andragogy / Self-directed Learning	Adult Learning Theory – Children and Adults learn differently. Knowles is credited with being a fundamental influence in the development of the Humanist Learning Theory and the use of learner constructed contracts or plans to guide learning experiences. Knowles believed that people must continue to learn throughout their lives and it should be the mission of all schools to produce lifelong learners.	Knowles' andragogy was premised on at least four crucial assumptions about the characteristics of adult learners: Self-concept and self-directed learning; Experience as a resource for learning; Readiness to learn; Orientation to learning shifting from subject-centeredness to problem-centeredness; and, Motivation to learn is an internal process. Malcolm Knowles' put the idea of self-directed learning into packaged forms of activity that could be understood by educators and learners. His five step model involved: Diagnosing learning needs; Formulating learning needs; Identifying human material resources for learning; Choosing and implementing appropriate learning strategies; and, Evaluating learning outcomes.	Aligns with ID9® Framework: Internal Performance Consulting approach.
Donald Kirkpatrick	Born 1917	• 4 Levels of Learning Evaluation	Kirkpatrick is best known for creating a highly influential 'four level' model for training course evaluation. Kirkpatrick's ideas were first published in 1959 in a series of articles in the US Training and Development Journal but are better known from a book he published in 1975 entitled "Evaluating Training Programs." At times, there is confusion about the measurement of learning (level 2) versus behavior (level 3). Often the assumption is that trainees did not learn anything because they are not behaving any differently than they did before training occurred. The training program evaluators might consider the environment (or other factors affecting the transfer or application of learning) at the trainee's workplace to determine if that could be a case for non-transfer of learning.	The four levels of Kirkpatrick's evaluation model are as follows: 1. Reaction - what participants thought and felt about the training (satisfaction; "smile sheets"). 2. Learning - the resulting increase in knowledge and/or skills, and change in attitudes. This evaluation occurs during the training in the form of either a knowledge demonstration or test. 3. Behavior - transfer of knowledge, skills, and/or attitudes from classroom to the job (change in job behavior due to training program). This evaluation occurs 3–6 months post training while the trainee is performing the job. Evaluation usually occurs through observation. 4. Results - the final results that occurred because of attendance and participation in a training program (can be monetary, performance-based, etc.).	Step 5: Topic Rotation Tool – Drawing together adult learning engagement methods and styles to assist in the transfer and application process. Step 6: Major Review – Repetition, Reflection and Review linked to learning objectives demonstrates retention of new learning and mastery of new knowledge. Step 8: Evaluation – the importance of assessing learning.

Author	Birth / Death	System / Model / Theory	Brief overview of contribution to theory	Theory linking to ID9®	Influence on ID9® concept and steps
David Ausubel	1918 – 2008	• Subsumption Theory and Advanced Organizer Theory	Ausubel advanced the concept of the impact of prior knowledge on new learning through Ausubel's Meaningful Learning Model. Moving from what is known to what is not known, i.e. unconsciously incompetent to conscientiously incompetent.	An advance organizer is information presented by an instructor that helps the student organize new incoming information. This is achieved by directing attention to what is important in the coming material, highlighting relationships, and providing a reminder about relevant prior knowledge. Ausubel distinguishes between two kinds of advance organizer: *comparative* and *expository*: • The main goal of comparative organizers is to activate existing schemas. Similarly, they act as reminders to bring into the working memory of what you may not realize is relevant. By acting as reminders, the organizer points out explicitly "whether already established anchoring ideas are non-specifically or specifically relevant to the learning material • In contrast, expository organizers provide new knowledge that students will need to understand the upcoming information. Expository organizers are often used when the new learning material is unfamiliar to the learner. They often relate what the learner already knows with the new and unfamiliar material—this in turn is aimed to make the unfamiliar material more plausible to the learner.	Step 4: Connect – activity designed to connect the learning to each participant. Step 5: Topic Rotation Tool – Drawing together adult learning engagement methods and styles to assist in the transfer and application process.
George Miller	1920 - 2012	• Miller's Law – the 'Magical Number 7"	Miller was the first to suggest memory chunking exists within the short term memory for the easy recall of knowledge. Miller suggested that an individual was able to immediately recall seven bits of knowledge. Later studies suggested seven bits for digit recall, six for letters and five for words, however recent research indicates that all memory recall is dependent upon context and size of the objects or numbers being recalled.	The Magical Number Seven, Plus or Minus Two: Some Limits on Our Capacity for Processing Information" is one of the most highly cited papers in psychology. Miller observed that the memory span of young adults is approximately seven items.	The number of steps in ID9® (9-step process) was influenced by Miller's work. Step 5: Topic Rotation Tool – Drawing together adult learning engagement methods and styles to assist in the transfer and application process.
Albert Bandura	Born 1925	• The founder of social learning theory and the theory of self-efficacy • The theory is related to Vygotsky's Social Development Theory and Lave's Situated Learning, which also emphasize the importance of social learning.	Bandura's research analyzed the foundations of human learning and the willingness of children and adults to imitate behavior observed in others. Bandura believed that self-efficacy beliefs (which are individual beliefs that they are capable of overcoming negative or phobic beliefs) mediated changes in behavior.	People learn through observing others' behavior, attitudes, and outcomes of those behaviors. Most human behavior is learned observationally through modelling: from observing others, one forms an idea of how new behaviors are performed, and on later occasions this coded information serves as a guide for action. Social learning theory explains human behavior in terms of continuous reciprocal interaction between cognitive, behavioral, and environmental influences.	Step 5: Topic Rotation Tool – Drawing together adult learning engagement methods and styles to assist in the transfer and application process.

Author	Birth / Death	System / Model / Theory	Brief overview of contribution to theory	Theory linking to ID9®	Influence on ID9® concept and steps
Allen Paivio	Born 1925	Dual-coding theory posits that visual and verbal information are stored separately in long term memory. Dual coding theory is complemented by the theory of Alan Baddeley, in which working memory is divided into a visuospatial sketchpad and a phonological loop.	The dual coding theory (DCT) suggests that visual and verbal information act as two distinctive systems. The expected additive memory benefit of dual coding has been confirmed in numerous experiments which also suggested that the nonverbal code is mnemonically stronger (contributes more to the additive effect) than the verbal code.	Paivio's work has implications in many areas including human factors, interface design, as well as the development of educational materials.	Step 5: Topic Rotation Tool – Drawing together adult learning engagement methods and styles to assist in the transfer and application process.
Eric Kandel	Born 1929	Memory storage in neurons	Long and short term memory. 'learning is experience and experience is memory'.	Kandel researched how behavior is capable of being modified by learning and used it to explore how learning occurs and how memories are stored in the neural circuitry of that behavior. Kandels study is pivotal in the ID9® process for increasing retention which leads to changing behavior through learning as well as his work on how different forms of learning and memory relate to each other at the cellular level. Specifically how short-term memory converted to long-term memory in the brain.	Step 5: Topic Rotation Tool – Drawing together adult learning engagement methods and styles to assist in the transfer and application process. Step 6: Major Review – Repetition, Reflection and Review linked to learning objectives demonstrates retention of new learning and mastery of new knowledge
Edward de Bono	Born 1933	Father of Lateral Thinking and Creativity: Six Thinking Hats; Lateral Thinking; The Power of Perception; Focus on Facilitation; Simplicity; The Six Value Medals; and Mind Mapping	Edward de Bono is the world's leading authority on conceptual thinking as the driver of organizational innovation, strategic leadership, individual creativity, and problem solving. 'Six Thinking Hats' is an important and powerful technique that is used to look at decisions from a number of important perspectives. This forces you to move outside your habitual thinking style, and helps you to get a more rounded view of a situation. Mind Maps are the ideal tool for effectively accessing natural creativity and harnessing that creativity for effective problem solving. The main branches of the Mind Map can be used in a variety of ways to support thinking. The only limit to the ways in which Mind Maps can be used is the imagination.	Edward De Bono's CoRT Thinking and Six Thinking Hats emphasize the importance of creativity to problem solving and decision making.	Step 5: Topic Rotation Tool – Drawing together adult learning engagement methods and styles to assist in the transfer and application process.
Jean Lave	Born 1939	• Theories of Situated Learning and Community of Practice.	Situated learning is learning that takes place in the same context in which it is applied. Lave and Wenger (1991) argue that learning should not be viewed as simply the transmission of abstract and decontextualized knowledge from one individual to another, but a social process whereby knowledge is co-constructed; they suggest that such learning is situated in a specific context and embedded within a particular social and physical environment.	Choice of learning process by which to deliver content.	ID9® is a constructivist approach to learning design that encourages collaborative experiential learning. ID9® includes training and review activities and social learning techniques integrated within all steps of the process.

Author	Birth / Death	System / Model / Theory	Brief overview of contribution to theory	Theory linking to ID9®	Influence on ID9® concept and steps
John Favell	Published 1979	• Metacognition; Metacognitive knowledge, reflection and experiences	Metacognition is a form of cognition, a second or higher order thinking process which involves active control over cognitive processes. It can be simply defined as thinking about thinking or as a "person's cognition about cognition". This definition emphasizes the executive role of metacognition in the overseeing and regulation of cognitive processes. Executive processes are those responsible for the goal-directed processing of information and selection of action, and for the implementation and monitoring of task-specific cognitive processes. Metacognition plays an important role in oral communication of information, oral persuasion, oral comprehension, reading comprehension, writing, language acquisition, attention, memory, problem solving, social cognition and various types of self-control and self-instruction. Metacognition has influence within areas of social learning theory, cognitive behavior modification, personality development, and education. Metacognitive knowledge is that segment of your stored knowledge that has to do with people as cognitive individuals and with their diverse cognitive tasks, goals, actions, and experiences. An example would be a child's acquired belief that unlike many of her friends, she is better at arithmetic than at spelling. Metacognitive experiences are any conscious cognitive or reflective experiences that accompany and pertain to any intellectual enterprise. An example would be the sudden feeling that you do not understand something another person just said.	"Metacognition refers to understanding of knowledge, an understanding that can be reflected in either effective use or overt description of the knowledge in question". (Brown, 1987, p. 65). This definition calls attention to an important aspect of metacognition: awareness of one's own knowledge or understanding of knowledge. It can be said that a learner understands a particular cognitive activity if she can use it appropriately and discuss its use. But there are in fact different degrees of understanding, as it is not unusual for learners to use knowledge effectively without being able to explain how they did so. To account for this variability, the term "metacognitive person" is often used to represent a person who is aware of her own knowledge (as well as its limitations).	ID9® is a constructivist approach to learning design that encourages collaborative experiential learning. ID9® includes training and review activities and social learning techniques integrated within all steps of the process. Metacognitive reflection is an ID9® program level balance check.
Bernice McCarthy	Published 1980	• 4MAT	McCarthy's 4MAT approach identifies the diversity of learners and connects them, no matter their level, to any type of material, emphasizing real-world applications as an essential component of in-depth understanding. This concept-based approach to curriculum and instructional planning promotes high-quality teaching and learning. Most educators consider Bernice McCarthy's work to be a key contribution to the development of the learning styles movement.	*McCarthy* drew on the research of Jung, Paiget, Vygotsky, Dewey, Lewin and Kolb to create an instructional system that would progress through the complete learning cycle using strategies that would appeal to all learners.	Step 5: Topic Rotation Tool – Drawing together adult learning engagement methods and styles to assist in the transfer and application process.

Author	Birth / Death	System / Model / Theory	Brief overview of contribution to theory	Theory linking to ID9®	Influence on ID9® concept and steps
Jay Cross	unavailable	• Cross coined the terms "eLearning" and "workflow learning." A pioneer in both the practice and theory of technology in learning	Jay Cross is CEO of Internet Time Group and founder of the Workflow Institute. A thought leader in learning technology, informal learning, performance improvement, and organizational culture. The importance of informal learning. Cross highlighted the major spend on learning is via formal training when the majority of learning occurs informally.	Adaptation of the ID9® 9-step process from classroom and live instructor led training to create eID9® – the adapted process suited for eLearning.	Adaptation of the ID9® 9-step process from classroom and live instructor led training to create eID9® – the adapted process suited for eLearning.
Robin Fogarty	unavailable	• Metacognition and Metacognitive Reflection	Metacognition is thinking about how we think about how we know and about how we learn. Fogarty defines metacognition as "thinking about thinking." She adds that "to have awareness and control over your own thinking one may plan metacognitively, monitor progress metacognitively, or evaluate metacognitively. Thus, the three areas, planning, monitoring, and evaluating provide the appropriate framework for self-reflection." We know that facilitating is improved by careful planning (future), by monitoring our craft (present), and by evaluation (past). Developing these self-reflective practices is at the heart of metacognition leading to the construction of individual meaning. Our participants also need to develop metacognitive strategies to improve their learning and we can help them with this process by weaving metacognitive practices into our training environment.	"Metacognition refers to understanding of knowledge, an understanding that can be reflected in either effective use or overt description of the knowledge in question" (Brown, 1987, p. 65). This definition calls attention to an important aspect of metacognition: awareness of one's own knowledge or understanding of knowledge. It can be said that a learner understands a particular cognitive activity if she can use it appropriately and discuss its use. But there are in fact different degrees of understanding, as it is not unusual for learners to use knowledge effectively without being able to explain how they did so. To account for this variability, the term "metacognitive person" is often used to represent a person who is aware of her own knowledge (as well as its limitations).	ID9® is a constructivist approach to learning design that encourages collaborative experiential learning. ID9® includes training and review activities and social learning techniques integrated within all steps of the process. Metacognitive Reflection is an ID9® program level balance check.
Atkinson-Shiffrin Memory Model	Published 1968	• The Atkinson-Shiffrin Multi-store Memory Model	Atkinson-Shiffrin proposed human memory involves a sequence of three stages: Sensory memory, Short-term memory and Long-tern memory	This is the first significant levels of processing memory model delineated in the mid-to-late 1960s, in which it is postulated that humans process sensory data and information from the environment through three distinct levels: sensory memory, short-term memory and long-term memory. Previous theories of how people remember and learn focused on a simple model in which information either goes directly into short-term memory or long-term memory. Using ID9® the more levels experienced, the deeper the processing that occurs.	ID9® is a constructivist approach to learning design that encourages collaborative experiential learning ID9® includes training and review activities and social learning techniques integrated within all steps of the process.

Author	Birth / Death	System / Model / Theory	Brief overview of contribution to theory	Theory linking to ID9®	Influence on ID9® concept and steps
Black & Wiliam	Published 1998	• Inside the Black Box: Raising Standards through Classroom Assessments	Black and Wiliam studied Formative and Summative assessment and concluded firm evidence shows that formative assessment is an essential component of classroom work and that its development can raise standards of achievement. Formative assessment is assessment that is meant to guide both teachers and students toward the next steps in the learning process. Summative assessments (unit tests, final exams, standardized tests, entrance exams etc.) are the assessment of the learning and summarize the development of learners at a particular time.	Black and Wiliam's formative assessment suggests that facilitators confirm a learner's level of new knowledge during a learning intervention and alter their teaching in-line with these results. The use of review activities progressively confirms learning progress prior to completion of the intervention. William and Black (1995) claimed that all assessments have the potential to serve a summative function but some have the additional capability of serving formative functions.	Step 5: Topic Rotation Tool – Drawing together adult learning engagement methods, review activities and learning styles to assist in the transfer and application process. Step 6: Major Review – Repetition, Reflection and Review linked to learning objectives demonstrates retention of new learning and mastery of new knowledge.
Peter Honey and Alan Mumford	Published 2000	• Learning Styles / Learning Cycle	Two adaptations were made to Kolb's experiential model. Honey & Mumford published the learning styles helper's guide in 2000 based on Kolb's LSI, however Honey and Mumford's learning cycle slightly differs from Kolb's: • Having an experience • Reflecting on it • Drawing their own conclusions (theorizing) • Putting their theory into practice to see what happens Based on the result, the learners can then move around the cycle again, jump in any part of the cycle, and then quit when they deem them self as successful (learned the task or material).	Similar to Kolb's ELM and LSI some elements of the H&M Learning Cycle, based on reflection and learning application, are included in the ID9® process, however the full H&M Learning Cycle process is not used in its entirety.	Step 5: Topic Rotation Tool – Drawing together adult learning engagement methods, review activities and learning styles to assist in the transfer and application process.

Appendix B:
Constructivism Terms, Theories and Models

By Catherine Mattiske

The learning paradigm Constructivism is one of the four main paths of learning theory. The three others behaviourism, cognitivism and humanism have influenced ID9® however the ID9® Framework and Process has been designed by Mattiske (1997) as a Constructivist approach to adult learning and instructional design. It is recommended that further reading into these terms, theories and models which create the constructivism pathway be explored for a deeper understanding of the constructivist approach.

Constructivism

Accommodation

Active Learning

Activity Theory

Andragogy

Appraisal theories interaction

Assimilation

Barriers to learning

Bodily kinesthetic intelligence

Case-based reasonsing

Chain of Resonse model

Chaos theory

Co-emergence

Cognitive apprenticeship

Cognitive coaching

Cognitive flexibility

Cognitive structure

Cohort groups

Collaboration

Collaborative learning

Community of practice

Complex systmes

Concept mapping

Conceptual landscape

Conceptual map

Constructionism

Constructivist learning environment

Conversation theory

Curriculum as experience

Cybernetics

Developmental learning

Dialectic method

Differentiation

Discovery learning

Dynamic assessment

Emotion theory

Enactivism

Engaged learning

Equlibration

Existential intelligence

Experienced-based learning

Facial action coding system

Generative learning

Genetic epistemology

Godel's theory of incompleteness

Inquiry-based learning

Insightful learning

Instructionism

Interiorization

Interpersonal intelligence

Intrapersonal intelligence

Knowledge media design

Learner-centric

Learning web

Legitimate peripheral participation

Logical-mathematical intelligence

Mental constructs

Metamathematics

Mindtools

Minimalism

Minimalist model

Multiple intelligences

Musical intelligence

Naturalist intelligence

Nurnberg funnel

Observational learning

Pansophism

Pedagogy

Personal curriculum design

Problem-based learning

Project zero

Psychological tools

Reciprocal determinism

Reductive bias

Scaffolded knowledge integration framework

Scaffolded learning

Schemata

Self-directed learning

Self-efficacy theory

Self-reflection

Self-regulated learning

Shared cognition theory

Situated cognition theory

Situated learning

Social and cultural artifacts

Social cognitive conflict

Social development theory

Social learning theory

Socio-cognitive conflict

Socio-constructivist theory

Sociocultural theory

Solo taxonomy theory

Spatial intelligence

Spatial reasoning

Spiralled organization

Staged self-directed learning model

Teachback

Verbal-linguistic intelligence

Zone of proximal development

Index

Lightning Source UK Ltd.
Milton Keynes UK
UKOW06f1207160114

224738UK00005B/5/P